Probability Is the Very Guide of Life

Probability Is the Very Guide of Life

The Philosophical Uses of Chance

EDITED BY
Henry E. Kyburg, Jr.,
and Mariam Thalos

OPEN COURT
Chicago and La Salle, Illinois

To order books from Open Court, call 1-800-815-2280
or visit www.opencourtbooks.com.

Open Court Publishing Company is a division of Carus Publishing Company.

First printing 2003

Printed and bound in the United States of America.

Library of Congress Cataloging-in-Publication Data

Probability is the very guide of life / edited by Henry E. Kyburg, Jr. and Mariam Thalos.

p. cm.

Includes bibliographical references and index.

ISBN 0-8126-9513-5 (pbk. : alk. paper)

1. Probabilities. I. Kyburg, Henry Ely, 1928- II. Thalos, Mariam, 1962-

QA273.18 .P749 2003

519.2—dc21

2003000725

Contents

Acknowledgments vii

Introduction: The Philosophical Uses of Probability ix

PART I: PROBABILITY, FREQUENCY, AND INFERENCE

1. Reichenbach, Reference Classes, and Single-Case 'Probabilities' 3
James H. Fetzer

2. Direct Inference and the Problem of Induction 33
Timothy McGrew

3. Objective Modality and Direct Inference 61
Isaac Levi

4. Severe Testing as a Guide for Inductive Learning 89
Deborah G. Mayo

5. Bayesian Meets Frequentist: A Marriage Made in California 119
James R. Henderson

6. Probability as a Guide in Life 135
Henry E. Kyburg, Jr.

PART II: PROBABILITY AND DECISION

7. A Dilemma for Objective Chance 153
Phil Dowe

8. Simpson's Paradox: A Logically Benign, Empirically Treacherous Hydra 165
Gary Malinas

9. Conditional Probability Is the Very Guide of Life 183
Alan Hájek

10. Causal Generalizations and Good Advice 205
Christopher Hitchcock

PART III: PROBABILITY AND CAUSATION

11. Instrumental Probability 235
Clark Glymour

12. What Is Wrong with Bayes Nets? 253
Nancy Cartwright

13. Don't Take Unnecessary Chances! 277
Henry E. Kyburg, Jr.

14. The Reduction of Causation 295
Mariam Thalos

PART IV: WIDER APPLICATIONS OF PROBABILITY

15. Is It a Crime to Belong to a Reference Class? 331
Mark Colyvan, Helen M. Regan, and Scott Ferson

16. Explaining Things Probabilistically 349
Wesley C. Salmon

Index 358

Acknowledgments

We gratefully acknowledge permission to reproduce the following copyrighted material, originally appearing in *THE MONIST*, vol. 84, no. 2, April 2001, "Probability as a Guide to Life." The essays listed below are copyright © 2001, *THE MONIST: An International Quarterly Journal of General Philosophical Inquiry*, Peru, Illinois, U.S.A. 61354. Reprinted by permission.

Chapter 2, Timothy McGrew, "Direct Inference and the Problem of Induction."

Chapter 3, Isaac Levi, "Objective Modality and Direct Inference."

Chapter 6, Henry E. Kyburg, Jr., "Probability as a Guide in Life."

Chapter 8, Gary Malinas, "Simpson's Paradox: A Logically Benign, Empirically Treacherous Hydra."

Chapter 10, Christopher Hitchcock, "Causal Generalizations and Good Advice."

Chapter 11, Clark Glymour, "Instrumental Probability."

Chapter 12, Nancy Cartwright, "What Is Wrong with Bayes Nets?"

Chapter 16, Wesley C. Salmon, "Explaining Things Probabilistically."

Chapter 1, James H. Fetzer, "Reichenbach, Reference Classes, and Single-Case 'Probabilities,'" is reprinted from W. C. Salmon, ed., *Hans Reichenbach: Logical Empiricist*, 187–219.

Chapter 15, Mark Colyvan, Helen M. Regan, and Scott Ferson, "Is It a Crime to Belong to a Reference Class?," was first published in *The Journal of Political Philosophy* 9, no. 2 (June 2001). Reproduced with permisson of Blackwell Publishing Ltd.

Introduction

1. Intellectual Origins of the Essays Assembled Here

In this introduction we shall array a family of fundamental questions pertaining to probability, especially as it has been judged to bear upon the guidance of life. Applications and uses of probability theory need either to address some or all of these questions, or to tell us why they don't. The essays assembled in this volume bring integrative perspectives on this family of questions. We asked the authors to describe in their own voices the intellectual histories of their contributions, so as to shed further light upon the philosophical interest of their projects, and their particular integrative approaches, within the broader context we have sketched. The authors' comments precede the essays.

2. Fallibility Rediscovered

Centuries ago David Hume struck a deep chord that has been resonating ever since. While philosophical predecessors and contemporaries enjoyed confidence in the human capacity to know our environment, whether by means of the senses or by means of reason, Hume insisted instead upon a philosophical account of how we pull this off—how we succeed in getting beyond the most superficial of sensory information, by means of a combination of the evidence of the senses and the power of reason, and (though aware of his continental contemporaries' rationalist solutions to the question) he contended that no such account has ever been produced. "Nature," he wrote, "has kept us at a great distance from all her secrets, and has afforded us only the [direct] knowledge of a few superficial qualities of objects; while she conceals from us those powers and principles on which the influence of those objects entirely depends" (*Enquiry Concerning Human Understanding*).[1]

Hume's contemporaries were very much in agreement with one another on the proposition that nature's secrets can be unlocked, although they might have disagreed on the key to that achievement. Thinkers on the continent (like Descartes and Leibniz) held that the key—the foundation of knowledge—lies fundamentally in the power of reason, while many of Hume's own compatriots held that the key lies instead in the evidence of the senses. Their confidence in human access to nature's secrets served as foundation for unexamined faith in the principle that the future shall resemble the past—the principle on which Hume's arguments cast a long shadow of doubt. Against his contemporaries and the preponderance of his predecessors, Hume resolutely maintained that confidence in our opinions vis-à-vis nature's secrets is thoroughly unfounded—while nonetheless affirming that confounding human nature foists this confidence upon us, and indeed that this (baseless) confidence serves our mundane interests surpassingly well. It is not without a strong measure of irony then that he wrote: "only a fool or madman will ever pretend to dispute the authority of experience, or to reject that great guide of human life."[2] And indeed he seemed to favor the proposal that experience makes many of those opinions to which we cling with undeserved confidence, "merely probable."

Hume's legacy is in part the lesson that the proposition to the effect that the future shall resemble the past is probable at best, never certain. It is a legacy that faces up to the fallibility of human knowledge, under the very best of circumstances. To be sure, Aristotle before him would doubtless have affirmed this thesis of fallibility. But Hume had to rediscover it. For intervening between Aristotle and Hume was a Roman empire, which was followed by an epoch in which the Christian Church controlled dissemination of intellectual ideas, and then by an age of Reason Alone ushered in by dissolution of Church rule over Reason. Hume's legacy to us is, in part, a rediscovered fallibility, a rediscovered empiricism, which is by its nature more vigorous than the original. It is more vigorous in that it urgently presses the question of the sources of fallibility. Indeed it amounts to discovery of the qualifier "probable" as an entire field for philosophical—as against purely mathematical—inquiry. Before Hume it was a term for which there existed only the most negligible philosophical market.

One thing is unshakably certain: we cannot have unshakable certainty. So perhaps belief in some proposition pertaining to the future is a form of wagering, on something that is not certain but probable. This leads to substantive philosophical questions about the meaning of probability statements, and their applications to actual day-to-day instances. And it leads too to questions as to the relationship between knowledge and wagering.

3. Possibility and Probability

The theory of probability grew up in gaming rooms. One of the first serious studies of probability was performed in the mid-1500s by an Italian physicist and mathematician named Giralamo Cardano, who was perhaps the first to think about chance events in a systematic way. He discovered that the likelihood of getting a particular sum when rolling two dice (assumed fair and distinct from one another) exactly equals the number of ways of obtaining that sum, divided by the total number of possible ways that the pair can fall. Thus he could say that the likelihood of securing a 7, on any given roll of fair dice, is exactly 6/36, that it is the largest likelihood for any sum on a roll of dice, and that this likelihood is exactly 1.5 times as large as the likelihood of turning up a 9 or a 5. These facts had been known, no doubt, for thousands of years; but only as lore, never as founded upon principles.

It would be another century before the next conceptual landmark in the field of probability would emerge: the notion of *expected outcome*. In 1657 the Dutch physicist Christiaan Huygens proposed a precise formula for computing the expected outcome of a game. It would be the sum of all possible outcomes, weighted by the relative chance of each occurring. So for example, in a lottery with two equally likely monetary payoffs, *a* and *b*, the expected outcome (in monetary units) of a ticket is $\frac{1}{2}(a) + \frac{1}{2}(b)$. In a lottery that is equally likely to pay one of either 0 or $1000, the expected outcome is $500. And the expected outcome, said Huygens, is a "fair" asking price: a ticket in such a lottery is worth $500, on the open market. Should one always be prepared to pay the fair asking price? What kind of sense does it make, to ask what price one should pay to undertake a risky venture? Is there a price on risk itself? To answer these and related philosophical questions, we require a theory of decision under risk. Such a theory would take nearly three centuries to become fully articulated, as it did with publication in the 1940s of John von Neumann and Oskar Morgenstern's *Theory of Games and Economic Behavior*.[3]

With the rise of mercantilism, a special form of gambling became important: *insurance*. Insurance rates were not based on the counting of possible cases, à la Cardano, but on the relative frequencies known through experience. Uncertainty became a practical matter, not just for gamers, whose probabilities could be computed on the basis of numbers of possible cases, but also in business. And through this route it made its way into science itself. The mathematics of probability came to be developed for use in a number of scientific areas, from the treatment of errors of measurement, to biology and astronomy. The great mathematician and astronomer Laplace recognized the essential circularity of defining probability as a ratio of possible cases—it only works if the cases are *equally probable*. He therefore proposed a *principle of indifference*, according to which two symmetrical alternatives would be assigned the same probability.

Although there was some discussion of the meaning of the term "probability" before the twentieth century, the three standard views were articulated mainly after 1928. Richard von Mises in 1928 identified probability with limiting frequency: the probability of the kind of event K, within the collective C, is p, just in case the limiting relative frequency of events of kind K among the individuals of an initial segment of C, approaches p as longer and longer initial segments of C are considered. This interpretation of probability reflects the concern with relative frequency. Probability statements, on this view, are empirical statements, concerning frequencies or limits of frequencies in the real world. They are true or false, absolutely and without qualification, and independent of every corpus of propositions, believed or entertained.

At the opposite end of the spectrum of definitions we find those of Carnap and his followers. According to this approach, probability represents a kind of partial entailment. This is a view not unlike Laplace's, except that here inconsistency is avoided through requiring that the cases denote the most detailed possible stipulations of ways the world might be. These stipulated ways the world might be were called *state descriptions.* So a state description specifies, for every individual and every property term of the language in use, whether or not the property term applies to that individual; and for every pair of individuals, and every two-place relation, whether or not those individuals stand in that relation; and so on.

On the Carnapian approach each state description is assigned a measure —for example, each state description in a finite language could be assigned the same measure. Every statement of the language is equivalent to a disjunction of state descriptions. Thus every statement has a measure determined by the sum of the measures of the state descriptions whose disjunction it is equivalent to. Then, for an agent with background knowledge *K*, the probability of a statement *S*, *prob(S|K)* is the ratio of the measure of *S* and *K* to the measure of *K*. This is the degree of *rational* belief the agent with background *K* ought to have in *S*.

The third main interpretation of probability is the subjective or Bayesian interpretation, developed by the philosopher Frank Ramsey and independently also by the probabilist, Bruno de Finetti. This view is similar to Carnap's logical view, but without the Carnapian proviso to the effect that state descriptions are assigned measures on logical grounds. Probabilities here are tied directly to individual choices or predispositions to choose: the probability of the statement S, for John, is the amount he would pay for a ticket that would return $1.00 in case S turned out to be true. Thus the probability of securing a one on the next roll of a die, for John, is *1/3* just in case he would pay $0.33 for a ticket that would return him $1 if that roll did in fact result in a one. Bayesians insist that the probabilities of a rational individual, over any finite algebra of statements, should satisfy the axioms of the probability calculus, either as a matter of consistency or as a matter simply of immunity to manipulation by others.

As a guide to life, each of these three interpretations of probability suffers shortcomings. The probability of a certain kind of event, on the frequency interpretation, depends on the particular collectivity, class or sequence in which is it regarded as embedded. The probability that the insurance applicant Fred survives for ten years depends on whether he is considered a forty-year-old smoker, a forty-year-old College Professor, a skier, . . . There are many collectivities and classes to which he belongs, each with a *different* frequency of ten-year survival. By contrast, subjective probability is a direct reflection on the subject whose probability it is. According to the subjective-Bayesian account of probability, any distribution of probabilities will do, provided only that it satisfy the axioms of the calculus and refrains from assigning the extreme values of 0 and 1 to uncertain propositions. There is no requirement here that a probability assignment be constrained by any facts of the world. And the logical interpretation of probability—the third proposal canvassed above and developed by Carnap and his followers—never became settled. Optimism amongst logical theorists gradually faded: they never identified grounds *ex ante* on which to found probability assignments to state descriptions in a useful language.

Thus despite the optimism mid twentieth century, there was found no simple solution to the problem of applying probability as an integral part of a recipe for guiding life. The frequency interpretation countenanced multiple values of probability, pending identification of the relevant reference class; the subjective interpretation could accommodate any consistent values whatever, but did not dispel discomforts expressed by detractors vis-à-vis its deference to whim and vagary; and the question amongst logical theorists went in the end unanswered. Where there is advisement at all (amongst the frequency theorists), there is altogether too much—so much as to undo consistency. And where consistency is possible (among the subjectivists), there is too much freedom, and the choice amongst possibilities left up to groundless, arbitrary whim.

4. Probability and Belief-as-Decision

At about the time of Huygens, the French mathematician Blaise Pascal appealed to the notion of *expected value* to commend belief in God, as a form of decision-making. He therefore pioneered the idea that believing is a form of wagering. Assuming that the *value* of a wager is equal to the sum of the stakes involved in each of winning and losing (normally with opposite affective signs), weighted by the relative likelihoods of each, Pascal argued that since the stakes if God exist are infinite (on the one side there is eternal blessing minus small inconveniences of attending church and the small cost of candles, on the other side there is eternal damnation outweighing the pleasures of a finite earthly existence passed one's own way), then it is definitely worth believing even if the likelihood of God existing is itself very small. Besides taking for granted that one can think of believing as a form of choosing, this early argument assumes that the value to someone, of a wager, is the same as the fair asking price, itself equated (just as Huygens equated it) with the expected outcome. But there is cause here to tread with some caution.

Daniel Bernoulli, writing in 1738, argued that it is wrong to equate expected outcome with the value of a wager to the risk-taker. The example he used to drive the message home was introduced twenty-five years earlier by his brother Nicolas, and is now known as the St. Petersburg Paradox (with capital letters serving to caution that one must exercise one's very best judgment when accepting any particular solution to it). Peter promises Paul that he will toss a fair coin as many times as it takes for it to land heads, and will pay Paul one dollar if it lands heads on the first trial, two if it lands heads on the second, four if it lands heads on the third, 8 if it lands heads on the fourth, and so on (that is, 2^{n-1} dollars, where n is the trial number on which it finally turns up heads). How much should Paul be willing to pay for an opportunity to play this game? Bernoulli, for his part, asserted that no reasonable person would pay more than $20 to play the game, although its expected outcome is infinite ($\frac{1}{2} \times \$1 + \frac{1}{4} \times \$2 + \frac{1}{8} \times \$4 + \frac{1}{16} \times \$8 + \ldots = \infty$). And he explained this empirical fact by arguing—and defending it as rational—that people do not determine how much to pay for an opportunity on the basis of expected outcome, but rather on what he referred to as *expected utility*.

Aiming to explain also why people of good sense refuse fair bets (such as, for example, an equal chance of winning or losing some large sum of money S), instead of being simply indifferent between accepting and refusing them, Bernoulli originated the doctrine we now refer to familiarly as the *diminishing marginal utility of money*. This doctrine states that the value, to someone, of one more monetary unit will be strictly smaller than the value, to that same person, of one he currently holds. The effect is that my millionth dollar is worth much less to me than my tenth, or my hundredth, or even my thousandth (possibly because when one has only ten, or one hundred, dollars, one has much less in the way of a discretionary budget than if one had one million dollars).

The idea that it is rational to pay more or less than the "fair" or "market" price (understood as the expected outcome), establishes that *value* and *good* are distinct things. Value is *set* by *us*, under the prevailing conditions, upon those goods, commodities, and services that are on offer. Goods (and services too) are created and destroyed, where by contrast value is set and withdrawn. This is a metaphysical distinction. It implies that goods and values belong to different metaphysical realms or categories. This separation of good and value does not presuppose monism (the doctrine that there is only one species of intrinsic goods—goods sought or worth seeking for their own sake—of which one can have more or less). It presupposes, instead, that *value* is conferred and not found in the objects valued. And it leaves open entirely the question of what makes a good what it is—what makes a good a good. The doctrine that value is conferred rather than discovered also descends from Hume, and is taken on by the (utilitarian) architects of decision theory who come after him.[4] The cornerstone of this edifice, whose foundation was laid by the British utilitarians (for example, Jeremy Bentham and John Stuart Mill) and which was brought to completion by von Neumann and Morgenstern, is the doctrine of expected utility—to the effect that the supremely rational decision maker maximizes expected utility, not expected value.

Now if believing can be a form of wagering, as Pascal suggested, then it is a form of decision making, and hence subject to the doctrine of expected utility. Belief formation becomes a specimen of practical reasoning, and the distinction between theoretical reasoning and practical reasoning as nonoverlapping forms of reason—a distinction that was insisted upon with nary a second thought before the nineteenth century—disappears. This is the Bayesian turn, which was in many ways anticipated by Karl Popper.[5]

Bayesianism is an uneasy contemporary marriage between eighteenth-century empiricism, on the one side, and modern decision theory, on the other side. Bayesianism, like many of its rivals, divides reasoning *ab initio* into two kinds: theoretical (or disciplinary) reasoning and practical reasoning. Practical reasoning has the function of controlling action or decision: its point is to figure out what to do. This is contrasted with disciplinary reasoning, whose aim is to figure out how things stand in the world, rather than what to do about them. Bayesians moreover maintain that disciplinary and practical reasoning operate independently—each without consultation with the other. This (if true) preserves the impartiality of scientific disciplines, by way of ensuring that the opinions we (as scientists) hold as to how things stand in the world, are not influenced by how we might wish things stood (our utilities). And this, of course, guarantees that science and other theoretical achievements committed within a disciplinary setting are never tainted by wishful thinking.

Now Bayesians also believe that all reasoning, even disciplinary reasoning, is at bottom a form of decision making, to which a cost-benefit calculus applies at the ground floor. Thus, while the Bayesian marriage between theoretical reason and practical reason is supposed to be a marriage of equals, it really is not. And so the contemporary Bayesian, against the likes of Hume, Descartes, Carnap, and Kant, maintains the idea that the fundamental imperatives for all of human life are practical, and that disciplinary reasoning ultimately resolves into practical reasoning. Everything in the cognitive cornucopia, according to the Bayesian, is poured out, in the first instance, as a guide to life.

5. Probability and Causality

Hume defined the notion of cause twice over, within the space of paragraphs: once in terms of necessary connections or secret powers connecting events together in time, and a second time in terms of how human impressions of objects in the world are related. In the first instance we have a cause as "an object, followed by another, and where all objects similar to the first are followed by objects similar to the second" (*Enquiry Concerning Human Understanding*).[6] In the second, a cause is "an object followed by another, and whose appearance always conveys the thought to that other." This definition twice over could be interpreted (as many have suggested) as a reductionist strategy, in which the notion of cause is reduced to that of a chance- or probability-raiser. For we can harmonize Hume's two definitions through the proposal that a cause (by definition) functions to render its effect more likely or more probable. So that (once again) probability should serve as a guide to life, by serving as a guide to making the shortest, most cost-effective, or in some other way best, beeline to our (human) objectives.

Hume's remarks about causation, besides creating a crisis in the theory of knowledge, created a stir also in the discipline of metaphysics, by drawing attention to the fact that too little attention had been given to discussion of the metaphysical referent of the term "cause," understood in Aristotle's sense of "efficient cause." To be sure, Malebranche and Leibniz treated the question of how it is possible to have world of causes alongside an omnipotent and omniscient God, but they did not elaborate on what the term "cause" refers to. The debate Hume sparked on this point rages today, if anything more than ever before, with the Humean occupying a distinctive position in the spectrum.

The Humean reduction falls nowadays under a larger class of proposals that can be termed reductionistic. The reductionist seeks to identify the core of the concept of cause, with a central function of the causal concept in the economy of human life. The most resilient reductionist proposal extant today is traceable to Hume himself. It claims for its foundation the idea that causal facts are nothing more than configurations of probability relations—specifically, facts about certain factors improving the chances of others. This is the proposal that lies behind all probabilistic accounts of causality. Probabilistic accounts draw heavily upon highly sophisticated statistical analyses. They confer upon the notion of chance—or at any rate that of probability—a fundamental role to play in the universe with which humans must cope, both practically and scientifically. And so they both service and cultivate a class of coping sciences—the engineering sciences, under which fall all the medical and clinical disciplines.

But inference from statistical data to causal hypothesis is treacherous, fraught with danger and drama. One of the most well known problems is Simpson's Paradox, and is famously illustrated by a certain constellation of incidents at Berkeley. The graduate school at Berkeley was once accused of discriminating against women in admissions, so that the question was raised, "Does being a woman cause one to be rejected at Berkeley?" The accusation rested on the numbers: women seeking graduate admission at Berkeley were rejected at a much higher rate than men. But when the data were more closely scrutinized, it was found that in a majority of the 85 graduate departments, the probability of admission for women was just about the same as for men, and in some even higher for women than for men. The reason for the overall rate of rejection of women being higher, is simply that women tended to apply to departments with higher rejection rates overall than men did. This illustrates the reality that inference from numbers to causes, even if possible in principle, is very difficult.

6. The Larger Uses of Probability

In life, the more probable routinely happens more often than the less probable—if there's anything in a name. But this only underscores the fact that sometimes the less probable happens. Does this require explanation? Does nature owe us an explanation when the less likely happens in preference to the more likely? This question raises, albeit in a narrower context than usual, the question of what explanation consists in, and the role of probability in explanation. And it raises in an oblique fashion the question of the relationship between giving explanation and attending to relations of cause and effect. At the center of the debate over explanation are those who equate explanation-giving with the illumination of causes. Naturally, their adversaries separate the terms of this equation. However this debate plays itself out, the question will still remain as to how knowledge of probabilities should bear upon issues of moral and legal responsibility. Are we entitled to use statistical knowledge in assessing guilt? How shall we use probabilities responsibly, on the way to framing scientific explanations? And how shall we use them responsibly in the courtroom?

NOTES

1. David Hume, *Enquiry Concerning Human Understanding*, sec. IV, part II.

2. Hume, *Enquiry Concerning Human Understanding*, sec. IV, part II, para. 8–10.

3. John von Neumann and Oskar Morgenstern, *Theory of Games and Economic Behavior* (Princeton: Princeton University Press, 1944).

4. It isn't true, therefore, that the Humean is not in a position to make a distinction between wanting and valuing, as Gary Watson suggests in the much-cited article "Free Agency," *Journal of Philosophy* 72 (1975): 205–20. In fact, the Humean *must* make that distinction—and does—for the sake of her utility theory.

5. See Mariam Thalos, "*The Logic of Scientific Discovery* by Karl Popper," in *The Classics of Western Philosophy*, ed. J. Gracia, G. Reichberg, and B. Schumacher (Blackwell Publishers, 2002).

6. Hume, *Enquiry Concerning Human Understanding*, sec. VII.

PART I

Probability, Frequency, and Inference

1

Reichenbach, Reference Classes, and Single-Case 'Probabilities'

JAMES H. FETZER

The problem of the single case has haunted probability theoreticians, especially those with an objective orientation, since they (Mises and Reichenbach, for example) tend to assume that probabilities are to be defined extensionally and collectively. Thus, the definition of a "collective" (or of a "normal sequence") presupposes that the reference class is infinite, since otherwise the conditions imposed cannot be met on purely logical grounds alone. But even given infinite sequences, the relationship between the infinite long run and the finite short run, much less the single case, remain problematic.

The single-case propensity approach, which defines probabilities as single-case causal tendencies of probabilistic strength, supplies an interpretation that is not only meaningful for the single case but also for the short run and the long run, as finite and as infinite sequences of single cases. Moreover, as the arguments elaborated here establish, the reference-class problem yields only degenerate probabilities equal to zero or to one on extensional collectivist accounts, where overcoming these problems requires an ontological conception that is both intensional and distributive in character.

—*J. H.*

Perhaps the most difficult problem confronted by Reichenbach's explication of physical probabilities as limiting frequencies is that of providing decision procedures for assigning singular occurrences to appropriate reference classes, that is, *the problem of the single case.*[1] Presuming the

Reprinted from W. C. Salmon, ed. *Hans Reichenbach: Logical Empiricist*, 187–219.

symmetry of explanations and predictions is not taken for granted, this difficulty would appear to have two (possibly nondistinct) dimensions, namely: the problem of selecting appropriate reference classes for *predicting* singular occurrences, that is, the problem of (single-case) prediction, and the problem of selecting appropriate reference classes for *explaining* singular occurrences, that is, the problem of (single-case) explanation. If the symmetry thesis is theoretically sound, then these aspects of the problem of the single case are actually nondistinct, since any singular occurrence should be assigned to one and the same reference class for purposes of either kind; but if it is not the case that singular occurrences should be assigned to one and the same reference class for purposes of either kind, then these aspects are distinct and the symmetry thesis is not sound.[2]

The decision procedure that Reichenbach advanced to contend with the problem of the single case, that is, the policy of assigning singular occurrences to "*the narrowest reference class for which reliable statistics can be compiled*," moreover, strongly suggests that one and the same reference class should serve for purposes of either kind. Reichenbach himself primarily focused attention on the problem of (single-case) prediction, without exploring the ramifications of his resolution of the problem of the single case for the problem of (single-case) explanation.[3] The theories of explanation subsequently proposed by Carl G. Hempel and by Wesley C. Salmon, however, may both be viewed as developments with considerable affinities to Reichenbach's position, which nevertheless afford distinct alternative solutions to the problem of (single-case) explanation.[4] In spite of their differences, moreover, when Hempel's and Salmon's formulations are understood as incorporating the frequency criterion of statistical relevance, they appear to be saddled with theoretical difficulties whose resolution, in principle, requires the adoption of an alternative construction.

The purpose of this paper is to provide a systematic appraisal of Reichenbach's analysis of single-case 'probabilities' *with particular concern for the frequency conceptions of statistical relevance and of statistical explanation,* especially as they may be related to the theories of explanation advanced by Hempel and Salmon. Among the conclusions supported by this investigation are the following:

(a) that the frequency criterion of relevance is theoretically inadequate in failing to distinguish between two distinct kinds of 'statistical relevance';

(b) that reliance upon this defective criterion of relevance suggests that, on frequency principles, there are no irreducibly statistical explanations; and,

(c) that these difficulties are only resolvable within the frequency framework by invoking epistemic contextual considerations.

As a result, taken together, these reflections strongly support the contention that the problem of (single-case) prediction and the problem of (single-case) explanation require distinct (if analogous) resolution, that is, that the symmetry thesis is unsound; and indirectly confirm the view that the meaning of *single-case* probabilities should be regarded as fundamental, where a clear distinction may be drawn between *causal* relevance and *inductive* relevance on the basis of a statistical disposition conception, that is, that Reichenbach's limiting frequency construction should be displaced by Popper's propensity interpretation for the explication of probability as a physical magnitude.

1. Reichenbach's Analysis of Single-Case 'Probabilities'

The theoretical foundation for Reichenbach's analysis of the single case, of course, is provided by the definition of 'probability' itself: "In order to develop the frequency interpretation, we define probability as the *limit of a frequency* within an infinite sequence."[5] In other words, the probability r of the occurrence of a certain outcome attribute A within an infinite sequence of trials S is the limiting frequency with which A occurs in S, that is,

(I) $P(S, A) = r =_{df}$ the limit of the frequency for outcome attribute A within the infinite trial sequence S equals r.

Reichenbach himself assumes no properties other than the limiting frequency of A within S as necessary conditions for the existence of probabilities and thereby obtains an interpretation of the broadest possible generality.[6] It is important to note, however, that Reichenbach envisions *finite* sequences as also possessing 'limits' in the following sense:

> Notice that a limit exists even when only a finite number of elements x_i belongs to S; the value of the frequency for the last element is then regarded as the limit. This trivial case is included in the interpretation and does not create any difficulty.[7]

One justification for the inclusion of such 'limits', moreover, is that when the sequence S contains only a finite number of members, those members may be counted repetitiously an endless number of times to generate trivial limiting frequencies.[8]

As the basis for a theoretical reconciliation of these concepts, therefore, let us assume that a sequence *S* is *infinite* if and only if *S* contains at least one member and the description of its reference class does not impose any upper bound to the number of members of that class on syntactical or semantical grounds alone. Although 'limits' may be properties of finite sequences under this interpretation, they are not supposed to be properties of single individual trials *per se* and may only be predicated of single individual trials *as a manner of speaking:*

> I regard the statement about the probability of the single case, not as having a meaning of its own, but as representing an elliptical mode of speech. In order to acquire meaning, the statement must be translated into a statement about a frequency in a sequence of repeated occurrences. The statement concerning the probability of the single case thus is given a *fictitious meaning*, constructed by a *transfer of meaning from the general to the particular case.*[9]

Strictly speaking, therefore, probabilities are only properties of single trials as members of reference classes collectively; but Reichenbach nevertheless countenances referring to 'probabilities' as properties of such trials distributively "not for cognitive reasons, but because it serves the purpose of action to deal with such statements as meaningful."[10] Indeed, in order to distinguish the meaning of 'probability' with respect to the occurrence of singular trials and of infinite trial sequences, Reichenbach introduces a different term, that is, 'weight', for application to the single case.

In spite of this difference in meaning, the numerical value of the weight to be assigned to attribute *A* as the outcome of a singular trial *T*, in principle, is determined by the limiting frequency with which *A* occurs within a trial sequence of kind *K*, where $T \in K$. The existence of a single-case weight for the occurrence of attribute *A* thus requires (i) the existence of an infinite sequence of trials of kind *K* (ii) with a limiting frequency for *A* equal to *r*, where (iii) it is not the case there exists some other infinite sequence of kind *K* such that the limiting frequency for *A* is not equal to *r*; hence, '$P(K, A) = r$' is true if and only if there exists an infinite sequence of trials of kind *K*, then the limiting frequency for outcomes of kind *A* is equal to *r* .[11] In effect, therefore, every single individual trial *T* that happens to be a trial of kind *K* with respect to the occurrence of attribute *A* must be regarded as a member of a unique trial sequence *K* consisting of all and only those single trials that are trials of a kind *K* with respect to the occurrence of attribute *A* must be regarded as a member of a unique trial sequence *K* consisting of all and only those single trials that are trials of kind K with respect to the occurrence of outcome attribute *A*; otherwise, violation of the uniqueness condition would generate explicit contradictions of the form, '$P(K, A) \neq P(K, A)$'.[12]

Any single individual trial, however, may be exhaustively described if and only if *every* property of that trial is explicitly specifiable including, therefore, the spatial and the temporal relations of that instantiation of properties relative to every other. Let us assume that any single individual trial T is a property of some object or collection of objects x such that, for each such individual trial, 'Tx' is true if and only if '$F^1x \cdot F^2x \cdot \ldots$', is true, where '$F^1$', '$F^2$', . . . , and so on are predicates designating distinct properties of that single individual trial. Then the single individual trial T is subject to exhaustive description, in principle, if and only if there exists some number m such that F^1 through F^m exhausts every property of that single individual trial; otherwise, the single individual trial T is not exhaustively describable, even in principle, since there is no end to the number of properties that would have to be specified in order to provide an exhaustive description of that trial T. The last time I turned the ignition to start my car, for example, was a single individual trial involving a 1970 Audi 100LS 4-door red sedan, with a Kentucky license plate, a recorded mileage of 88,358.4 miles, that had been purchased in 1973 for $2600.00 and driven to California during the summer of the same year, and so on, which was parked in the right-most section of a three-car wooden garage to the rear of a two-story building at 159 Woodland Avenue in Lexington, on a somewhat misty morning at approximately 10:30 A.M. on 12 March 1976, one-half hour after I had drunk a cup of coffee, and so forth. As it happened, the car would not start.

The significance of examples such as this, I surmise, has two distinctive aspects. On the one hand, of course, it indicates the enormous difficulty, in principle, of providing an exhaustive description of any such individual trial; indeed, it strongly suggests *a density principle for single trial descriptions*, that is, that for any description '$F^1x \cdot \ldots \cdot F^mx$' of any singular trial T that occurs during the course of the world's history, there exists some further description '$F^1x \cdot \ldots \cdot F^nx$' such that the set of predicates {'F^1', . . . , 'F^m'} is a proper subset of the set of predicates {'F^1', . . . , 'F^n'}.[13] On the other hand, it is at least equally important to notice that, among all of the properties that have thus far been specified, only some *but not all* would be viewed as contributing factors, i.e., as relevant variables, with respect to the outcome attribute of starting or not, as the case happened to be; in other words, even if this single individual trial is not exhaustively describable, it does not follow that the *causally relevant* properties of this trial arrangement T are themselves not exhaustively describable; for the properties whose presence or absence contributed to bringing about my car's failure to start would include, perhaps, accumulated moisture in the distributor, but would not include, presumably, my wearing a flannel overshirt at the time. It is at least logically possible, therefore, that among the infinity of properties that happened to attend this single individual trial, only a finite proper subset would exhaust all those exerting any influence upon that outcome attribute on that particular occasion.

The theoretical problem in general, therefore, may be described as follows, namely: for any single individual trial *T*, (i) to determine the kind of trial *K* that *T* happens to be with respect to the occurrence of outcome attribute *A*; and, (ii) to ascertain the limiting frequency *r* with which attribute *A* occurs within the infinite sequence of trials of kind *K*, if such a sequence and such a limit both happen to exist. The theoretical 'problem of the single case', therefore, is precisely that of determining the kind of trial *K* that any single individual trial *T* happens to be with respect to the occurrence of an outcome attribute of kind *A*, that is, the problem of the selection of a unique reference sequence *K* for the assignment of a unique individual trial *T*. Reichenbach's solution to this problem is therefore enormously important to his analysis of the single case:

> We then proceed by considering *the narrowest class for which reliable statistics can be compiled.* If we are confronted by two overlapping classes, we shall choose their common class. Thus, if a man is 21 years old and has tuberculosis, we shall regard the class of persons of 21 who have tuberculosis [with respect to his life expectancy]. Classes that are known to be irrelevant for the statistical result may be disregarded. A class *C* is irrelevant with respect to the reference class *K* and the attribute class *A* if the transition to the common class *K* • *C* does not change the probability, that is, if $P(K \cdot C, A) = P(K, A)$. For instance, the class of persons having the same initials is irrelevant for the life expectation of a person.[14]

A property C is *statistically relevant* to the occurrence of an attribute *A* with respect to a reference class *K*, let us assume, if and only if:

(II) $P(K \cdot C, A) \neq P(K, A)$;

that is, the limiting frequency for the outcome attribute *A* within the infinite sequence of *K* • *C* trials differs from the limiting frequency for that same attribute within the infinite sequence of K trials itself.[15]

Since a unique individual trial *T* is supposed to be assigned to the narrowest reference class *K* "for which reliable statistics can be compiled," it seems clear that for Reichenbach, at least, a decision of this kind depends upon the state of knowledge $\mathcal{K}$ of an individual or collection of individuals *z* at a specific time *t*, that is, the set of statements $\{\mathcal{K}\}$ accepted or believed by *z* at *t*, no matter whether true or not, as follows:

> Whereas the probability of a single case is thus made dependent on our state of knowledge, this consequence does not hold for a probability referred to classes. . . . The probability of death for men 21 years old concerns a frequency that holds for events of nature and has nothing to do with our knowledge

> about them, nor is it changed by the fact that the death probability is higher in the narrower class or tuberculous men of the same age. The dependence of a single-case probability on our state of knowledge originates from the impossibility of giving this concept an independent interpretation; there exist only substitutes for it, given by class probabilities, and the choice of the substitute depends on our state of knowledge.[16]

Reichenbach allows that statistical knowledge concerning a reference class K may be fragmentary and incomplete, where the problem is one of "balancing the importance of the prediction against the reliability available." Nevertheless, as a general policy, Reichenbach proposes treating an individual trial T as a member of successively narrower and narrower reference classes K^1, K^2, . . . and so on, where each class is specified by taking into account successively more and more statistically relevant properties F^1, F^2, and so forth, where $K^1 \supset K^2$, $K^2 \supset K^3$, and so on and $P(K^1, A) \neq P(K^2, A)$, $P(K^2, A) \neq P(K^3, A)$, and so forth.

Reichenbach observes that, strictly speaking, the choice of a reference *class* is not identical with the choice of a reference *sequence*, since the members of that class may be ordered in different ways, which my sometimes differ in probability.[17] The intriguing question, however, is precisely how narrow the appropriate class in principle should be if our knowledge of the world were complete:

> According to general experience, the probability will approach a limit when the single case is enclosed in narrower and narrower classes, to the effect that, from a certain step on, further narrowing will no longer result in noticeable improvement. It is not necessary for the justification of this method that the limit of the probability, respectively, is = 1 or is = 0, as the hypothesis of causality [i.e., the hypothesis of determinism] assumes. Neither is this necessary *a priori*; modern quantum mechanics asserts the contrary. It is obvious that for the limit 1 or 0 the probability still refers to a class, not to an individual event, and that the probability 1 cannot exclude the possibility that in the particular case considered the prediction is false. Even in the limit the substitute for the probability of a single case will thus be a class probability. . . .[18]

The evident reply on Reichenbach's analysis, therefore, is that the appropriate reference class K relative to a knowledge context $\mathcal{K}zt$ containing every sentence that is true of the world and no sentence that is false would be some reference class K^i where $T \in K^i$ and, for every class K^i such that $T \in K^j$ and $K^i \supset K^j$, it is not the case that $P(K^i, \mathrm{A}) \neq P(K^j, A)$; that is, with respect to attribute A for trial T, K should be an *ontically homogeneous reference class* in the sense that (i) $T \in K$; (ii) $P(K, A) = r$; and (iii) for all subclasses K^j of K to which T belongs, $P(K^j, A) = \mathrm{r} = P(K, A)$.

Notice that the class K itself is not necessarily unique with respect to the set of properties $\{F^i\}$ specified by the reference class description of K;

for any class K^j such that $K \supseteq K^j$ and $K^j \supseteq K$ (where K is an ontically homogeneous reference class relative to attribute A for trial T) will likewise qualify as an ontically homogeneous reference class relative to attribute A for trial T even though the set of properties $\{F^j\}$ specified by the reference class description of K^j differs from that for K, that is, $\{F^i\} \neq \{F^j\}$. Consequently, although any classes K and K^j which happen to be such that $K \supseteq K^j$ and $K^j \supseteq K$ will of course possess all and only the same trial members and will therefore yield the same frequencies for various specific attributes with respect to those same trial members, their reference class descriptions, nevertheless, will not invariably coincide. From this point of view, therefore, the resolution of the reference class problem by assigning a single case to an ontically homogeneous reference class does not provide a unique *description* solution but rather a unique *value* solution. Nevertheless, on Reichenbachian principles, it may be argued further that there *is* a unique description solution as well as a unique value solution, namely: that any single individual trial T should be assigned to the *narrowest* class, that is, *the class whose description includes specification of the largest set of properties of that individual trial,* "for which reliable statistics can be compiled."

The largest set of properties of an individual trial T that might be useful for this purpose, of course, is not logically equivalent to the set of all of the properties of that individual trial; for any individual trial T may be described by means of predicates that violate the provision that reference classes may not be logically limited to a finite number of members on syntactical or semantical grounds alone. Let us therefore assume that *a predicate expression is logically impermissible for the specification of a reference class description* if (a) that predicate expression is necessarily satisfied by every object or (b) that predicate expression is necessarily satisfied by no more that a specific number N of objects during the course of the world's history.[19] Predicates that happen to be satisfied by only one individual object during the course of the world's history, therefore, are permissible predicates for reference class descriptions so long as their extensions are not finite on logical grounds alone, as, for example, might be any predicate expression essentially requiring proper names for its definition or such that the satisfaction of that expression by some proper name would yield a logical truth.[20] Let us further assume that no predicate expression logically entailing the attribute predicate or its negation is permissible. Then the largest set of permissible predicates describing a single trial T is not logically equivalent to the set of all of the properties of that individual trial; but nevertheless it will remain the case that, in general, such *narrowest* reference class descriptions are satisfied by only one individual event during the course of the world's history *as a matter of logical necessity.*[21]

These considerations suggest an insuperable objection to the applicability, in principle, of the frequency interpretation of probability; for if it is true that each individual trial T is describable, in principle, by some set of predicates such that (i) every member of that set is a permissible predicate for the purpose of a reference class description and (ii) that reference class description itself is satisfied by that individual trial alone, then the indispensable criterion of statistical relevance is systematically inapplicable for the role it is intended to fulfill. For under these circumstances, every individual trial T is the solitary member of reference class K* described by a reference class description consisting of the conjunction of a set of permissible predicates $F^1, F^2, \ldots, F^n$, that is, $\{F^n\}$, where, moreover, lacking any information concerning the statistical relevance or irrelevance of any property of any singular trial—other than that the attribute A did occur (or did not occur) on that particular trial—it is systematically impossible to specify which of the properties of the trial T are statistically relevant and which are not; for the occurrence of that outcome, whether A or not-A, in principle, *must be attributed to the totality of properties present at that individual trial.*[22] Reliable statistics, after all, are only as reliable as the individual statistics upon which they are based; so *if the only statistical data that may be ascertained, in principle, concern the occurrence of outcome attributes on singular trials where each singular trial is the solitary member of a reference class, there is no basis for accumulating the 'reliable statistics' necessary for the applicability of the frequency criterion.* Of each individual trial $T^1, T^2, \ldots$, it is possible in principle to specify a homogeneous reference class description $K^{*1}, K^{*2}, \ldots$; but since each trial is the solitary member of its particular reference class, it is impossible to employ the frequency criterion to ascertain which properties, if any, among all of those present on each such singular trial, are statistically irrelevant to it outcome.

The theoretical problem of the single case, let us recall, requires, for any single individual trial T, (i) to determine the kind of trial K that T happens to be with respect to the occurrence of outcome attribute A; and, (ii) to ascertain the limiting frequency r with which attribute A occurs in the infinite sequence of trials of kind K, when such a sequence and such a limit both happen to exist. With respect to any single individual trial T that actually occurs in the course of the world's history, however, these conditions are, in effect, automatically satisfied; for (i) any such trial T may be described by some set of permissible predicates $\{F^n\}$ specifying a kind of trial K^* of which T is the solitary member, where, nevertheless, (ii) the reference class K^* is not logically limited to any finite number of members and Reichenbach's limit concept for infinite sequences of this kind is trivially satisfied by 0 or 1. Any other such singular trial T^i, after all, may likewise be described by some set of permissible predicates, that is, $\{F^i\}$, where

$\{F^i\} \neq \{F^n\}$, a condition of individuation that distinct events surely have to satisfy. With respect to each such singular trial *T*, of course, outcome attribute *A* either occurs or does not occur. Assume that *T* belongs to reference class *K* for which the probability of *A* is $\neq 0$ and $\neq 1$; that is, (a) $T \in K$; and, (b) $P(K, A) = r$, where $0 \neq r \neq 1$. Then there necessarily exists a subclass of that class K^* such that $P(K^*, A) = 0$ or $= 1$, namely: the class specified by any set of permissible predicates $\{F^n\}$ of which trial *T* is the solitary member. Hence, since $P(K^*, A) \neq P(K, A)$ and $K \supset K^*$, the properties differentiating between K^* and *K* are statistically relevant with respect to the occurrence of attribute *A*, necessarily, by the frequency criterion; moreover, for any such reference class *K* such that (a) $T \in K$ and (b) $P(K, A) = r$, where $0 \neq r \neq 1$, it is theoretically impossible that *K* is a homogeneous reference class for trial *T* with respect to attribute *A* in Reichenbach's sense. Indeed, on the basis of the frequency criterion of statistical relevance, such an assumption is always invariably false.

The point of the preceding criticism, therefore, may be stated as follows: The only data available for ascertaining the reliable statistics necessary for arriving at determinations of the statistical relevance or irrelevance of any property F^i with respect to any outcome attribute *A* is that the frequency with which outcome *A* accompanies trials of kind $K \cdot F^i$ differs from that with which *A* accompanies trials of the kind *K*. Every single individual trial T^i occurring during the course of the world's history may be described as a member of some K^* reference class specified by at least one conjunction of permissible predicates K^{*i} that is satisfied by that individual trial. As a necessary logical truth, every such trial happens to belong to one and only one *narrowest* class of this kind; however, since the K^* reference classes are not likewise limited to any finite number of members, the occurrence of the attribute *A* may still be assigned a probability, which, in this case, will be = 1 or = 0, depending upon whether that outcome occurred or failed to occur on that individual trial. The frequency criterion of statistical relevance, presumably, should permit distinguishing between the statistically relevant and irrelevant properties of each such trial. However, *since each trial* T^i *happens to be different in kind*, the only conclusion supported by that criterion of relevance is that every single property distinguishing those individual trials with respect to the occurrence of a specific attribute *A* is statistically relevant to the occurrence of that outcome; for those properties certainly 'made a difference', insofar as in one such case the attribute *A* occurred, while in another such case *A* did not occur. Thus, under circumstances of this kind, it is systematically impossible to obtain the reliable statistics necessary to support determinations of statistical relevance; for in the absence of that statistical evidence, such 'conclusions' merely take for granted what that evidence alone is capable of demonstrating.

2. Salmon's 'Relevance' Account of Statistical Explanation

It is interesting to observe that Reichenbach himself tended to focus upon the problems involved in the *prediction* of singular events rather than those involved in their *explanation*. The differences that distinguish explanations from predictions, however, may figure in significant ways within the present context; for if it happens to be the case that the purpose of a prediction is to establish grounds for *believing that* a certain statement (describing an event) is true, and the purpose of an explanation is to establish grounds for *explaining why* an event (described by a certain statement) occurs, that is, if predictions are appropriately interpreted as *reason-seeking* why-questions, while explanations are appropriately interpreted as *explanation-seeking* why-questions, it might well turn out that at least part of the problem with the frequency criterion of statistical relevance is that it is based upon an insufficient differentiation between explanation and prediction contexts.[23] Consider the following:

(a) Reason-seeking why-questions are relative to a particular epistemic context, that is, a knowledge context $\mathcal{K}zt$ as previously specified, where, with respect to an individual hypothesis H whose truth is not known, *a requirement of total evidence* may appropriately be employed according to which, for any statement S belonging to $\mathcal{K}zt$, *S is inductively relevant to the truth of H* if and only if the inductive (or epistemic) probability EP of H relative to $\mathcal{K}zt \cdot S$ differs from the inductive probability of H relative to $\mathcal{K}zt \cdot -S$, that is,

$$\text{(III)}\ EP(\mathcal{K}zt \cdot S, H) \neq EP(\mathcal{K}zt \cdot -S, H);$$

where, in effect, any statement within $\mathcal{K}zt$ whose truth or falsity makes a difference to the inductive probability of an hypothesis H must be taken into consideration in determining the inductive probability of that hypothesis.[24]

(b) Explanation-seeking why-questions are relative to a specific ontic context, that is, the nomological regularities and particular facts of the physical world W, where, with respect to the explanandum-event described by an explanandum statement E whose truth is presumably known, *a requirement of causal relevance* should appropriately be employed according to which, for any property F belonging to W, *F is explanatorily relevant to the occurrence of E* (relative to reference class K) if and only if the physical (or ontic) probability PP of E relative to $K \cdot F$ is not the same as the physical probability of E relative to $K \cdot -F$, that is,

$$\text{(IV)}\ PP(K \cdot F, E) \neq PP(K \cdot -F, E);$$

where, in effect, any property whose presence or absence relative to reference class K makes a difference to the physical probability of an explanandum-event E must be taken into consideration in constructing an adequate explanation for that event.[25]

If predictions belong to the epistemic reason-seeking context, then it is entirely plausible to take into account any property whose presence or absence changes the inductive probability of an hypothesis H with respect to a knowledge context $\mathcal{K}zt$; indeed, a requirement of total evidence would require that any such property G of any individual object x belonging to the knowledge context $\mathcal{K}zt$ has to be taken into consideration in calculating the inductive probability of any H where the statement G^* attributing G to x is such that

$$\text{(V)}\ EP(\mathcal{K}zt \cdot G^*, H) \neq EP(\mathcal{K}zt \cdot -G^*, H);$$

where, as it might be expressed, the statistical relationship between property G and the attribute property A described by the hypothesis H may be merely one of statistical correlation rather than one of causal connection, i.e., it is not necessary that G be a property whose presence or absence contributes to bringing about the occurrence of an outcome of kind A relative to some reference class K.

It is not at all obvious, however, that the frequency criterion provides any theoretical latitude for differentiating between statistical relations of these quite distinctive kinds; on the contrary, it appears as though any factor at all with respect to which frequencies differ is on that account alone 'statistically relevant' to the probability of an hypothesis H or an explanandum E, respectively, without reflecting any theoretical difference between the explanation-seeking and the reason-seeking situations themselves. If every member of the class of twenty-one-year-old men K were also a member of the class of tuberculous persons T, for example, then the property of being tuberculous would be statistically irrelevant to the outcome attribute of death D. But although this property might reasonably be ignored for the purpose of prediction (as a matter of statistical correlation), it would not be reasonable to ignore this property for the purpose of explanation (when it makes a causal contribution to such an individual's death). If there is a significant difference between these kinds of situations, therefore, then those principles appropriate for establishing relevance relations within one of these contexts may be theoretically inappropriate for establishing relevance relations within the other. Perhaps the crucial test of the utility of Reichenbach's criterion of statistical relevance is found within the context of explanation rather than the context of prediction; for an examination of the statistical relevance account of explanation advanced by Salmon may provide an opportunity to evaluate the criticisms of that principle thus far considered.

Salmon departs from Reichenbach's formulations, not in deviating from his criterion of statistical relevance, but rather in assigning a single case not to the *narrowest* relevant class but to the *broadest* relevant class instead:

> If every property that determines a place selection is statistically irrelevant to A in K, I shall say that K is a homogeneous reference class for A. A reference class is homogeneous if there is no way, even in principle, to effect a statistically relevant partition without already knowing which elements have the attribute in question and which do not. . . . The aim in selecting a reference class to which to assign a single case is not to select the narrowest, but the widest, available class. . . . I would reformulate Reichenbach's method of selection of a reference class as follows: choose the broadest homogeneous reference class to which the single event belongs.[26]

Precisely because Salmon preserves the frequency criterion of relevance, his own formulations encounter difficulties analogous to those previously specified; but the introduction of the concept of a partition and of a 'screening-off' rule may be viewed as significant contributions to the frequency theory of explanation as follows:

(i) On Salmon's analysis, *a partition of a reference class* K is established by a division of that class into a set of mutually exclusive and jointly exhaustive subsets by means of a set of properties $F^1, F^2, \ldots F^m$ and their complements where each ultimate subset of that class $K \cdot C^1$, $K \cdot C^2, \ldots, K \cdot C^n$ is homogeneous with respect to the outcome attribute A.[27] This procedure may be regarded as effecting a refinement in the application of Reichenbach's criterion, since it thus assumes that a property C is *statistically relevant* to the occurrence of attribute A with respect to a reference class K if and only if:

$$\text{(II*)}\ P(K \cdot C, A) \neq P(K \cdot -C, A);$$

that is, the limiting frequency for the outcome attribute A within the infinite sequence of $K \cdot C$ trials differs from the limiting frequency for that same outcome within the infinite sequence of $K \cdot -C$ trials.

(ii) Furthermore, a property F *screens off a property* G with respect to an outcome attribute A within the reference class K if and only if:

$$\text{(VI)}\ P(K \cdot F \cdot G, A) = P(K \cdot F \cdot -G, A) \neq P(K \cdot -F \cdot G, A);$$

where the equality between the limiting frequency for A within the classes $K \cdot F \cdot G$ and $K \cdot F \cdot -G$, on the one hand, establishes that the property G is not statistically relevant with respect to attribute A within the reference class $K \cdot F$; and the inequality between the limiting frequency for A within the class $K \cdot -F \cdot G$ and classes $K \cdot F \cdot G$ and $K \cdot F \cdot -G$, on the other hand, establishes that the property F is statistically relevant with respect to the attribute A within the reference class $K \cdot G$.[28]

Salmon consolidates these ingredients as the foundation for his explication of explanation on the basis of the principle that screening-off properties should take precedence over properties which they screen off within an explanation situation.[29] According to Salmon, an explanation of the fact that x, a member of the reference class K, is a member of the attribute class A as well, may be provided by fulfilling the following set of conditions, that is,

(1) $K \cdot C^1, K \cdot C^2, \ldots, K \cdot C^n$ is a homogeneous partition of K relative to A;

(2) $P(K \cdot C^1, A) = r^1, P(K \cdot C^2, A) = r^2, \ldots, P(K \cdot C^n, A) = r^n$;

(3) $r^i = r^j$ only if $i = j$; and,

(4) $x \in K \cdot C^m$ (where $m \in \{1, 2, \ldots, n\}$).[30]

Consequently, the appropriate reference class to specify in order to explain an outcome A for the trial T is the ontically homogeneous reference class $K \cdot C^m$ such that (a) $T \in K \cdot C^m$; (b) $P(K \cdot C^m, A) = r^m$; and, (c) for all homogeneous reference classes $K \cdot C^1, K \cdot C^2, \ldots, K \cdot C^n$ relative to outcome, A, $r^i = r^j$ only if $i = j$, which, presumably, is intended to insure that there is one and only one reference class to which T may appropriately be assigned, namely: the *broadest* one of that kind. From this point of view, therefore, Salmon provides a unique description solution as well as a unique value solution to the single case problem.

Salmon's conditions of adequacy, let us note, are sufficient for the purpose of assigning individual trials to broadest homogeneous reference classes *only if* broadest homogeneous reference classes may be described by means of what may be referred to as *disjunctive properties*, that is, predicate expressions of the form, '$K \cdot F^1 \vee F^2 \vee \ldots \vee F^n$', where a statement of the form '$P(K \cdot F^1 \vee F^2 \vee \ldots \vee F^n, A) = r$', is true if and only if '$P(K \cdot F^1, A) = P(K \cdot F^2, A) = \ldots = P(K \cdot F^n, A) = r$' is true, as Salmon himself has explicitly pointed out.[31] Otherwise, Salmon's conditions would be theoretically objectionable, insofar as it might actually be the case that there is an infinite set of reference classes, $\{K \cdot C^i\}$, whose members satisfy conditions (1) and (2) only if they do not satisfy condition (3), and conversely. The difficulty with this maneuver as a method of preserving Salmon's conditions (1) through (4) as sufficient conditions of explanatory adequacy, however, is that it entails the adoption of *a degenerating explanation paradigm*; for the occurrence of attribute A on trial T may be explained by referring that trial to a successively more and more *causally heterogeneous* reference class under the guise of the principle of reference class homogeneity. For if condition (3) is retained, then if, for example, the division of the class of twenty-one-year-old men K on the basis of the properties of having tuberculosis F^1 or heart disease F^2 or a brain tumor F^3 establishes a subclass such that, with respect to the attribute of death D, $P(K \cdot F^1 \vee F^2 \vee F^3, D) = r$ is an ultimate subset of the homogeneous partition of that original class, that is, $\{K \cdot F^1 \vee F^2 \vee F^3\} = \{K \cdot C^m\}$, then the explanation for the death of an individual member i of class K resulting from a brain tumor, perhaps, is only explainable by identifying i as a member of class $K \cdot C^m$, that is, as a member of the class of twenty-one-year-old men who either have tuberculosis or heart disease or a brain tumor.

The significance of this criticism appears to depend upon how seriously one takes what may be referred to as *the naïve concept of scientific explanation for singular events*, namely: that the occurrence of an outcome A on a single trial T is to be explained by citing *all and only* those properties of that specific trial which contributed to bringing about that specific outcome, that is, a property F is *explanatorily relevant* to attribute A on trial T if and only if F is a *causally relevant* property of trial T relative to attribute A.[32] From this perspective, Salmon's explication of explanation is theoretically objectionable for at least two distinct reasons:

First, *statistically relevant* properties are not necessarily *causally relevant* properties, and conversely.[33] If it happens that the limiting frequency r for the attribute of death D among twenty-one-year-old men K differs among those whose initials are the same F when that class is subject to a homogeneous partition, then that property is explanatorily relevant, necessarily, on the basis of the frequency criterion of statistical relevance; and it might even happen that such a property screens-off another property G, such as having tuberculosis, in spite of the fact that property G is causally relevant to outcome D and property F is not. Indeed, Salmon himself suggests that "relations of statistical relevance must be explained on the basis of relations of causal relevance,"[34] where relations of statistical relevance appear to fulfill the role of evidential indicators of relations of causal relevance.[35]

Second, the admission of disjunctive properties for the specification of an ultimate subset of a homogeneous partition of a reference class does not satisfy the desideratum of explaining the occurrence of an outcome A on a single trial T by citing *all and only* properties of that specific trial, whether causally relevant, statistically relevant, or otherwise. This difficulty, however, appears to be less serious, in principle, since a modification of Salmon's conditions serves for its resolution, namely: Let us assume that a reference class description 'K' is *stronger than* another reference class description 'K +' if and only if 'K' logically entails 'K +', but not conversely.[36] Then let us further assume as new condition (3*) Salmon's old condition (4), with the addition of a new condition (4*) in lieu of Salmon's old condition (3) as follows:

(4*) $K \cdot C^m$ is a strongest homogeneous reference class;

that is, the reference class description '$K \cdot C^m$' is stronger than any other reference class description '$K \cdot C^j$' (where $j \in \{1, 2, \ldots, n\}$) such that $x \in K \cdot C^j$.[37] The explanation of the death of an individual member *i* of class *K* resulting from a brain tumor, therefore, is thus only explainable by identifying *i* as a member of a *strongest* class $K \cdot C^m$, that is, as a member of the class of twenty-one-year-old men who have brain tumors, which is a broadest homogeneous reference class of the explanatorily relevant kind, under this modification of the frequency conception.

It is important to observe, however, that none of these considerations mitigates the force of the preceding criticism directed toward the frequency criterion of statistical relevance itself. For it remains the case that any single trial *T* which belongs to a reference class *K* for which the probability of the occurrence of attribute *A* is $\neq 0$ and $\neq 1$ will likewise belong to innumerable subclasses $K \cdot C^j$ of *K* and, indeed, *T* itself will necessarily belong to some subclass K^* of *K* such that $P(K^*, A) = 0$ or $= 1$, which, on Salmon's own criteria, requires that trial *T* be assigned to K^*, so long as K^* is a broadest (or a strongest) ultimate subclass of a homogeneous partition of the original class *K*. In effect, therefore, those properties that differentiate trial *T* as a member of class *K* from all other trial members of that class, a partition for which the probability for attribute *A* within every one of its ultimate subclasses (whether strongest or not) is $= 0$ or $= 1$, necessarily. And this result itself may be viewed as reflecting a failure to distinguish those principles suitable for employment within the context of prediction, promoted by (what appears to be) the mistaken identification of statistical relevance with explanatory relevance.

It should not be overlooked that the properties *taken to be* statistically relevant to the occurrence of attribute *A* on trial *T* relative to the knowledge context $\mathcal{K}zt$ are not necessarily those that actually *are* statistically relevant to that attribute within the physical world. For this reason, Salmon's analysis emphasizes the significance of the concepts of *epistemic* and of *practical* homogeneity, which, however, on Salmon's explication, actually turn out to be two different kinds of *inhomogeneous* reference classes, where, for reasons of ignorance or of impracticality, respectively, it is not possible to establish ontically homogeneous partitions for appropriate attributes and trials.[38] Salmon's analysis thus does not provide an explicit characterization of the conception of reference classes that are believed to be homogeneous whether or not they actually are; nevertheless, there is no difficulty in supplementing his conceptions as follows: Let us assume that a reference class K is an ***epistemically homogeneous reference class*** with respect to attribute A for trial T within the knowledge context $\mathcal{K}zt$ if and only if the set of statements $\{\mathcal{K}\}$ accepted or believed by z at t, considerations of truth all aside, logically implies some set of sentences, $\{S\}$, asserting (a) that $T \in K$; (b) that $P(K, A) = r$; (c) that for all subclasses K^j of K to which T belongs, $P(K^j, A) = r = P(K, A)$; and (d) that it is not the case that there exists some class $K^i \supset K$ such that $P(K^i, A) = r = P(K, A)$. The satisfaction of conditions (a), (b), and (c), therefore, is sufficient to fulfill the epistemic version of the concept of an ***ontically homogeneous*** reference class K for trial T with respect to attribute A, while satisfaction of (d) as well is sufficient to fulfill the epistemic version of the ***broadest homogeneous*** reference class for T relative to A, within the knowledge context $\mathcal{K}zt$. In order to differentiate this concept from Salmon's original, however, let us refer to this definition as the *revised* conception of epistemic homogeneity, while acknowledging the theoretical utility of both.

3. Hempel's Revised Requirement of Maximal Specificity

The conclusions that emerge from the preceding investigation of Salmon's own analysis of statistical explanation support the contention that, on the frequency criterion of statistical relevance, statistical explanations are only ***statistical*** relative to a knowledge context $\mathcal{K}zt$, that is, as the matter might be expressed, "God would be unable to construct a statistical relevance explanation of any physical event, not as a limitation of His power but as a reflection of His omniscience."[39] It is therefore rather intriguing that Salmon himself has strongly endorsed this conclusion as a criticism of *Hempel's* ***account*** of statistical explanation, for as the following considerations are intended to display, the fundamental difference between them is that Hempel's explicit relativization of statistical explanations to a knowledge context $\mathcal{K}zt$, as it were, affirms *a priori* what, on Salmon's view, is *a posteriori* true, namely: that for probabilities r such that $0 \neq r \neq 1$, the only homogeneous reference classes are epistemically homogeneous. What Salmon's criticism fails to make clear, however, is that this difficulty is a necessary consequence of adoption of the frequency criterion of statistical relevance for any nonepistemic explication of explanation, including, of course, Salmon's own ontic explication. Additionally, there are at least two further important issues with respect to which Hempel's analysis and Salmon's analysis are distinctive, in spite of their initial appearance of marked similarity.

In order to establish the soundness of these claims, therefore, let us consider the three principal ingredients of Hempel's epistemic explication. First, Hempel introduces the concept of an *i-predicate* in $\mathcal{K}zt$ which, in effect, is any predicate 'F^m' such that a sentence '$F^m i$' asserting the satisfaction of 'F^m' by the individual *i* belongs $\mathcal{K}zt$, regardless of the kind of property that may be thereby designated.[40] He then proceeds to define *statistical relevance* as follows:

> 'F^m' will be said to be *statistically relevant* to 'Ai' in $\mathcal{K}zt$ if (1) 'F^m' is an *i*-predicate that entails neither 'A' nor '$-A$' and (2) $\mathcal{K}zt$ contains a lawlike sentence '$P(F^m, A) = \mathrm{r}$' specifying the probability of 'A' in the reference class characterized by 'F^m'.[41]

Insofar as sentences of the form, '$P(F^m, A) = r$', are supposed to be *lawlike*, it is clear that, on Hempel's analysis, (a) their reference class descriptions must be specified by means of permissible predicates and (b) these sentences are to be understood as supporting subjunctive (and counterfactual) conditionals.[42] Salmon likewise assumes that the limiting frequency statements that may serve as a basis for statistical explanations are lawlike, although the theoretical justification for attributing counterfactual (and subjunctive) force to these sentences should not be taken for granted, since it may entail the loss of their extensionality.[43]

The condition that the knowledge context $\mathcal{K}zt$ contain a set of probability statements, of course, might be subject to criticism on the grounds that it requires $\mathcal{K}zt$ to contain an enormous number of lawlike sentences.[44] This objection lacks forcefulness, however, when the following are considered, namely:

(i) the sentences belonging to $\mathcal{K}zt$ are accepted or believed by *z* at *t*, i.e., they represent what *z* takes to be the case;

(ii) this set of sentences, therefore, may be believed to be exhaustive with respect to attribute *A* and trial *T*, whether that is actually true or not; and,

(iii) presumably, this explication is intended to specify the conditions that must be fulfilled in order to provide an adequate explanation relative to a specified knowledge context without presuming that these conditions are always (or even generally) satisfied.

Second, Hempel defines the concept of *a maximally specific predicate 'M' related to 'Ai' in* $\mathcal{K}zt$ where 'M' is such a predicate if and only if (a) 'M' is logically equivalent to a conjunction of predicates that are statistically relevant to 'Ai' in $\mathcal{K}zt$; (b) 'M' entails neither 'A' nor '$-A$'; and, (c) no predicate expression stronger than '*M*' satisfies (a) and (b), that is, if '*M*' is conjoined with a predicate that is statistically relevant to '*Ai*' in $\mathcal{K}zt$, then the resulting expression entails '*A*' or '–*A*' or else it is logically equivalent to '*M*'.[45] Thus, for outcome *A* on trial *T*, '*M*' is intended to provide a description of that trial as a member of reference class *K* determined by the conjunction of every statistically relevant predicate 'F^m' of trial *T* with respect to outcome *A*, that is, '*M*' is the conjunction of all and only the statistically relevant *i*-predicates (or the negations of such *i*-predicates) satisfied by trial *T* in $\mathcal{K}zt$.

Third, Hempel formulates the *revised requirement of maximal specificity* as follows: An argument

$$\text{(VII)} \qquad \begin{array}{l} P(F, A) = r \\ \\ Fi \\ \hline\hline Ai \end{array} \; [r],$$

where *r* is close to 1 and all constituent statements are contained in $\mathcal{K}zt$, qualifies as an explanation of the explanandum-phenomenon described by the explanandum-sentence '*Ai*' (or of the fact that *i* is a member of the attribute class *A*), within the knowledge context $\mathcal{K}zt$, only if:

(RMS*) For any predicate, say '*M*', which either (a) is a maximally specific predicate related to '*Ai*' in $\mathcal{K}zt$ or (b) is stronger than '*F*' and statistically relevant to '*Ai*' in $\mathcal{K}zt$, the class $\mathcal{K}$ contains a corresponding probability statement, '$P(M, A) = r$', where, as in (VII), $r = P(F, A)$.[46]

Since a predicate expression 'F^j' is stronger than a predicate expression 'F^i' if and only if 'F^j' entails but is not entailed by 'F^i', moreover, a predicate which is logically equivalent to the conjunction of '*F*' with *any other permissible i-predicate* 'F^k' such that $\mathcal{K}zt$ contains the corresponding probability statement, '$P(F \cdot F^k, A) = r$', will satisfy condition (b) of this requirement, provided that, as in (VII), $r = P(F, A)$.

The motivation of Hempel's introduction of a requirement of this kind, let us recall, was the discovery that *statistical explanations* suffer from a species of explanatory ambiguity arising from the possibility that an individual trial *T* might belong to innumerable different reference classes K^1, K^2, . . . for which, with respect to a specific attribute *A*, the probabilities for the occurrence of that outcome may vary widely, that is, the reference class problem for single-class explanations. In particular, Hempel has displayed concern with the possibility of the existence of alternative explanations consisting of alternative explanans that confer *high probabilities* upon both the occurrence of an attribute A and its nonoccurrence $-A$, relative to the physical world itself or a knowledge context $\mathcal{K}zt$, a phenomenon which cannot arise in the case of explanations involving universal rather than statistical lawlike statements.[47] However, it is important to note that there are *two* distinct varieties of explanatory ambiguity, at least one of which is not resolved by Hempel's maximal specificity requirement. For although Hempel provides a unique *value* solution to the single-case problem (which entails a resolution to the difficulty of conflicting explanations which confer high probabilities upon their explanandum sentences), Hempel's approach does not provide a unique *description* solution to the reference class problem, a difficulty which continues to afflict his conditions of adequacy for explanations invoking universal *or* statistical lawlike statements within an epistemic *or* an ontic context. Hempel's explication, therefore, appears to afford only a restricted resolution of one species of statistical ambiguity, which, however, does not provide a solution to the general problem of explanatory ambiguity for explanations of either kind. For explanations involving universal laws as well as statistical laws continue to suffer from the difficulties that arise from a failure to contend with the problem of providing a unique *description* solution for single-case explanations.

Hempel resolves the problem of statistical ambiguity, in effect, by requiring that, within a knowledge context $\mathcal{K}zt$ as previously specified, the occurrence of outcome attribute A on trial T is adequately explained by indentifying a reference class K such that (a) $T \in K$; (b) $P(K, A) = r$; and, (c) for all subclasses K^j of K to which T belongs, $P(K^j, A) = r = P(K, A)$; but he does not require as well that (d) it is not the case that there exists some class $K^i \supset K$ such that $P(K^i, A) = r = P(K, A)$. For on the basis of condition (b) of (RMS^*), if, for example, the probability for the outcome death D within the reference class of twenty-one-year-old men who have tuberculosis K is equal to r and the probabilities for that same outcome within the reference class $K \cdot F^1$, $K \cdot F^1 \cdot F^2$, . . . of twenty-one-year-old men who have tuberculosis K and who have high blood pressure F^1 and have blue eyes F^2, . . . are likewise equal to r, then the explanation for the occurrence of death for an individual who belongs not only to class K but to class $K \cdot F^1$ and to class $K \cdot F^1 \cdot F^2$ and so on is adequate, *regardless of which of these reference classes is specified by the explanans in that single case.*[48] Consequently, on Hempel's explication, there is not only no unique explanation for the occurrence of such an explanandum outcome but, if the density principle for single trial descriptions is sound, *there may be an infinite number of adequate explanations for any one such explanandum*, on Hempel's explication. And this surprising result applies alike for explanations invoking laws of universal form, since if salt K dissolves in water A as a matter of physical law (within a knowledge context or without), then table salt $K \cdot F^i$ dissolves in water, hexed table salt $K \cdot F^1 \cdot F^2$ dissolves in water, . . . as a matter of physical law as well; so if a single trial involves a sample of hexed table salt an adequate explanation for its dissolution in water may refer to any one of these reference classes or to any others of which it may happen to belong, providing only that, for all such properties F^i, it remains the case that all members of $K \cdot F^i$ possess the attribute A as a matter of physical law.

Comparison with Salmon's explication suggests at least two respects in which Hempel's provides theoretically objectionable conditions of adequacy. The first, let us note, is that Hempel's requirement of maximal specificity (*RMS**) does not incorporate any appropriate relevance criteria that would differentiate statistically relevant from statistically irrelevant properties in the sense of principle (II*). For Hempel has defined the concept of statistical relevance so generally that a property F^i such that there exists some probability r with respect to the attribute A where $P(F^i, A) = r$ necessarily qualifies as 'statistically relevant' independently of any consideration for whether or not there may exist some class K such that $K \supset F^i$ and $P(K, A) = r = P(F^i, A)$; in other words, *Hempel's concept of statistical relevance is not a relevance requirement of the appropriate kind.*[49] In order to contend with this difficulty, therefore, major revision of Hempel's definition is required along the following lines:

> 'F^m' will be said to be *statistically relevant* to 'Ai' relative to 'K' in $\mathcal{K}zt$ if and only if (1) 'F^m' and 'K' are *i*-predicates that entail neither 'A' nor '$-A$'; (2) $\mathcal{K}zt$ contains the lawlike sentences, '$P(K \cdot F^m, A) = r^i$' and '$P(K \cdot -F^m, A) = r^j$'; and, (3) the sentence, '$r^i \neq r^j$', also belongs to $\mathcal{K}zt$.

The second is that Hempel's explication of explanation is incapable of yielding a unique description solution to the single-case problem because it is logically equivalent to the *revised concept of epistemic homogeneity,* that is, the epistemic version of the concept of an *ontically homogeneous* reference class, rather than the epistemic version of the concept of a *broadest homogeneous* reference class. There appears to be no reason, in principle, that precludes the reformulation of Hempel's requirement so as to incorporate the conditions necessary for fulfilling the desideratum of providing a unique description solution (for arguments having the form (VII) previously specified) as follows:

(*RMS***) For any predicate, say 'M,' (a) if 'M' is weaker than 'F' and is statistically relevant to 'Ai' in $\mathcal{K}zt$, then the class $\mathcal{K}$ contains a corresponding probability statement asserting that $P(M, A) \neq r$; and, (b) if 'M' is stronger than 'F' and is statistically

> relevant to 'Ai' in $\mathcal{K}zt$, then the class $\mathcal{K}$ contains a corresponding probability statement asserting that $P(M, A) = r$; where, as is in (VII), $r = P(F, A)$.

Condition (*RMS***), therefore, not only requires that any property of trial *T* that is statistically relevant to '*A*' but nevertheless not explanatorily relevant must be excluded from an adequate explanation of that outcome on that trial in $\mathcal{K}zt$, but also requires that trial *T* be assigned to the ***broadest*** homogeneous reference class of which it is a member, in the sense that '*F*' is the *weakest* maximally specific predicate related to '*Ai*' in $\mathcal{K}zt$. Moreover, on the reasonable presumption that the definition of a maximally specific predicate precludes the specification of reference classes by *nontrivial* disjunctive properties, that is, disjunctive properties that are not logically equivalent to some nondisjunctive property, these conditions actually require that trial *T* be assigned to the *strongest* homogeneous reference class of which it is a member. From this point of view, therefore, the reformulation of Hempel's requirement appears to provide a (strongest) unique description solution as well as a unique value solution to the single case problem within the spirit of Hempel's explication.

The revised formulation of Hempel's requirements (incorporating appropriate relevance conditions and (*RMS***) as well) and the revised formulation of Salmon's requirements (incorporating his original conditions (1), (2), and (3*), together with new condition (4*) as well), of course, both accommodate the naïve concept of scientific explanation to the extent to which they satisfy the desideratum of explaining the occurrence of an outcome *A* on a single trial *T* by citing *all and only relevant properties of that specific trial.* Neither explanation, however, fulfills the expectation that a property *F* is *explanatorily* relevant to outcome *A* on trial *T* if and only if *F* is *causally* relevant to outcome *A* on trial *T*, so long as they remain wedded to the frequency criterion of statistical relevance. Nevertheless, precisely because Hempel's explication is *epistemic*, that is, related to a knowledge context $\mathcal{K}zt$ that may contain sentences satisfying the conditions specified, it is not subject to the criticism that the only adequate explanations are *non*-statistical, that is, those for which probability $r = 0$ and $r = 1$. On the other hand, it *is* subject to the criticism that there are no *non*-epistemic adequate explanations for which probability $r \neq 0$ and $r \neq 1$, that is, there are no ontic (or true) *statistical* explanations. As it happens, this specific criticism has been advanced by Alberto Coffa, who, while arguing that Hempel's epistemic explication is necessitated by (1) implicit reliance upon the frequency interpretation of physical probability, in conjunction with (2) implied acceptance of a certain 'not unlikely' reference class density principle, unfortunately neglects to emphasize that Salmon's *ontic* explication is similarly afflicted, precisely because the fatal flaw is not to be found in the *epistemic*-ness of Hempel's explication but rather in *reliance on the frequency criterion of statistical relevance for any ontic explication.*[50]

If Coffa's argument happens to be sound with respect to Hempel's rationale, then it is important to observe that, provided (1) is satisfied and (2) is true, there are, *in principle*, no nonepistemic adequate explanations for which probability $r \neq 0$ and $r \neq 1$; that is, an epistemic explication is not only *the only theoretically adequate kind of an explication*, but an explication remarkably similar to Hempel's specific explication appears to be *the only theoretically adequate explication.* So if it is not the case that an epistemic explication of the Hempel kind is the only theoretically adequate construction, then either (1) is avoidable or (2) is not true. Intriguingly, the density principle Coffa endorses, i.e., the assumption that, for any specific reference class K and outcome A such that trial $T \in K$, there exists a subclass K^i of K such that (i) $T \in K^i$, and (ii) $P(K^i, A) \neq P(K, A)$ is demonstrably false, since for all subclasses K^i such that $K \supseteq K^i$ and $K^i \supseteq K$, this principle does not hold, that is, it does not apply to *any* homogeneous reference class K, whether or not T is the only member of K.[51] Insofar as every distinct trial is describable, in principle, by a set of permissible predicates, $\{F^n\}$, such that that trial is the solitary member of the kind K^* thereby defined, however, evidently Coffa's density principle is not satisfied by even *one single trial* during the course of the world's history. Coffa's principle is plausible, therefore, only so long as there appear to be *no* homogeneous reference classes; once the existence of reference classes of kind K^* is theoretically identified, it is obvious that this density principle is false. Nevertheless, another density principle in lieu of Coffa's principle does generate the same conclusion, namely: the density principle for single trial descriptions previously introduced. Coffa has therefore advanced an unsound argument for a true conditional conclusion, where, as it happens, by retaining one of his premises and replacing the other, that conclusion does indeed follow, albeit on different grounds.

In his endorsement of Coffa's contentions, Salmon himself explicitly agrees that, on Hempel's explication, there are no *nonempistemic* adequate explanations for which probability $r \neq 0$ and $r \neq 1$; thus he observes, "There are no homogeneous reference classes except in those cases in which *either* every member of the reference class has the attribute in question *or else* no member of the reference class has the attribute in question."[52] With respect to his own explication, in contrast, Salmon remarks, "The interesting question, however, is whether under any other circumstances K can be homogeneous with respect of A—e.g., if one-half of all K are A."[53] It is Salmon's view, in other words, that Hempel's position entails an *a priori* commitment to determinism, while his does not. But the considerations adduced above demonstrate that determinism is a consequence attending the adoption of the frequency criterion of statistical relevance alone, that is, determinism is as much a logical implication of Salmon's own position as it is of Hempel's. This result, moreover, underlines the necessity to draw a clear distinction between *statistical* relevance and *causal* relevance; for, although it is surely true that two distinct events are describable, in principle, by different sets of permissible predicates, it does not follow that they are necessarily not both members of a *causally homogeneous* reference class K for which, relative to attribute A, $P(K, A) = r$ where $0 \neq r \neq 1$, even though, as we have ascertained, they may *not* both be members of some *statistically homogeneous* reference class K^* for which, with respect to attribute A, $P(K^*, A) = r$, where $0 \neq r \neq 1$. Although it is not logically necessary *a priori* that the world is deterministic, therefore, adoption of the frequency criterion of statistical relevance is nevertheless sufficient to demonstrate determinism's truth.

When the reformulated versions of Salmon's and Hempel's explications which entail assigning each singular trial T to the 'strongest' homogenous reference class K of which it is a member (with respect to attribute A) are compared, the revised Hempel explication provides, in effect, a meta-language formulation of the revised Salmon object-language explication, with the notable exception that the Hempel-style explication envisions explanations as arguments for which high probability requirements are appropriate, and the Salmon-style explication does not. The issue of whether or not explanations should be construed as arguments is somewhat elusive insofar as there is no problem, in principle, in separating *explanation-seeking* and *reason-seeking varieties of inductive arguments*, that is, as sets of statements divided into premises and conclusions, where the premises provide the appropriate kind of grounds or evidence for their conclusions.[54] But however suitable a high probability requirement may be relative to the reason-seeking variety of inductive argument, there appear to be no suitable grounds for preserving such a requirement relative to the explanation-seeking variety of inductive argument in the face of the following consideration, namely: that *the imposition of a high probability requirement between the explanans and the explanandum of an adequate explanation renders the adequate explanation of attributes that occur only with low probability logically impossible, in principle.*[55] Indeed, it appears altogether reasonable to contend that no single consideration militates more strongly on behalf of conclusive differentiation between 'inductive arguments' of these two distinct varieties that this specific consideration.

The theoretical resolution of these significant problems, therefore, appears to lie in the direction of a more careful differentiation between principles suitable for employment within the explanation context specifically and those suitable for employment within the induction context generally. The problem of single-case explanation, for example, receives an elegant resolution through the adoption of the *propensity* interpretation of physical probability; for on that explanation,

(VIII) $P^*(E, A) = r =_{df}$ the strength of the dispositional tendency for any experimental arrangement of kind *E* to bring about an outcome of kind *A* on any single trial equals *r*;

where, on this statistical disposition construction, a clear distinction should be drawn between *probabilities* and *frequencies*, insofar as frequencies display but do not define propensities.[56] The *propensity criterion of causal relevance*, moreover, provides a basis for differentiating between causal and inductive relevance relations; for, on the propensity analysis, a property *F* is *causally relevant* to the occurrence of outcome *A* with respect to arrangements of kind *E* if and only if:

(IX) $P^*(E \cdot F, A) \neq P^*(E \cdot -F, A)$;

that is, the strength of the dispositional tendency for an arrangement of kind $E \cdot F$ to bring about an outcome of kind *A* differs from the strength of the dispositional tendency for that same outcome with an arrangement of kind $E \cdot -F$ on any single trial. By virtue of a probabilistic, rather than deductive, connection between probabilities and frequencies on this interpretation, it is not logically necessary that probabilities vary if and only if the corresponding frequencies vary; but that

(X) $P(E \cdot F, A) \neq P(E \cdot -F, A)$;

i.e., that long- (and short-) run frequencies for the attribute *A* vary over sets of trials with experimental arrangements of kind $E \cdot F$ and $E \cdot -F$, nevertheless, characteristically will provide information which, although neither necessary nor sufficient for the truth of the corresponding probability statement, may certainly qualify as inductively relevant to the truth of these propensity hypotheses.[57]

On the propensity conception, it is not the case that every distinct trial *T* must be classified as a member of a *causally homogeneous* reference class $\{K^*\}$ of which it happens to be the solitary member merely because *T* happens to be describable by a set of permissible predicates $\{F^n\}$ such that *T* is the only member of the corresponding *statistically homogeneous* reference class. Consequently, a single individual trial *T* may possess a statistical disposition of strength *r* to bring about the outcome *A* (a) whether that trial is the only one of its kind and (b) whether that outcome actually occurs on that trial or not. On this analysis, the question of determinism requires an *a posteriori* resolution, since it is not the case that, on the propensity criterion of causal relevance, any two distinct trials are therefore necessarily trials of two different causally relevant kinds. And, on the propensity criterion of causal relevance, it is not the case that the only adequate explanations for which the probability $r \neq 0$ and $\neq 1$ are invariably epistemic; for a set of statements satisfying the revised Salmon conditions (1) through (4*) or the corresponding revised Hempel conditions (in their ontic formulation) will explain the fact that *x*, a member of *K*, is also a member of *A*, provided, of course, those sentences are true.[58] For both explications, thus understood, may be envisioned as fulfilling the theoretical expectations of the naive concept of scientific explanation, where the only issue that remains is whether or not, and, if so, in what sense, statistical explanations should be supposed to be inductive arguments of a certain kind.

Perhaps most important of all, therefore, is that Reichenbach's frequency interpretation of physical probability, which was intended to resolve the problem of providing an objective conception of physical probability, has indeed contributed toward that philosophical desideratum, not through any demonstration of its own adequacy for that role, but rather through a clarification of the conditions that an adequate explication must satisfy. For the arguments presented above suggest:

(a) that *the concept of explanatory relevance* should be explicated relative to a requirement of causal relevance;

(b) that *the requirement of causal relevance* should be explicated relative to a concept of physical probability; and,

(c) that *the concept of physical probability* should be explicated by means of the single-case propensity construction;[59] and, moreover,

(d) that *the concept of inductive relevance* should be explicated relative to a requirement of total evidence;

(e) that *the requirement of total evidence* should be explicated relative to a concept of epistemic probability; and,

(f) that *the concept of epistemic probability* should be explicated, at least in part, by means of the long-run frequency construction.[60]

If these considerations are sound, therefore, then it is altogether reasonable to suppose that the recognition of the inadequacy of the frequency conception as an explication of *physical* probability may ultimately contribute toward the development of an adequate explication of *epistemic* probability, where the frequency criterion of statistical relevance is likely to fulfill its most important theoretical role.

JAMES H. FETZER
University of Minnesota, Duluth

NOTES

* The author is grateful to Wesley C. Salmon for his valuable criticism of an earlier version of this paper.

1. Hans Reichenbach, *The Theory of Probability* (Berkeley: University of California Press, 1949), esp. pp. 366–78.

2. For the same attribute *A* on the same trial *T* in the same world *W* or knowledge context $\mathcal{K}$zt. Recent discussion of the symmetry thesis is provided by Adolf Grünbaum, *Philosophical Problems of Space and Time* (New York: Alfred A. Knopf, 1963; 2nd ed. 1973, ch. 9) and in James H. Fetzer, "Grünbaum's 'Defense' of the Symmetry Thesis," *Philosophical Studies* (April 1974): 173–87.

3. Reichenbach apparently never explicitly considered the question of the logical structure of statistical explanations; cf. Carl G. Hempel, "Lawlikeness and Maximal Specificity in Probabilistic Explanation," *Philosophy of Science* (June 1968): 122.

4. Especially as set forth in Hempel, "Maximal Specificity," pp. 116–33; and in Wesley C. Salmon, *Statistical Explanation and Statistical Relevance* (Pittsburgh: University of Pittsburgh Press, 1971).

5. Reichenbach, *Probability*, p. 68.

6. Reichenbach, *Probability*, p. 69.

7. Reichenbach, *Probability*, p. 72.

8. Cf. Hilary Putnam, *The Meaning of the Concept of Probability in Application to Finite Sequences* (University of California at Los Angeles, unpublished dissertation, 1951).

9. Reichenbach, *Probability*, pp. 376–77.

10. Reichenbach, *Probability*, p. 377.

11. This condition may be viewed as circumventing the problems posed by the requirement of randomness that might otherwise be encountered; but issues of randomness (or normality) will not figure significantly in the following discussion.

12. As will be explained subsequently, this condition imposes a unique *value* solution but does not enforce a unique *description* solution to the problem of the single case.

13. Assuming, of course, an unlimited supply of predicates in the object language. A different *density principle for reference classes* is discussed in section 3.

14. Reichenbach, *Probability*, p. 374. Variables are exchanged for convenience.

15. It is not assumed here that '$P(K, A)$' stands for '$P(K \cdot -C, A)$'; see section 2.

16. Reichenbach, *Probability*, p. 375.

17. Reichenbach, *Probability*, p. 376.

18. Reichenbach, *Probability*, pp. 375–76.

19. More precisely, perhaps, the term 'object' may be replaced by the term 'event' (or 'thing') to preserve generality; cf. Hempel, "Maximal Specificity," p. 124.

20. An extended discussion of this issue is provided by Hempel, "Maximal Specificity," pp. 123–29.

21. If a "narrowest" reference class description is satisfied by more than one distinct event, then it is not a *narrowest* class description, since there is some predicate 'F^i' such that one such event satisfies 'F^i' and any other does not; otherwise, they would not be distinct events. This conclusion follows from the principle of identity for events and may therefore be characterized as a matter of logical neces-

sity; cf. James H. Fetzer, "A World of Dispositions," *Synthese* (April 1977): 397–421. A reference-class description may be satisfied by no more than one distinct event, however, without being a narrowest reference class description. Thus, an ontically homogeneous reference class may have only one member but is not therefore logically limited to a finite number of such members.

22. There are therefore two theoretical alternatives in specifying a homogeneous reference class for the single individual trial T with respect to outcome A, namely: (a) a reference-class description 'K^*' incorporating only *one* predicate 'F^i' (or a finite set of predicates {'F^n'}) satisfied by that individual trial alone; or, (b) a reference-class description 'K^*' incorporating *every* predicate 'F^i', 'F^j', . . . satisfied by that individual trial alone. Since the set of predicates {'F^i', 'F^j', . . .} satisfied by that individual trial alone may be an infinite set (and in any case will be a narrowest reference-class description), alternative (a) shall be assumed unless otherwise stated. Note that $P(K^*, A) = P(F^i, A) = P(F^j, A) = \ldots = P(F^i \cdot F^j, A) = \ldots$, but nevertheless each of these predicates turns out to be statistically relevant.

23. Cf. Carl G. Hempel, in *Aspects of Scientific Explanation* (New York: The Free Press, 1965), pp. 334–35; and Fetzer, "Grünbaum's 'Defense'," pp. 184–86.

24. This requirement is discussed, for example, in Hempel, *Aspects*, pp. 63–67.

25. The relationship between the requirement of *total evidence* and a requirement of *explanatory relevance* (whether causal or not), moreover, is a fundamental issue. See in particular, Hempel, *Aspects*, pp. 394–403; Salmon, *Statistical Explanation,* pp. 47–51 and pp. 77–78; and esp. Hempel, "Maximum Specificity," pp. 120–23.

26. Salmon, *Statistical Explanation,* p. 43. Variables are exchanged once again.

27. Salmon, *Statistical Explanation,* p. 42–45 and pp. 58–62.

28. Salmon, *Statistical Explanation,* p. 55.

29. Salmon, *Statistical Explanation,* p. 55.

30. Salmon, *Statistical Explanation,* pp. 76–77.

31. Wesley C. Salmon, "Discussion: Reply to Lehman," *Philosophy of Science* (September 1975): 398.

32. Where the role of laws is to certify the relevance of *causes* with respect to their *effects*; cf. James H. Fetzer, "On the Historical Explanation of Unique Events," *Theory and Decision* (February 1975), esp. pp. 89–91.

33. Cf. J. Alberto Coffa, "Hempel's Ambiguity," *Synthese* (October 1974): 161–62.

34. Salmon, "Reply to Lehman," p. 400.

35. Wesley C. Salmon, "Theoretical Explanation," in *Explanation*, ed. Stephan Körner (London: Basil Blackwell, 1975), esp. pp. 121–29 and pp. 141–45.

36. Cf. Hemple, "Maximal Specificity," p. 130.

37. This result may likewise be obtained by prohibiting the specification of any homogeneous reference class by *nontrivial* disjunctive properties, which is apparently implied by Hempel's definition of a maximally specific predicate, as discussed in section 3.

38. Salmon, *Statistical Explanation,* p. 44.

39. Cf. Wesley C. Salmon, "Comments on 'Hempel's Ambiguity' by J. Alberto Coffa," *Synthese* (October 1974): 165.

40. Hempel, "Maximal Specificity," p. 131.

41. Hempel, "Maximal Specificity," p. 131. Variables are again exchanged.

42. Cf. Hempel, *Aspects*, pp. 338–43; and Hempel, "Maximal Specificity," pp. 123–29.

43. Salmon, *Statistical Explanation,* p. 81. Reichenbach's epistemological program, including (a) the verifiability criterion of meaning, (b) the rule of induction by enumeration, and (c) the pragmatic justification of induction, suggest a profound commitment to establishing wholly extensional truth conditions for probability statements, an effort that may be regarded as culminating in his introduction of the "practical limit" construct. For discussion of certain difficulties attending the reconciliation of these desiderata, see James H. Fetzer, "Statistical Probabilities: Single Case Propensities vs Long Run Frequencies," in *Developments in the Methodology of Social Science,* ed. W. Leinfellner and E. Köhler (Dordrecht: D. Reidel Publishing Co., 1974), esp. pp. 394–96.

44. Cf. Henry E. Kyburg, Jr., "Discussion: More on Maximal Specificity," *Philosophy of Science* (June 1970): 295–300.

45. Hempel, "Maximal Specificity," p. 131.

46. Hempel, "Maximal Specificity," p. 131.

47. Hempel, *Aspects,* pp. 394–96; and Hempel, "Maximal Specificity," p. 118.

48. As his own examples illustrate; cf. Hempel, "Maximal Specificity," pp. 131–32.

49. This contention may be taken to be Salmon's basic criticism of Hempel's view; cf. Salmon, *Statistical Explanation,* pp. 7–12 and esp. p. 35.

50. Coffa, "Hempel's Ambiguity," esp. pp. 147–48 and p. 154.

51. Coffa, "Hempel's Ambiguity," p. 154. Niiniluoto interprets Coffa's density principle analogously, concluding that it is true *provided* all the subclasses K^i of K required to generate these reference classes happen to exist. Ilkka Niiniluoto, "Inductive Explanation, Propensity, and Action," in *Essays on Explanation and Understanding,* ed. J. Manninen and R. Tuomela (Dordrecht, Holland: D. Reidel Publishing Co., 1976), p. 346 and pp. 348–49.

52. Salmon, "Comments of Coffa," p. 167.

53. Salmon, "Comments of Coffa," p. 167.

54. Cf. James H. Fetzer, "Statistical Explanations," in *Boston Studies in the Philosophy of Science,* vol. XX, ed. K. Shaffner and R. Cohen (Dordrecht: D. Reidel Publishing Co., 1974), esp. pp. 343–44.

55. Cf. Salmon, *Statistical Explanation,* pp. 9–10; Fetzer, "Statistical Explanations," pp. 342–43; and esp. Richard C. Jeffrey, "Statistical Explanation vs Statistical Inference," in Salmon, *Statistical Explanation,* pp. 19–28.

56. Among those adhering to one version or another are Peirce, Popper, Hacking, Mellor, Giere, and Gillies. See, for example, Karl R. Popper, "The Propensity Interpretation of Probability," *British Journal for the Philosophy of Science* 10 (1959): 25–42; James H. Fetzer, "Dispositional Probabilities," in *Boston Studies in the Philosophy of Science,* vol. VIII, ed. R. Buck and R. Cohen (Dordrecht: D. Reidel Publishing Co., 1971), pp. 473–82; R. N. Giere, "Obective Single-Case Probabilities and the Foundations of Statistics," in *Logic, Methodology, and Philosophy of Science,* ed. P. Suppes et al. (Amsterdam: North Holland Publishing Co., 1973), pp. 467–83; and the review article by Henry E. Kyburg, "Propensities and Probabilities," *British Journal for the Philosophy of Science* (December 1974): 358–75.

57. See, for example, Ian Hacking, *Logic of Statistical Inference* (Cambridge: Cambridge University Press, 1965); Ronald N. Giere, "The Epistemological Roots of Scientific Knowledge," in *Minnesota Studies in the Philosophy of Science,* vol. VI, ed. G. Maxwell and R. Anderson, Jr. (Minneapolis: University of Minnesota Press, 1975), pp. 212–61; and James H. Fetzer, "Elements of Induction," in *Local Induction,* ed. R. Bogdan (Dordrecht: D. Reidel Publishing Co., 1976), pp. 145–70.

58. Hempel's specific explication is not the only adequate explication (or the only adequate kind of an explication), therefore, precisely because condition (1)—reliance upon the frequency interpretation of physical probability—is not the only theoretical option. While Hempel's and Salmon's explications are both logically compatible with either the frequency or the propensity concepts, the choice between them is not a matter of philosophical preference but rather one of theoretical necessity (although Salmon suggests otherwise; cf. Salmon, *Statistical Explanation,* p. 82). For related efforts in this direction, see James H. Fetzer, "A Single Case Propensity Theory of Explanation," *Synthese* (October 1974): 171–98; and James H. Fetzer, "The Likeness of Lawlikeness," *Boston Studies in the Philosophy of Science*, vol. XXXII, ed. A. Michalos and R. Cohen (Dordrecht: D. Reidel Publishing Co., 1976). Also, note that even when Hempel's conception is provided an ontic formulation (by deleting the conditions that render statistical explanations inductive arguments for which a high probability requirement within a knowledge context $\mathcal{K}zt$ is appropriate), it is still not the case that Hempel's explication and Salmon's explication are then logically equivalent. For Salmon's (original) conditions may be criticized as requiring the explanans of (at least some) explanations to be "too broad," while Hempel's conditions even then may be criticized as permitting the explanans of (at least some) explanations to be "too narrow." Consequently, the relationship between Hempel's and Salmon's requirements is more complex than I previously supposed; cf. Fetzer, "A Propensity Theory of Explanation," pp. 197–98, note 25, and Fetzer, "Statistical Explanations," p. 342. For convenience of reference, finally, we may refer to the model of explanation elaborated here as the *causal-relevance* (or C-R) explication, by contrast with Hempel's (original) *inductive-statistical* (or I-S) model and with Salmon's (original) *statistical-relevance* (or S-R) model examined above.

59. It is significant to note, therefore, that Hempel himself has endorsed the propensity interpretation of physical probability for statistical "lawlike" sentences; Hempel, *Aspects*, pp. 376–80, esp. p. 378, note 1. Hempel's view on this issue is critically examined by Isaac Levi, "Are Statistical Hypotheses Covering Laws?," *Synthese* 20 (1969): 297–307; and reviewed further in Fetzer, "A Propensity Theory of Explanation," esp. pp. 171–79. Salmon, in particular, does not believe that the choice between the propensity and the frequency conceptions of physical probability is crucial to the adequacy of his explication of explanation, contrary to the conclusions drawn above; Salmon, *Statistical Explanation,* p. 82.

60. It is also significant to note that Hempel has recently expressed the view that Reichenbach's policy of assigning singular occurrences to "the narrowest reference class" should be understood as Reichenbach's version of the requirement of total evidence *and that the requirement of total evidence is not an explanatory relevance condition*; "Maximal Specifity," pp. 121–22. From the present perspective, moreover, Hempel's own revised requirement of maximal specificity (*RMS**), when employed in conjunction with the frequency interpretation of statistical probability, may itself be envisioned as applying within the *prediction context* generally rather than the *explanation context* specifically; indeed, for this purpose, Hempel's original definition of statistical relevance would appear to be theoretically unobjectionable, provided, of course, that these probability statements are no longer required to be *lawlike.* See also Fetzer, "Elements of Induction," esp. pp. 150–60.

2

Direct Inference and the Problem of Induction

TIMOTHY McGREW

It is truth very certain that, when it is not in our power to determine what is true, we ought to follow what is most probable.

—Rene Descartes, *Discourse on the Method*, III, 4

One of the greatest challenges to the notion of probability as a rational guide to life is Hume's famous assault on inductive inference. Granting that we have knowledge of such matters of fact as lie within our immediate experience, and granting that we can typically sort these into appropriate classes, Hume nevertheless denies that we can use our experience to form rational expectations regarding the future or, more generally, matters of fact lying outside of our experience.

Many contemporary philosophers have acquiesced in Hume's skeptical conclusion and moved away from global epistemological questions in the direction of naturalized epistemology. But a stubborn minority insists that Hume was wrong from the start. In my essay, I meet Hume head-on with an exposition and defense of direct inference as a cogent, though probabilistic, means of ampliative reasoning. Stressing the importance of the distinction between rationality and mere success and the indispensibility of an epistemic conception of randomness, I address a wide range of objections and argue that none of them undermines the rationality of direct inference. I conclude that, given such premises as Hume was willing to grant, the problem of induction turns out to have a nonskeptical internalist solution after all.

—T. M.

* * *

It would be difficult to overestimate the influence Hume's problem of induction exercises on contemporary epistemology. At the same time, the problem of induction has not perceptibly slowed the progress of mathematics and science. This ironic state of affairs, immortalized by C. D. Broad's description of induction as "the glory of science" and "the scandal of philosophy,"[1] ought in all fairness to give both sides some pause. And on occasion, it does: the mathematicians stop to concede that Hume has not yet been answered,[2] the scientists worry about randomization of experiments,[3] and inductive skeptics stir uneasily in their chairs at the mention of certain mathematical theorems that seem palpably to have bearing on the problem.[4]

But even when there is some cross-pollination between fields, there is depressingly little sign of consensus on the underlying problem. Part of the difficulty lies in the babble of conflicting interpretations of probability, which has grown markedly worse since Broad's time.[5] Part of it lies in the structure of Hume's original argument, which scarcely makes direct contact with the mathematically sophisticated approach of contemporary statisticians and probabilists.[6] And no small part of it lies in the conviction of a considerable number of philosophers that Hume's problem, or at any rate a refurbished modern version thereof, is quite simply and clearly insoluble.[7]

I aim to show that this pessimism is unfounded. To this end I will articulate and defend the epistemic legitimacy of a very simple form of direct inference; a version so minimal, indeed, that the celebrated questions of confirmational conditionalization do not arise.[8] This is tantamount to sidestepping the delicate issue of competing reference classes, surely one of the most difficult problems facing any comprehensive theory of inductive inference. This might at first blush seem to leave a project too modest to be of interest, but as we shall see even this minimal appeal to direct inference is enormously controversial. And small wonder. For I will argue that the form of direct inference I am defending provides the key to the refutation of Humean skepticism—theoretical and practical, historical and modern—regarding induction.

Hume and "Hume's Problem"

Hume's own account of the problem of induction has both theoretical and practical dimensions. The theoretical worry is quite straightforward and constantly repeated: since the falsehood of any nondemonstrative proposition is clearly conceivable, how are we, on the basis of our experience, to infer the truth of any such "matter of fact" that lies outside our experience?[9] Lacking demonstrative proof, we find our reasoning attended with some uncertainty; and though we customarily do draw conclusions regarding unknown matters of fact, Hume offers us in the end only a psychological explanation for this practice rather than the rational justification for which we might have hoped.

A salient passage in the *Abstract* exhibits several strands in Hume's critique of inductive inference:

> 'Tis evident, that Adam with all his science would never have been able to demonstrate, that the course of nature must continue uniformly the same, and that the future must be conformable to the past. What is possible can never be demonstrated to be false; and 'tis possible the course of nature may change, since we can conceive such a change. Nay, I will go farther, and assert, that he could not so much as prove by any probable arguments, that the future must be conformable to the past.[10]

Several issues intersect in this passage. The first is Hume's famous conceivability criterion of logical possibility. Some contemporary commentators on Hume have found this utterly unacceptable.[11] I think Hume's principle is not so easily dismissed,[12] but we can bypass this dispute if we grant the point that various empirical claims are logically contingent. This is all that is needed to create the problem of induction as Hume conceives it.

The second issue is central and constitutes the core of all Humean challenges to induction: it is Hume's claim that no "probable arguments" will underwrite our concluding that a given logically possible proposition is false. But beneath the apparent simplicity of this challenge lie several presuppositions that must be unearthed and reconstructed before the basic problem can be seen clearly. Despite its modern sound, Hume's phrase "probable arguments" does not refer to arguments in which the premises provide less than a guarantee for the conclusion; rather, Hume uses the phrase to denote *deductive* arguments with contingent premises.[13] Recognition of this fact clears up several puzzling features of Hume's discussion. The emphasis he lays on the Uniformity of Nature, for example, makes sense from this perspective: it is an attempt, ultimately unsuccessful, to insert a contingent lemma between the premises and the conclusion in order to create a valid deductive argument. Similarly, his reiterated claim that a connection between matters that lie within our experience and those that do not cannot be found a priori becomes clear and even obvious on a deductive model: adding a necessary truth to the premises will not strengthen the argument.

The interpretive point that Hume is working with a limited conception of "probable inference," though hardly original, has important consequences for the problem of induction. It has become obvious in the 250 years since the publication of the *Enquiry* that this restriction, taken literally, would render any reasonable solution to the problem of induction impossible by ruling out the possibility of learning from experience.

Nondemonstrative inference, even granting *arguendo* that it is epistemically legitimate, is not in general monotonic: adding further premises to a nondemonstrative argument may drastically undermine support for the conclusion. Nonmonotonicity is a feature we need for a plausible theory of inductive inference. Precisely because (as Hume never tires of pointing out) our conclusions may be false despite the favorable data, we must be able to weaken the support for those conclusions by enlarging our experience—discovering, say, a black swan or a white raven. Deductive inference, however, is monotonic: adding further premises cannot invalidate a deductive argument. Any interesting version of the problem of induction must therefore be reconstructed in a fashion that does not restrict us to deductive inference forms but leaves open at least the epistemic possibility of genuinely justificatory nondeductive forms of inference.

Reconstructing the technical challenge in this way casts the problem of induction in a different light. For one thing, it renders pointless Hume's own dilemma for inductive inference— that the premise added to the argument would be question-begging if it stated a matter of fact but useless if it expressed a relation of ideas. Once the skeptical problem is reformulated to allow for a nondeductive inference form, the presupposition of this dilemma collapses.

Nevertheless, something of the spirit of Hume's dilemma survives this reconstruction. The epistemic principle that connects the premises and conclusion of an inductive argument must be in some sense rationally defensible: but how can any such defense be mounted? In particular, if the defense of the epistemic principle itself depends essentially on contingent features of our world lying beyond our immediate experience, then the problem of induction engenders a regress: for by what means are we to infer that our world possesses the contingent feature in question? If, on the other hand, the epistemic principle is to be defended wholly a priori, then it is incumbent on the epistemologist to produce a purely logical or mathematical principle adequate to the task. And in view of the vagaries of the physical universe, which owes us no cooperation in our inductive enterprise, this has seemed to many inductive skeptics about as promising as an attempt to square the circle.

One way of putting the skeptical challenge regarding any form of inference is the question: "Granted that these premises are true, and that this inference form links them to the indicated conclusion; granted also that I prefer truth to falsehood; why should these facts commend the conclusion to me?" For deductive argumentation, we appear to have a simple and gratifying answer: "Because it is guaranteed that in accepting the conclusion you will *never* believe falsely." And this defense of deduction is arguably certifiable a priori. But precisely because the premises of a nondeductive inference form do not guarantee the truth of the conclusion, it is difficult to justify what appears to be the parallel response: "Because it is guaranteed that, in accepting the conclusion, you will *usually* believe truly."[14] Whether this renders the reconstructed problem of induction insoluble or is merely a red herring is a matter to which we will return.

The problem just outlined, though difficult, sets up only the minimal conditions for anything that is to count as an answer to the problem of induction. A stronger challenge is posed by specific examples Hume brings up of inductive extrapolation: reasoning from past sunrises to sunrise tomorrow, from the previous consumption of nourishing bread to the conclusion that it will nourish at another time, or from the fact that natural laws have not been violated in one's own experience to a reasonable skepticism regarding claims that they were violated at some other time. Though Hume does not stress the point, there is an implicit challenge here to produce more than a minimal validation of induction. The news that Professor Reichenfraassen, by dint of a lifetime's study and intense concentration, managed on one occasion to sustain for five minutes a justified belief on the basis of premises that did not entail its truth would strike us as being of limited interest. The practical challenge is to produce a validation of a principle of induction that is relevant to the justification of typical (and, prereflectively, well-justified) beliefs on such grounds as we commonly have.

Hume's challenge is as interesting for what he allows as for what he contests. He takes it for granted that in such situations we may unambiguously identify the right reference class—sunrises and loaves of bread, for instance. In this he shows a surprising streak of common sense. For although the selection of a reference class is not always a straightforward matter and sometimes creates serious problems, there do seem to be many cases in ordinary life where a single reference class strikes us as obviously right and all rivals as obviously wrong. Justifying our spontaneous preference in such simple cases is itself a significant philosophical undertaking. But it is not Hume's problem.

Many of Hume's examples of inductive extrapolation have an additional feature that seems to make them particularly difficult candidates for justification: they move from premises in the past and present tense to a conclusion regarding the future. Opponents of direct inference have seized upon this point to create a modal barrier against any statistical extrapolation into the future. If it is ever legitimate to argue from the properties of a sample to those of an unsampled member of the population, so runs the objection, this is only because each member of the population had an equal chance of being selected in the sample. But by definition, one *cannot* sample the future. Future ravens had no chance to be included in one's evidence; the probability that a raven not yet conceived is included in any past sample is simply zero. The sample is not, as a result, truly random with respect to the set of all ravens, and it therefore has no bearing on the future.[15]

We have, then, both a theoretical and a practical problem of induction. The challenge posed by the theoretical problem is to produce a method of inference in which, although the premises do not logically entail the conclusion, they do render it genuinely probable in an epistemically significant sense. The practical challenge grants that the problem of the reference class is often, from a practical standpoint, unproblematic but requires a method of inference that sanctions extrapolation from a uniform sample to the presence of the property in question in an unexamined member of the population. And the practical problem has, as a particularly interesting special case, the projection of past data into the future.

Inverse and Direct Inference

A long tradition, stretching from Bernoulli and Bayes to Howson and Urbach, identifies the inference from sample to population as an exercise in "inverse" reasoning. From this standpoint, the structure of our inference makes use of Bernoulli's theorem, also known as the "Law of Large Numbers," in reverse. A Bayesian reconstruction runs thus: we are seeking the probability that the frequency with which feature X occurs in a population lies within a small interval ϵ of the value p, given that an n-fold sample exhibits X with frequency p (where m is the number of members in the sample exhibiting X, and p=m/n).[16] More formally, we are seeking

$$P((Fx(Pop) = (p \pm \epsilon)) \,/\, (Fx(Smp) = p) \ \&\ (S(Smp) = n))$$

for pertinent values of p, ϵ, and n. From a Bayesian standpoint, we find this by expanding in the usual fashion:

$$\frac{P((Fx(Pop) = (p \pm \epsilon)) \,/\, (S(Smp) = n)) \times P((Fx(Smp) = p) \,/\, (Fx(Pop) = (p \pm \epsilon)) \ \&\ (S(Smp) = n))}{P((Fx(Smp) = p) \,/\, (S(Smp)=n))}$$

Bernoulli's theorem allegedly supplies us with the right-hand term in the numerator. Unfortunately, as early critics of inverse inference were quick to point out, the left term of the numerator and (tacitly) the denominator both invoke a prior probability that the proportion of X's in the population lies within ϵ of p.[17] How such priors are to be acquired is the fundamental problem of Bayesian inference; its apparent intractability is doubtless the chief stone of stumbling for non-Bayesians.

Actually, matters are complicated even with regard to the least controversial aspect of the Bayesian expression. What Bernoulli's theorem actually supplies is not the right-hand term of the numerator in the Bayesian expression,

$$P((Fx(Smp) = p) \,/\, (Fx(Pop) = (p \pm \epsilon)) \,\&\, (S(Smp) = n)),$$

but rather

$$P((Fx(Smp) = (p \pm \epsilon)) \,/\, (Fx(Pop) = p) \,\&\, (S(Smp) = n)).$$

The former expression, unlike the latter, requires us to specify a probability distribution over possible values of Fx(Pop)—a function that might vary sharply within a small interval around p.

I do not propose here to survey Bayesian responses to these difficulties, much less to adjudicate disputes about their adequacy. What I want to investigate instead are the prospects for a very different approach to inductive extrapolation that does not invoke prior probabilities and inverse inference but rather utilizes *direct* inference and Bernoulli's theorem to calculate

$$P((Fx(Pop) = (p \pm \epsilon)) \,/\, (Fx(Smp) = p) \,\&\, (S(Smp) = n)).$$

The method, if defensible, should hold interest for all but the most committed subjectivists.

Direct inference is perhaps the simplest and most natural expression of a "degree of entailment" interpretation of probability. Given that the frequency of property X in a population G is p, and the knowledge that *a* is a random member of G with respect to possession of X, the probability that *a* is an X is p.[18] Put more exactly,

$$P(Xa \,/\, (Ga \,\&\, Fx(G) = p)) = p.$$

Clearly, much depends on the clauses ensuring that *a* is a random member of G with respect to possession of X. We will return to this qualification in due course.

The intuitive appeal of direct inference comes out strongly in simple examples. Donald Williams, a passionate advocate of direct inference, describes it in terms of the "intermediate cogency of proportional syllogisms."[19] Just as the classical syllogism warrants our concluding, from

1. All G are X
2. *a* is a G

with full assurance, that

3. *a* is an X

so the proportional syllogism, subject to the restrictions mentioned above, licenses our inference from

1′. m/n G are X
2′. *a* is a G

with assurance m/n, that

3′. *a* is an X.

As Williams points out, we use the classical syllogism but rarely: our major premises are not of the form "All falling barometers portend storms" or "All red-meated watermelons are sweet" but rather the more modest form that falling barometers *generally* portend storms and *most* red-meated watermelons are sweet.

> In the cadres of the traditional deductive logic, these changes make a fatal difference: the propositions that falling barometers generally portend a storm and that the barometer is now falling entail, strangely enough, nothing whatever about an impending storm. . . . Impatient with this finicking of the logician, the native wit of mankind has jauntily transcended the textbook formulas, has found the principle self-evident that if *All M is P* makes it certain that any one M will be P, then *Nearly all M is P* makes it nearly certain, and has quite satisfactorily predicted its storms and purchased its melons accordingly.[20]

Indeed, the classical syllogisms Barbara and Celarent, with a singular minor premise, can readily be seen as limiting cases of the proportional syllogism when m = n and m = 0, respectively.[21] From this point of view, statistical syllogisms constitute a spectrum of inferences, each moving from statistical information to singular statements about members of the relevant class. The conclusion, as in the traditional syllogism, is always categorical, but the strength of the argument varies with the proportion cited in the major premise.

The notion of the statistical syllogism as a generalized form of the traditional one admitting intermediate grades of logical cogency is attractive, and a substantial number of philosophers have incorporated something like it in their treatment (though not always their justification) of inductive inference.[22] But granting for the moment the rationality of such direct inference, we have still to account for the truth of the major premise. How can we come by the knowledge that m/n ravens are black? In particular, how are we to come by it in a fashion that does not examine all ravens *seriatem*, including the one named *a*, so that in the last analysis direct inference falls prey to an analogue of Sextus Empiricus's complaint about the traditional syllogism—that to complete the enumeration required to establish the major premise, we will have to make use of the conclusion, thus rendering the subsequent argument circular?[23]

Strictly speaking, we cannot guarantee the major premise without examining all of its instances. But as Williams points out, we can circumvent this problem by a clever combination of Bernoulli's "Law of Large Numbers" and a second direct inference. Crudely but briefly put, Bernoulli's theorem says that most large samples differ but little from the population out of which they are drawn—where "most" indicates a satisfyingly high percentage and "little" a gratifyingly small deviation from the true value, provided that "large" is sufficiently great. We may stipulate a small margin ϵ such that a sample is said to "match" a population just in case

$$|p - m/n| \leq \epsilon ,$$

which is to say, the difference between the true proportion p and the observed sample proportion m/n is less than or equal to ϵ. It is a simple matter then to choose a sample size n great enough that at least a proportion α of the possible n-fold samples will match the population to the stipulated degree of precision. The formula

$$n \geq .25\ (\epsilon^2(1 - \alpha))^{-1}$$

gives the desired sample size.[24] For example, with ϵ =.05 and α =.95, a sample of 2000 suffices. Given the sample size and the width of the interval, on the other hand, we can calculate the degree of confidence α simply by rearranging terms:

$$\alpha = 1 - .25\ (n\,\epsilon^2)^{-1}.$$

A lovely feature of this equation is that it does not mention p: we can calculate the confidence level without knowing the actual proportion in the population. It is easy to show that the likelihood of a "match" is worst when p = .5; so the constant .25, the maximum value of the product p(1 – p), represents the "worst case scenario"—α will clearly be higher for any lower value of this term. By using this value, we can insure that our confidence levels are never overly optimistic.

Armed with an n-fold sample of balls (from the statistician's ubiquitous urn), 95% of which are red, we are in a position to reason as follows:

1*. At least α of n-fold samples exhibit a proportion that matches the population
2*. S is a random n-fold sample with respect to matching the population

════ [with probability $\geq \alpha$]

3*. S matches the population
4*. S has a proportion of .95 red balls

———

5*. p lies in the interval $[.95 - \epsilon, .95 + \epsilon]$

The move from 1* and 2* to 3* is a direct inference, its major premise being underwritten by Bernoulli's theorem.[25] The move from 3* and 4* to 5* incorporates the information regarding the sample proportion and the definition of matching. But 5* is not quite the simple statistical statement we are accustomed to dealing with: rather, it states that the proportion of red balls in the urn lies in the interval $[.95 - \epsilon, .95 + \epsilon]$. Provided that ϵ is small, however, the lower boundary of this interval is still a healthy majority. We can now extend the argument to predictive inference regarding an as yet unsampled ball from the urn:

6*. *a* is a random ball from this urn with respect to redness

════ [with probability in the interval $[.95 - \epsilon, .95 + \epsilon]$]

7*. *a* is red

Prima facie, this is a cogent response to Hume's challenge. There is no use caviling at 1*, which is a mathematical truism. From 2* and 4*, which state the size and composition of our sample, and 6* (which merely identifies *a*), we may draw a conclusion regarding an as-yet-unexamined member of the population with a reasonably high level of confidence. And by increasing the size of the sample, we can render the interval arbitrarily small without reducing the confidence level. Hence, an increase in sample size will allow us to take the sample proportion as an arbitrarily good estimate for p.

This solution is of more than academic interest. Hume himself grants that we have experience of bread nourishing us and of the sun rising. If we may take our experience to be a sample, then it appears that we possess all the tools necessary to make a rational defense of everyday extrapolations against Humean skepticism. But philosophical battles are not so easily won. Virtually every aspect of the argument just presented has been called into question. To these objections we now turn.

Linear Attrition

A surprisingly common objection to direct inference, particularly in sampling examples, is that it reflects merely a linear elimination of alternatives and therefore offers no information regarding unexamined cases. A. J. Ayer suggests this in his description of a sampling experiment without replacement:

> If there are a hundred marbles in a bag and ninety-nine of them are drawn and found to be green, we have strong confirmation for the hypothesis that all of the marbles in the bag are green, but we have equally strong confirmation for the hypothesis that 99 per cent of the marbles are green and 1 per cent some other colour.[26]

In other words, drawing 99 balls from this bag gives us information precisely regarding the 99 balls in question, nothing more, nothing less. No matter how extensive our sample, the veil of ignorance always stands between us and the unsampled remainder.

John Foster, in his excellent book on Ayer, faithfully reproduces this criticism and explicates it with a clarity that leaves no interpretive questions. Mathematical arguments designed to show that favorable instances increase the probability of a generalization, says Foster, reflect

> merely the trivial fact that, with each new favorable instance, there are fewer cases left in which the generalization could fail. The point is seen most easily if we focus on the example of drawing balls from a bag. Let us assume, for simplicity, that we already know that there are ten balls in all and that each is either black or white. When we have drawn one ball and found it to be black, we have more reason to believe that all the balls are black, simply because there are now only nine possible counter-instances remaining. . . . This has nothing to do with induction, since it does not involve using the examined cases as a basis for predicting the properties of the unexamined cases. It tells us that the probability that *all* the balls are black increases, as the number of black balls drawn increases, but not that the probability that the *next* ball drawn will be black increases, as this number increases. Thus it does not tell us that, having drawn nine balls, we are entitled to be more confident about the colour of the tenth ball than when we first began the experiment.[27]

Fred Dretske raises a similar concern about inferring regularities from uniform instantial data: "Confirmation is not simply raising the probability that a hypothesis is true: it is raising the probability that the unexamined cases resemble (in the relevant respects) the examined cases."[28] His suggestion is that we ought to infer laws of nature directly, since they simultaneously explain the data we already have and imply something about, so to speak, the data we do not have.

In each case, the implication is that a direct inference does not do the job required. Ayer and Foster are concerned that the data conveyed by a sample speak only for themselves and not for the unexamined cases; Dretske is concerned that a direct inference, since it does not conclude with something stronger than a statistical generalization, will not allow the data to speak as they ought. In either case, the promised probabilities are a will-o'-the-wisp.

All of this is half right. Surely, an inductive argument is of no value unless it gives us, on the basis of examined cases, a justification for our beliefs regarding unexamined ones. But as an explication of the mathematical rationale for direct inference, the thesis of linear attrition is demonstrably wrong. To see this, we need only shift to sampling from Ayer's bag with replacement—creating, in effect, an indefinitely large population with a fixed frequency. No finite sample with replacement, no matter how large, ever amounts to a measurable fraction of this population. Yet as we have seen, using direct inference and Bernoulli's theorem it is simple to specify a sample size large enough to yield as high a confidence as one likes that the true population value lies within an arbitrarily small (but nondegenerate) real interval around the sample proportion.

The thesis of linear attrition resembles an intuitively plausible error to which many beginning students of statistics are prone, namely, the mistake of thinking that the value of information in a sample is a function of the proportion of the population sampled.[29] In fact, the relative proportion of the population sampled is not a significant factor in these sorts of estimation problems. It is the sheer amount of data, not the percentage of possible data, that determines the level of confidence and margins of error. This consideration sheds some light on the worry raised by Peter Caws:

> Scientific observations have been made with some accuracy for perhaps 5,000 years; they have been made in quantity and variety only for about 500 years, if as long. An extrapolation (on inductive grounds) into the past suggests that these periods represent an almost infinitessimal fraction of the whole life of the universe.[30]

Caws is certainly right to doubt whether every present regularity may properly be extrapolated into the misty past. But the grounds of such doubt have to do with our concrete evidence for differing conditions in the past rather than with the small fraction of time in which we have sampled the aeons. When we have no reason to believe conditions were relevantly different—as in the case, say, of certain geological processes—we may quite rightly extrapolate backwards across periods many orders of magnitude greater than those enclosing our observations.

Randomness, Fairness, and Representative Samples

Or may we? There is a sharp division of opinion on the question of randomness, and the defense of direct inference sketched above takes its stand on what is, admittedly, the more thinly populated side of the line. For four decades Henry Kyburg has stood almost *solus contra mundum* in his insistence that randomness is epistemic, that it is a primitive notion rather than something to be defined in terms of probability, and that in conjunction with statistical data it yields probabilities without "fair sampling" constraints. I think he is right; and an examination of the problems generated by the standard definition of randomness indicates why Kyburg's approach is so important.

The standard statistical approach defines "randomness" in terms of equiprobability: a selection of an n-fold set from a population is random just in case every n-fold set is as likely to have been drawn from that population as any other.[31]

"But surely," runs the argument, "it is incumbent upon the defenders of direct inference to make some sort of defense of the claim that the sample selected was no more likely to be chosen than any other. The assumption is not generally true. Elementary textbooks are replete with examples of bias in sampling. To assume without argument that one's sample is unbiased is more than imprudent: in effect, it attempts to manufacture valuable knowledge out of sheer ignorance."

No other single criticism is more widely canvassed or more highly regarded in the literature. Apropos of an example involving a sample of marbles selected one each from 1000 bags, each of which contains 900 red and 100 white balls, Ernest Nagel urges that while Bernoulli's theorem

> does specify the probability with which a combination belonging to M [the set of all possible 1000-fold samples, one from each bag] contains approximately 900 red marbles, it yields no information whatever concerning the proportion of combinations satisfying this statistical condition that may be *actually selected* from the 1000 bags — unless, once more, the independent factual assumption is introduced that the ratio in which such combinations are *actually selected* is the same as the ratio of such combinations in the set M of all *logically possible* combinations.[32]

Without a special assumption of "fair sampling," we are vulnerable to the possibility that some samples may be much more likely to be selected than others; and perhaps the ones most likely to be selected are highly unrepresentative. Isaac Levi explicitly urges the need for such restrictions on direct inference in his critique of Kyburg.

> Suppose X knows that 90% of the Swedes living in 1975 are Protestants and that Petersen is such a Swede. Imagine that X knows nothing else about Petersen. On Kyburg's view, X should assign a degree of credence equal to .9 to the hypothesis that Petersen is a Protestant.
>
> I see no compelling reason why rational X should be obliged to make a credence judgment of that sort on the basis of the knowledge given. X does not know whether the way in which Petersen came to be selected for presentation to him is or is not in some way biased in favor of selecting Swedish Catholics with a statistical probability, or chance, different from the frequency with which Catholics appear in the Swedish population as a whole. . . .
>
> For those who take chance seriously, in order for X to be justified in assigning a degree of credence equal to .9 to the hypothesis that Petersen is a Protestant on the basis of direct inference alone, X should know that Petersen has been selected from the Swedish population according to some procedure F and also know that the chance of obtaining a Protestant on selecting a Swede according to procedure F is equal to the percentage of Swedes who are Protestants.[33]

Here is a pretty puzzle. We set out initially in search of a form of inference that would supply something we lacked: a rationally defensible ascription of probabilities to contingent claims on the basis of information that did not entail those claims. If we are required for the completion of this task to have in hand already the probability that this particular sample would be drawn (and indeed an identical probability for the drawing of each other possible sample), or information on the "chance" of obtaining a given sort of individual from the population (above and beyond frequency information), then the way is blocked. Direct inference is impaled on the empirical horn of Hume's dilemma.

The first step toward answering this criticism is to distinguish a "fair" sample from a "representative" one.[34] Fair samples are drawn by a process that gives an equal probability to the selection of each possible sample of that size; a representative sample exhibits the property of interest in approximately the same proportion as the overall population from which the sample is drawn. To insist on a guarantee that the sample be *representative* in this sense is to demand something that turns induction back into deduction, for if we are certain that the sample is representative, we know *eo ipso* approximately what the population proportion is.

If representativeness is too much to demand, however, fairness seems at first blush to be a just requirement. We should like to avoid biased (i.e., unrepresentative) samples; and since most large samples are representative, a selection method that gives each such sample equal probability of being selected yields an agreeably high probability that a given sample is representative. Fair sampling will on occasion turn up samples that are wildly unrepresentative. But constraints of the sort outlined by Levi, if we could be sure they held good, would assure us that in the long run these biased samples will make up only a small proportion of the total set of samples.

Here again, however, the road to an a priori justification of induction appears closed. For under the demands of fair sampling, we cannot rely on the direct inference unless we know that each possible sample was equally likely to be chosen. And that is itself a contingent claim about matters that transcend our observational data and stands, therefore, in need of inductive justification. An infinite regress looms.

The point can be put in another way. Levi requires that X know Petersen has been selected by a method F that has a .9 chance of selecting Protestants from the population of Swedes. But what does "chance" mean here? Surely it does not mean that 90% of the *actual* applications of F result in the selection of Protestants from among Swedes. For this would reduce the problem to another direct inference, this one about instances of F rather than about Swedes, and if this sort of answer were satisfactory there would have been no need to appeal to F in the first place.[35]

Perhaps sensible of this difficulty, Michael Friedman has tried to rescue a notion of objective chance by appealing to the set of actual and physically possible applications of a method, arguing that if the ratio of successes in such a set is favorable then we may say that the objective chance of success is high—and hence, in Friedman's terminology, that the method is "reliable"—regardless of the ratio of actual successes.[36] But this approach is open to three serious objections. First, it is unclear that there is a definite ratio of successes to trials for the set of all actual and physically possible applications of an inferential method: for there may be infinitely many physically possible applications, and hence an infinite number both of successes and of failures. Second, waiving this difficulty, many of our applications of inductive methodology may yield theories and empirical claims that are accepted at present but not *independently* certifiable as true. Hence, the ratio of successes to trials even among our actual applications may prove impossible to estimate without begging the question. Third, even if this problem can be circumvented, we are left with the question of how to estimate the proportion of successes among actual *and physically possible* applications of the method. To do so by deriving the "reliability" of our inductive methods from extant scientific theories tangles us up in epistemic circularity, for those theories have nothing to commend them except that we have arrived at them by our inductive methods. Friedman is, I think, overly optimistic about the epistemic worth of such appeals.[37] On the other hand, if we are to estimate the frequency of inferential successes from our actual experience, we are back to direct inference once again. If simple direct inference is not epistemically acceptable, we are back to fair sampling constraints. And fair sampling constraints will not rescue induction.

Contrary to common wisdom, however, an assumption of fairness is *not* necessary for the epistemic legitimacy of the inference from sample to population. What is required instead is the condition that, relative to what we know, there be nothing about this particular sample that makes it less likely to be representative of the population than any other sample of the same size. And this is just a particular case of the general requirement for direct inference that the individual about which the minor premise speaks be a random member of the population with respect to the property in question.[38]

Even some critics of direct inference have recognized the justice of this point. Wisdom, for example, points out that it accords well with practical statistical work.

> We know in practical affairs that we must take random samples. But this is because we utilise existing knowledge. If we know of some circumstance that would influence a sample, we must look for a sample that would be uninfluenced by it. . . . Now all this is only to say that *we avoid using a sample that is influenced in a known way*. . . . If we demand that they should be random in some further sense, it is either a demand for knowledge of 'matching' or for additional knowledge about the influences that might affect the sample—the one would render statistical inference superfluous, the other is worthy in the interests of efficiency but does not come into conflict with Williams' argument. After all, *probability is used when all available knowledge has been taken account of and found insufficient.*[39]

An example makes this plain. Every Friday afternoon at 3:30 p.m. sharp, Professor Maxwell emerges from his office, strides down the hall to the freshly-stocked vending machine, inserts the appropriate amount of coin of the realm, and punches the button for a Coke. Because of the way the machine is designed, he will of course get the can resting at the bottom of the column: it is *that* can, no other, that will emerge. Yet given the information that one of the fifty cans in the vertical column is a Mello Yello and the other forty-nine are Coke, he is still justified in placing the probability that he will get a Coke at 98%. True, Maxwell is not equally likely to get any of the various cans stacked within the machine: his selection is not fair. But the Mello Yello is, on his information, a random member of the stack of cans with respect to position. Consequently, the can at the bottom is, on his information, a random element of the stack with respect to being a Coke.

The contrary intuition that demands fairness depends, I submit, on a Cartesian worry rather than a Humean one: it conflates the presence of possibilities with the absence of probabilities.[40] If Maxwell sees that the machine has just been stocked by Damon, a resentful former logic student, he may harbor reasonable doubts that the can at the bottom is a Coke; it may not be a random member of the stack with respect to that property. (It may be a random member of the set of objects deliberately placed in someone's path by a practical joker intent on upsetting his victim's expectations—a set in which the frequency of anticipated outcomes is rather different!) But in the absence of some definite contrary evidence, the mere *possibility* that some can or other of the fifty might have been chosen deliberately to be placed at the bottom does not, in itself, provide information that changes the *probabilities* obtained by direct inference. And the fact that possibilities do not eliminate probabilities is a point that Descartes himself, for all his skeptical arguments, recognized very clearly.

The same considerations apply, mutatis mutandis, to sampling. The possibility that we might be sampling unfairly, like the logical possibility that Maxwell's nemesis Damon has maliciously stacked the machine to trick him, cannot be eliminated a priori. But in the absence of concrete evidence that, for example, places the about-to-be-selected sample in a different and more appropriate reference class, mere possibilities should not affect our evaluation of epistemic probabilities.

Appearances notwithstanding, this is not a retreat to the old principle of indifference; nor is it vulnerable to the charge, to which some advocates of that principle have exposed themselves, that it manufactures knowledge out of ignorance. Indifference assigns equal probabilities to each element of a set on the basis of symmetry considerations, and a drawing method from that set is baptized "random" in terms of that assignment. On the account advocated here, by contrast, randomness is not parasitic on probability. To say that *a* is a random member of class F with respect to having property G, relative to my corpus of knowledge K, does invoke symmetry considerations. But when combined with knowledge of the frequency of G's among the F's, epistemic symmetry yields probabilities that reflect the relevant empirical information rather than reflecting hunches, linguistic symmetries, or preconceived predicate widths. It is a consequence of this view that, in situations of complete ignorance regarding the proportion of F's that are G's, symmetry by itself yields no useful probability information. This is an intuitively gratifying result. Epistemic symmetry conjoined with ignorance yields ignorance; conjoined with knowledge, it yields symmetrical epistemic probabilities.

Success versus Rationality

The foregoing defense of randomness as a basis for assigning probabilities raises a fresh difficulty. The sort of "probability" that can be gotten from randomness and statistical information regarding a reference class is relativized, in the very definition of "randomness," to the state of our knowledge; and this strikes some critics as too much of a retreat from the goal of arriving at true beliefs. As a consequence, so runs the objection, any defense of induction predicated on epistemic probability fails to address the true problem—the problem of future success.

This criticism recalls our reconstructed version of Hume's dilemma: "Granted that these premises are true and that the conclusion is linked to them by a direct inference; why should that fact make the conclusion probable for me, in a sense that commends it to me if I prefer truth to falsehood?" By analogy with the natural answer regarding deductive inference, it would be at least prima facie satisfying to answer that direct inference guarantees a high proportion of future successes. But without fair sampling constraints, which as we have seen would only engender a regress, direct inference offers no such guarantee. Hao Wang puts the challenge succinctly when he notes that on an epistemic interpretation of probability

> we shall at no stage be able to pass from a certain frequency being overwhelmingly probable to it being overwhelmingly frequent. That is to say, on any nonfrequency interpretation we have no guarantee that on the whole and in the long run the more probable alternative is the one that is more often realized.[41]

And again, criticizing Williams's a priori interpretation of probability, Wang asks:

> [W]hat guarantees induction to lead us more often to success than to disappointment,—granted that we can justify inductive generalizations with high probability on some a priori ground? . . . a principle of induction which might always lead to disappointment does not seem to be what is wanted. . . . the conclusions reached in such fashion need not guarantee success, on the whole and in the long run, of our actions guided by them as predictions. In granting that we know a priori that a large sample very probably has nearly the same composition as the whole population, we must not forget that here what are known to be more probable need not be those which are on the whole and in the long run more often realized.[42]

Predictably, this line of criticism is advanced most vigorously by those who insist that both the definition of probability and the legitimacy of induction are bound up inextricably with contingent claims about the nature of the physical world. Nagel makes it clear that what makes Williams's justification of induction unacceptable to him is precisely this failure to guarantee success.

> For without the assumption, sometimes warranted by the facts and sometimes not, that a given method of sampling a population would actually select all sam-

> ples of a specified size with roughly the same relative frequency, arithmetic can not assure us that we are bound to uncover more samples approximately matching the population than samples that do not.[43]

Why should such a "guarantee" or an "assurance" seem a compelling requirement for the justification of induction? Russell, in his defense of a finite frequency interpretation of probability, offers a clue. If we are obliged to admit that the improbable may happen, then

> a probability proposition tells us nothing about the course of nature. If this view is adopted, the inductive principle may be valid, and yet every inference made in accordance with it *may* turn out to be false; this is improbable, but not impossible. Consequently, a world in which induction is true is empirically indistinguishable from one in which it is false. It follows that there can never be any evidence for or against the principle, and that it cannot help us to infer what will happen. If the principle is to serve its purpose, we must interpret "probable" as meaning "what in fact usually happens"; that is to say, we must interpret a probability as a frequency.[44]

But the moral drawn here confuses success with rationality. What Russell means by a world in which induction is "true" is, apparently, one in which inductive reasoning works well. Since it might turn out that all of our samples are unrepresentative, our extrapolations from them might all be hopelessly wide of the mark. This is, however, a reversion to the Cartesian worry. It is possible to get a large but unrepresentative sample, just as it is possible to draw the one black ball from an urn of a million, 999,999 of which are white. But it would be irrational to expect this, given no further relevant information; and it is equally irrational to expect our samples to be unrepresentative and our inductions, in consequence, unsuccessful.

This conflation of Humean and Cartesian worries underlies Russell's complaint that such a principle "cannot help us to infer what will happen." If we demand a guarantee of success, or at any rate a guarantee of a high frequency of future successes, then we are indeed out of luck: that sort of "help" is not forthcoming. No amount of reasoning will turn contingent propositions into necessary ones. But rationality requires both less and more than this: less, because it is logically possible that a rational policy of nondemonstrative inference may always lead us astray; and more, because no accidental string of successes can in and of itself establish a policy of inference as rational. Perhaps the real value of surveying our success frequencies is that it gives us a rough gauge of the "uniformity of nature" in a sense that, while post hoc and therefore not useful for justifying induction, is at least tolerably clear.

Ironically, a guarantee of a high proportion of successes is not only unavailable but would be useless to the apostles of success without a subsequent appeal to unvarnished direct inference.[45] This is not merely because in the long run we are all dead: it applies even to an ironclad guarantee that 99% of all of the inductions we make in the next year will be true. For in applications, it is always *this* induction, this particular instance, that is of importance. Even if it were granted that the proportion of successes among our inductions in the next year is .99, and that this application of inductive methodology is, given our present evidence, a random member of the class of those inductions with respect to its success, why should these facts confer any particular epistemic credibility upon the notion that this induction will be successful? The rationality of direct inference is so fundamental that it cannot even be criticized in this fashion without a covert admission that it is rational.

Once we have seen this, we are freed from the trap of thinking that a proper justification of induction must necessitate future success. The correct response to the modern Humean challenge regarding probabilities is to distinguish it from Cartesian anxiety over possibilities and, having done so, to point out the way in which direct inference is underwritten by the symmetry of epistemically equivalent alternatives with respect to concrete frequency data. That symmetry offers no binding promises with respect to the future, no elimination of residual possibilities of failure. But our probabilistic extrapolations are apt to fail *only* if our samples have been unrepresentative; and despair over this bare possibility is, at bottom, an instance of the same fallacy that drives the credulous to purchase lottery tickets because of the *possibility* of winning. To see this fixation on possibilities aright is to understand the legitimacy of direct inference and to recognize that the probabilities it affords us are, in every sense of the term, rational.

Sampling the Future: The Modal Barrier

Granting that the rationality of direct inference is logically independent of its record of successes, it is subject to what appears at first sight to be a severe limitation: it applies only to the population *from which we are sampling*, and that population often seems much more restricted than the scope of our conclusions. C. D. Broad raises this consideration to cast doubt on any approach to the problem of induction that takes its cue from observed samples, both because of our "restricted area of observation in space" and because of the "distinction of past and future cases"—by which he means quite simply that the probability of our having met any future crow is zero.[46] It is impossible to sample the future. Wisdom picks up on Broad's criticism to supply a vivid image of the modal barrier that apparently blocks the use of direct inference from the past and present to the future:

> [I]f some balls in an urn were sewn into a pocket, we could not get a fair sample—or rather we could not get a sample at all. Likewise the 'iron curtain' between the present and the future invalidates inductive extrapolation about the composition of things behind the curtain—we cannot sample them from this side.[47]

This objection has a plausible ring, but it proves extraordinarily difficult to give a detailed explanation of just why the modal barrier should block direct inferences. There is a metaphysical thesis, going back to Aristotle, that future tense contingent statements have no present truth value.[48] This seems strong enough to scotch direct inference regarding the future, but it goes well beyond the modal barrier raised by Broad and Wisdom; indeed, it is difficult to see how the problem of induction could even arise with respect to the future if we run no risk of speaking falsely when we make contingent claims in the future tense. Traditionally, the chief motivation for this approach has been the fear that allowing contingent claims about the future to be true in the present would commit us to fatalism.[49] It is by now widely acknowledged that there are serious problems with the reasoning behind this charge.[50]

But even if fatalism did follow from the unrestricted law of excluded middle, the attempt to salvage human freedom by denying the truth of future contingents seems to be a cure nigh as evil as the disease. For in a great many contexts where freedom matters to us it is bound up with *deliberation*, and deliberation involves, ineliminably, the consideration of possible but avoidable future courses of action and their possible but avoidable future consequences. If future contingents have no truth values, then deliberation is a sham. This is not a plausible way to rescue human freedom.

The real attractions of the modal barrier lie elsewhere. Ayer, for example, grants as an arithmetical truism that an omniscient being who made every possible selection precisely once would necessarily find that most of his samples were typical.

> It hardly needs saying, however, that we are not in this position. . . . So far from its being the case that we are as likely to make any one selection as any other, there is a vast number of selections, indeed in most instances the large majority, that it is impossible for us to make. Our samples are drawn from a tiny section of the universe during a very short period of time. And even this minute portion of the whole four-dimensional continuum is not one that we can examine very thoroughly.[51]

To extricate ourselves from this predicament, says Ayer, we require

> two quite strong empirical assumptions. They are first that the composition of our selections, the state of affairs which we observe and record, reflects the composition of all of the selections which are available to us, that is to say, all the states of affairs which we could observe if we took enough trouble; and secondly that the distribution of properties in the spatio-temporal region which is accessible to us reflects their distribution in the continuum as a whole.[52]

He is prepared to grant the first assumption, provided that we have taken some precautions to vary our samples and test our hypotheses under different conditions to safeguard against bias. But the second one he finds deeply problematic. The problem is not just that we are intuitively disinclined to extrapolate our local sample billions of years into the future or billions of light-years across the visible universe. That problem can be resolved by restricting the field of our conjectures to our local cosmic neighborhood and the relatively near future, and such a restriction may guarantee that our sample is typical of the local region of spacetime. If we approach the matter in this fashion, then

> we can be certain, and that without making any further assumptions, that in many cases the percentages with which the characters for which we are sampling will be distributed among [the populations in which we are interested] will not be very different at the end of the future period from what they are now. This will be true in all those cases in which we have built up such a backlog of instances that they are bound to swamp the new instances, however deviant these may be. But this conclusion is of no value to us. For we are interested in the maintenance of a percentage only in so far as it affects the new instances. We do not want to be assured that even if these instances are deviant the final result will be much the same. If we make the time short enough, we know this anyway. We want to be assured that the new instances will not be deviant. But for this we do require a non-trivial assumption of uniformity.[53]

Ayer's adroit exposition almost succeeds in concealing the fact that he has smuggled in the thesis of linear attrition once again. The problem arises not because the unsampled instances are future, but rather because they are unsampled, and we want to be assured that the unsampled instances are not deviant. "New instances" are the ones about which we have no information. If this objection works at all, it will work regardless of their temporal position. The modal barrier is simply the veil of ignorance seen from a particular point of view.

This analysis of the objection casts doubt on Ayer's distinction between the two assumptions he thinks we need. If we are going to be worried about the unrepresentativeness of our sample regarding the far reaches of spacetime on the grounds that those far reaches may be deviant, then why not also be worried about unexamined ravens in the local wood at the dawn of the twenty-first century, since they may be deviant as well? That we have varied the conditions of our observations is no defense against this possibility, for we wish (following Ayer's example) to know not merely that our sample is representative of the whole spatiotemporally local population but that it is representative of the unexamined instances within that population. And however uniform our sample heretofore, we cannot eliminate what Wisdom calls "the theoretical [problem] of making an inference about unexamined things in view of the possibility that the universe might play some trick that would wreck our best calculated expectations."[54]

Thus the thesis of linear attrition, and with it the modal barrier, are grounded in the Cartesian worry about possibilities that we have already met; for the fear that the universe might "trick" us is plainly a reversion to Maxwell's apprehensions regarding Damon. Why, to use Wisdom's own analogy, should we believe that the balls sewn into a pocket in the bag are specially unrepresentative of the whole? To be sure if we had some information to that effect then epistemic randomness would be violated and we would not use direct inference. But Wisdom leaves no doubt that fear of the bare *possibility* that our samples might be unrepresentative lies at the root of his inductive skepticism, for in his critique of Williams he explicitly repeats the objection:

> It is true that in the absence of knowledge of factors influencing a sample we rightly use that sample as a guide and that with such knowledge we rightly reject a sample. But here the position is that we do not know whether or not there is an influence at work and we think it possible there may be. In view of this doubt we cannot regard the sample as a guide that has the required statistical reliability.[55]

Such is the moral of our extended examination of the problem of induction. In case after case, the challenges to direct inference reduce to the fundamental objection that the possibility of error has not been eliminated. The thesis of linear attrition, the demand for fairness constraints, the insistence on a guarantee of success and despair of breaching the modal barrier are all variants on the same underlying theme: the fear "that the universe might play some trick" on us. To such an objection there is in the final analysis only one answer, as old as Herodotus:

> There is nothing more profitable for a man than to take counsel with himself; for even if the event turns out contrary to one's hope, still one's decision was right, even though fortune has made it of no effect: whereas if a man acts contrary to good counsel, although by luck he gets what he had no right to expect, his decision was not any the less foolish.[56]

TIMOTHY MCGREW
Western Michigan University

NOTES

1. In a 1926 lecture on "The Philosophy of Francis Bacon," reprinted in Broad, C. D., *Ethics and the History of Philosophy* (New York: Humanities Press, 1952). The comment appears on p. 143.

2. For example, Harold Jeffreys, *Theory of Probability*, 2nd ed. (Oxford: Oxford University Press, 1948), p. 395; I. J. Good, *The Estimation of Probabilities* (Cambridge, MA: MIT Press, 1965), p. 16.

3. For a classic reference, see R. A. Fisher, *The Design of Experiments* (New York: Hafner, 1971; originally published in 1935).

4. See, for instance, Edwin Hung's discussion of sampling and the Law of Large Numbers in his undergraduate textbook *The Nature of Science: Problems and Perspectives* (New York: Wadsworth, 1997), pp. 276–77, 292–94.

5. Useful surveys of the conflicting schools regarding the interpretation of probability and its relation to statistics, coming from theorists of various persuasions, may be found in Howard Raiffa, *Decision Analysis* (Reading, MA: Addison-Wesley, 1968), Alex Michalos, *Principles of Logic* (Englewood Cliffs, NJ: Prentice Hall, 1969), J. R. Lucas, *The Concept of Probability* (Oxford: Oxford University Press, 1970), J. L. Mackie, *Truth, Probability, and Paradox* (Oxford: Oxford University Press, 1973), Henry Kyburg, *Logical Foundations of Statistical Inference* (Boston: D. Reidel, 1974), and Roy Weatherford, *Philosophical Foundations of Probability Theory* (Boston: Routledge & Kegan Paul, 1982).

6. See, for example, D. C. Stove, "Hume, Probability, and Induction," *Philosophical Review* 74 (1965): 160–77.

7. Notable representatives of this viewpoint are Karl Popper, *Conjectures and Refutations* (New York: Harper and Row, 1963) and three philosophers of science heavily influenced by Popper: J. O. Wisdom, *Foundations of Inference in Natural Science* (London: Methuen & Co., 1952), John Watkins, *Science and Skepticism* (Princeton: Princeton University Press, 1984), and David Miller, *Critical Rationalism* (Chicago: Open Court, 1994). But skeptical worries about induction also drive non-Popperians to pessimistic epistemological conclusions, as in A. J. Ayer's *Probability and Evidence* (London: Macmillan, 1973) and *The Central Questions of Philosophy* (New York: William Morrow and Co., 1973) and Richard Fumerton's recent book *Metaepistemology and Skepticism* (Lanham, MD: Littlefield Adams, 1995).

8. See Isaac Levi, "Direct Inference," *Journal of Philosophy* 74 (1977): 5–29, Kyburg's reply, "Randomness and the Right Reference Class," *Journal of Philosophy* 74 (1977): 501–21, Levi's response "Confirmational Conditionalization," *Journal of Philosophy* 75 (1978): 730–37, and Kyburg's rebuttal "Conditionalization," *Journal of Philosophy* 77 (1980): 98–114. There are further details in Radu Bogdan, ed., *Profile of Kyburg and Levi* (Dordrecht: D. Reidel, 1981) and "Epistemology and Induction," in Kyburg's collection *Epistemology and Inference* (Minneapolis: University of Minnesota Press, 1983). Not all versions of direct inference violate confirmational conditionalization: see, e.g., John Pollock, *Nomic Probability and the Foundations of Induction* (New York: Oxford University Press, 1990), p. 137, n.16. The issue is important but does not affect the discussion here.

9. David Hume, *An Enquiry Concerning Human Understanding*, ed. Eric Steinberg (Indianapolis: Hackett, 1977), p. 15 f.; *A Treatise of Human Nature*, 2nd ed., ed. P. H. Nidditch (Oxford: Oxford University Press, 1978), Book I, sec. 3, part 11 *et passim.*

10. Hume, in Nidditch, ed., *Treatise*, p. 651.

11. See, e.g., Barry Stroud, *Hume* (London: Routledge and Kegan Paul, 1977), p. 50.

12. See the doubts raised regarding Stroud's counterexample and Putnam-style "Twin Earth" cases in Timothy and Lydia McGrew, "Psychology for Armchair Philosophers," *Idealistic Studies* 23 (1999): 147–57.

13. Stove has an enlightening discussion of this point in "Hume, Probability, and Induction."

14. R. M. Sainsbury suggests that this is the sort of response we should like to give regarding induction as well; see his discussion in *Russell* (London: Routledge & Kegan Paul, 1979), p. 173.

15. Critics of direct inference typically present this point as an intuition pump for skepticism about the move from sample to population in general. The classic formulation of the criticism can be found in C. D. Broad's famous 1918 paper "The Relation Between Induction and Probability," reprinted in *Induction, Probability, and Causation: Selected Papers* (Dordrecht: D. Reidel, 1968). John O. Wisdom explicitly draws the parallel between predicting the future and drawing inferences regarding the unsampled members of the population in *Foundations of Inference in Natural Science*, pp. 217–18.

16. This statement simplifies slightly: the upper and lower margins need not be identical, as Keynes points out in his *Treatise on Probability* (London: Macmillan, 1963), pp. 338–39. Provided that p(1 – p)n is large enough, the asymmetry is negligible, but it will not affect the discussion here if we select ϵ so as to yield a conservative estimate of the probability that the true frequency of X in the population lies within that interval around p. In the finite case a unique shortest interval is always computable.

17. This prior may be assumed to be independent of the mere size of our sample, though some critics of direct inference, construing it as an inverse inference, have maintained that it may not be independent of the sample frequency of m/n. See Patrick Maher, "The Hole in the Ground of Induction," *Australasian Journal of Philosophy* 74 (1996): 423–32. But this criticism is blocked by the requirement of epistemic randomness discussed below.

18. There is some terminological variability in the use of the phrase "direct inference." Carnap, in *Logical Foundations of Probability* (Chicago: University of Chicago Press, 1950), sec. 94, uses it to denote the inference from the known constitution of a population to the most probable constitution of a *sample* drawn from that population. My usage in this paper resembles that in more recent discussions, e.g., Kyburg, "Epistemology and Induction," in *Epistemology and Inference*, pp. 221–31. Unless otherwise noted I take direct inference to be *simple*, i.e., made without dependence on "fairness" constraints. This issue is taken up in detail below. Note that 'p' may take interval values of the form [a, b], where $0 \leq a \leq b \leq 1$. Point values for p may be construed as degenerate intervals where a = b.

19. Donald Williams, *The Ground of Induction* (New York: Russell & Russell, 1963), p. 39.

20. Williams, p.8.

21. That general statements may be construed as limiting cases of probability statements is also stressed by R. B. Braithwaite, *Scientific Explanation* (Cambridge: Cambridge University Press, 1968), p. 152.

22. Roy Harrod indicates that he is in "substantial agreement" with Williams's position in *Foundations of Inductive Logic* (New York: Harcourt, Brace & Co., 1956), pp. xv, 103 ff., etc., though his own system is in some respects idiosyncratic. Max Black adopts a version of the statistical syllogism in "Self-Supporting Inductive Arguments," *Journal of Philosophy* 55 (1958): 718–25. Stephen Toulmin advocates his own informal version of the statistical syllogism in *The Uses of Argument* (Cambridge: Cambridge University Press, 1958), pp.109 ff., though he tends to confuse the strength of the inference with the strength of the conclusion (see p. 139). Simon Blackburn endorses a pair of weaker, qualitative claims analogous to results derivable from the statistical syllogism in *Reason and Prediction* (Cambridge: Cambridge University Press, 1973), pp. 126 ff. Paul Horwich, though a self-professed "therapeutic Bayesian," suggests supplementing coherence with a form of direct inference (couched, of course, in terms of "degree of belief") in *Probability and Evidence* (Cambridge: Cambridge University Press, 1982), pp. 33–34. J. L. Mackie exploits direct inference in his contribution to a 1979 Festschrift for A. J. Ayer, "A Defence of Induction," reprinted in Mackie, *Logic and Knowledge* (Oxford: Oxford University Press, 1985), pp. 159–77. D. C. Stove endorses and elaborates upon Williams's position in the first half of *The Rationality of Induction* (Oxford: Oxford University Press, 1986). John Pollock develops a detailed theory of direct inference, incorporating sevaral variations on the statistical syllogism, in *Nomic Probability and the Foundations of Induction*. The most extensive, probing, and systematic exploitation of direct inference is found in Henry Kyburg's work, spanning more than four decades from "The Justification of Induction," *Journal of Philosophy* 53 (1956): 394–400 and *Probability and the Logic of Rational Belief* (Middletown, CT: Wesleyan University Press, 1961) to the present.

23. Arthur Prior gives a useful sketch of this controversy in his article "Logic, Traditional," in *The Encyclopedia of Philosophy*, ed. P. Edwards (New York: Macmillan and Free Press, 1968), vol. 5, pp. 41–42.

24. Note that there is a minor slip in the otherwise excellent discussion of this formula in Deborah Mayo, *Error and the Growth of Knowledge* (Chicago: University of Chicago Press, 1996), p. 170: it is α, not $(1 - \alpha)$, that represents the desired confidence level.

25. If the need arises, we can get an even more generally applicable result by replacing Bernoulli's theorem with Tchebyshev's inequality: given *any* distribution of data, not less than $1 - (1/n^2)$ of the distribution lies within n standard deviations of the mean. The estimates yielded by Tchebyshev's inequality are generally more cautious than those derived using Bernoulli's theorem, and in a wide range of cases needlessly so. But they have the advantage that they are essentially independent of constraints on the distribution. See William Feller, *An Introduction to Probability Theory and its Applications*, vol. 1, 2nd ed. (New York: John Wiley & Sons, 1957), pp. 219–21.

26. Ayer, *The Central Questions of Philosophy*, p. 178.

27. John Foster, *A. J. Ayer* (London: Routledge & Kegan Paul, 1985), p. 211. Foster brings this example up to counter a version of Bayes's Theorem, but it has more direct bearing on direct inference.

28. Dretske, "Laws of Nature," *Philosophy of Science* 44 (1977): 258.

29. Those interested in speculations on the history of probability might want to investigate the possibility that Keynes, by introducing his Principle of Limited Variety and thereby attempting to ground enumerative induction in eliminative inference, fostered the confusion visible in the thesis of linear attrition.

30. Peter Caws, *The Philosophy of Science* (New York: D. Van Nostrand & Co., 1965), p. 265.

31. See, e.g., Bhattacharyya and Johnson, *Statistical Concepts and Methods* (New York: Wiley, 1977), pp. 86–87. Similar definitions can be found in almost any statistics text.

32. Nagel's review appears in *Journal of Philosophy* 44 (1947): 685–93. The quoted remark appears on p. 691.

33. Levi, "Direct Inference," pp. 9–10.

34. There is an unfortunate tendency in some introductory textbooks to use these terms interchangeably. See, e.g., Hung, *The Nature of Science*, p. 277, and Robert M. Martin, *Scientific Thinking* (Orchard Park, NY: Broadview Press, 1997), where the following definition appears on p. 55: "A **REPRESENTATIVE SAMPLE** is a sample that is likely to have close to the same proportion of the property as the population." The introduction of "is likely" here blurs the distinction between fairness and representativeness.

35. This point is raised in a slightly different form by Kyburg in "Randomness and the Right Reference Class," p. 515.

36. Michael Friedman, "Truth and Confirmation," *Journal of Philosophy* 76 (1979): 361-82. Reprinted in *Naturalizing Epistemology*, ed. Hillary Kornblith (Cambridge, MA: MIT Press, 1985), pp. 147–67. See pp. 153–54.

37. Friedman, "Truth and Confirmation," pp. 154–57. The appeal to epistemically circular arguments is characteristic both of inductive defenses of induction and of externalist epistemologies: the arguments, both pro and con, show remarkable similarities. For attempted inductive justifications of induction, see Braithwaite, *Scientific Explanation*, and Max Black, *Problems of Analysis* (Ithaca: Cornell University Press, 1954), ch. 11. Braithwaite's approach is criticized in Kyburg, "R. B. Braithwaite on Probability and Induction," *British Journal for the Philosophy of Science* 35 (1958-9): 203–20, particularly pp. 207–8, and Wesley Salmon critiques Black's use of epistemic circularity, which he terms "rule circularity," in *Foundations of Scientific Inference* (Pittsburgh: University of Pittsburgh Press, 1969), pp. 12–17. For appeals to epistemic circularity on behalf of epistemic externalism, in addition to Friedman see William Alston, "Epistemic Circularity," *Philosophy and Phenomenological Research* 47 (1986), reprinted in Alston's collection *Epistemic Justification* (Ithaca: Cornell University Press, 1989), pp. 319–49, and his recent book *The Reliability of Sense Perception* (Ithaca: Cornell University Press, 1993). For criticism, see Timothy and Lydia McGrew, "Level Connections in Epistemology," *American Philosophical Quarterly* 34 (1997): 85–94, and

"What's Wrong with Epistemic Circularity," *Dialogue* 39 (2000): 219–39, and Fumerton, *Metaepistemology and Skepticism*.

38. Strictly speaking, we should say "or better than random." The inference demands simply that the individual not be *less* likely to be representative than any other individual. But typically our evidence that a given individual is no less likely to be representative than any other is simply that it is a random member of the set and hence no more likely to be representative either.

39. Wisdom, *Foundations of Inference in Natural Science*, p. 216.

40. This point was noted by Williams, pp. 69, 149, though he unfortunately expounded it in a manner that did not sharply distinguish direct from inverse inference (see especially p. 149).

41. Hao Wang, "Notes on the Justification of Induction," *Journal of Philosophy* 44 (1947): 701–10. The quotation appears on p. 703.

42. Ibid., pp. 705–6.

43. Nagel, p. 693.

44. Bertrand Russell, *Human Knowledge: Its Scope and Limits* (New York: Simon and Schuster, 1948), p. 402.

45. This point is made forcefully in Kyburg, "The Justification of Induction."

46. Broad, *Induction, Probability, and Causation: Selected Papers*, pp. 7–8.

47. Wisdom, *Foundations of Inference in Natural Science*, p. 218.

48. *De Interpretatione*, ch. 9.

49. See Steven Cahn, *Fate, Logic, and Time* (New Haven: Yale University Press, 1967) for a useful historical discussion and a defense of the view that fatalism is an inevitable consequence of the ordinary (temporally indifferent) formulation of the law of excluded middle.

50. L. Nathan Oaklander provides a careful and persuasive evaluation of the fatalism problem in *Temporal Relations and Temporal Becoming: A Defense of a Russellian Theory of Time* (Lanham, MD: University Press of America, 1984), pp. 195–220.

51. Ayer, *Probability and Evidence*, pp. 41–42. The reference here to the four-dimensional continuum is, of course, incompatible with the denial of future contingents.

52. Ibid., p. 42.

53. Ibid., p. 43.

54. Wisdom, *Foundations of Inference in Natural Science*, p. 217.

55. Ibid., p. 218.

56. Herodotus, *History*, vii, 10. Quoted in Keynes, p. 307.

3

Objective Modality and Direct Inference

ISAAC LEVI

I have long been at least a dualist about applications of probability theory. One main kind of application of the calculus is in characterizing the evaluation by an agent of the expected values of the options available to him or her. That kind of evaluation invokes a notion of credal, personal,or subjective probability. Another kind of application concerns the use of probability distributions in the formulation of statistical hypotheses in the natural and social sciences. Both types of application invoke the notion of a space of possibility. In the case of subjective probability, the corresponding notion is that of doxastic or serious possibility. In the case of statistical probability, the corresponding notion is that of ability or possibility for the dual notion of a sure-fire disposition and the idea of a sample space. Certainty of the truth of statistical probabilities of outcomes of experiments of a given kind supports judgments of subjective probability conditional on the supposition that an experiment of the given kind is implemented. Certainty of the truth of a sample space attribution supports judgments of serious possibility conditional on a similar supposition. I examine the analogue of direct inference in the modal case. I argue against the widely held view that because abilities and dispositions are attributed truly or falsely of systems, the judgments of conditional modality supported by them should be construed as carrying truth values and requiring a possible-worlds semantics to supply truth conditions for them.

—I. L.

* * *

1. Sample Spaces

In chapter I of his celebrated *Foundations of Probability*, A. N. Kolmogorov proposed an axiomatic treatment of the mathematical theory of probability—the approach that assimilated probability theory into measure theory (Kolmogorov 1950). Kolmogorov followed his statement of the axioms with an account of how "we apply the theory of probability to the actual world of experiments" (pp. 4–5).

According to Kolmogorov, "there is assumed a complex of conditions *S* which allows of any number of repetitions." In addition, there are posited a definite set of events Ω called "elementary events" "which could take place as a result of the establishment of the conditions *S*." Kolmogorov seems to be saying that the inquirer makes two presuppositions: (a) Whenever the system he is examining is subject to an experiment where conditions of type *S* are realized, exactly one type of result belonging to the set Ω of types of results Kolmogorov called "elementary events" is realized. (b) For each elementary event ω in Ω, it is possible *for* the system to yield ω on an experiment of kind *S*.

Presupposition (a) asserts that the system x under study has a surefire disposition to realize exactly one of the elementary events in the set Ω when conditions of kind *S* are satisfied. Presupposition (b) implies that it is possible for x to realize every member of Ω on a trial of kind *S*. It is possible for x to realize ω on a trial of kind *S* if and only if x *lacks* the surefire disposition to *fail* to realize ω on a trial of kind *S*.

Consider, for example, a coin. The coin has a surefire disposition to land on the surface of the Earth upon being gently tossed close to the surface of the Earth. But a thin coin with two sides marked heads and tails lands on the surface of the Earth if and only if it lands heads on the surface of the Earth or lands tails on the surface of the Earth. If so, the coin with the surefire disposition to land on the surface of the Earth upon being tossed close to the surface also has a surefire disposition to land either heads on the surface of the Earth or tails on the surface of the Earth upon being so tossed. The coin has the ability to land in each of these two ways on a toss. In that case, the set Ω consists of two elementary events. Each of these results "could take place as a result of the establishment of the conditions *S*"—to wit the tossing of the coin.

According to Kolmogorov's terminology, an event is represented by a set of elementary events. To say that an event E occurs is to say that exactly one of the elementary events belonging to the set E occurs. This characterization of events is always relative to the conditions *S*. It is possible for an event E to occur on x's realizing conditions *S* if and only if there is an elementary event relative to *S* belonging to E. That is to say, E is not empty relative to *S*.

In applying the mathematical theory of countably additive probability to such a system x, real numbers are assigned to a "field" ***F*** of events (sets of elementary events) relative to ***S*** so that the conditions imposed by the axioms of the mathematical theory of probability are satisfied by the assignment. In effect, the assignment of such real values according to a probability measure μ to a field of events relative to a trial of kind ***S*** is the representation of a stochastic property of the system x.

The field ***F*** will not, in general, be the power set of Ω. That is because a countably additive probability measure cannot be defined over all members of the power set of Ω when Ω is nondenumerably infinite. This is troublesome. If x is able to respond in manner ω on a trial of kind ***S*** for each and every ω in Ω, surely x is able to realize an event ***E*** of which ω is a member on a trial of kind ***S***. This is so no matter what subset of Ω containing ω a member ***E*** happens to be. The restriction of events assigned probability to a field of measurable events does not seem defensible. Whatever the merits of countable additivity might be, it should not impose restrictions on judgments of objective possibility.

Although the hidden agenda of this discussion concerns probability, officially this discussion is about objective modality. I appeal to Kolmogorov to point out the importance of a *space Ω of possible outcomes of a trial of kind **S*** or of a *sample space* to Kolmogorov's characterization of objective, statistical probability.

It is important to emphasize that Kolmogorov's account of objective physical or statistical probability does not equate such probability with some sort of disposition or ability. Attributing a probability distribution to points in a sample space Ω relative to a trial of kind ***S*** presupposes that the system under study has a sample space relative to the given kind of trial. Different systems may have a similar sample space relative to ***S*** but differ in the objective probability distribution over Ω. So attributing an objective probability to a system relative to a kind of trial presupposes a congeries of dispositions and abilities but adds some additional information without implying the presence of additional dispositions or abilities.

In spite of the differences between the approaches of Kolmogorov and R. von Mises to the interpretation of physical probability, the centrality of the notion of a space of possible outcomes of a trial of kind S is common to both views. The salient difference between the Kolmogorovian school and the Von Mises school concerns the understanding of how a probability value is to be assigned to events carved out of the sample space. Both views share a commitment to some notion of objective possibility or ability relative to a trial of some kind and a dual notion of objective compulsion, necessity, or disposition relative to a kind of trial.

One might be in a position to specify these modal properties of systems or set-ups without being able to identify the probabilities appropriate to possible outcomes of experiments. Perhaps, no such probabilities are coherently ascribed. Or, if they are intelligible, they are unknown. Sample spaces relative to experiments can be discussed without reference to chances (i.e., objective or statistical probabilities relative to kinds of trials).[1]

Attributions of a sample space to system x is relative to trials of kind *S*. The sample space for normal die *a* on a throw will be showing 1, 2, 3, 4, 5, or 6. On a throw yielding an odd number of points, the sample space is 1, 3, or 5. Both sample space attributions are true of the same die at the same time. And they remain true of die *a* when the die is tossed and shows an odd number of points.

The relativity of attributions of sample spaces to trials of kind *S* has ramifications for the relevance of full belief in the truth of such attributions to judgments of doxastic or serious possibility concerning the outcome of a trial of kind *S*. X fully believes that the normal die *a* is going to be tossed. Should X judge it seriously possible that *a* will land showing a 2? That will depend on the additional information available to X. If X is certain that the die will be tossed in a manner yielding an odd number of spots, the answer is clearly negative. But if he is ignorant of any information about the outcome (that is to say, he does not have information about the kind of trial except that it is a tossing onto the surface), he should judge the prospect of showing a 2 to be a serious possibility.

In this essay, I shall focus on direct inference from information about *sample spaces* that contain information about surefire dispositions and abilities to judgments of subjective or serious possibility and impossibility. The parallel and more complicated issue of direct inference from information about objective probability to subjective probability will be taken up briefly at the end of the paper.

2. Dispositions, Abilities, Sample Spaces, and Kinds of Trials

We may plausibly claim that coin *a* invariably lands heads up or tails up on a toss *given that it has the surefire disposition to do so*. The universal regularity we can invoke here is that any coin having the surefire disposition that is tossed near the surface of the earth invariably lands heads up or lands tails up.

Some coins do not have that disposition. They have the ability to land on their edge when tossed near the surface of the earth. Coins with heads on both sides do not have the disposition to land heads or tails on a toss. Unlike "normal" coins, they lack the ability to land tails on a toss. They have the surefire disposition to land heads on a toss. Yet deviant coins of both kinds may sometimes land heads or tails every time in the actual history of tossing they are made to endure.

There is no universal regularity between coins being tossed near the surface of the earth and landing heads or tails. Coins possessing the surefire disposition to land heads-or-tails on a toss near the surface of the earth invariably land heads or tails when tossed. Coins with thick edges lack the disposition. Whether or not they always land heads or tails, their doing so is not explanatory. Causality cannot be explicated by appealing to a constant conjunction between tossings and landings heads or tails. We need to appeal to the presence of the disposition to land heads or tails as well.

Appealing to dispositional properties to account for causality smacks of the hidden springs and mechanisms that Hume decried. And it intimates vacuous explanation of the sort allegedly found in appealing to the dormitive virtue of opium when explaining why someone who took opium went to sleep.

Neither of these objections is decisive. Consider first the issue of hidden springs and mechanisms. Disposition predicates are, to be sure, not thereby completely interpreted in terms of test behavior. The disposition predicate 'D(R/S)' (to be read as "is disposed to respond in manner R on a trial of kind S") may be taken as a primitive term characterized by the following postulate:

(1) $D(R/S)x \supset [Sx \supset Rx])$

Condition (1) fails to secure necessary and sufficient satisfaction conditions for the disposition predicate 'D(R/S)' in terms of test behavior. Where is the sin in this?

Inquirers are not prevented from finding out that attributions of dispositions are true of systems by an appeal to test behavior. Of course, the appeal may need to be supplemented by additional information present in an inquirer's state of full belief. Or the inquirer may resort to drawing ampliative inferences. The information obtained in this fashion may be fully believed and, hence, judged to be certain by X. But it will be vulnerable to being given up to a greater degree than (1). There need be no well entrenched general principle affording a sufficient satisfaction condition in terms of test behavior for the predicate 'D(R/S)'.

Let us grant then that (1) is postulated to be a law. Its postulation is defended by noting that some things respond in manner R when S′d and others do not. The difference between the two sorts of things is marked by the presence of different dispositions—that is to say, properties constrained by lawlike generalizations such as (1).

An ability predicate 'A(R/S)x' (x is able to R upon being S′d) is the dual of the surefire disposition predicate 'D(R/S)'. A(R/S)x if and only if

$\sim D(\sim R/S)x$. '$A(R/S)$' has sufficient satisfaction conditions in terms of test behavior given by (2).

$$(2)\quad Sx \wedge Rx \supset A(R/S)x.$$[2]

In lieu of necessary conditions, attributions of abilities assure the serious possibility of test outcomes unless the inquirer has relevant information preventing such possibility.

Disposition and ability predicates are useful for the purpose of offering explanations. Condition (1) can be used in order to explain why x responded in manner R after being S′d. It had the disposition to respond in this manner. (1) has the form of a covering law. Provided that we are prepared somehow to assert the disposition statement in the antecedent of (1) we can offer explanations.

Disposition and ability predicates suffer often from a serious liability. Because (1) is postulated and at the same time used as a covering law, the putative explanations are vacuous in the sense in which explanatory appeals to dormitive virtue are. There is no well-entrenched satisfaction condition given, independent of appeal to (1) itself, to test for the presence or absence of the disposition. Moreover, in the absence of other pertinent background information, there may be no grounds for asserting the presence of a disposition independent of running a trial of kind S and recording a result of kind R. In this rather narrow sense, dispositions seem useless for prediction and are useful for explanation only on the basis of the behavior to be explained.

The postulation of (1) alone is not the trouble. Rather it is this postulation combined with the absence of any other principles or postulates characteristic of an explanatorily sophisticated and integrated theory. If, for example, necessary and sufficient satisfaction conditions for the disposition predicate were provided by appealing to the details of microstructure as elaborated in some microtheory, the discontent might be removed. This would be so even if necessary and sufficient satisfaction conditions for the disposition term in terms of test behavior were not provided. Or if the disposition and ability predicates remained theoretical predicates in a rich and explanatorily acceptable system, the objections to the use of such predicates would dissipate. Such additional lore might even render the disposition attributions predictively useful.

Thus, the defects in disposition and ability predicates in scientific inquiry, when such predicates are considered defective, are defects in their use for explanatory purposes. Such defects need not, however, deter us from treating them as being true or false of systems, set-ups, or objects. In this sense, we can be as "realist" as can be about dispositions and abilities.

The explanatory drawbacks of disposition and ability predicates need not deter a responsible inquirer from using disposition predicates in covering law explanations. To the contrary, inquirers introduce disposition predicates for use in stopgap covering law explanations. Disposition and ability predicates (and predications of statistical probability) are "placeholders" in stopgap explanation and prediction pending future investigation that integrates such predicates more adequately into theory (Levi and Morgenbesser 1964; Levi 1980, ch. 11). The fact that they are placeholders accounts for their vacuity in explanation. Yet it also allows for their use in stopgap explanations in spite of such vacuity. We need not be deterred from using them for purposes of explanation *as long as the stopgap character of the explanation is recognized and taken seriously as relevant to the direction of further inquiry.*

According to the placeholder view, disposition predicates are used in explanation in an objectionably vacuous manner when there is no recognition of the need for further inquiry aimed at integrating such predicates into an explanatorily more adequate theory.

As an example of such objectionable use consider cases where the predicate "is rational" is taken to be a disposition to obey principles of rational belief, desire, and choice for the purpose of explaining human behavior. Those who think of principles of rationality as explanatory have good reason to favor such a view, for otherwise they lack "covering laws" to invoke in developing such explanations. Authors, like D. Davidson (1980, ch. 14), who adopt this view sometimes insist that there are no psychophysical principles allowing for the reduction of psychology to physics. This suggests that integrating the predicate "is rational" in a more comprehensive theory is hopeless. Fulfilling the promise to cash out the promissory note is abandoned. We may have to rest content with the vacuous covering laws as Davidson is resigned to do. In my opinion it would be preferable to abandon the view that principles of rationality explain behavior.

One may well ask what constitutes adequate integration into theory. I have no definite answer. Of course, the theory should be part of the established body of full beliefs or, perhaps, of the shared beliefs of the community to which the inquirer belongs. It should also fulfill the demands of a research program to which the inquirer or the community subscribe to some satisfactory degree. In my judgment, the relativity of adequate integration to a research program precludes the possibility of a standardized characterization of adequate integration. The adoption of a research program is not the endorsement of the truth of some metaphysical scheme. It is rather the adoption of a value commitment that is open to revision in the ongoing activity of inquiry. When inquirers disagree concerning the conditions demanded for explanatory adequacy, the disagreement is often a disagreement about the aims that the given inquiry ought to be promoting informed, perhaps, by information already available about the extent to which realizing a given program is feasible.

It may, perhaps, be possible to identify some minimal and very weak conditions on the adequacy of any explanatory research program. And, perhaps someday, something may be said about how inquirers committed to competing programs may engage in joint inquiry to iron out their differences. But the status of disposition, ability, and sample space predications as placeholders relative to research programs remains secure.

I shall not pursue this notion of a "placeholder" construal of disposition predicates, ability predicates, and chance predicates here. (Levi and Morgenbesser 1964; Levi 1980, ch. 11). It does, however, have one advantage. It allows us to recognize that dispositions, abilities, and chances are true or false of things as Peirce's "Scotist Realism" insists without indulging in the occult aspects of this idea to which he seems to have been addicted.

One respect in which the realism I am advocating here is quite earnest concerns the question of suspension of judgment.

Consider the following three scenarios:

Case 1: Coin *a* is a thin coin with heads on one side and tails on another. It has a surefire disposition to land on the surface of the earth upon being tossed near the surface. Relative to this kind of trial, the coin has a sample space consisting of two points, heads up and tails up. X is certain of all of this and is in addition certain that coin *a* is tossed at t. X has no other (relevant) information.

Case 2: Coin *b* is again a thin coin. But X is in suspense at to whether it has two heads or two tails. So X is in suspense as to whether *b* has a surefire disposition to land heads up or a surefire disposition to land tails up. X is certain that *b* does not have a sample space consisting of landing heads up and landing tails up on a toss. X is in suspense as to whether *b* has a sample space on a toss containing the singleton {heads up} or the singleton {tails up}. X is certain of this and is in addition certain that *b* is tossed at t. X has no other relevant information.

Case 3: There are two coins *c* and *d* in a bag. X is certain that *c* is two headed and that *d* has two tails. X selects a coin from the bag blindfolded and tosses it. Relative to this kind of experiment (type S), X is certain that the sample space relative to selecting a coin from the bag and tossing it is {selecting *c* & heads up, selecting *d* & tails up}. Given the model, {tails up, heads up} and {selecting *c*, selecting *d*} are equivalent representations of this sample space. Relative to the experiment of tossing *c* or *d* (type S′), X should be in suspense as to whether the sample space is {heads up} or is {tails up}.

If one focuses attention exclusively on judgments of serious possibility and impossibility concerning outcomes of the toss at t, there is nothing to distinguish the three cases. Even though the objective modalities figuring in the three cases are taken to be different, X should be certain that the coin in question will land heads or tails and should be in suspense as to which alternative is true. Both alternatives are serious possibilities. Someone with strong antirealist proclivities might question the significance of the differences allegedly obtaining.

The complaint is misguided. Relative to a kind of trial consisting of tossing the coin twice at t, the subjective modal judgments about hypotheses concerning outcomes in the three cases should be different. To be sure, it will be necessary to appeal to further elaborations of the information about the objective modalities in the two cases. In case 1, X knows that the sample space for a relative to two tosses has four points {HH, TT,TH and TT}. In cases 2 and 3, it is {HH, TT} and case 3 may be elaborated to {HH&b, TT&c}.

Elaborations that bring out these differences introduce extra assumptions about objective modalities relative to new kinds of trials. In the examples considered here, these assumptions seem plausible. But consider a glass bottle. In case 1′, X is convinced that the bottle can be broken into 5 pieces and can be broken into 10 on being dropped on a smooth surface. In case 2′, X is in suspense as to whether it is disposed to break into 5 pieces or disposed to break into 10 pieces on being dropped. Case 3′ is a case where X selects blindfolded one of two bottles, one of which is fragile and the other not. In these cases, dropping the bottle twice is not an implementable experiment. The point to emphasize is that whether additional tests can discriminate between the three cases depends on additional background assumptions.

Case 3 can be used to illustrate another important feature of disposition, ability, and sample space attributions. Describing a kind of trial disjunctively (describing it as of kind S′ in case 3) does not automatically commit X to a sample space attribution even though X is committed to attributing sample spaces relative to each of the disjoined trials. (X is committed to a sample space relative to the description of the kind of trial as tossing coin *c*. X is committed to a sample space relative to the description of the kind of trial as tossing coin *d*. X is not committed to a sample space relative to the kind of trial as tossing either *c* or tossing *d*.)

Notice, however, that the kind of trial described as selecting a coin from the bag and tossing it is describable as selecting a coin from the bag and tossing it where the coin selected is *c* or the coin selected is *d*. And relative to this disjunctive characterization, a sample space is attributable to the bag. The reason is that the disjuncts are themselves events in the sample space relative to selecting one of the coins from the bag and tossing it.

Finally, consider kinds of trials S that are made more specific by adding more qualifications. If X is certain that *f* has the surefire disposition to R upon being S′d, then adding further specificity T to the characterization of the trial of kind S implies that *f* is disposed to R upon being T′d as well as S′d.

Suppose that *f* has the ability to R′ on a trial of kind S. It does not follow that f has the ability to R′ on a trial of kind S&T. But if it does not, f has the surefire disposition not to R′ on a trial of kind S&T.

Suppose that *g* has the sample space Ω on a trial of kind S. It does not follow that *g* has that sample space on a trial of kind S&T. What does follow is that *g* has a sample space $\Omega' \times \Omega$ relative to S&T.

For example, coin *f* may have the ability to land heads on a toss and also to land tails on a toss. Add to the characterization of tossing that it is tossing where the initial mechanical and boundary conditions of the tossing are specified to be heads inducing. According to classical mechanics, the coin will land heads. When the initial and boundary conditions are specified to be tails inducing *f* will land tails. Relative to such a more specific kind of trial, the coin has the surefire disposition to land heads (or to land tails as the case might be) and, hence, continues to have the ability to do so. But it lacks the ability to land tails (heads). And the two-element sample space relative to S has been reduced to a unit set.

The important point to emphasize about the remarks in the last paragraph are these: that claiming that *f* has the ability to R on being S′d may be true even though *f* is determined to fail to R upon being S&T′d. In this sense, it is objectively possible for *f* to R upon being S′d even though the trial correctly described as a trial of kind S is determined according to some more specific elaboration of the process to fail to R. *Pace* Bernoulli and Laplace, objective possibility is compatible with an underlying determinism provided care is taken to relativize objective possibility and necessity to kinds of trials or conditions.

3. Conditionals

Peirce tended to think that predicating dispositional properties of things is equivalent to asserting so called "counterfactual" or "subjunctive" conditionals. To say that the coin has a surefire disposition to land heads or tails up on a toss is to say that if it were tossed, it would land heads up or tails up. As Peirce saw, if dispositions and abilities are treated in a realist vein, so must the conditionals that are entailed by them. And as empiricists like Berkeley, Mill, and Russell appreciated, when the specification of truth conditions in terms of test behavior seems hopeless, modal notions like the appeal to conditional and unconditional judgments of possible truth and falsity become irresistible. We need truth conditions semantics for conditionals if conditionals are equivalent to disposition and ability statements. And the equivalence seems desirable; for in that way necessary and sufficient truth conditions for disposition and ability statements in terms of (conditional) judgments of test behavior become available. This line of reasoning drives many into the madness of possible worlds semantics in general and the introduction of some "closest worlds" semantics for conditionals in particular.

We need to look at this a little more closely.

If-sentences are sometimes understood to predicate true of things primitive theoretical predicates characterized by postulates of the forms (1) and (2). As such, these sentences are rephrasals of disposition statements. V. Dudman has pointed out that this is especially so when the "if"-sentences are "generalizations" of the types illustrated by "If it drops, it breaks," "if it dropped, it broke." If disposition statements carry truth values, so do such generalizations (Dudman 1985).

Sentences like "if it had been dropped, it would have broken," "if it were dropped, it would break," or "if it drops, it will break" are quite distinct grammatically from generalizations. Perhaps, in spite of this, they can be used in effective communication with the same understanding as generalizations can. Dudman thinks that, as a matter of fact, English speakers normally do not do so. I think he is right.

For the sake of such freedom of expression, I do not want to argue for prohibiting anyone from using subjunctive conditionals or future indicatives as attributions of dispositions if that facilitates communication. However, I am under the impression that such conditionals generally express modal judgments of serious possibility and impossibility on a supposition. Conditional sentences of the form "If x were S′d, x might (would) R" express the modal judgment that x might R (that x might not R) *on the supposition made for the sake of the argument that x is S′d.* Here is how I think such judgments ought to be construed.

Let us represent, agent X's state of full belief by a deductively closed theory <u>K</u> in some regimented language <u>L</u>. Three cases can be distinguished.

(1) The Open Case: X is in suspense as to whether system *a* is subject to trial of kind S or not. That is to say, X is committed to recognizing there being a fact of the matter as to whether *a* is subject to a trial of kind S. X's mind concerning this issue is not made up.

(2) *The Belief Contravening Case:* X is certain that a trial of kind *a* has not been conducted on x.

(3) *The Belief Conforming Case:* X is certain that a trial of kind S has been conducted on *a*.

To suppose that *a* is S′d in the open case is to expand K̲ by adding a sentence expressing that *a* is subject to a trial of kind S. If the sentence "*a* does not R" is inconsistent with the expansion, the modal judgment that *a* would or must R is made conditional on the supposition. If the sentence "*a* does not R" is consistent with the expansion, the modal judgment that *a* might not R is made conditional on the supposition.

In the belief-contravening case, K̲ is first contracted by removing the claim that a trial of kind S has not been conducted on x. This is to be done so that the loss of informational value is kept at a minimum. The contraction is then treated like the open case. Add the supposition and then make the modal judgment.

In the belief-conforming case, K̲ is first contracted by removing the claim that a trial of kind S has been conducted on x. Again, loss of informational value should be kept to a minimum. As before, treat the contraction like the open case. Add the supposition and make the modal judgment.

To repeat, I do not intend to legislate linguistic usage. There are other candidate construals of suppositional reasoning and the associated conditionals on offer. In particular, there is the view that provides closest worlds semantics for conditionals along the lines of R. Stalnaker (1968) or, more impressively, of D. Lewis (1973). And there is a variant of the view I have just sketched according to which supposing that x is S′d in the belief-conforming case is to base modal judgment on K̲ itself. This is suppositional reasoning based on AGM revision after the notion of revision made famous in a justly celebrated paper of Alchourrón, Gärdenfors and Makinson (1985). I have called suppositional reasoning along the lines I have sketched, reasoning based on *Ramsey* revision (Levi 1996).

I agree with Peirce and Mellor (1991, ch. 6) that attributions of dispositions and abilities are true or false. My concern is to question reasoning from realism about dispositions and abilities to the conclusion that conditional sentences expressing modal judgments on suppositions carry truth values.

If such reasoning were cogent, the epistemic account I have sketched of modal judgment conditional on a supposition based on Ramsey revision would be undermined. Replacing Ramsey revision by AGM revision cannot help. Nor does the use of an epistemized version of closest world analysis (invoking imaging transformations of belief-states). Such conditional modal judgment lacks truth value whereas the conditionals allegedly entailed by disposition and ability statements would have truth values. Realism about dispositions would then seem to support the cogency of attempts to supply truth conditions for conditionals as closest worlds semantics does.

My contention is this: Dispositions *in the sense in which it is desirable to allow for a realistic construal of dispositions in scientific inquiry* do *not* entail "would" conditionals carrying closest-worlds truth conditions. Abilities (duals of dispositions) do not entail closest-world "might" conditionals.[3] Whatever other applications closest-worlds semantics may have, they do not contribute to the understanding of dispositions. The following considerations argue for this view.

4. The Monotonicity of Dispositionality and the Nonmonotonicity of Closest-Worlds Conditionals

Consider a disposition predicate 'D(R/S)x'. Assuming it true of an object *a*, it should also be true of *a* that it has the disposition 'D(R/S∧T)x'. That is to say, this should be so if disposition predicates are placeholders in universal generalizations serving as stopgap covering laws.

Some may complain that disposition predicates in natural languages do not have the strict construal that I am taking disposition predicates to have. A lump of sugar has a disposition to dissolve upon immersion in water—except when the water is already saturated with sugar.

What this point establishes is that the lump of sugar lacks the disposition to dissolve upon immersion in water. It only has the ability to dissolve upon immersion in water. It may have the disposition to dissolve upon immersion in unsaturated water.

But surely sugar is water soluble. Quite so! But what does "soluble" mean? There are two dimensions of ambiguity here. First, there is the question of whether "soluble" means capable of dissolving or being disposed to dissolve. Second, we need to identify the test conditions relative to which the ability or disposition in question is claimed to hold.

In spite of the opportunities for equivocation available here, the placeholder account of dispositions and abilities makes one thing clear. Disposition terms are introduced as primitives with the Carnapian reduction sentences like (1) as postulates in order to provide stopgap universal generalizations for purposes of explanation. This function would be undermined if disposition terms were not "surefire." And this feature requires that the disposition not be undermined as trial conditions are strengthened. In this sense, dispositionality is monotonic.[4]

However, assuming that conditionals carry truth values (as closest-worlds conditionals do), they should be "variably strict implications," as Lewis rightly notes. That is to say, they are nonmonotonic. Adding additional qualifications to the prodosis of the conditional may undermine the conditional. "If x were S∧T, x might fail to R" might be true even though "if x were S, x would R" is true.

Thus, “If this match were struck, it would light” could be true according to Lewis while “If this match were struck in the absence of oxygen, it would light” is false.

By way of contrast, either it is false that this match has the surefire disposition to light upon being struck or it is true that this match has the surefire disposition to light upon being struck in the absence of oxygen. I conjecture that most of us think that the match lacks both dispositions. Yet we think that the match has the surefire disposition to light upon being struck under conditions *C*. We are not ready, however, to spell out the conditions *C* (although, perhaps, we can specify some of the conditions). In spite of our ignorance, we may coherently be convinced that the conditions *C* are satisfied on some occasions and that the match is disposed to light when struck under conditions *C*.

We are then committed, so I submit, to endorsing the view that the match is disposed to light when struck under conditions *C* by Bill Clinton or under conditions *C* when D is true regardless of what D asserts. (If D is inconsistent with claiming that the match is struck under conditions *C*, then a test characterized by striking of the match under conditions *C* when D is true is never realized. No inconsistency is threatened.) This is the monotonicity property of dispositionality. And it is a consequence of the placeholder view of dispositions according to which disposition predicates are theoretical primitives characterized by postulates of type (1) that require integration into theory through further investigation.

According to the closest-worlds account of the semantics of conditionals favored by David Lewis (1973), conditionals are “variably strict.” If dispositions are equivalent to conditionals so construed, disposition statements must be variably strict as well. If they are variably strict, they must be nonmonotonic. Since they are monotonic, they do not entail truth value-bearing closest-world conditionals. *A fortiori,* the thesis that disposition statements are equivalent to closest-worlds conditionals is untenable.

5. The Nonmonotonicity of Ability and the Centering Condition

Consider the overworked example of coin tossing. Coin x has the ability to land heads on a toss. But it lacks the ability to land heads on a toss by Morgenbesser. That is to say, it has a surefire disposition to *fail* to land heads on a toss by Morgenbesser.

Let it be true that coin x is tossed by Morgenbesser and lands tails. The fact that this happens does not undermine the fact that at the time of this occurrence the coin had the ability to land heads on a toss.

Shall we say that the ability of the coin x entails the judgment that if the coin were tossed, it might have landed heads? That is to say (according to closest-worlds analysts), in at least one closest world to the actual world that is a coin-tossing world, the coin lands heads. Given that the actual world is a coin-tossing world where Morgenbesser tosses the coin and the coin lands tails, the former condition cannot hold. According to Lewis's semantics, when the closest world to the actual world in which the coin is tossed by Morgenbesser is the actual world, that world is the uniquely closest such world (according to the "centering condition").

Abandoning the centering condition does not alter the situation. No matter what requirement on the nearness of possible worlds to the actual world is imposed, either the set of closest worlds includes at least one case where the coin lands heads or no such cases. According to the first alternative, the "might land heads" conditional is true and the "would land tails" conditional is false. According to the second alternative, the "might" conditional is false and the "would" conditional is true. But *both* the conditionals should be true if the corresponding disposition and ability statements are true and Morgenbesser tosses the coin. Lewis's theory (and other closest-worlds and selection function theories) must do one of two things:

(1) Declare the following to be an inconsistent triad: (a) that the coin is able to land tails on a toss, (b) that the coin is constrained to land heads on a toss by Morgenbesser, and (c) that the coin is tossed by Morgenbesser.

(2) Recognize the consistency of the triad but deny that disposition statements are equivalent to conditionals.

Insisting that the ability and disposition attributions together with the claim that Morgenbesser tosses the coin form an inconsistent triad is untenable. That is to say, it is untenable if the attribution of the ability to land heads on a toss to the coin is to be neutral with respect to whether the process of coin tossing can be correctly redescribed according to a deterministic model.

James Bernoulli insisted in *Ars Conjectandi* that there can be neither objective possibility nor objective probability if there is objective necessity—that is, determinism. One of the concerns of those introducing notions of objective or statistical probability in the nineteenth century was to characterize objective probability so that its use in characterizing macroprocesses could be neutral with respect to whether these macroprocesses might be described microscopically in a neutral fashion.

To relativize probability attributions to kinds of trials was critical to such views. And this called for relativizing attributions of dispositions and abilities to kinds of trials as well. The attribution of the ability to land heads on a toss is neutral with respect to whether the coin toss can be redescribed as a deterministic process or as an indeterministic one. We may coherently acknowledge that coin *a* has the ability even if we also think that situating the coin in a certain mechanical state and subject to appropriate boundary conditions constrains it to land tails and believe that the coin is so situated upon being tossed by Morgenbesser. If we think that the best contemporary physical theory is not deterministic, we can also allow for the ability.

Relativizing ability and disposition attributions to kinds of trials allows for this kind of neutrality, however, only if triads of the kind illustrated above are not incoherent. Equating disposition and ability statements with corresponding closest-world conditionals requires that such triads be inconsistent. Neutrality with respect to underlying determinism requires that ability statements should not be equated with closest-world might-conditionals and disposition statements should be differentiated from closest-world would-conditionals.

These considerations argue against providing some variant of closest-world semantics for disposition and ability statements if one seeks to secure the neutrality of macroscopic indeterminism with respect to microscopic determinism. They do not show that disposition or ability statements and corresponding conditional statements cannot be used interchangeably but only that truth conditions cannot be spelled out for statements of these kinds along the lines of closest-worlds semantics when they are so equated.

6. Suppositional Modal Judgments Lack Truth Value

Advocates of closest-world or selectionist semantics take their intended target to be sentences that express conditional judgments of *de dicto* modality. Such sentences are sometimes cast in the allegedly subjunctive mood. (Examples: If the coin had been tossed near the surface of the Earth, it would have landed on the surface. If the coin had been tossed near the surface of the Earth, it might have landed heads.) Gibbard (1980), like Dudman, thinks that this holds for so-called "future indicative" sentences as well. (Examples: If the coin is tossed near the surface of the Earth, it will land on the surface. If the coin is tossed near the surface of the Earth, it may land heads.) In such conditional judgments, the "if"-clause expresses a supposition made for the sake of the argument. A judgment as to whether a given proposition is possible or impossible is made relative to the supposition.

This leads to the third objection to equating disposition and ability attributions with conditional judgments of possibility and impossibility on a supposition adopted for the sake of the argument. Such conditional judgments of possibility and impossibility are best understood as judgments of serious or doxastic possibility and impossibility. Like all judgments of serious possibility and impossibility, judgments of serious possibility conditional on suppositions lack truth values (Levi 1996, 3.4). Attributions of dispositions and abilities carry truth values. Hence, such attributions cannot be equivalent in truth value with conditionals that express such conditional modal judgments and they cannot entail such conditionals.

Modal realists have often seemed to take for granted that conditional judgments of modality must carry truth values precisely because disposition and ability statements that support them do. I have already sought to undermine this argument by noting that the current favorite accounts of truth conditions for judgments of conditional modality preclude equating disposition and ability statements with such conditionals. These arguments did not beg the question as to whether conditional modal judgments are truth-valued or not. They do undermine attempts to support the use of truth value-bearing conditionals along the lines of closest-worlds semantics by an appeal to truth value-bearing conditionals. This then leaves us open to appeal to an account of conditional modal judgments that construes them as judgments of serious possibility and impossibility conditional on a supposition.

To defend such a view it remains necessary to be responsive to the demand for clarification of the respect in which conditional modal judgments that lack truth values are supported by truth value-bearing attributions of disposition and ability.

As I understand such conditional modal judgments, they express epistemic or subjective modal judgments on a supposition (the supposition that S is true) relative to a body of information or state of full belief **K**. The inquirer judges the possibility or impossibility that x R's relative to a transformation of the inquirer's state of belief **K** by incorporating the supposition that x is S′d in a way that minimizes the loss of valuable information required to preserve consistency and logical closure.

If a judgment carries a truth value without being a logical truth or (if there be such) a conceptual truth or falsity, the inquiring agent should be in a position to coherently suspend judgment as to the truth of the judgment. But the inquiring agent cannot be in doubt concerning judgments of serious possibility. Assuming that h carries a truth value, X may fully believe that h, be in suspense with respect to h, or fully believe that ~h. In the first two cases, X is committed to judging it possible that h is true. In the latter case, X is committed to judging it impossible that h. X cannot suspend judgment as to whether it is possible that h or impossible that h. So neither the judgment that it is possible that h nor its negation can carry a truth value. On this understanding, unconditional judgments of modality the inquirer cannot coherently suspend judgment as to whether it is possible (impossible) that x R's (fails to R). A similar argument applies to conditional modal judgments where the inquirer's current state of full belief transformed into another potential state of full belief by supposing it true that x is S′d.

My claim is that X's judgment that it is possible that h lacks a truth value where by "X's judgment" I mean *the propositional attitude* expressed by X's sincere utterance "h might be true." The *attitude* lacks a truth value. The biographical judgment that X has that attitude does carry a truth value. So does the claim that it is possible that h according to X's state of full belief. This latter claim may be rephrased as saying that X's state of full belief K *supports* X's judgment that it is seriously possible that h. And we may be interested in spelling out truth conditions for such claims. X's state of full belief K supports the judgment that it is possible that h if and only if the potential state of full belief represented by that h is consistent with K. Notice that K supports the judgment that it is possible that h without in any way entailing it.

Modal judgments on a supposition of the sort expressed by "if you drop the vase, it will (may) break" or "if you were to drop the vase, it would (might) break" or "if you had dropped the vase, it would have (might have) broken" differ from unconditional modal judgments in that the judgments of possibility and impossibility are relative to transformations of the current state K of full belief. Such a transformation *T*(K,h) stipulates that the new potential state of full belief should include the supposition that h (you drop the vase) is true. The judgment of possibility or impossibility is made relative to the resulting potential state of full belief. The same considerations that argue against unconditional judgments of serious possibility carrying truth values apply here as well.

On this understanding of conditional judgments of modality, disposition, ability, and sample space statements, which, I concede, do carry truth values, cannot entail conditional modal judgments.

Disposition, ability, and sample space statements can *support* conditional modal judgments in the sense that when the inquirer's state of full belief has as a consequence a disposition (ability) statement of some sort and meets other conditions, the inquirer is committed to appropriate conditional judgments of possibility or impossibility. Spelling out the conditions on the inquirer's state of full belief that are needed is the task of an account of direct inference from full belief that relevant disposition and ability statements are true to modal judgments conditional on suppositions that certain experiments are instituted.

Surefire dispositions and their duals are theoretical primitives relative to the test behavior they relate to. So, therefore, are the predicates characterizing systems in terms of the "elementary events" that the systems under study are capable of displaying in response to experiments of the kind specified. I shall call such predicates or properties *sample-space* predicates. They specify responses that it is possible for system x to make to a "stimulus" or "input" of some kind as well as responses that are precluded. Such sample-space predicates are understood to be promissory notes for predications better integrated into theory than the sample-space predicates initially are. Although they are understood "realistically" from the outset because they are taken to be true or false of things, they may fail to be adequate as resources for explanation. In this sense they serve as placeholders in stop-gap explanations pending improved integration into theory.[5]

By way of contrast, conditional judgments of modality are judgments of possibility or impossibility relative to transformations of the inquirer's current state **K** of full belief (or the corpus of sentences $\underline{K}$ closed under logical consequence used to represent **K**) by suppositions of various kinds. The supposition that h is true is used to revise $\underline{K}$ so as to insure that a new corpus $T(\underline{K},h)$ is obtained that is "successful" in containing h. If and only if g $\in$ $T(\underline{K},h)$ is ~g judged impossible on the supposition that h is true. If and only if g $\notin$ $T(\underline{K},h)$ is ~g judged possible on the supposition that h is true. This is the format that characterizes a Ramsey Test for the acceptability of conditional judgments of modality on a supposition in a sense that conforms to Ramsey's own practice.

To further clarify the notion of judging possibility and impossibility on a supposition, it is necessary to elaborate further on the character of the transformation involved. Several candidates have been proposed. Some of them are not rivals to one another but reflect differences in the uses to which supposition is put. (See Levi 1996, ch. 2, for an elaboration of the ideas sketched here.)

For example, arguments from suppositions appear in reductio proofs and are expressed by so called "pure indicatives." In such cases, we cannot expect the transformation T to be *consistency preserving*. To be consistency preserving, we require that $T(\underline{K},h)$ not only be successful but also that it be consistent if $\underline{K}$ and h are each consistent even when h is inconsistent with $\underline{K}$. So-called subjunctive conditionals as well as so-called future indicatives customarily are used to express modal judgments on suppositions that transform $\underline{K}$ in a consistency preserving manner. Consistency-preserving supposition applies in three kinds of cases where both h and $\underline{K}$ are consistent:

(1) The open case: h and ~h are both consistent with $\underline{K}$.

(2) The belief-contravening case: h is inconsistent with $\underline{K}$.

(3) The belief-conforming case: ~h is inconsistent with $\underline{K}$.

According to F. P. Ramsey, in the open case, $T(\underline{K},h) = \underline{K}^{+}_{h} = Cn(\underline{K} \cup \{h\})$ where $Cn(x)$ are the logical consequences of the set of sentences x. Transformations of this kind are *preservative in the open case.*

Ramsey did not spell out the details of the transformation he favored for the other two cases. Two candidates have been proposed:

AGM revision $(\underline{K}^{*}_{h})$:

In the belief-contravening case, $\underline{K}^{*}_{h} = [\underline{K}^{-}_{\sim h}]^{+}_{h}$. Here $\underline{K}^{-}_{\sim h}$ is the deductively closed set of sentences obtained by removing ~h while minimizing loss of informational value. To fully come to grips with this *contraction* transformation, the details of how informational value and loss of informational value is to be evaluated need to be elaborated. I shall not examine this matter here.

In the belief-conforming case, $\underline{K}^{*}_{h} = \underline{K} = \underline{K}^{+}_{h}$. Transformations of this kind are *preservative in the belief-conforming case.*

In sum, AGM revision is preservative in the open case and in the belief-conforming case. Preservation cannot be practiced in the belief-contravening case without abandoning consistency preservation. So AGM hews to preservation as best one can short of violating consistency preservation.

Ramsey revision $(\underline{K}^{*r}_{h})$:

In the belief-contravening case. $\underline{K}^{*r}_{h} = \underline{K}^{*}_{h}$.

In the belief-conforming case, $\underline{K}^{*r}_{h} = [\underline{K}^{-}_{h}]^{+}_{h}$.

If in the belief-conforming case, removing h and then returning it yields $\underline{K}$ again (the so-called "Recovery Condition"), there is no difference between Ramsey and AGM revision. But if the Recovery Condition is not satisfied, then Ramsey revision is not preservative in the belief-conforming case in contrast to AGM revision.

There is good reason to think that the Recovery Condition is not always satisfied. Consider the following example.

On the supposition that the coin is tossed at a given time, the coin would land on the surface but it might and it might not land heads up. According to the AGM version of the Ramsey Test, if the inquirer X already knew that the coin was tossed and landed heads, X could not allow that the coin might and might not land heads up on the toss. The same is true according to Ramsey revision if the Recovery Condition holds. Presystematic judgment testifies strongly in favor of Ramsey revision *without* Recovery.

Whatever the merits of this argument might be, both AGM and Ramsey revision are superior to what has been called imaging because they are both preservative in the open case.[6]

That is to say, the *Ramsey revision* $\underline{K}^{*r}_{\text{coin is tossed}}$ by adding the supposition that the coin is tossed to $\underline{K}$ is a new deductively closed corpus obtained from $\underline{K}$ as follows:

If neither "the coin is tossed" nor its negation is in $\underline{K}$, $\underline{K}^{*r}_{\text{coin is tossed}} = \underline{K}^{+}_{\text{coin is tossed}}$ = the deductive closure of adding "the coin is tossed" to $\underline{K}$ or the *expansion* of $\underline{K}$ by adding "the coin is tossed."

If "The coin is not tossed" is in $\underline{K}$, $\underline{K}$ is *contracted* by removing "the coin is not tossed" in a manner that minimizes loss of valuable information from among all the potential contraction strategies specified by the problem under investigation. The result is $\underline{K}^{-r}_{\text{the coin is not tossed}}$. Expand the result by adding "the coin is tossed." The net of these transformations is the revision by adding "the coin is tossed."

If "the coin is tossed" is in $\underline{K}$, $\underline{K}$ is contracted by removing "the coin is tossed." The sentence "the coin is tossed" is then added to the result in an expansion.

F. P. Ramsey spelled out conditions for endorsing conditional modal judgments in the case where the condition spelled out in the prodosis of the conditional was taken to be in suspense. His characterization was essentially the one specified in the first clause mentioned above. For the belief-contravening case corresponding to the second clause and the belief-conforming corresponding to the third clause, he invoked a derivability-from-laws approach. The notion of Ramsey revision cited above is based on taking Ramsey's approach to open conditionals and generalizing it to cover belief-contravening and belief-conforming supposition as well. Ramsey, it seems clear, did not think that (*de dicto*) possibility should be reified any more than *de dicto* probability should. Whether one passes such judgments relative to one's current state of full belief or relative to a supposition adopted purely for the sake of the argument, the judgment is neither true nor false.

Space does not permit a more elaborate survey of consistency-preserving conditionals according to either the AGM revision or Ramsey revision approaches just briefly sketched. (Further discussion of the ideas about supposition conforming to this approach may be found in Levi 1996 and Arló Costa and Levi 1997.) The aim here was to indicate that there are indeed alternatives to the view that consistency-preserving suppositional reasoning is expressed in truth value-bearing conditional judgments. Many authors have maintained that so-called "pure indicative" conditionals lack truth values. I contend that consistency-preserving conditionals (typically "subjunctive" conditionals) lack truth values as well. Hence, disposition and ability statements that are truth value-bearing cannot entail them.

Disposition and ability statements can, however, support conditional modal judgments. That is to say, full belief that disposition or ability statements are true constrain the inquirer to make subjective modal judgments of certain kinds and not others in conformity with certain principles of doxastic rationality.

The situation is parallel to the way full belief in the truth of statements of objective, statistical probability constrain judgments of subjective or credal probability. I should like to close this discussion with some remarks on "direct inference" from objective to subjective modality as an introduction to direct inference from objective to subjective probability.

7. Modal Direct Inference

The system or "set-up" *a* has the sample space property $SP(\Omega/S)$ if and only if the following three conditions hold:

(1) *a* is $D(R_\Omega/S)$. *a* is disposed to realize at least one of the outcomes represented by a point in Ω.

(2) If ω and ω' are two distinct points in Ω, *a* is $D(\sim(R_\omega \& R_{\omega'})/S)$. *a* is incapable of realizing two outcomes represented by distinct points in Ω.

(3) For every $\omega \in \Omega$, *a* is $A(R_\omega/S)$

Information that a trial of kind S also satisfies condition T is *irrelevant with respect to objective modality* relative to sample space property $SP(\Omega/S)$ and set-ups of kind G if and only if all set-ups G that are $SP(\Omega/S)$ are $SP(\Omega/S\&T)$.

Information that a trial of kind S also satisfies condition T is relevant with respect to objective modality relative to sample space property $SP(\Omega/S)$ precisely because some systems of kind G are $SP(\Omega'/S\&T)$ where $\Omega' \subset \Omega$ and these very same systems are $SP(\Omega/S)$

With this understood, suppose that X fully believes that the following holds:

(a) *a* is $SP(\Omega/S)$.

(b) *a* is subject to a trial of kind S&T.

The central problem of modal direct inference is to spell out conditions under which X ignore the extra information that the trial of kind S is also of kind T and judge that any outcome R_ω where $\omega \in \Omega$ is subjectively or seriously possible relative to X's state of full belief. This problem parallels the problem of stochastic direct inference where X has information about the objective statistical probability over Ω relative to S and wants to determine whether the extra information about T may be ignored in determining subjective probability.

Given that X fully believes that (a) and (b), there are three cases to consider:

> *Case 1:* X fully believes that the extra information about T is irrelevant with respect to objective modality (relative to *SP*(Ω/S)).

Provided that X has no additional information above and beyond the information that experiment of kind S was implemented under conditions T, X is warranted in judging it seriously possible that an outcome of type R_ω will occur for every $\omega \in \Omega$.

> *Case 2:* X fully believes that the extra information about T is relevant with respect to objective modality (relative to (*SP*(Ω/S)) and has definite information as to what Ω′ is in *SP*(Ω′/S&T).

With the same proviso as before, X is warranted in judging it subjectively impossible that an outcome of type R_ω for every ω in Ω but not Ω′.

> *Case 3:* X is in doubt as to whether the extra information about T is irrelevant or relevant with respect to objective modality (relative to *SP*(Ω/S)). X should judge each R_ω to be seriously possible for $\omega \in \Omega$.

> *Case 4:* X is certain that T is relevant with respect to objective modality (relative to *SP*(Ω/S)) but is not definite as to what Ω′ is in *SP*(Ω′/S&T)

X should rule out as subjectively impossible all R_ω's for ω in Ω but recognized by X not to be in Ω′ and should judge all other R_ω's ($\omega \in \Omega$) to be seriously possible whether these be recognized to be members of Ω′ or not.

Observe that the recommendations for each of the four cases are based on the criterion of serious possibility according to which a hypothesis is judged possible relative to a state of full belief if and only if it is consistent with it. According to this view, the judgments of serious possibility that are grounded in the information (a) and the fact that the system *a* is subject to a trial of kind S are mandated also when the information that the experiment of kind S is also of kind T as long as the extra information does not imply the objective impossibility of the outcomes represented by points in Ω. That is to say, the agent X should make judgments of subjective possibility that are grounded in the information available concerning trials of kind S&T where S&T is the strongest information about the trials in question available to X that is modally relevant.

Direct inference from beliefs about sample spaces to judgments about serious possibility undergirds direct inference to judgments about subjective probability from beliefs about objective probabilities. It also supports explanation how possible.

Consider a situation where X fully believes that a fair coin has been tossed 1000 times and landed heads up each time. X can provide a covering law explanation of why it was to have been expected that the coin landed on the surface 1000 times by noting that it has a surefire disposition to do so on being tossed 1000 times and using the appropriate type (1) sentence as the covering law. But X cannot explain via covering law why it was to have been expected that the coin landed heads up each time. An explanation how possible is available. Landing heads up 1000 times is in the sample space relative to the kind of trial described as being tossed 1000 times. The coin has the ability to behave this way on a 1000 toss trial. If one supposes for the sake of the argument that the coin is tossed 1000 times and models such supposition along the lines favored by Ramsey revision, X will give up the claim that the coin was tossed 1000 times and with that the claim that it landed heads 1000 times. After restoring the judgment that the coin was tossed 1000 times and as long as there is no additional relevant information interfering with modal direct inference one can judge that coin might have landed heads up 1000 times. X might say, "Since the coin was tossed 1000 times, it might have landed heads every time."

De Finetti (1963) and Kyburg (1963, 1974) deny that objective probabilities exist. De Finetti undertook to replace judgments about objective probability with judgments about subjective probability and thereby to dispense with the notion of objective probability altogether. For him, no question of direct inference from belief about objective probability to judgment of subjective probability is supposed to arise. Kyburg replaces judgments of objective probability by judgments of relative frequency in finite sets. In Kyburg's view, there is a form of direct inference from belief about such relative frequencies and the membership of objects in given classes to judgments of what he calls epistemological probability. Nonetheless, direct inference as I have characterized it is ignored because there can be no knowledge of objective, physical probabilities.

The challenge I pose to skeptics about objective probability is whether they adopt the same view concerning sample space attributions that they take towards objective probability attributions?

ISAAC LEVI
Columbia University

NOTES

1. Similar structures arise in discussions of decision making. Decision-maker X has a set of options X is able to implement by choice or through X's deliberation. However, in this case, there is good reason to deny that objective statistical probabilities are well defined.

2. Carnap (1950) and many others who deployed his notion of bilateral reduction sentences to characterize disposition predicates thought that the following condition holds:

(2′) $Sx \wedge Rx \supset D(R/S)x$.

The sufficient condition for the presence of the ability in (2) became a sufficient condition for the presence of the ability. Obtaining heads on a single toss of a coin is not sufficient for its having the surefire disposition to land heads on a toss. It is true that data about the behavior of magnets rotating in copper coils might warrant coming to the conclusion that such experiments will under appropriate conditions invariably induce an electric current. But this conclusion is not entailed by the data specified alone. It is either entailed by some theory of electromagnetism or is obtained by some series of well-designed repetitions of the experiment. As a general practice, therefore, it is unwise to claim that conditions like (2′) are part of the axiom set associated with the disposition predicate 'D(R/S)x'. Perhaps through inquiry sufficient conditions and even necessary and sufficient satisfaction conditions for disposition predicates in terms of test behavior may be uncovered, although this, in general, does not appear to be the case.

3. Assuming a closest-world semantics for "would" and "might" conditionals, the thesis that dispositions entail the corresponding closest-world "would" conditionals and abilities entail the corresponding "might" conditionals holds if and only if disposition statements are equivalent to the corresponding "would" conditionals.

4. *Pace* C. Martin and D. Lewis, this precludes so-called "finkish" dispositions. There would be no point to the introduction of disposition predicates such as "fragile" if they were not associated with postulates of form (1). I grant that in the course of inquiry, disposition terms may be integrated into theories and, indeed, might be integrated by equating them with bases. In that event, there is no further need for a placeholder. If the erstwhile disposition term continues to be used as a shorthand characterization of the basis, it remains the case that it no longer serves the distinctive function of disposition terms serve as placeholders. Having equated the fragility of a certain type of glass with a certain type of basis, "is fragile" is no longer a disposition predicate in the placeholder sense. Finkishness arises if it is discovered that experiments of kind S on the basis are followed by a modification of the basis. We have a choice. Give up the equation of the disposition with the basis and retain the thesis that fragile glass breaks when subject to trials of the given kind or retain the equation and speak of finkishness. The latter option is indeed available and may be used when the disposition term is well integrated theoretically. But in that case, the disposition term has ceased to be dispositional for the simple reason that it has ceased to serve the function for which it was

initially designed. I agree with Lewis that attributions of dispositions do not entail closest-world conditionals. But they do not entail conditionals precisely because they cannot be finkish and serve their function as placeholders.

5. I am uncomfortable with Hugh Mellor's commitment to the significance of the distinction between "real" properties versus "Cambridge properties" and nonprojectible properties. I do think they are real in the sense that they are true or false of the systems of which they are predicated, that inquirers may be in suspense as to whether objects do or do not have them and may evaluate hypotheses claiming that various systems do or do not have such and such dispositions with respect to probability.

6. Keep in mind that the belief states being transformed do not contain any modal or conditional judgments. As argued previously, such judgments do not carry truth values. The conditional expressing a modal judgment in the case where the supposition h is open according to the corpus K is supported by K depending upon the modal evaluation of the consequent g relative to the expansion of K by adding the supposition. Imaging allows violations of this condition unless special restrictions are imposed on comparative similarity relativizing it to K.

REFERENCES

Arló Costa, H., and I. Levi. 1996. "Two Notions of Epistemic Validity." *Synthese* 1–9: 217–62.

Alchourrón, C., P. Gärdenfors, and D. Makinson. 1985. "On the Theory of Logic Change: Partial Meet Functions for Contraction and Revision." *Journal of Symbolic Logic* 50: 510–30.

Carnap, R. 1950. *Testability and Meaning*. Reprinted by the Graduate Philosophy Club, Yale University, with corrections and additional bibliography of the paper published in *Philosophy of Science* 3 (1936) and 4 (1937).

Cartwright, N. 1983. *Why the Laws of Physics Lie*. Oxford: Oxford University Press.

Davidson, E. 1980. *Actions and Events*. Oxford: Oxford University Press.

De Finetti, B. 1963. "Foresight: Its Logical Laws, Its Subjective Sources." In *Studies in Subjective Probability*, ed. H. Kyburg and H. Smokler. New York: Wiley.

Dudman, V. H. 1985. "Towards a Theory of Predication in English." *Australasian Journal of Linguistics* 5: 143–93.

Elster, J. 1999. *Alchemies of the Mind*. Cambridge: Cambridge University Press.

Gibbard, A. 1980. *Ifs*, edited by W.L.Harper, R. Stalnaker and G.Pearce, pp. 211–47. Dordrecht: Reidel.

Kolmogorov, A. N. 1950. *Foundations of the Theory of Probability*. Translated by N. Morrison. Translation of *Grundbegriffe der Wahrscheinlichkeitrechnung, Ergebnisse Der Mathematik 1933*. New York: Chelsea Publishing Company.

Kyburg, H. E. 1961. *Probability and the Logic of Rational Belief*. Middletown, Conn.: Wesleyan University Press.

———. 1973. *The Logical Foundations of Statistical Inference*. Dordrecht: Reidel.

Levi, I. 1980. *The Enterprise of Knowledge*. Cambridge, Mass.: MIT Press.

———. 1996. *For the Sake of the Argument.* Cambridge: Cambridge University Press.

Levi, I., and Morgenbesser, S. 1964. "Belief and Disposition." *American Philosophical Quarterly* 1: 221–32.

Lewis, D. 1973. *Counterfactuals.* Cambridge, Mass.: Harvard University Press.

Mellor. D. H. 1991. *Matters of Metaphysics.* Cambridge: Cambridge University Press.

Stalnaker, R. C. 1968. "A Theory of Conditionals." In *Studies in Logical Theory,* pp. 98–112. Oxford: Blackwell.

4

Severe Testing as a Guide for Inductive Learning*

DEBORAH G. MAYO

In the late 1970s, switching my doctoral dissertation topic from the philosophical foundations of deductive logic to the foundations of inductive logic did not seem all that radical a shift, a fact which says a lot about the conception of induction that gripped (and still mostly grips) philosophers. In this conception, inductive inference takes the form of what may be called a "logic of confirmation": rules for assigning degrees of probability or confirmation to claims and hypotheses on the basis of statements of evidence, assumed at the start. Given this conception of the task, answering the "guide to life" question turns on scrutinizing various definitions of probability to evaluate their appropriateness for measuring degrees of confirmation, generally by applications of the definition of conditional probability (whether absolute or comparative). This is basically how the problem was put by the philosopher who first introduced me to the "guide to life" problem, Wesley Salmon (1966). But my conception of what was needed for probability to be a relevant guide for induction underwent a "paradigm shift" soon after finding myself (accidentally) in a class on mathematical statistics. This shift had two parts.

(1) A methodology for genuinely inductive or "ampliative" inference, I came to see, required tools for generating and analyzing data—it could not start out with "given data." In this way the (modeled) data could serve to reliably probe hypotheses (deliberately) framed in terms of (aspects of) the data generating process. In contrast to the philosophers' image, inductive inference need not be like

* I dedicate this paper to the memory of Wesley Salmon to whom I am indebted, both for his clear explanations, over the years, of the "guide to life" problem, and for encouraging me to pursue this avenue toward its solution.

building a tower, each level as shaky as what went before: properly collected and cleverly used, we can obtain highly reliable results on the basis of highly shaky data. (2) Probability, or rather, probabilistic models, have a central role to play, not to supply degrees of confirmation to hypotheses, but to quantify, model, and control the frequencies with which given outcomes would occur under varying (statistical) hypotheses. This is the basis for calculating error probabilities—the heart of standard statistical methods, for example, Neyman-Pearson (N-P) tests and estimates. However, these methods have themselves been the object of considerable philosophical criticism and controversy and answering them, I found, required reformulating N-P methods.

The key was to see how error probabilities may be used to characterize the probativeness or severity of tests. By the time this attempt grew into the experimental testing account of Error and the Growth of Experimental Knowledge *(Mayo 1996), the picture had diverged sufficiently from the N-P model to deserve a new name. The error statistical account seems about right. In that work, however, I still shied away from using the word "induction," as if allowing that term to have been co-opted by the logic of confirmation construal. This paper represents a break from that former constraint, and is made explicit in what I call the "severity principle." The conception of induction as severe testing, while it has never been made fully explicit by philosophers or statisticians, seems to me to underlie the real "logic" guiding inductive learning both in ordinary life and the life of science.*

—D. M.

* * *

1. Introduction and Overview: Probability as a Guide to Life

Probability has had a central role to play in philosophical accounts of induction, confirmation, and statistical reasoning; and a key criterion in judging those accounts is how well they apply to the actual tasks of reaching inferences, assessing data, and making decisions on the basis of incomplete evidence. Probability, or more accurately, accounts based on probabilistic ideas, it is often said, should be "a guide for life," but *what exactly does that require?*

Although probability may be looked upon as giving guidance for a variety of tasks, what interests me here is its use in guiding inductive inference in some sense. I am interested, roughly, in the questions:

- *Can we use probability as a guide for extending our knowledge?*
- *Can probabilistic ideas be guides for making reliable claims on the basis of limited data? (that is, guides for ampliative inference or induction)?*

If an account affords a way to answer these questions affirmatively, it would seem pretty clearly to serve as a guide for inductive learning, both in ordinary life as well as in the life of science. To tackle them we are immediately led to prior questions as to the nature of inductive inference, or more specifically, to ask: *What is the role of probability in inductive inference?*

Inductive Inference as a Logic of Confirmation

Philosophers, by and large, have regarded the role of probability in induction as supplying one or another measures of evidential weight—degrees of probability, belief, support, confirmation, and the like—to be assigned to claims and hypotheses on the basis of statements of data or evidence that are assumed to be given at the outset. Just as the rules of deductive logic guide us to true conclusions, given the truth of a set of premises, inductive logic, or a logic of confirmation, it might be thought, should guide us to probable conclusions, given the truth of a set of premises or statements of evidence.[1] We can refer to all such inductive logics as *logics of confirmation*. This view has intrinsic plausibility, especially from the perspective of logical empiricist philosophies of science, and one can see how it sets the stage for the way philosophers of confirmation have generally tackled the "guide to life" question.

If probability enters to supply a logic of confirmation, then answering the "guide to life" question revolves around scrutinizing various definitions of probability to evaluate their appropriateness as guides for assigning degrees of confirmation (absolute or comparative), generally by applications of Bayes's theorem from probability theory. The philosopher by whom I was first introduced to this conception of the guide to life problem, Wesley Salmon (1966), saw early on the difficulties faced by the logical, subjective, and frequency conceptions of probability for this task. For Salmon, in order for an interpretation of probability to provide a logic of confirmation that is adequate as "a guide of life," it must (1) supply a method for determining the values of probabilities (his criterion of "ascertainability"), and (2) have practical predictive significance (his criterion of "applicability") (Salmon 1966, p. 64).[2] I begin with a quick sketch of his assessment.

Logical Probability and Inductive Logic. The inductive logics of the type developed by Carnap held out the promise to supply an objective guide for measuring the degree of confirmation in hypotheses—at least to many of us in the mid- to late-1970s—even in the face of the much-discussed problems, paradoxes, and conflicting choices of confirmation. In Carnapian inductive logics, initial probability assignments are to be based on a choice of language and on intuitive, logical principles, giving *logical probabilities*, which could then be updated (given the statements of evidence) by means of Bayes's Theorem. The fact that the resulting degrees of confirmation were analytic and a priori—while lending them their air of objectivity—at the same time proved to be the central weakness of such confirmation theories as guides for life, for example, as guides for empirical frequencies—as Salmon warned:

> Given any hypothesis h and any consistent evidence statement e, the degree of confirmation c(h,e) can be established by computation alone. . . . The question is: *How can statements that say nothing about any matters of fact serve as "a guide of life"?* . . .
>
> How can a synthetic statement about the past, in conjunction with an analytic degree of confirmation statement, tell us anything about the future? How in particular can it serve as any kind of guide to prediction, decision, and action? (Salmon 1966, pp. 75–76)

Subjective and Personalist Accounts. Interpreting probability as measuring subjective degree of belief, as in subjective or personalist Bayesian views, might perhaps be seen as supplying a guide for how to consistently update one's beliefs given a series of prior degrees of belief. But since conflicting beliefs could therefore be warranted for different Bayesian agents with different priors, this would not fill the bill for those who, like Salmon, seek an objective (intersubjective) guide for inductive inference: "The personalistic theory therefore leaves entirely unanswered our questions about inductive inference. It tolerates any kind of inference from the observed to the unobserved. This amounts to an abdication of probability from the role of 'a guide of life'" (Salmon 1966, p. 82).

Probability as Relative Frequency in a Long-Run. Frequentist logics of confirmation have not fared much better, even in the hands of frequentist-leaning Salmon. The familiar frequentist rule, to infer claims about the long-run frequencies of A's that will be B's, on the basis of the observed frequencies of A's that have been B's—enumerative induction or the "straight rule"—Salmon grants, "will work if any method will" (1966, p. 87), but it is not the only rule with this characteristic. Most importantly, hypotheses of interest in science are generally either true or false, so what sense can we give to their relative frequency of truth? Salmon, following Reichenbach, offers an interesting suggestion. The suggestion is that the prior probabilities of the hypotheses needed for Bayes's theorem "can be understood as our best estimates of the frequencies with which certain kinds of hypotheses succeed" (Salmon 1990, p. 187). In giving a prior probability assignment to hypotheses H, in other words, a scientist would strive to give an estimate of the relative frequency with which hypotheses "relevantly similar" to H are successful. Such an assessment, Salmon proposed, would measure the plausibility of H. But what is to count as a "relevantly similar hypothesis to H"? Successful in what respects? For how long? The reference class problem becomes acute, and it is one Salmon never satisfactorily answered.[3] Moreover, it is not clear why the plausibility or reasonableness of a given hypotheses H would be given by the relative frequency with which hypotheses appropriately similar to H have succeeded in the past, even assuming we knew this value, and even allowing that H was randomly drawn from the population of relevantly similar hypotheses.[4] We want a guide as to whether we are warranted in inferring that *this* hypothesis, H, will succeed in subsequent applications or trials. For this we need to consider how well H itself has stood up to testing, rather than how rarely hypotheses similar to it have proved successful.

Frequentism in Testing (Rather Than in a Logic of Confirmation)

What does this leave us with? What if we retain a frequentist account of probability but reject the assumption that if probability is to guide inductive inference it will be by guiding the assignment of degrees of support or probability to hypotheses? In other words, what if we reject the assumption that the goal is a "logic of confirmation" to begin with? One need not look far to find approaches that do just that. In standard statistical methodology, probabilities are assigned, not to hypotheses, but to the inference methods themselves, to assess the relative frequency with which a given type of test or estimation procedure would lead to an erroneous inference in some series of applications. These probabilities of error are, appropriately enough, called *error probabilities.*

Neyman and Pearson Frequentist Statistics. Neyman and Pearson methods, for example, developed in the 1930s, give us tests that control at low values the long-run probabilities of making errors in rejecting and accepting statistical hypotheses (type I and type II errors, respectively). However, one can grant that these methods control error probabilities and still question their relevance as "a guide of life," whether in science or in everyday life. The NP methodology does not supply a logic of confirmation, as I am using that term. Error probabilities such as the probabilities of type I and type II errors, confidence levels, or significance levels do not supply assignments of probability or confirmation to hypotheses, and if one interprets them as if they do, it is easy to obtain unsatisfactory and even contradictory results. Therefore, if one adheres to the assumption that only by providing a final measure of confirmation or probability to hypotheses can a statistical account be a relevant guide for inference, one will be led to reject N-P tests as failing this task. N-P statistics is intended as a guide for error frequencies rather than a logic of confirmation.

Obviously, merely recognizing this altered goal is not yet to render frequentist statistics a satisfactory guide for induction. We need a different conception of inductive inference for which error statistical methods can supply guides. For the most part, however, philosophical discussions of probability as a guide to life do not address the question of the role that frequentist error probabilities might play in induction.[5] The tendency to assume that an inductive account must come in the form of a logic of confirmation has led most philosophers to inadvertently suppose that the problems a frequentist notion faces when used in a logic of confirmation, apply also to frequentist notions of testing, or to *frequentist statistics.* Thus N-P methods are given short shrift.[6] Matters were not helped by the fact that N-P methods are standardly couched not as rules for inductive inference but rather as rules for "inductive behavior."

Tests as Guides for Inductive Behavior. Jerzy Neyman, co-founder of Neyman-Pearson (N-P) methods, deliberately distinguished the aim of N-P tests from accounts claiming to supply means to assign degrees of probability to hypotheses. He recommended that statistical tests be regarded as rules for deciding whether to adopt a given *action* with respect to a phenomenon. In this view, statistical tests succeed as guides for inductive behavior by providing rules for action that ensure we will avoid making erroneous decisions too often in the long run.

> To decide whether a hypothesis, *H*, of a given type be rejected or not, calculate a specified character, x, of the observed facts; if $x>x_0$ reject *H*; if $x<x_0$ accept *H*. Such a rule tells us nothing as to whether in a particular case *H* is true when $x<x_0$ or false when $x>x_0$. But it may often be proved that if we behave according to such a rule . . . we shall reject *H* when it is true not more, say, than once in a hundred times, and in addition we may have evidence that we shall reject *H* sufficiently often when it is false. (Neyman and Pearson 1933, p. 142)

If one takes seriously Neyman's remark that a statistical test "tells us nothing as to whether in a particular case *H* is true, then one may rightly wonder how tests can be guides for using data as evidence in testing hypotheses or in reaching inductive inferences. Indeed, it might be thought that the issue of whether these tests can provide guidance for induction is closed, since Neyman himself can be heard to deny that the tests serve this role. But the issue is not so simple. Despite Neyman's penchant for behavioristic talk, it is clear that there are other interpretations for statistical tests and these other interpretations might let us view them as guides for inductive inference, albeit not in the form of logics of confirmation. At the same time it must be admitted that there is a great deal of controversy as to what such an "inferential" or "evidential" interpretation of tests might be, and the entire issue is mired in decades-long controversy and vehement disagreement. The goal of this discussion is to propose we start afresh and consider what kinds of guidance we need in making inferences in the face of limited evidence and error.

Error Statistics as a Guide to Inductive Learning. Supposing, as I do, that the methodology of Neyman-Pearson tests, and more generally the formal and informal cognate methods I put under "error statistics," supply guides for reliable inductive inference, our compacted overview suggests an open path for showing this: we need to show how they provide methods for reliable inductive learning, without supplying degrees of confirmation and without being limited to ensuring low long-run probabilities of erroneous decisions. When we use probabilities either to learn from data or to evaluate if a single hypothesis is warranted by evidence, I maintain, we are in need, not of a way to assign the claim a degree of probability, however interpreted. Rather, statistical measures are needed to quantify *how far* a given hypothesis is from a correct model of (an aspect of) a phenomenon, and how *severely hypotheses* pass given tests.

Granted, for any body of data there is in general more than one hypothesis with which it is compatible or in accordance—after all, that is why we say an inference from limited data is inductive and not deductive. Nevertheless, it does not follow that all such equally compatible hypotheses are equally well tested, and we may be able to discuss the warrantedness of given hypotheses according to the probativeness or severity of the tests each has passed. Let us move away for a moment from formal accounts, and begin with an informal consideration of how these severity considerations arise in familiar appraisals.

2. Induction as Severe Testing in Contrast to Logics of Induction

Suppose we are testing how well a student, Isaac, has mastered first-order symbolic logic. A test that required doing truth tables, translations, and proofs in propositional and quantified logic would be regarded as more difficult to pass than one which only required a few truth tables: it would be regarded as more searching, more probing, and more severe. That Isaac has passed the highly severe test, it seems clear, indicates he has mastered more of the material of first-order logic than having merely passed the less severe test. A passing and even a perfect score is easier and more likely to have come about with the less severe test than the more severe one, even among students who have not mastered the bulk of the course material. We deny that the student's passing score warrants inferring he fully masters the material if we learn that even students who mastered very little of the material would very probably have scored as high or even higher than he did; and in so doing, we are demanding that a test be *severe*. When we infer, on the other hand, that Isaac knows at least most of the material on the grounds that he would scarcely have done as well as he did were he not to know at least that much, we are making an inference based on a *severe test*.

The same reasoning abounds in science. Does the recent report of increased mortality among Monarch butterflies fed on leaves from genetically modified (GM) corn[7] supply good evidence that *H*: GM corn harms Monarch butterflies? Not if such a reported correlation turns out to have been fairly typical, even if the mortality rates were unaffected by the transgenic pollen, that is, even if *H* were false. *When we reason this way, we are demanding a hypothesis pass a severe test with data* **x** *before regarding* **x** *as a good indication or good evidence for H.*

To infer from data **x** to a hypothesis *H* on the grounds that *H* has passed a severe test with **x**, is a case of what I will call an *inference from severe testing*. I propose that warranted procedures for using data to infer claims that go beyond the data—that is, warranted inductions—be regarded as cases of inference from severe testing. Inductive learning, in this view, proceeds by testing hypotheses and inferring those which pass probative or severe tests—tests which very probably would have unearthed some error in the hypothesis *H*, were such an error present. A methodology for induction, accordingly, is a methodology for arriving at severe tests, and for scrutinizing inferences by considering the severity with which they have passed tests. Far from wishing to justify the familiar inductive "straight rule" from an observed correlation between A and B to an inference that all or most A's are B's in a given population, we can see that such a rule would license inferences that had not passed severe tests: it would be a highly unreliable rule. An induction following this pattern will be warranted, I claim, only when the inference has passed a severe test with the observed correlation: It is warranted just when the test did a good job of ruling out the ways it can be an error to go from the sample correlation to the population.

If we wish to capture these intuitions about induction or ampliative inference by means of probabilistic ideas, we find ourselves in need of methods that differ from familiar logics of confirmation wherein inductive inference takes the form of probability assignments to hypotheses on the basis of evidence. Whereas probability enters in obtaining a quantitative assessment of severity, it arises not to provide a degree (of belief, weight, support, or confirmation) to the hypothesis, but to characterize the overall test procedure with respect to its effectiveness for probing errors of interest. In contrast to *logics of confirmation or induction,* a methodology for severe testing cannot begin with given statements of evidence but requires enough information about how the data were generated, and about the specific testing context, to assess the overall severity with which a claim or hypothesis may be inferred.

It seems to me that there are aspects of evidence considered crucially relevant, both in day-to-day reasoning and in science, which are not properly accounted for in logics of confirmation but which are easily explained in an account that views induction as severe testing. Most importantly, identifying severity as the goal of induction, we begin to see how to get around what has most often been taken as posing a serious obstacle to arriving at inductive or ampliative inferences reliably. While it is true that intermediary inferences are often required to arrive at inductive evidence, far from posing a threat to reliability, these become the source of avoiding these very threats. In contrast to the image of building a tower with each floor at least as shaky as the inferences on which it is built, a properly inferred inductive result is far more reliable than any of the "premises." This is the heart of what allows induction—understood as severe testing—to be genuinely ampliative; to come out with more than is put in.

3. Severe Tests

From our examples in section 2, we can identify what is required for a hypothesis or prediction *H* to have passed a good or severe test with data **x**. Although, minimally, a passing result requires a good agreement between data **x** and hypothesis *H*, more is required besides. In addition to finding a "good fit" between data **x** and hypothesis *H*, we need to be able to say that the test was really probative—we need to show that so good a fit between data **x** and *H* is very improbable if it is a mistake to regard **x** as evidence for *H*. So we can say:

*Hypothesis H passes a severe test T with **x** if,*

(i) **x** agrees with or "fits" *H* (for a suitable notion of fit), and

(ii) with very high probability, test T would have produced a result that fits *H* less well than **x** does, if *H* were false or incorrect.[8]

Some points of clarification will be important to avoid anticipated misunderstandings.

Avoiding Anticipated Misunderstandings

1. A severity assessment is always relative to the hypothesis that "passes." It is commonly assumed that a severity assessment attaches to the test itself—but doing so leads to untoward results. Once cannot answer the question: how severe is test *T*? without including the particular inference that is claimed to have passed the test, if any. A test may severely pass one hypothesis and not another, even among the hypotheses under consideration. For example, observing a (statistically) significant increase in mortality in butterflies fed GM corn might severely pass the hypothesis that there is an increased risk to butterflies fed GM corn; but failure to observe an increase does not severely pass the hypothesis that there is zero increased risk (that is, as the slogan warns: no evidence of risk is not the same as evidence of "no risk").

2. Severity is based on assessing error probabilities. Existing quantitative measures of support, confirmation, or the like may be evaluated by means of the severity requirement because each supplies one or another measures of "fit" (as in condition [i] of severity). For any such measure of fit between **x** and *H*, we must also ask: *how often would so good a fit occur, under the assumption that H is false?* The probability the test would pass a hypothesis *H*, under the assumption that *H* is false, is an *error probability* or error frequency. If this error probability is very low, the severity with which *H* passes is high. It is the crucial role of error probabilities that differentiates this severe testing approach from other accounts of induction.

3. Finding that a hypothesis *H* severely passes test T with data x does not license a posterior probability assignment to *H*. This is a notion that will play no role in the frequentist account I favor. So, we are not open to the charge confronting frequentist logics of confirmation, as discussed in section 1, namely that since hypotheses are regarded as true or false and it would make no sense (except for very special cases) to assign them probabilities other than the trivial ones, 0 or 1. But I wish to go further: even if we allow attempts to formulate a problem so that "even a frequentist" can speak of the probability of *H* being true, a high posterior probability of *H* given e will not give us what we need for *H* passing a test severely.

Suppose a disease is so rare in a given population, that one would rarely err by declaring any randomly selected member of this population U is free of the disease. Even though it is very improbable that a randomly selected person from U has the disease the hypothesis "the person randomly selected is disease-free" has not passed a severe test, in the sense I have defined it. Why? Because the person being declared disease-free—call her A—had *no chance* of having her disease detected even if it were present. Therefore, the assertion: "A is disease-free" has passed a test with *minimal* (that is, 0) severity![9] Note how this is applicable to the "lottery paradox."[10]

4. **The severity condition (ii) is not the same as saying that x is very improbable given not-H.** That is, condition (ii) is not merely asserting that P(**x**; H is false) is low,[11] where "P(**x**; H is false)" is to be read: "the probability of **x** under the assumption that H is false." For a familiar example, H_1 might be that a coin is fair, and **x** the result of n flips. For any **x** one can construct a hypothesis H_2 that makes the data maximally likely, for example, H_2 can assert that the probability of heads is 1 just on those tosses that yield heads, 0 otherwise. P(**x**;H_1) is very low and P(**x**;H_2) is high, however, H_2 has not passed a severe test because one can always construct some *such maximally likely hypothesis or other* to perfectly fit the coin toss data, even though this maximally likely H_2 is false, and in fact the coin is perfectly fair (that is, H_1 is true). The test such an H_2 passes has minimal severity.[12]

4. Popperian Severity

It was Popper who is best known for insisting upon severe tests, and while the above intuitions about tests are Popperian in spirit, Popper never adequately captured the severity notion. Although Popper offered various formal definitions which would *potentially* measure the degree to which **x** corroborates H, C(H,**x**), in order for it to actually measure corroboration, Popper claimed, **x** would have to be the result of a severe test.

> In opposition to [the] inductivist attitude, I assert that C(H,**x**) must not be interpreted as the degree of corroboration of H by **x**, unless **x** reports the results of our sincere efforts to overthrow H. The requirement of sincerity cannot be formalized—no more than the inductivist requirement that e must represent our total observational knowledge. (Popper 1959, p. 418. I substitute his h, e with **x** and H, respectively, for consistency with my notation.)

Under "inductivist" Popper includes Bayesians both of Carnapian and subjective varieties, as well as those holding variants of induction by enumeration. The important kernel of rightness here is that these inductive logics of evidential relationship made it too easy to find inductive support for hypotheses: their measures of evidential relationship may be satisfied without satisfying the requirement of severity. There is a formal counterpart to this claim: All such algorithms lack formal niches through which to pick up on aspects of the evidence that are relevant for assessing if the test was really good at probing H's errors, that is, for assessing severity in my sense. *Unfortunately, Popper's algorithm was similarly lacking.*

According to Popper, data **x** was to pass *H* severely if: *H* fits or entails data **x** and **x** is improbable "without" *H* or under the assumption that *H* is false. But his formal measures never got beyond measures of fit, such as requiring that

P(**x**;*H*) = high (or maximal)

P(**x**;*H* is false) = low.

(A weaker variant of the second requirement is sometimes understood as requiring only that without *H*, **x** is improbable). Popper never saw how error probabilistic notions, as in clause (ii) of severity, permit what sound like psychological intentions of the tester to be captured rigorously.

An even more crucial difference between the approach I am putting forward and Popper's is that Popper recoiled from endorsing anything that could be considered induction. Even where a hypothesis had passed a test that is severe by Popper's lights—even if it is highly corroborated—he regarded this as at most a report of the hypothesis's past performance. Although many would agree with Salmon's charge that, "modus tollens without corroboration is empty; modus tollens with corroboration is induction" (Salmon 1966, 26), Popper adamantly denied that even highly corroborating results afford positive evidence for a hypothesis's correctness or reliability. As such, Popperian corroboration never answered the challenge to show why we should follow his prescription to accept or prefer the most highly corroborated hypothesis, and thus never showed his rule: "prefer the best tested hypothesis" provides any kind of guide for reliable learning.

5. The Severity Principle as Inferring to the Absence of an Error

In contrast, in our view, when a hypothesis *H* has passed a highly severe test we can infer that the data x provide good evidence for the correctness of *H*. We may refer to this inductive principle as *the severity principle:*

> *Severity Principle.* Data **x** (produced by process G) provides a good indication or evidence for hypothesis *H* (just) to the extent that test T severely passes *H* with **x**.

Hypothesis *H* is regarded (or modeled) as a claim about some aspect of the process that generated the data, G. According to the severity principle, when hypothesis *H* has passed a highly severe test (something that may require several individual tests taken together), we can *regard it as supplying good* grounds that we have ruled out the ways it can be a *mistake* to regard **x** as having been generated by the procedure described by *H*.[13] The inductive inference from passing a severe test reflects an informal argument which we may call *arguing from error*, and what we infer on the basis of *H*'s passing a severe test is an *inference to the absence of a specific error.*

> *Inference to the absence of an error:* It is learned that an error is absent when a procedure of testing with an extremely high probability of signaling the *presence* of the error if in fact the error is present, nevertheless does not signal the error but instead yields a result that accords with the *absence* of the error.

A test "signals" the presence of the error by giving rise to an outcome that either fails *H* or is interpreted as a poor fit with *H*. Hence, the inference to the absence of an error really just instantiates what is given in the severity principle:

> If a hypothesis or claim "passes" a test that with very high probability it would not have passed, unless it were true or free of a specific error, then its passing is a good indication that the hypothesis or claim is correct (or free of the specific error).

Thus we can infer something positive from passing *H* severely: that a particular error is absent (or is no greater than a certain amount). (An analogous argument is used to infer the *presence* of an error. See Appendix.)

The intuition underlying the severity principle is a familiar one: we have a good indication that we are correct about a claim or hypothesis, whether in science or in day-to-day learning, just to the extent that we have ruled out the ways we can be wrong in taking the claim or hypothesis to be true. Such a critical stance demands that an inductive account be directed toward supplying tools, not to quantify our subjective opinions, but to avoid being misled by our subjective opinions. An account of induction, once viewed as severe testing, must supply intersubjective methods capable of addressing skeptical doubts (of others as well as ourselves), and thus must set the stage for others to check, debate, and extend the inferences reached. The main quantitative aspect of this task is shifted from assessing how well a hypothesis explains, agrees with, or is instantiated by data, to how capable the test is at revealing disagreements, counterinstances, and errors not yet probed.

6. Learning from Errors

Although specific methods and rules about their use are numerous, I maintain that they are all tied to detecting and avoiding a handful of error types (although there is nothing firm about this list):

- mistaking chance effects or spurious correlations for genuine correlations or regularities
- mistakes about a quantity or value of a parameter
- mistakes about a causal factor
- mistakes about the assumptions of the data or experiment.

There is a corresponding localization of what one is entitled to infer severely: "*H* is false," in applying the severity requirement, does not refer to the so-called Bayesian catchall—all hypotheses other than *H*, but rather a specific error that the hypothesis *H* is *denying*. If *H* states a given effect is systematic—of the sort brought about more often than by chance—then not-*H* states it is due to chance; if *H* states a parameter is greater than some value *c*, not-*H* states it is less than *c*; and so on. How specific the error hypothesis is depends upon what is required to ensure a good chance of learning something of interest.

Granted, unlike evidential-relation logics, our account must recognize that there may be uncertainty as to whether we have any kind of evidence for a hypothesis—we clearly cannot begin with "given evidence." Nevertheless, we may know a good deal about how the type of data can be mistaken as evidence for *H*. We have to become shrewd inquisitors of errors, interact with them, simulate them (with models and computers), amplify them: *we have to learn to make them talk.*

By understanding induction as severe testing we can see how the kind of day-to-day strategies for learning from mistakes receive systematic treatment by means of a host of experimental strategies and methodological rules (for generating and analyzing data) such as: controlled and double-blind trials, randomization, varying the data, predesignating properties to be tested, splitting up or partitioning inquiries to ask one question at a time. Since the rules are claims about strategies for avoiding mistakes and learning from errors, their appraisal turns on understanding how methods enable avoidance of specific errors. Hence an inductive methodology of severe testing will focus on understanding the properties of tools for generating, modeling and analyzing data—properties which, while empirical, are objective.

To illustrate, suppose one were interested in estimating the proportion in the U.S. population who have some property, say, stands opposed to the

U.S. going to war with Iraq. If I take a random sample of 1,000 or so (in the manner done in polling), I have *created* a connection between the proportion who say "do not go to war" in my sample and the proportion with this property in the U.S. population at that point in time. The general connection between a randomly selected sample proportion and the population proportion is a genuine empirical relationship. For instance, the sample proportion will differ from the population proportion by more than 2 standard deviations less than 5% of the time. Hence, according to the severity principle, the sample proportion, x, permits inferring, with severity .95, that the population proportion is within 2 standard deviations of x.[14]

7. Statistical Methods as Tools for Severe Testing

In practice, informal and qualitative arguments may be all that are needed to approximate the severity argument—even in science. Indeed many of the strongest severity arguments are of a qualitative variety. A familiar example is Hacking's (1983) "argument from coincidence" for taking dense bodies as a real effect, not an artifact. "If you can see the same fundamental features of structure using several different physical systems, you have excellent reasons for saying, 'that's real' rather than, 'that's an artifact'" (Hacking 1983, p. 204). We can argue that, if it were an artifact, it is highly improbable that numerous instruments and techniques would have conspired to make all of the evidence appear as if the effect were real. In short, we severely argue to infer the absence of the artifact error, and we do so without any formal statistical model.

However, in order to serve as the basis for a reliable guide for induction, we have to be very clear about how to simulate and subtract out errors, how to arrive at reliable claims from (suitably massaging) highly shaky data, and how to utilize statistical models to articulate such counterfactual claims as what "would have occurred with high probability were such and such the case." Here is where I see formal ideas from probability and statistics arising: they provide systematic means for (a) expressing real-life errors in terms of a handful of statistical models and statistical hypotheses within those models, (b) generating and modeling actual observations so as to bear upon the statistical hypotheses, for example, by means of tests and estimation procedures.

Philosophers of "confirmation" and induction were right to look to formal probabilistic ideas, but for a genuinely ampliative account, one should turn neither to formal logic nor to probabilistic logics of evidential relationship, but to the methodology of standard statistics (for example, Neyman-Pearson and Fisherian statistical tests and estimation procedures).

These methods were developed to ensure control of error probabilities of tests without any assignments of prior probabilities to hypotheses. Given the new emphasis philosophers have placed on taking their cues from relevant sciences, it is surprising epistemologists and philosophers of induction have paid that little attention to the ongoing advances in statistics—the body of methods to which scientists regularly appeal in making inductive inferences with limited data. The philosophy of induction and of evidence seems to be the one field that has not taken advantage of the growing move to apply to our philosophical problems the results from the relevant empirical sciences, or else has assumed the relevant sciences are limited to psychology and biology.

Having said this, I wish to state plainly that I do not consider appealing to standard statistical techniques a panacea for arriving at an adequate guide for inductive learning. These methods are fraught with philosophical controversies of their own, as I pointed out in section 1. However, I think an important role for philosophers of science is to address these criticisms, as they are actually played out in practice, especially in such fields as ecology, economics, risk assessment, psychology, and many others. In numerous scientific forums in which these issues about evidence, inference, observation, and induction are debated, it seems to me, philosophical insights are badly needed and too rarely present.

Even as we may wish to move away from and reinterpret many features of formal statistical tests—and as will be seen below, I definitely do—they provide several insights on which we can capitalize for our task of severe testing. From formal error statistical tests we learn that it is impossible to assess reliability or severity with just statements of data and hypotheses divorced from the experimental context in which they were generated and modeled. Minimally, we need to consider three main elements of experimental inquiry which we can represent as three types of models: *the primary hypotheses of interest, the data*, and *the experiment* that link the others by means of test procedures.

1. A scientific hypothesis or question is probed by setting out a statistical hypothesis H, couched as a claim about the data-generating source G. As a statistical hypothesis, H must assign probabilities to the different experimental outcomes, that is, for any outcome $\mathbf{x}$, H tells us the "probability of $\mathbf{x}$ *under* H," written $P(\mathbf{x};H)$.[15]

2. A statistical test is a rule for classifying the possible outcomes by telling us which to take as "rejecting," and which "accepting," various hypotheses. The cornerstone of Neyman-Pearson (N-P) tests is to ensure that, whichever hypothesis is true, the probability of erroneously rejecting or accepting them may be controlled at specified low values.

3. The control of error probabilities depends on the data **x** satisfying the assumptions of the statistical model; that is P(**x**; H) must apply to the data **x** we happen to have.

The *primary question* in our transgenic corn example above might be: *Does transgenic pollen harm Monarch butterflies in the field?* It is tackled by observing the difference in mortality rates between treated and control larvae. One considers a standard statistical hypothesis often called a null (or error) hypothesis:

> H_0: there is no difference in mortality rate between treated and control larva.

H_0 asserts, in other words, that *it is an error* to take as genuine any observed increase in mortality between a sample fed GM pollen (treated) and a sample not so fed (controls). (That is, H_0 asserts that any observed difference is "due to chance"—due to the normal variabilities that result even if all larva are treated in exactly the same way.)

The mortality rate was observed to be much higher in the GM-fed larva than in the controls: the data were in very good accordance with alternative hypothesis H*:

> H^*: mortality rates are higher in treated as opposed to untreated larva.

But the researchers need to ask:

> How frequently would so good an accordance with H^* arise under the assumption that the data arose from a process correctly described by H_0?

The answer is the *statistical significance level* (or p-value) of the observed difference *x*. The smaller the significance level the further the data are from H and the better they fit H^*.[16] As such, an intuitively plausible statistical test takes this form:

> Reject H_0 and accept H^* iff the statistical significance level of **x** reaches some small value α.

By definition, the probability of an α-level statistical difference, under the assumption that H_0 is true is equal to α, i.e.,

> P(Test T rejects H_0; H_0) $\leq \alpha$.

Thus, the test ensures that the probability of an erroneous rejection of the null hypothesis H_0 (i.e., a *type I error*) is no more than α.[17]

Following Neyman, such tests are often framed as decision rules with low long-run error probabilities, leading to the questions we noted in section 1 regarding their appropriateness as guides for inference. It is at this point that we can link those initial concerns about the "guide to life" question with our discussion of how we might view induction as severe testing. For, if we think of inductive inference as an inference to the absence of an error, as an inference to a severely passed hypothesis, we see how statistical hypothesis tests supply guides for severe tests, and not merely good decision rules with low long-run errors.

By requiring the significance level to reach some very small value, α, before rejecting H_0 and accepting H^*, the test ensures that whenever H_0 is rejected, alternative H^* may be inferred with severity *at least* $1 - \alpha$. (To "infer H^* with high severity $(1 - \alpha)$", it must be remembered, does *not* mean H^* is assigned a high measure of probability or support, but that H* has passed a test with severity $1 - \alpha$.) Note that "H^* is false," within this testing context, is identical to "H_0 is true." To elucidate the gist of this argument, I will hazard putting it in terms of a kind of statistical analogy to *modus tollens*, despite some distortion.[18] Given the *severity principle*, we argue:

> If the hypothesis H_0 is correct (about the process generating the data **x**) then, with probability $1 - \alpha$, **X** would *not* be statistically significant at level α.
>
> **x** is statistically significant at level α.
>
> Therefore, "reject H_0" and infer that **x** is good evidence that H^* [19]

I shall return in the Appendix to a more rigorous sketch of the reinterpretation of statistical tests that I am recommending.

Guiding Substantive Inductive Inference. Clearly, the data taken to severely pass the inference about the risk GM corn poses to Monarchs in conditions of the lab (where they have no other choice of food but the GM corn) do not automatically extend to what happens in the field. One has not probed and ruled out those errors by means of the test in the lab, and this lets us see that distinct tests would be needed for such an extrapolation. Such additional probes may be tackled by adding "higher level" hypotheses to the low level one considered here—making for an extended "hierarchy" of models and hypotheses. Formal statistical methods and models serve to guide the choice of model in which to embed a given question by providing standard or "canonical models" of given error types.

Justifying Assumptions. Justifying inductive inferences understood as severe testing is a matter of showing the existence of severe tests, or showing a particular inference is warranted with severity. To this end, it is easy to explain the importance of certain procedures for data generation, for example, randomization.[20] Even where such before-data procedures are absent, the goal of running a severe test directs one to alternative means for checking, and satisfying test assumptions, something which any full-blown inductive account would need to incorporate. Using the test procedure in question and deliberately violating one or another assumptions, it can be checked that we have a procedure that would, with high probability, detect these violations just when they are present. This permits arguing to the absence (or presence) of an error—where this time the "error" concerns a violation of a test assumption. Once we have a handful of such canonical procedures, we can rely on them to build an increasingly probative and varied arsenal to simulate and detect violations of assumptions.[21]

8. Concluding Remarks

If we view induction as severe testing then the "guide to life" challenge becomes a matter of showing how probabilistic methods, models, and tools supply tools for making reliable inferences based on severe tests. By reframing the guide to life challenge in this way, the twin concerns of "ascertainability" and "applicability," I think, may be satisfied—although here I have only set the stage for how to carry out that project. The Appendix sketches how the needed assessments are ascertainable by a suitable use of frequentist statistical tests and, simultaneously, how statistical tests are applicable to inductive learning, but many questions remain.

Having altered the role of probability in induction, from assessing how well confirmed hypothesis H is, I can well imagine the reader asking, does not the frequentist still have to face many of the same problems? I think, in fact, they do, but in forms that admit solutions that escaped the degree of confirmation frequentist. The familiar problem of how to choose the *reference class* reappears as that of specifying and validating the probability model for the test. The problem of how to show the relevance of long-run frequencies to particular inferences and *single hypotheses or cases* reappears as well, in the guise of justifying the "severity principle." The latter problem, the more difficult of the two, demands spelling out precisely what is licensed when we say that a hypothesis H has passed test T with high severity.

That a hypothesis passes severely may license claims of very different forms, according to the nature of the primary hypothesis H that severely passes. Minimally, the induction to H tells us that what H asserts about experimental applications is correct: that H is correct in what it says about what would be expected in future applications of (or interactions with) the specified phenomenon (whether real or hypothetical). But when we make an inference to *H*, we are also making an inference to aspects of the particular phenomenon or case.

Consider our logic student, Isaac. Suppose Isaac has been given numerous logic tests, probing different areas of logic, all of which he passed with flying colors. Do his test scores indicate he has mastered most of first order logic? Yes if he passes severe test after test—where it is known that a student who has not mastered logic would almost surely not have managed to pass all of these tests as well as Isaac did. It is not merely that following the rule: *if a student obtains high passing grades on a great many difficult logic tests, then infer that the student has mastered most of logic*, would very infrequently lead to erroneous pronouncements in the long run of testing students. It is also that the knowledge of the characteristics of the tests this student has passed teaches us about *this student*—about his mastery of logic. More generally, knowledge of a test's capabilities to detect errors teaches us about aspects of the process that produced the test results. That is the basis underlying the severity principle which licenses inductively inferring claims from information about the severity of the tests they passed.

Viewing statistical tests from this perspective, we see that the real value of being able to control error probabilities at small values is not the desire to have a good track record in the long run—although such a long-run justification is still available (and in several contexts may be perfectly apt). It is, rather, because of how this guides us to severely probe, and make correct inductive inferences about, the process underlying the data in front of us.

DEBORAH G. MAYO
Virginia Tech

Appendix

Outline of an Interpretation of N-P Tests as Guides for Ascertaining the Severity of Inferences

In this Appendix, I attempt to flesh out the key aspects of the severity reinterpretation with reference to a very familiar statistical test. The test involves taking a random sample of size n, $X_1, \ldots X_n$ where each X_i is distributed normally with unknown mean μ and known standard deviation σ = 1 to conduct a one-sided test of $H_0 : \mu = 0$ against $H_1 : \mu > 0$.

The N-P test, in its naked mathematical form, is a rule which tells us for each possible outcome $\mathbf{X} = X_1, \ldots X_n$ whether to "accept H_0" or reject H_0 and accept H_1. There is a distance measure $d(\mathbf{X})$ with which the test rule is defined. In particular, the uniformly most powerful UMP test T_α is

Test T_α: Reject H_0 iff $d(X) \geq c_\alpha$

where $d(\mathbf{X}) = (\bar{X} - \mu_0)n^{.5}/\sigma$ and $\bar{X}$ is the sample mean. Equivalently,

Test T_α: Reject H_0 iff $\bar{X}\ \mu_0 + c_\alpha \sigma_x$

where $\sigma_x = \sigma / n^{.5}$. Setting α = .02 corresponds to a ca of approximately 2, and with n = 100, $\sigma_x = .1$. So $d(\mathbf{X})$ would be statistically significant (at the .02 level) whenever $d(\mathbf{X}) > 2$. Therefore, Test $T_{.02}$ takes the mathematical form:

Test $T_{.02}$: reject H_0 whenever $\bar{X} \geq .2$.

This test, however, is far too coarse: one really wants tests with suitably low error probabilities for particular discrepancies from H_0, and one would also like to go beyond the classifications "accept"/"reject" to take into account specific data **x**. Viewing the goal of tests to be severity, it is easy to extend the N-P testing framework to serve these purposes. Although N-P tests are framed in terms of a hypothesis being "rejected" or "accepted," both results will correspond to "passing" some hypothesis or, rather, some hypothesized discrepancy, enabling us to have a single notion of severity which applies to both. Post-data—once the data are in—we use the observed **x** that leads to 'reject' or 'accept' H_0 in order to assess the actual severity with which specific discrepancies from H_0 pass the given test. 'Accept H_0' in this one-sided test, for example, will correspond to an inference that the data indicates the discrepancy from H_0 is less than a given amount, whereas 'Reject H_0' will license inferences about the extent of the positive discrepancy that is *severely indicated* by data **x**. The basic idea of a hypothesis H passing a severe test with data **x**, recall, is that it is highly improbable that H would have passed so well, if in fact H is false (or a specified discrepancy exists). Let us begin with a "metastatistical" rule for interpreting "reject H_0" with Test $T_{.02}$:

A. Rule of Rejection:

(RR) (i) A statistically significant difference (from 0) as large as d(**X**) is a *good indication* that μ exceeds μ′ just to the extent that it is very probable that test T_α would have resulted in a smaller difference if μ were as small as μ′. i.e., d(**X**) indicates μ > μ′ to the extent that severely passes μ ≥ μ′.

From (RR)(i) we get a companion rule for what an observed difference does *not* indicate:

(RR) (ii) d(**X**) is a *poor indication or poor evidence* that μ > μ′ if it is very probable that test T_α yields so large a difference even if μ is no greater than μ′.

By stipulating that H be rejected only if the difference is statistically significant at some small level, note, it is assured that such a rejection—*at minimum*—warrants hypothesis H_1, that μ exceeds μ_0, which in our example is 0. Rule (RR) (i) makes this plain. To get a feel for the "customized" interpretations that are licensed, consider some particular outcomes that lead to rejecting H_0:

Reject H_0

Case 1: let $\bar{X} = .2$. From rule RR we have:

Infer with severity .98 that $\mu > \bar{X} - 2(.1)$

$$\mu > 0$$

Infer with severity .84 that $\mu > \bar{X} - 1(.1)$

$$\mu > .1$$

and so on.

The companion part of rule (RR) tells us which discrepancies from 0 are *not* licensed by an outcome that falls just at the cut-off for rejection. For example, the severity with which $\bar{X} = .2$ passes hypothesis H: $\mu > .3$ is .16, so it is a poor indication that the discrepancy from 0 is that large.

If the statistically significant outcome exceeds the cut-off point, this is reflected in the extent of the discrepancy that one can regard as having severely passed. Unlike standard N-P practice, we do not report both rejections of H_0 identically. For example,

Case 2: let $\bar{X} = .3$. From rule RR we have:

Infer with severity .999 that $\mu > 0$

Infer with severity .98 that $\mu > .1$.

From the companion part of rule (RR) we have:

The severity with which $\bar{X} = .3$ passes hypothesis H: $\mu > .3$ is .5.

The outcome in case 2 is still a poor indication that the discrepancy from 0 is that large, but the severity is not at low as in case 1.

Consider now the case where the statistical test outputs 'accept H_0' beginning with: $\mu = \mu_0$. We know that this does not license the inference that μ is exactly μ_0—that μ does not exceed μ_0 at all, because the probability of such a negative result is high even if there is some discrepancy from μ_0. Nor will it license ruling out discrepancies against which the test is too insensitive to detect. However, we may find a positive discrepancy γ that can be well ruled out. Combining both parts, we get the metastatistical rule of acceptance, RA:

B. Rule of Acceptance: RA:

(RA) If d($\boldsymbol{x}$) is not statistically significant, but there is a very high (low) probability that test T_α would have produced a more statistically significant difference, if μ exceeds $\mu_0 + \gamma$, then the result is (is not) good grounds for inferring $\mu \leq \mu_0 + \gamma$.

To have just one example, let $\bar{X} = .1$. From rule RA we have:

Infer with severity .98 that $\mu < .3$.

We also have,

Infer with severity .3 that $\mu < .05$.

To apply this latter result, suppose on the basis of the "negative" result, $\bar{X} = .1$, someone proposes to infer, "This result is evidence that the null hypothesis is true, or if there are any discrepancies from 0, this is evidence that it is less than .05.". Since the severity with which $\mu < .05$ passes this test is only .3, we would criticize such an interpretation of this negative result as unwarranted—and we would do so on objective grounds. Such a negative result would occur 70% of the time, even if $\mu \geq .05$; it thereby fails to provide grounds for ruling out this discrepancy. The severity assessment makes this type of critique systematic.

Note that by ensuring ahead of time that the test has high power to detect an alternative μ', it is assured than any "acceptance of H_0" licenses, with high severity, $\mu < \mu'$. (That is because, were $\mu = \mu'$, the test would, with high probability, have resulted in a more statistically significant $d(\mathbf{x})$ than we observed.) This immediately shows how we would respond to the often heard charge that setting the probabilities for the type I and II errors are arbitrary. Pre-data, the basis for choosing error characteristics of tests stem from the goal of ensuring it is capably of licensing given inferences severely. The grounds for specifying tests grows directly out of the inferences for which the test is to give guidance. We set the "worst case" values accordingly: small α ensures, minimally, that any rejection licenses inferring some discrepancy; large power against discrepancy γ ensures that failing to reject H_0 warrants ruling out, severely a discrepancy this large. Second, post-data, the severity assessment—however the test was chosen—allows for an objective interpretation of the results. While statistical tests cannot themselves supply the information as to which discrepancies are and are not of substantive importance, once supplied with the concept of severity, they can be used as guides to assess the extent of the discrepancies detected severely.

C. *We can summarize these two "metastatistical" rules for the case of test* T_a *as follows:*

(RR) Reject H_0 iff $d(x) > c_\alpha$

Infer with severity $1 - \varepsilon$: $\mu > \bar{X} - k_\varepsilon \sigma / n^{.5}$

Where $P(Z > k_\varepsilon) = \varepsilon$

or,

Infer with severity $1 - \varepsilon$: $\mu > \mu_0 + \gamma$

where $\gamma = (d(\mathbf{x}_0) - k_\varepsilon) s / n^{.5}$

(RA): Accept H_0 iff $d(\mathbf{x}) < c_\alpha$

Infer with severity $1 - \varepsilon$: $\mu \leq \bar{X} - k_\varepsilon \sigma / n^{.5}$

where $P(Z > k_\varepsilon) = \varepsilon$.

or,

Infer with severity $1 - \varepsilon$: $\mu \leq \mu_0 + \gamma$

where $\gamma = (d(\mathbf{x}_0) + k_\varepsilon)\sigma / n^{.5}$

NOTES

1. C.S. Peirce, anticipating modern error statistical conceptions, distinguished between the use of probability in deductive or analytic inference and its use in inductive or synthetic inference: "In the case of analytic inference we know the probability of our conclusion (if the premises are true), but in the case of synthetic infernces we only know the degree of trustworthiness of our proceeding" (2.693).

2. Strictly speaking, Salmon identifies the "guide to life" criterion with that of "applicability," but since without ascertainability the notion pretty clearly will fail as a guide to life, I combine them here.

3. Salmon recommended a comparative Bayesian account in order to cancel out the need to assess P(e|not-H).

4. I discuss this in Mayo 1996, chapter 4.

5. Exceptions include the group we may call "philosophers of statistics": e.g., Braithwaite, Giere, Gillies, Kyburg, Hacking, Levi, Seidenfeld, Fetzer.

6. Wesley Salmon explains this as due to the fact that philosophers in search of a logic of confirmation rejected any account that was itself based on empirical assumptions, e.g., random sampling (private conversation). Other explanations are that philosophers of induction and confirmation tend to operate apart from statistical practitioners, and the fact that those philosophers who did take up Neyman-Pearson methods, (e.g, Hacking 1965) were highly critical of the methods for scientific inference.

7. It is the pollen from corn genetically altered to control certain pests that is placed on the leaves for this experiment. The GM corn is intended to kill the European corn borer by naturally producing the (BT) pesticide. The corn borer is the "targeted" species, whereas the Monarch butterflies are "untargeted."

8. Equivalently, (ii) can be written as (ii′) with very low probability, test T would have produced a result that fits H as well as (or better than) x does, if H were false or incorrect.

9. This relates to a common criticism against significance test reasoning. A statistically significant difference from a null hypothesis (e.g., GM corn poses 0 increased risk to Monarchs), say at the .02 level, is taken as evidence of increased risk (severity .98) by the error statistician even though, the critic alleges, the frequentist posterior probability of the null is high. According to the critic, approxi-

mately 50% of the null hypotheses tested are true, from which it follows that the probability that the null "no risk" hypothesis is true even given it would be rejected at a small significance level is "at least 22%—and typically over 50%" (Berger 2003). Firstly, our frequentist would deny that any given null gets a prior probability of x just because it was selected (randomly) from a pool of nulls, x% of which are true—for the same reason we rejected Salmon's attempt to assign frequentist priors earlier. But suppose that we grant that evidence that we would regard as severely indicating some increased risk might correspond to a Bayesian posterior to "no risk" that is not low—it may (with appropriately high priors to the null) be high. Far from taking that as evidence against significance tests (or severity assessments) as guides for induction, we take it as grounds for denying that such posteriors are the guides we need in appraising scientific claims. This is precisely what Fisher argued (Fisher 1956/73; Mayo 1997, 2003).

10. Henry Kyburg is famous for having propounded this paradox. The "evidence," x, is that a person A has bought a ticket in a lottery with only a one in a million chance of having her ticket drawn as the winner. Even though P(A will win; given evidence x) = very low, their intuition is that x is not really good grounds for inferring A will not win. The intuition is correct; it's the way of assessing reliability that is at fault. x is not good evidence for thinking that person will not win the lottery because there is no chance that evidence would be found for inferring the person will win, even if the person's ticket is the winning ticket! So the inference has passed a test with minimal severity.

11. Bold x indicates that the data may be a vector $(x_1, x_2, \ldots, x_n)$. The requirement of "fit" in (i) may be cashed out as a requirement about *likelihoods*, in particular, it requires that P(x; *H*) be higher than P(x ; *H* is false). It is important to see that P(x; *H*) differs from a conditional probability; there is no assumption that a prior probability assignment to *H* exists or is meaningful.

12. This was what led Hacking (1972) to reject the "likelihood" account he had previously promoted.

13. The procedure licensed by the severity principle is reliable in this sense: There is a low probability it will license inferring *H* with high reliability, when *H* is (specifiably) false. One may regard the inductively inferred *H* as reliable provided one is careful about how to interpret this. Take the case of *H* as a statistical hypothesis: an assertion of the relative frequency of outcomes in specified experimental applications. That *H* is reliable would mean, roughly, that such applications of *H* would yield given results about as often as *H* asserts. I shall have more to say about the nature of the inference to *H* at the end.

14. The standard deviation here is generally estimated from the sample, in which case it would properly be called the *standard estimate of the error* or the *standard error.*

15. This is not a conditional probability.

16. Here is the data report: "Larval survival after four days of feeding on leaves dusted with [genetically modified or GM] pollen was significantly lower than survival either on leaves dusted with untransformed pollen or on control leaves with no pollen" (*Nature* 399 [May 20, 1999]: 214). In particular, the observed difference in survival rates would occur no more than .08 % of the time, under the null hypothesis H_0—the *statistical significance level* of x was .008.

17. A "best" N-P test with significance level α is one which, at the same time, minimizes the probability of erroneously accepting H_0 (a type II error).

18. X refers to the random variable that takes on different values with different probabilities (under H_0). The actual value is written as **x**. The distortion is mainly that the first premise is not a material conditional or even a probabilistic conditional. It is an assertion about the probability that **X** would take values so far from what is expected under H_0 to be deemed statistically significant, under the assumption that H_0 is correct. It asserts that P(**X** would not be statistically significant at level α) = 1 – α.

19. Although I am considering the one-sided test here, the same argument can be given with a two-sided test, where H^* asserts there is either an increase or a decrease in risk. Also, more informative inferences to the extent of the increased risk indicated may be given, using the same pattern of reasoning.

20. Justifying randomization is well known to be deeply problematic for Bayesians. Note that randomization (e.g., in assigning treatments) is not the same as random (independent and identically distributed) sampling. Both procedures, and many others besides, get their justifications from seeing how (and when) they contribute to substantiating severity.

21. Methods for testing assumptions are manifold and are continually being developed; I can only touch on them ever so slightly here. *Nonparametric* tests are often appealed to because their validity does not depend on the distribution being assumed by test T. Very roughly, one finds a quantitative characteristic C of the data set **x** such that the probability of different values of C is given under just the hypothesis that the assumption, say randomness, holds. For example, in testing randomness in Binomial trials, C might be the number of consecutive occurrences of "successes" in n trials. Each such string of consecutive outcomes is called a *run*. Were **x** to arise from random process, then both too many and too few runs are very rare—it is highly probable these would *not* occur. (These indicate trends or cycles in the data). Hence, following the severity principle, those outcomes warrant inferring a violation of randomness. Conversely, to infer the absence of violations, one designs tests which, with high probability, would have detected the given violation if it were present. Putting such tests together is the basis for inferring, with severity, that the assumptions hold sufficiently well for substantiating the severity assessment of the primary test. While the literature on testing assumptions in statistics is huge, there is a need for a clear articulation of the reasoning which justifies such inferences in relation to the severity assessment for the primary inference. This is the focus of forthcoming work (Mayo and Spanos 2001).

REFERENCES

Braithwaite, R. 1953. *Scientific Explanation: A Study of the Function of Theory, Probability and Law in Science*. New York: Cambridge University Press.

Chalmers, A. 1999. *What is This Thing Called Science?* 3rd ed. Indianapolis, Ind.: Hackett.

Earman, J. 1992. Bayes or Bust? *A Critical Examination of Bayesian Confirmation Theory.* Cambridge, Mass.: MIT Press.

Edwards, W., H. Lindman, and L. Savage. 1963. "Bayesian Statistical Inference for Psychological Research." *Psychological Review* 70: 193–242.

Fetzer, J. H. 1981. *Scientific Knowledge: Causation, Explanation, and Corroboration.* Dordrecht, The Netherlands: D. Reidel.

Fisher, R. A. 1956/73. *Statistical Methods and Scientific Inference.* New York: Macmillan.

Giere, R. N. 1969. "Empirical Probability, Objective Statistical Methods. and Scientific Inquiry." In *Foundations of Probability Theory, Statistical Inference and Statistical Theories of Science*, vol. 2, edited by W. L. Harper and C. A. Hooker, 63–101. Dordrecht, The Netherlands: D. Reidel.

Gillies, D. 2000. *Philosophical Theories of Probability.* London: Routledge.

Glymour, C. 1980. *Theory and Evidence.* Princeton: Princeton University Press.

Good, I. J. 1983. *Good Thinking.* Minneapolis: University of Minnesota Press.

Hacking, I. 1965. *Logic of Statistical Inference.* Cambridge: Cambridge University Press.

———. 1972. "Likelihood." *British Journal for the Philosophy of Science* 23: 132–37.

———. 1980. "The Theory of Probable Inference: Neyman, Peirce and Braithwaite." In *Science, Belief and Behavior: Essays in Honour of R. B. Braithwaite*, ed. D. H. Mellor, pp. 141–60. Cambridge: Cambridge University Press.

———. 1983. *Representing and Intervening: Introductory Topics in the Philosophy of Natural Science.* Cambridge: Cambridge University Press.

Howson, C. 1997. "Error Probabilities in Error." *Philosophy of Science* 64 (PSA 1996 Proceedings). East Lansing, Mich.: Philosophy of Science Association.

Howson, C., and P. Urbach. 1989. *Scientific Reasoning: The Bayesian Approach.* La Salle: Open Court.

Kyburg, H. E., Jr. 1974. *The Logical Foundations of Statistical Inference.* Dordrecht: Reidel.

———. 1993. "The Scope of Bayesian Reasoning." In *PSA 1992*, vol. II, ed. D. Hull, M. Forbes, and K. Okruhlik. East Lansing, Mich.: Philosophy of Science Association.

Levi, I. 1980. *The Enterprise of Knowledge: An Essay on Knowledge, Credal Probability, and Chance.* Cambridge, MA: MIT Press.

Mayo, D. G. 1996. *Error and the Growth of Experimental Knowledge.* Chicago: University of Chicago Press.

———. 1997. "Response to Howson and Laudan." *Philosophy of Science* (June 1997): 323–33.

———. 1999. "Theory Testing, Statistical Methodology, and the Growth of Experimental Knowledge." In *In the Scope of Logic, Methodology and Philosophy of Science*, vol. I, ed. P. Gärdenfors, J. Wolenski, and K. Kijania-Placek, pp. 171–90. Dordrecht: Kluwer Press.

———. 2000. "Taking Bayesian Criticisms Seriously." In *Philosophical Aspects of Bayesianism*, ed. D. Corfield and J. Williamson. Oxford: Oxford University Press.

Mayo, D. G., and M. Kruse. 2001. "Principles of Inference and Their Consequences." In *Foundations of Bayesianism*, ed. D. Corfield and J. Williamson, pp. 381–403. Dordrecht: Kluwer Press.

Mayo, D. G., and A. Spanos. 2000. "A Post-data Interpretation of Neyman-Pearson Methods Based on a Conception of Severe Testing." Measurements in Physics and Economics Discussion Paper Series. London School of Economics, Centre for Philosophy of Natural and Social Science.

———. Forthcoming. "Severe Tests as Self-correcting: Testing the Assumptions of Statistical Tests."

Neyman, J. 1971. "Foundations of Behavioristic Statistics." In *Foundations of Statistical Inference*, ed. V. P. Godambe and D. A. Sprott, pp. 1–13 (comments and reply, pp. 14–19). Toronto: Holt, Rinehart, and Winston.

———. 1977. "Frequentist Probability and Frequentist Statistics." *Synthese* 36: 97–131.

Neyman, J., and E. S. Pearson. 1933. "On the Problem of the Most Efficient Tests of Statistical Hypotheses." In *Philosophical Transactions of the Royal Society* (A) (1933): 231, 289–337, as reprinted in J. Neyman and E. S. Pearson 1967, pp. 140–85.

———. 1967. *Joint Statistical Papers.* Berkeley: University of California Press.

Pierce, C. S. 1931–35. *Collected Papers.* Vols. 1–6, ed. C. Hartshorne and P. Weiss. Cambridge: Harvard University Press.

Popper, K. 1959. *The Logic of Scientific Discovery.* New York: Basic Books.

Reichenbach, H. 1971. *The Theory of Probability: An Inquiry into the Logical and Mathematical Foundations of the Calculus of Probability.* 2nd ed. Translated by E. Hutten and M. Reichenbach. Berkeley: University of California Press.

Rosenkrantz, R. 1977. *Inference, Method and Decision: Towards a Bayesian Philosophy of Science.* Dordrecht: Reidel.

Salmon, W. 1966. *The Foundations of Scientific Inference.* Pittsburgh: University of Pittsburgh Press.

———. 1990. "Rationality and Objectivity in Science, or Tom Kuhn Meets Tom Bayes." In *Scientific Theories,* ed. C. W. Savage, pp. 175–204. Minneapolis: University of Minnesota Press.

Seidenfeld, T. 1979. *Philosophical Problems of Statistical Inference: Learning from R. A. Fisher.* Dordrecht, The Netherlands: D. Reidel.

5

Bayesian Meets Frequentist: A Marriage Made in California

JAMES R. HENDERSON

The notion that the ideal way to use probability in making predictions is to begin with a frequentist approach, collect a critical mass of information to supply rational support for the adoption of prior probabilities, and then exploit Bayes's Theorem to forecast the future, is not uncommon or new. This method works well in many cases, but in some, those where the information collected is of a uniform nature (either event A always occurs under given conditions or it never does) and the only rational choice for the prior probability of event A occurring is an extreme value of either 0 or unity, no meaningful application of Bayes's Theorem involving event A is possible. As I am loathe to give up on this frequentist-Bayesian approach, my focus is on constructing a way to deal with these troublesome cases.

It is well known that any ampliative deductive argument is necessarily invalid. This sad fact (sad because ampliative deductive arguments would be ideal) forces us to be careful in how we make our arguments invalid. In practice, the invalidity generally works itself into our "deduction" when we assume that the future will look like the past. It turns out, however, that the key to marrying the frequentist and Bayesian approaches to probability in a general fashion involves assuming just the opposite—that the future is not like the past—at least sometimes.

—J. R. H.

* * *

1. Introduction

In “Are Humans Good Intuitive Statisticians after All? Rethinking Some Conclusions from the Literature on Judgment under Uncertainty,” Leda Cosmides and John Tooby suggest that humans employ an intriguing combination of frequentist and Bayesian approaches to probability theory in arriving at statistical conclusions in everyday life. It is well known that both the frequentist and Bayesian (subjective belief) schools of thought encounter problems when used as bases for an interpretation of probability. It is the purpose of this essay to explore the hybrid model they put forth and see if it passes philosophical muster as a proper interpretation of probability theory. Since Cosmides and Tooby start with a frequentist approach and shore it up with Bayesian tools, concentration will be given to the question, “Can the Cosmides and Tooby model handle single-case probabilities?” I will argue that it cannot, but I suggest that with a few adjustments their account is salvageable. It is important to note here that while Cosmides and Tooby put forth a descriptive view of cognition, I will not argue that the model I put forth is how humans actually think. It might be argued that this is how humans *should* think, but this is secondary to my main objective of solving the single-case problem. Hence, I will not make the prescriptive argument.

Cosmides and Tooby write in response to the conventional wisdom in psychology that the “common sense” of human beings does not work along the lines of a calculus of probability. Included in the psychological body of literature is Kahneman and Tversky’s “On the Psychology of Prediction” which says, among other things, that people use limited probabilistic “rules of thumb” (“heuristics”) in making judgments where knowledge is incomplete rather than using statistically sound procedures. These heuristics are sometimes quite precise but at other times can be wildly inaccurate (Kahneman and Tversky, p. 237). Indeed, “cognitive bias,” “normative fallacy,” “base-rate fallacy,” “overconfidence,” and “conjunction fallacy” have all entered the psychological lexicon to describe human error in probabilistic calculations (Cosmides and Tooby, p. 2).

Cosmides and Tooby argue that the errors in calculation that Kahneman and Tversky turned up are not due to shortcomings in intuitive mathematical ability but rather to the form of the problems given to experimental subjects. An example may clarify this. Casscells and Graboys posed the following medical diagnosis problem to their subjects:

> If a test to detect a disease whose prevalence is 1/1000 has a false positive rate of 5%, what is the chance that a person found to have a positive result actually

> has the disease, assuming that you know nothing of the person's symptoms or signs? ____% (Cosmides and Tooby, p. 21)

Eighteen percent gave the correct Bayesian response of 2%. However, when the question was re-worded using frequency terminology thus:

> 1 out of every 1000 Americans has disease X. A test has been developed to detect when a person has disease X. Every time the test is given to a person who has the disease, the test comes out positive (i.e., the "true positive" rate is 100%). But sometimes the test also comes out positive when it is given to a person who is completely healthy. Specifically, out of every 1000 people who are perfectly healthy, 50 of them test positive for the disease (i.e., the "false positive" rate is 5%).
>
> Imagine that we have assembled a random sample of 1000 Americans. They were selected by lottery. Those who conducted the lottery had no information of the health status of any of these people.
>
> Given the information above: on average, How many people who test positive for the disease will *actually* have the disease? ____ out of ____ (Cosmides and Tooby, p. 24)

something stunning happened: 56% gave the correct answer of 2%. When the following four "probe questions" were asked

1. How many of these 1000 people will have the disease?
2. How many of these 1000 people will have the disease AND test positive for it?
3. How many of these 1000 people will be healthy AND test positive for the disease?
4. How many of the 1000 people will test positive for the disease, whether they have the disease or not?

the number of correct responses rose to 76%.

In a series of experiments designed to show that the improvement in performance is due purely to the presentation of the problem (and that, therefore, people do reason in accordance with a calculus of probability when data are packaged in a frequentist fashion—the Frequentist Hypothesis, first advanced by Gigerenzer), Cosmides and Tooby convincingly maintain that statistical reasoning in humans is bolstered when problems are dealt with in a frequentist manner. From there it is only a short step for Cosmides and Tooby to argue that people are frequentists by nature and that, as such, we calculate in a way consistent with the calculus of probability.

2. The Frequency Interpretation

To get the flavor of the frequency interpretation of probability, consider a sequence of coin tosses. Let the first five tosses have outcomes THHTH (T = tails, H = heads). We say $F^5(T) = .4$; that is to say, $F^5(T) = 2/5$ because two of the first five tosses came out "tails." Define

$$F^n(T) = (\#\text{ of occurrences of "tails"})/n,$$

where n is the total number of tosses. Using the standard mathematical definition of a limit, define

$$F^\infty(T) = \lim_{n \to \infty} F^n(T).$$

If the coin in our example is fair, $F^\infty(T) = .5$. We may now give a technical frequentist definition of probability: "[P]robability is defined in terms of the limit of relative frequency of the occurrence of an attribute in an infinite sequence of events" (Salmon 1979, p. 83). In the language of our example, the probability of tails is $F^\infty(T)$.

There are obvious problems with this interpretation from a practical standpoint, and some not-so-obvious problems from a theoretical standpoint. This in itself is hardly surprising. Indeed, if this conception were free of difficulty, the problem of interpreting the calculus of probability would not exist.

From a practical standpoint, there seems to be no way to ascertain the probability of many events. Given the first billion or so terms of a sequence ($F^1(T), F^2(T), \ldots, F^{1{,}000{,}000{,}000}(T)$), there is no way to find the limit unless we are given a formula for generating the terms (needless to say, this is hardly ever the case). In fact, the limit, regardless of the known terms, can be anywhere from 0 to 1, inclusive.

This might not be as devastating a shortcoming as one might imagine. Bertrand Russell points out that what makes probability useful is that many times we must make judgments from a position of partial ignorance. Though "ignorance is not involved in the concept of probability, [probability] would still have the same meaning for omniscience as for us" (Russell, pp. 353, 354). In other words, probability is used to solve problems of the form "*Given datum A*, what is the likelihood of an occurrence of B?" Given that we are faced with problems in a state of ignorance as Russell says, why should we be guaranteed an answer? We don't need an infinite sequence to see that sometimes there are no answers (or too many answers) to be had. Consider:

> A car travels one mile in a period of time between one and two minutes in duration. What is its most likely average speed?

We may argue that since between one and two minutes elapsed, a period of 1.5 minutes is most likely. This yields an average speed of 40 mph. Similarly, we could say that the car had an average speed between 30 mph and 60 mph, so an average speed of 45 mph is most likely. There are now two answers given, and, further, we had no right to assume "most likely" values of 1.5 minutes and 45 mph. The fact is we simply don't have enough information for a unique, "best" answer. It may be asked why we should expect one. More technically, if probability is a function, it is not necessarily defined on all domains (i.e., over all data sets). That is, we need not demand that *every* data set yield a single, best answer to a given probabilistic question. Just as the natural logarithm function, given by $y = \ln(x)$, is not defined over all real numbers, probability need not be defined over all data sets. Since $\ln(x)$ doesn't have an output for all x, why should probability have an output for all data sets?

More problematic is the charge that the frequency interpretation is useless in the face of the single-case problem. Recall that probability is defined in terms of an infinite sequence, so when we ask for the probability of, say, a "tail" on a *particular* toss of a coin, the frequentist must argue that the probability involves the limit associated with an infinite sequence of this particular toss. This is plainly meaningless, and the problem is well known to Cosmides and Tooby (Cosmides and Tooby, p. 3).

3. The Bayesian Interpretation

Bayesians view probability as an individual's subjective degree of confidence in a hypothesis, and they freely admit these degrees of confidence may vary from person to person. That is, two perfectly rational people may believe to different degrees that, for instance, the Yankees will win their next game against the Red Sox—Smith may be 70% sure of this outcome, while Jones is only 55% certain. The probability, then, of a Yankees win for Smith is .7 while for Jones it is only .55; Bayesians accept that there is no objective measure of probability apart from a person's degree of belief. Now, the object of Bayesian inference is to calculate the probability of a hypothesis given a data set and background information, $P(H|D.B)$, through the use of Bayes's Theorem. The theorem itself may be stated thus:

$$P(H|B.D) = P(H|B) \times P(D|H.B) \,/\, P(D|B), \text{ where } P(D|B) \neq 0.$$

If we give H, D, and B the following interpretation,

H: Hypothesis

B: Background information (highly confirmed observational and theoretical conclusions already in hand)

D: New observational data

we can pronounce on the (prior) probability of a hypothesis. But P(H|D.B) is in part a function of P(H|B). "This means that different people can draw entirely different conclusions from one and the same experiment" (Cosmides and Tooby, p. 6). As an example of this, consider Smith and Jones, two statisticians who observe one hundred tosses of a coin. Of the one hundred tosses, fifty-one result in "heads" and forty-nine result in "tails." Smith believes the coin is fair, but Jones believes it is slightly biased towards "heads." This appears to violate the notion that probability is a function whose range is the closed interval [0, 1] (here 'function' is construed in the narrow, mathematical sense—it maps a point of its domain to a single point in its range). That is, it seems to do violence to the idea that a unique probability results from a single data set. This, however, is not a fair criticism; Bayesians define probability as an *individual's* subjective degree of confidence. Hence, as long as Smith (or Jones) doesn't believe that the coin is simultaneously both fair and biased, a unique result is obtained (that is to say, as long as, say, Smith doesn't form a subjective degree of confidence that the coin is fair and, on the same evidence, a subjective degree of confidence that the same coin is biased, no violation of probability *as a function* occurs; the fact that Smith and Jones may disagree on their conclusions as to the nature of the coin doesn't come into play because they are different individuals).

More troubling for Bayesians is that defining probability as subjective degree of belief allows for violations of the probability calculus. Salmon reports that "[c]ertain seventeenth-century gamblers . . . believed more than they disbelieved in getting at least one double six in twenty-four throws [of two dice]. . . . Computation showed . . . that the probability of getting double six, under the conditions specified, is less than one half" (Salmon 1979, p. 68). Here is a specific instance of a subjective degree of confidence that is not in accord with calculated values of probability. The gamblers had a subjective degree of belief of over 50% that a double six would occur within 24 throws; straightforward calculations (and empirical evidence) demonstrate that their degrees of belief should have been below 50%. It is now widely accepted that when intuitions (those of the gamblers in this case) disagree with the probability calculus (the calculated values of probability), the intuitions are wrong (Cosmides and Tooby, p. 2), so we see that the Bayesian approach is susceptible to demonstrably incoherent conclusions.

4. Cosmides and Tooby's Hybrid Interpretation

Cosmides and Tooby begin by pointing out that Bayes's Theorem is an elementary result of the axioms of probability. As such, use of it is open to subjectivists and frequentists alike since the axioms

> can be interpreted in a number of ways, and both the subjectivist and frequentist interpretations of probability are consistent with these axioms. One can use Bayes' rule to calculate the probability of a single event . . . which entails *interpreting* probability as a subjective degree of confidence. But one can also use Bayes' rule to calculate a relative frequency. . . . In this second case, one interprets probability as a frequency: the inputs to the equation are frequencies, and the output is a frequency. (Cosmides and Tooby, p. 8, their emphasis)

Having established that Bayes's Theorem is available to statisticians of all stripes (this is uncontroversial), Cosmides and Tooby argue that humans begin the decision making procedure by arranging observed data in a frequentist manner ("we were successful 5 out of the last 20 times we hunted in the north canyon" [Cosmides and Tooby, pp. 15, 16]). It is convincing that people would in fact collect data in this way, for "[n]o sense organ can discern that if we go to the north canyon, there is a .25 probability that today's hunt will be successful" (Cosmides and Tooby, p. 15). It was to our ancestors' advantage not to immediately convert these data into a single-event probability for three reasons:

> (1) A judgment based on large numbers of observations is more reliable than one based on a small number (1 out of 4 versus 25 out of 100). The number of observations is lost in the conversion to .25.
>
> (2) Updating information is trivial in a frequentist representation. 5 out of 20 becomes 5 out of 21 after an unsuccessful hunt; transforming .25 is considerably more difficult. Further, if two data sets are collected separately, it is easy to combine them into a larger, more comprehensive set.
>
> (3) Reference classes may be constructed or reconstructed after the fact in frequentist representations. If we hunted in the north canyon 100 times and the last 20 were successful 5 times, but the last 20 hunts were in winter, we could easily construct summer and winter hunting reference classes. Each of these could be supplemented the following year. (Cosmides and Tooby, p. 16)

Reason (1) above alludes to the search for sufficient statistics. A sufficient statistic is one that condenses a data set so that information is not lost (Mood, Graybill, and Boes, p. 301). For purposes of lending credence to a judgment or updating a data set, the number of observations is necessary (notice here that the order of successes and failures, for instance, is not viewed as important in any reference class; hence, 2 out of 5 carries all the information in S(uccess), F(ailure), F, S, F). It is clearly more efficient to memorize "5 out of 20" than to memorize an ordered sequence of 20 successes and failures. It is worth mentioning that ".25, 20 observations" carries all the information of "5 out of 20" and could be supplemented just as easily.

Reason (3) recognizes the desirability of homogeneous reference classes. A reference class is homogeneous if it is impossible to relevantly partition it (Salmon 1990, p. 63). That is, the class of summer hunts is homogeneous if whenever it is partitioned (say, into rainy summer and dry summer hunts), the partitions each have the same ratio of successful to unsuccessful hunts. It is obviously to one's advantage to know where to hunt and, say, when to hunt. If the north canyon is only full of game in the summer while the south canyon is bountiful in the winter, information more important to a hunter-gatherer society is hard to imagine.

After a "critical mass" of data has been collected, the relative frequency may be used as input for Bayes's rule. Cosmides and Tooby claim that "[w]hen fed into an appropriate decision rule, a frequency representation can easily produce a subjective degree of confidence" (Cosmides and Tooby, p. 16). It is vital that the frequency representation be recast as a subjective degree of belief if the single-case problem is to be solved. Otherwise, the output of Bayes's rule would be a frequency still vulnerable to the shortcomings of all frequencies. If the output is a subjective degree of confidence, the single-case problem is not a concern. It should here be noted, then, that a subtle shift has taken place. The frequency representation that is the output of Bayes's rule is now being interpreted as a *subjective degree of belief.* Is this justified? In short, yes. *Anything* may serve as the basis of a subjective degree of belief, precisely because it is subjective. The shift might just as easily have been made before Bayes's rule was employed. That is, once a critical mass of data had been collected, this frequency could have been interpreted as a degree of belief and then plugged into Bayes's rule. The output, then, would likewise be a degree of belief. As this will simplify the language to be used, and it is equivalent to Cosmides and Tooby's position with respect to calculating prior probabilities, we will proceed as if the change in interpretation had been made prior to the application of Bayes's rule.

5. Observations

We mentioned at the end of section 3 that the subjective belief interpretation allowed incoherent assignments of probability insofar as it admits of bad betting strategies, but Cosmides and Tooby said that the subjective belief model was in harmony with the axioms of probability. This conflict is merely terminological (and common [Salmon 1979, p. 68]). If we take Cosmides and Tooby to be inputting mere subjective degrees of confidence into Bayes's rule, we do them an injustice. If one sees a coin tossed one thousand times with all but one outcome "heads," one might still believe the coin is fair—one might see this as only a highly atypical string of tosses. Indeed, if a fair coin is tossed often enough (true, a very great many times), such a subsequence is possible. This, however, is not what Cosmides and Tooby prescribe. The procedure for generating input for Bayes's rule they lay out is better described as "logical" than "subjective." Salmon says that in the logical interpretation of probability, "probability measures the degree of confidence that would be rationally *justified by the available evidence*" (Salmon 1979, p. 68, my emphasis). Notice here that while we speak of subjective degrees of confidence, it is not subjective at all. The prior probabilities generated by the method of Cosmides and Tooby represent "an objective logical relation between statements that formulate evidence and other statements . . . whose truth or falsity is not fully determined by the evidence" (Salmon 1979, p. 68). In the one-thousand-coin-toss example just described, Cosmides and Tooby could not infer that the coin is fair. Instead, they would be forced to assume a degree of confidence of .001 for a result of "tails" (if they considered one thousand tosses a sufficient sample). Therefore, the fact that the subjective belief model allows for bad betting strategies is unimportant for our purposes; Cosmides and Tooby do not avail themselves of it. The logical interpretation, on the other hand, involves no violations of the probability calculus (Salmon 1979, p. 78).

It is at this stage that Cosmides and Tooby's method of generating input must be differentiated from two theories that, at first glance, resemble it strongly. They are Russell's Finite-Frequency Theory and Hans Reichenbach's Rule of Induction by Enumeration.

> The Finite-Frequency Theory starts from the following definition: Let B be any finite class, and A be any other class. We want to define the chance that a member of B chosen at random will be a member of A. . . . We define this probability as the number of Bs that are As divided by the total number of Bs. (Russell, pp. 350, 351)

An example will clarify this definition. Imagine we toss a coin ten times, and we wish to know the probability that, say, the seventh toss was a "tail." Further imagine that there were a total of six results of "tails" in the ten tosses. The total number of tosses (Bs) is ten, and the total number of "tails" (As) is six. Therefore, the probability that the seventh toss was a "tail" is 6/10 or .6.

While Cosmides and Tooby, like Russell, take a finitist approach, they are asking an entirely different (and more problematic) question. Rather than asking the probability of an event that has already occurred, they are asking for a prior degree of confidence for an event that has yet to happen. It is said to be more problematic for an obvious Humean reason: What can events in the past tell us about events in the future? It is clear that Russell's calculation applies to the situation for which he intends it, but it is not so obvious how it is of any help with Cosmides's and Tooby's problem. Fortunately for Cosmides and Tooby, all we really need from past events is a *starting point* from which to begin thinking about future events. From there, other tools are used (namely, Bayes's Theorem).

Reichenbach's Rule of Induction by Enumeration is a tool used by frequency theorists. It works like this: Given that $F^n(T) = m/n$, infer $F^\infty(T) = m/n$ (actually, this is Salmon's version of Reichenbach's rule); Reichenbach says to infer

$$m/n - \delta < F^\infty(T) < m/n + \delta \text{ for small, positive } \delta.$$

As Reichenbach gives no procedure for determining δ, Salmon eliminates it altogether (Salmon 1979, p. 138, n. 11). This is intuitively pleasing, and Reichenbach argues for it ingeniously: Either the sequence will converge or it will not (it has a limit or it doesn't). If it doesn't converge, *no* method for inferring a limit will work. If it does converge, given any small but positive δ, there is a number N such that $F^s(T)$ is within δ of the limit L for every s > N (technically,

$$|F^s(T) - L| < \delta, \text{ for all } s > N).$$

Another way: there is a point in the sequence where every term in the sequence which follows that point is closer to the limit than any pre-set positive distance. So no method of inference works if there is no limit, and this method works if there is one. There is no method for finding N (given δ) unless a rule for generating terms of the sequence is given, but as new data arrive, the inference may be suitably adjusted. Again, Cosmides and Tooby's goal is different from that of Reichenbach. Reichenbach seeks a final answer to a question of probability; Cosmides and Tooby are merely setting a position from which to start using an inferential tool. That is, Cosmides and Tooby only use finite strings of data to establish a subjective degree of confidence in a particular proposition P so that P may be further explored using Bayes's rule. This is a considerably less heady objective than that of Reichenbach, who, using the same finite string of data, seeks a unique and objective probability P. Hence, criticisms of Reichenbach (for instance, that no value of $F^{\infty}(T)$ is ever ruled out) do not apply to Cosmides and Tooby.

There is a problem with Cosmides and Tooby's account that cannot be solved within the parameters that they have laid down. Consider the following scenario. A hunter-gatherer society has a religious ritual that is performed once a year. One of their two sacred hunting grounds is secretly and randomly chosen by the high priest to be the site of the Hunt of the Gods. Of the twenty times the East Ground has been chosen, the hunt has been successful seven times; of the twenty hunts in the West Grounds, none has been successful. This year the hunt is successful. If the site of the hunt is unknown to the builders of the sacred pyre, what do they calculate the probability of the hunt having been held at the West Hunting Grounds to be? Taking the prior probabilities to be .35 (7/20) and 0 (0/20) for the success of hunts in the East and West Grounds, respectively, calculation yields a value of 0. In fact, no number of applications of Bayes's rule with these prior probabilities will ever give results other than certainty that the hunt occurred in the East Grounds; Bayes's rule is of no use to our hunter-gatherers in this situation. This highlights a general problem: Successive uses of Bayes's rule only converges to the true probability value of an event if the prior probabilities are non-0 and non-unitary (strictly between 0 and 1).

There are possibilities that are worse still. If the East Grounds, like the West, had never yielded a successful hunt, Bayes's rule would not only fail to admit evolution of posterior probabilities, the rule would not even be applicable. The fraction on the right side of the equation given in Bayes's Theorem would be 0/0, a disaster, mathematically speaking.

It may be argued that the two situations described can be solved in the same way: If one or more prior probability is 0, then a critical mass of observations has not been collected, and more observations would have to be made until the 0-probability event has finally been observed to occur. That is, Bayes's Theorem must not be brought into play until a non-0 prior probability has been established for each of the competing options. What if this never happens? What if, unbeknownst to our primitive society, one of the options is an impossibility? Generations would come and go, but no useful application of Bayes's rule would ever be admissable. True, the society would gather encyclopedic data, but it would all be of a frequentist sort, of such a nature as to not lend itself to use in Bayesian estimation and still frustratingly susceptible to the single-case problem. This is part of a general problem in their account. Cosmides and Tooby tell us that "[o]nce a frequency representation has been computed [from the data collected], it can serve as input to decision rules" (Cosmides and Tooby, p. 16), but how many observations are needed? Millions are not (necessarily) necessary, but Bayes's rule does no good until each event to be considered has a non-0 prior probability (until each event to be considered has been observed to occur at least once). This might never happen. On the other hand, if our society decides an event is impossible after many failed trials, it will be considered impossible forever more (for purposes of Bayesian inference) even if it is merely unlikely and had not occurred before a decision to form a prior degree of confidence was made. It must be pointed out here that use of Bayes's rule was seen as the solution to the single-case problem by Cosmides and Tooby. If they are not guaranteed the ability to apply it, they cannot claim to have solved the problem.

6. Solution

We should be very clear about the difficulty just discussed. It is not devastating to Cosmides and Tooby that there is no set number of observations that must be made before the frequentist data are transformed into a degree of confidence for use in Bayes's rule. Even if, say, the first one hundred trials do not yield a final probability measure of an event, repeated application of Bayes's rule (and the further collection of data that goes hand-in-hand with it) will allow for more accurate prior probabilities to be calculated. What *is* a concern for Cosmides and Tooby's account is that an event may not be given anything but a prior probability of 0 until it has been observed. Further, until an event has a non-0 prior probability it contributes nothing to any calculation of posterior probability using Bayes's rule. That is, no Bayesian inference that involves an event A may ever be meaningfully made until A has been observed at least one time.

A real life example may be illustrative. In 1911, Albert Einstein predicted light passing very near the sun would be deflected from its original path by .83 seconds of arc (Schneer, p. 312) in keeping with his 1905 special theory of relativity. In 1919 British astronomers mounted expeditions to observe a solar eclipse from a small town in northeast Brazil and an island in the Gulf of Guinea. They found the deflection of light rays from several stars was, within the experimental uncertainties, equal to what Einstein had predicted. Here is a situation *made* for Bayes's Theorem. There is a huge supply of background data from earlier study of light and gravity, a bold hypothesis, and stunning new data. Alas, Cosmides and Tooby cannot apply Bayes's rule in this case since there were never any observations of (or even attempts to observe) deflection of light in this manner. In 1922, when the results were confirmed, Cosmides and Tooby would *still* not be able to apply Bayes's rule (or at least not meaningfully). Either no prior probability of deflection of light could be ascertained because not enough observations had been made (in which case the rule could not be applied), or (taking the one success from the only trial in

1919) such deflection would be viewed as a certainty prior to application of the rule.

The difficulties of Cosmides and Tooby may be avoided by recognizing the fact that for meaningful applications of Bayes's Theorem to be made, an at least slightly open mind toward outcomes of experiments is necessary. That is, prior probabilities should take on values strictly between ("between" in a noninclusive sense) 0 and 1. It is laudable that Cosmides and Tooby wish to base their prior probabilities on all and only available evidence, but we have seen this can get in the way of using Bayes's rule, and, hence, solution of the single-case problem. To preserve the use of available evidence and keep prior probabilities from taking values of 0 or 1, a three-part rule may be proposed:

(I) If $n > 0$ trials have been run, and all trials have been unsuccessful, assume the $n+1^{st}$ trial is successful to set prior probability of the event occurring at $1/(n + 1)$.

(II) If $n > 0$ trials have been run, and all trials have been successful, assume the $n+1^{st}$ trial is unsuccessful to set prior probability of the event occurring at $n/(n + 1)$.

(III) If $n > 0$ trials have been run, and m trials have been successful (with $0 > m > n$), set the prior probability of the event occurring at m/n.

In the case of the 1919 eclipse, where no trials had been conducted, any value p (0, 1) for the prior probability could be argued for since there is no data to set a unique value. To avoid ambiguity, a default value of, say, .5 may be stipulated (though, admittedly, this seems unsatisfactory—indeed, most would have set a very low prior probability for the bending of light rays, but Einstein's degree of confidence was quite high). Rather, an alternative method of setting prior probabilities seems to be called for here. In a case where no trials of a particular case have been conducted, we may opt instead to set the prior probability of the truth of the theory that makes the prediction to be tested. That is, in the 1919 case we may try to establish a prior probability for the theory of relativity. This is simpler than it sounds. Only a finite number of experiments/observations (of any variety) have been conducted/made since the dawn of time, so necessarily only a finite number of experiments having anything to do with relativity have been conducted. Those which would have been predicted (or, those which are retrodicted) by the theory of relativity count as positive instances, and those not retrodicted by the theory count as negative instances. The ratio of positive instances to total instances gives the prior probability of the truth of the theory. For instance, if there are 15,000 total experiments done which are relevant to relativity theory, and 12,000 are retrodicted by it, the prior probability of Einstein's theory is 12,000/15,000, or .8. Thus, the prior probability of light rays bending could be set at .8 (similarly, if all 15,000 had been retrodicted by the theory, we would assume the 15001st trial violated the theory; if all 15,000 violated the theory, we would assume the 15001st trial was a success—though it seems unlikely anyone would still take it seriously). While it may be the case that light rays bend even though Einstein's theory is wrong, .8 would be a conservative prior probability, but slight errors are acceptable since we are not setting a final probability value for the theory based only on previous experiments.

Clearly, if one follows this new rule, only values in the open interval (0, 1) would be assigned as prior probabilities, but the weight of the number of observations would still be respected. For instance, if four trials had all been unsuccessful, a prior probability for the event of .2 (1/5) would be established, but if twenty trials had all been failures, the prior probability for the event would only be .0476 (1/21).

This rule must be justified, but the argument is a simple one. The rule only recognizes the finite nature of the data gathering process. It often happens that highly (but finitely) confirmed hypotheses turn out to be false (consider "All swans are white" and the discovery of black swans in Australia). It seems rational in the extreme to admit that propositions, no matter how well confirmed, *may* turn out to be false. Similarly, highly disconfirmed propositions may turn out to be true. The new rule (of assuming one more experiment that contradicts the rest) simply acknowledges these possibilities. Further, in the case of unanimously confirmed (or disconfirmed) hypotheses that have had many trials, the prior probability would be changed only slightly by the assumption of one only more test. In exchange for this small departure from the observed evidence, we receive the ability to use Bayes's rule in our calculations of probability and escape the single-case problem.

7. Summary

It is well known that both the frequentist and Bayesian accounts of probability are flawed when taken on their own: the frequency interpretation fails to account for single-case probabilities, and the Bayesian interpretation allows for violations of the probability calculus. Cosmides and Tooby have suggested a combination of these two approaches as an explanation of how humans actually calculate probabilities. They propose gathering information in a frequentist fashion and, when a sufficient bulk of data has been collected, using these data to set a subjective degree of confidence (though there is nothing subjective about it), or prior probability, for use in the inferential rule set out in Bayes's Theorem. It was hoped that the shortcomings of the frequentists and Bayesians would thus be overcome. The single-case problem is solved by application of Bayes's rule, and statistical incoherence is avoided by forcing assigned prior probabilities to conform to available data.

Unfortunately, requiring prior probabilities to reflect the data exactly doesn't always allow meaningful use of Bayes's rule (and sometimes it doesn't allow the use of it at all). These problems arise when prior probabilities are equal to 0, and unless Cosmides and Tooby are able to assure us the use of Bayes's rule, they can in no way claim to have solved the single-case problem. To ensure our access to Bayes's rule, I suggested a "legislation of open-mindedness," a rule that disallows the assignment of prior probabilities values of 0 or 1. This rule guarantees the use of Bayes's rule while, to a very large extent, preserving information gained from observation (and the more observations that have been made, the more information is preserved). This rule is justified by recognition of the finite nature of human observation; no number of observations—10, 100, or 1000 consecutive occurrences of event A in circumstance B—can make A a certainty given B. Hence, a rule is proposed to require that prior probabilities are never assigned extreme values.

In the case of testing a hypothesis on the basis of never before observed data (e.g., the 1919 observation of light bending), a data-based assignment of prior probability is impossible—there are no data upon which to base it. A default value of .5 was suggested, but this appears ad hoc, maybe to the extent that this proposed solution should be rejected. It is unfortunate that this is where the problem arises, because it is in just these situations where new theories are most rigorously tested; a bold prediction of a counter-intuitive experimental result provides the best opportunity to confirm or disconfirm a hypothesis. To avoid this problem, I suggested that rather than the hypothesis itself having a prior probability assigned, the theory that predicts it should be subjected to this treatment. In this way we may preserve our reliance on observed data to set appropriate prior probabilities.

JAMES R. HENDERSON
SUNY Buffalo

BIBLIOGRAPHY

Cosmides, Leda, and John Tooby. 1996. "Are Humans Good Intuitive Statisticians after All? Rethinking Some Conclusions from the Literature on Judgment under Uncertainty." *Cognition* 58: 1–73.

Gigerenzer, Gerd. 1991. "How to Make Cognitive Illusions Disappear: Beyond Heuristics and Biases." *European Review of Social Psychology* 4: 83–115.

Kahneman, D., and A. Tversky. 1973. "On the Psychology of Prediction." *Psychological Review* 80: 237–51.

Mood, Alexander, Franklin Graybill, and Duane Boes. 1974. *Introduction to the Theory of Statistics.* New York: McGraw-Hill.

Reichenbach, Hans. 1949. *The Theory of Probability.* Berkeley: University of California Press.

Russell, Bertrand. 1948. *Human Knowledge: Its Scope and Limits.* New York: American Book-Stratford Press.

Salmon, Wesley. 1979. *The Foundations of Scientific Inference.* Pittsburgh: University of Pittsburgh Press.

———. 1990. *Four Decades of Scientific Explanation.* Minneapolis: University of Minnesota Press.

Schneer, Cecil. 1960. *The Evolution of Physical Science.* Lanham: University Press of America.

6

Probability as a Guide in Life

HENRY E. KYBURG, JR.

As part of a general project to explore the practical consequences of adopting one interpretation or another of probability, it seemed appropriate to examine the role of probability as a guide to decision. Of course, it is as a factor in the computation of mathematical expectation that probability plays this role; but I felt that I could leave considerations of utility to one side while I concentrated on probability.

It is no real news that an interpretation of probability that identifies it with relative frequency runs headlong into the problem of the single case. Even if we contemplate a long finite sequence of decisions, that sequence itself can be construed as a single complex case. If we could resolve the problem of the reference class—the problem of deciding what frequency was relevant to the single case at issue—then we would be on the way to a solution.

One of the standard features of Bayesianism is that it tends to reduce degrees of belief to choices among actions in a quite behavioristic way. This suggests that, since the Bayesian construes probabilities as degrees of belief, there is a strong connection between the use of probability as a guide in life and the Bayesian interpretation of probability.

It struck me that there was something suspect about using choice behavior as a guide to probability, and probability as a guide to choice behavior. This suspicion was correct, and the strongest result in this paper is that despite its use in seminars for executives, the Bayesian approach has nothing to offer in the way of guidance. Given fixed utilities, any decision an agent is disposed to can be rationalized.

It will come as no surprise that I feel that the evidential interpretation of probability will yield the guidance we seek in life.

—H. E. K.

* * *

ABSTRACT

Bishop Butler (1736) said that probability was the very guide of life. But what interpretations of probability can serve this function? It isn't hard to see that empirical (frequency) views won't do, and many recent writers—for example, John Earman, who has said that Bayesianism is "the only game in town"—have been persuaded by various Dutch Book arguments that only subjective probability will perform the function required. We will defend the thesis that probability construed in this way offers very little guidance, Dutch Book arguments notwithstanding. We will sketch a way out of the impasse.

1. Introduction

Maimonodes wrote philosophy as a Guide for the Perplexed. There are many things that people are perplexed about: from the ultimate aim of life to the issue of whether to lead the ace of spades or a small club. Mathematical expectation is clearly relevant at one end of the extreme—there lies the classical gambling situation. But it has also been applied at the other end, for example, by Pascal in formulating his "wager." The mathematical expectation of an act A can be defined as follows:

$$Exp(A) = \sum_i P(O_i \mid A)U(O_i \mid A).$$

where we evaluate the expectation of act A as the sum of the products of the probability of each possible outcome of that act, multiplied by the utility of that outcome, given the act. The principle in question, which we all learned at our mothers' knees, is the principle of maximizing mathematical expectation: Given a choice of acts $A_1, A_2, \ldots A_m$ choose an act A_j such that $Exp(A_j)$ is maximal, that is, such that no other act yields a greater mathematical expectation. (It is worth observing already that this principle may not yield a unique act. Maybe it doesn't matter whether you lead a spade or a club; maybe it doesn't matter whether you marry Bill or Robert.)

Thus Pascal looked at the mathematical expectation of Believing: bliss, given that God exists multiplied by the perhaps small probability that God exists plus minor inconvenience, multiplied by the probability that God does not exist, and compared it to the mathematical expectation of Doubting: eternal suffering given that God exists, multiplied by the small probability that God exists, plus the savings in time and candles, multiplied by the probability that God does not exist.

There are two functions we need to think about. One is the utility function U, about which I'll have next to nothing to say, though utility raises a number of deep and important philosophical issues. The other is the probability function, on which I shall focus. There have been a number of ways of understanding probability. We will look at a very rough characterization of three main ways of approaching probability, and then explore the ramifications of these approaches when it comes to taking mathematical expectation as a guide to life.

2. History of Interpretations of Probability

The history of probability, in the quantitative sense—that is, in the sense in which it has been associated with chance—is a rather short one, as fundamental ideas go. The calculus of probability is associated with the name of the Chevalier de la Mere because of a problem he raised in connection with the fair division of the stakes in an incomplete game of chance. The date of the discussion was the seventeenth century (the participants were the Chevalier de la Mere, Pascal, and Fermat), but, of course, the question could not have been raised at all had there not been some understanding of the use of probability in the form of mathematical expectation as a guide in life—at least the life of gamblers.

The particular problem concerned the fair division of the stakes in a game of chance in which each of the two players had earned a certain fraction of the number of points required to win the game. The framing of the problem assumed implicitly that what was needed was an assessment of each player's *expectation*. The problem posed was to calculate that expectation in terms of the probability of each player winning each point. It is worth noting that the issue concerned the evaluation of probabilities, not the evaluation of utilities.

The first hundred years of the study of probability were concerned primarily with games of chance. (Serious questions about the meaning of "probability" were not raised until late in the nineteenth century; serious differences of opinion did not arise until the twentieth.) Now games of chance have a curious property: they involve just the same ideas that were to come to be involved in the conflicting interpretations of probability. That is, they involve aspects of long-run frequencies, aspects of logical entailment or evidence, and aspects of personal belief.

Everybody knows that a die lands with the one spot up a sixth of the time (unless it has been tampered with!). Almost everybody, except inspired gamblers, knows that the fact that a die has just landed with a one spot up does not affect the chance that it will land with a one spot up on the next toss. These chances correspond, intuitively, to long-run frequencies.

Almost everybody would take 1:5 to be the "fair" odds for betting on a one, *under most circumstances*. If, as is natural, "fair" is cashed out in terms of expectation (a bet at these odds renders the mathematical expectations of both parties the same), then if betting behavior is an indication of "degree of belief," under most circumstances one should have a degree of belief equal to 1/6 that the die will yield a one. This tradition is quite new, starting around 1930 with Frank Ramsey (1931) and Bruno de Finetti (1980) and has been widely pursued in recent years (Earman 1992; Skyrms 1966; Savage 1954; Jeffrey 1965).

A natural and intuitive heuristic for evaluating probabilities consists in "counting possibilities." Obviously this doesn't always work well (consider the loaded die) but it has seemed possible to refine it to become a tool for finding "objective" subjective probabilities: objective in the sense that they are determined by an arbitrary set of rules that could be agreed on by a group of agents. But they would still be arbitrary. This is the tradition that starts with Laplace (1951), and continues on through Harold Jeffreys (1930) to Rudolf Carnap (1950), and, in a slightly different direction, to E. T. Jaynes (1958).

2.1. *Frequency*

Frequency data, degrees of belief, plausible logical relations, all come to the same thing in the well-regulated gambling situations to which probability was initially applied. To make distinctions reasonably among the alternatives, we should consider less well-regulated domains: insurance, balls in urns, loaded dice, and so on. Typically in these situations our knowledge will be incomplete and approximate.

Consider insuring the life of Fred Smith, a 40-year-old man who smokes, avoids cholesterol, exercises, and comes from a long-lived family. Should we give him a thousand dollars' worth of insurance for a premium of forty dollars? Call this act A. We calculate:

$$Exp(A) = \sum_i P(O_i \mid A)\, U(O_i \mid A).$$

$$= P(D)(-\$960) + P(\neg D)(\$40)$$

Since in this simple case, $P(\neg D) = 1 - P(D)$ and it is plausible (for an insurance company) to take the utility of money to be proportional to its amount, all we need to evaluate the act of insuring Mr. Smith is the value of $P(D)$. But the frequency with which Mr. Smith dies in the coming year is either 0 or 1. We don't know which. If it is 0, we should insure him; if it is 1, we should decline to insure him. That's no help to us in making a decision. Perhaps it is not the frequency corresponding to the unique proposition at issue that we should be concerned with, but the frequency associated with some related class. For example, could we look at mortality tables? But Mr. Smith is not a member of any class covered by the mortality tables, since they concern only those who have already died.

We are missing a step: perhaps what we need is to *extrapolate* those frequencies from the mortality tables into the future. For example, we take the death rate of 43-year-old men from the table, and extrapolate it into the future. We assume that the future will be like the past, and that in the next few years, 43-year-old men will continue to die at the same rate.

A trivial problem is that we cannot expect that 43-year-old men will continue to die at *exactly* the same rate, or that the rate will remain unchanged with developments in nutrition, health care, and warfare. But under normal circumstances, at least for a while, we have reason to think the death rate will be close to its historical value.

The serious problem is that this approach is no help: Mr. Smith is a member of many classes for which we have statistics, and for which we can project the statistics into the future. Which class do we base our probability on? Reichenbach (1949) recognized this problem, and recommended that we use the "smallest" class about which we have "adequate" statistics.

The trouble with this recommendation is that the smallest class is small indeed: it will be the intersection of all the classes to which we know that Mr. Smith belongs—generally it will be the singleton of Mr. Smith—and we will have no useful frequency knowledge concerning this class that we can project. Even if this class is ruled out, for example, by Reichenbach's proviso that this be the smallest class *about which we have adequate statistics* we have a problem. We may have data about 43-year-old men, data about 43-year-old men who are smokers, data about 43-year-old men who exercise, but no data about 43-year-old men who both smoke and exercise.

In short, there are many known frequencies that may be taken to bear on Fred Smith's longevity, and the frequency theory of probability itself gives us no way of combining these frequencies. Nor could it, since these are merely the known frequencies, and the frequency interpretation of probability is concerned with all frequencies (all frequencies related to collectives, all frequencies related to a well-specified chance setup, etc.) and not just those that are (approximately) known.

These problems have not gone unnoticed by statisticians who have adopted an empirical interpretation of probability but who recognize the need for grounded decision making. Early among these writers was one of the fathers of modern statistics, Jerzy Neyman. An ardent frequentist, but married to no particular version of the frequency theory, Neyman recognized that no useful probability could be attributed to such propositions as Fred Smith's surviving for a year—that is, no probability other than 0 or 1; using these probabilities depends on our knowing whether he survives or not, which we don't.

What can we do, then? Neyman points out that while we can't be sure of the outcome of our deal with Fred, we can be *quite* sure of the outcome of a long series of similar deals with 43-year-old males. Put otherwise, we can characterize the *rule* according to which we give 43-year-old males a thousand dollars' worth of insurance for $40 in terms of its long-run properties.

More generally, we may look on statistics as yielding guides to "inductive behavior" (Neyman 1957; Neyman 1947). The function of statistical analysis is to help us to arrive at a general rule that has satisfactory long-run properties. For example, in the manufacture of monkey wrenches we do not want to ship defective wrenches. On the other hand, we do not want to spend all our profits in the inspection of the wrenches we ship. We compromise by inspecting a certain number of the wrenches in each crate of wrenches we ship. We withhold the shipment if more than *k* of the *n* wrenches in the sample are defective. This sampling inspection, under ordinary circumstances in which neither all nor none of the wrenches manufactured are defective, demonstrably reduces the proportion of defective wrenches shipped.

Is this using probability as a guide in life? It is at least arguable that it is not. Relative to the assumptions involved (that there is a fixed long-run rate at which defectives are manufactured, that they are produced *at random*, that they find their way into crates *at random*, and that the sampling is *random*—where each occurrence of "random" is given a long-run frequency interpretation—the reduction in the number of defective wrenches shipped is simply a logical consequence. True, it is a consequence that depends on probabilities construed as long-run frequencies, but the consequence itself is one that holds "with probability one."

Contrast the purchaser of a crate of wrenches. While the manufacturer is adopting a rule (the sampling inspection rule) with certain long-run consequences, the purchaser of the crate of wrenches might adopt his own rule: Reject the crate of wrenches if more than *k* of *n* sampled wrenches are defective. It is in fact the same rule . . . but what is it to the purchaser if the rule has certain long-run properties? He is not contemplating purchasing an unending sequence of crates of wrenches. He is considering purchasing the crate on the floor at his feet. What concerns him is what he knows about that particular crate—for example, that it was packed by Compulsive Karl, who can't help but look closely at each wrench as he packs it.

In short, the long-run performance of the inspection sampling rule is of interest to the manufacturer, but is only a question of probability by courtesy; the application of the rule to a particular crate of wrenches is what concerns the purchaser of that crate, and while this application is an application of probability as a guide in life, it depends on everything the purchaser knows, and not merely the long-run properties of the rule.

Almost the same problems face us when it comes to extending this approach to the testing of statistical hypotheses. Accepting and rejecting *particular* statistical hypotheses depends on more than the calculation of long-run frequencies. This has been emphasized in the frequentist statistical literature: the application of statistics requires mature statistical judgment. It has been argued (Mayo 1996) that controlling long-run errors—in the jargon of statistics, errors of type I and errors of type II—is what is essential to the growth of scientific knowledge. But as Mayo's book illustrates admirably, the question of *what* long-run error frequencies to apply to a particular case is not at all trivial.

The general problem of taking long-run frequencies to be a guide to life is that it is particular cases that we face in making life's decisions, and there are often all too many possible long-run frequencies that could be applied to a particular case. Each determines its own mathematical expectation.

2.2. Logic

An alternative interpretation of probability takes probability to be a logical relation between sentences. The first detailed treatment of probability along these lines is due to Carnap, who showed that once you have a probability measure (i.e., a nonnegative additive measure with a maximum value of 1) defined over all the sentences of a language, you can express conditional logical probabilities as the ratio of these measures: that is, the probability of sentence h, given total evidence e is the ratio of the measure of $h \wedge e$ to the measure of e.

But these probabilities are of little help to us, since there is so little agreement as to what a reasonable probability measure on the sentences of a formal language might be. If, as is common, we adopt a first-order language with an infinite number of atomic sentences, then no uniform measure is possible. Carnap, perhaps the most dedicated enthusiast of this approach, never settled on the measure of choice, and, toward the end of his life, drew closer and closer to the subjective interpretation of probability. We shall therefore, temporarily, postpone the discussion of the relation between mathematical expectation and "logical" probabilities.

2.3. Belief

To construe probability as a matter of subjective belief is the hallmark of the "Bayesian" approach to probability. It is this approach that seems to promise the most. Bayesianism is closely tied to decision theory from the outset: the degree of belief of an agent in *S* is behavioristically measured by the odds at which he would bet on *S*. Furthermore, this approach is politically correct: one person's opinion is as good as another's. Finally, according to many people John Earman is correct in calling Subjective Bayesian Probability "the only game in town."

Can Bishop Butler be vindicated by Bayesianism?

Let us examine Bayesian probability a little more closely. Your belief in *S* is identified with the odds at which you would be willing to bet on *S*. This crudely behavioristic idea is Ramsey's; even more crudely, it comes to this: the agent should put his money where his mouth is.

That degrees of belief are to conform to the laws of probability follows as a conclusion from "Dutch Book" arguments. Ramsey observed that if the agent's beliefs fail to satisfy the axioms of the probability calculus—in modern terms, if the beliefs, as determined by the money/mouth formula, are incoherent—then a "clever bookie" could present the agent with a set of bets under which the agent will lose, however the events turn out.

Canonical Example: Suppose the agent is willing to bet at 2:1 on heads, and also at 2:1 on tails. Poor agent! The Clever Bookie makes bets on both sides, and wins however the coin lands.

False! We supposed only that our agent was "incoherent"—that is, had degrees of belief that conflicted with the probability calculus, and that these degrees of belief could be interpreted behavioristically as his willingness to accept certain bets. We did *not* suppose that the agent was deductively incompetent. But if he is not deductively incompetent, he will not actually make both bets at once: having made the first bet, he will decline the second bet. Having made the second bet, he will decline the first bet. Quite independently of probability or partial belief, we already know that no rational agent will have a book made against him. This is not guidance from probability, but guidance from arithmetic.

A better way to construe the constraint of coherence is *dispositionally*: in effect we could require that the degrees of belief of the agent correspond to *posted odds*. That is, we *require* that the agent post odds on a field of events, and be willing to take either side of any bet at the posted odds. If the posted odds do not conform to the probability calculus, that is, if they are not coherent, the agent can be forced to lose. But why should the agent do any such thing? It is sometimes said that you can *force* an agent to do this: if worst comes to worst, you can put a gun to his head. But no, this won't work. To "force" the agent to post odds is precisely to apply utility sanctions that should be taken into account in the first place. The sanctions often contemplated quite swamp any agent's degrees of belief.

Nevertheless, we can achieve the same end, step by step, by stipulating that the dispositions should rationally be closed under composition: that is, if the agent is disposed to accept bet *A* and disposed to accept bet *B*, then he should be disposed to accept (bet *A* and bet *B*).

Complementation is more problematic. Composition requires that we be prepared to make any combination of bets that we are willing to make. This is perfectly compatible with being willing to offer odds of 1:2 on rain, and also odds of 1:2 against rain. This is exactly what real bookies (and real tote machines) actually do. It is how they make money. We get complementation by requiring that the agent's odds be construed equally as odds on or (inversely) as odds against an event. That would require that if we offer odds of 1:2 on rain, then we *must* offer odds of 2:1 against rain. Howson and Urbach (1993) achieve the same end by construing the agent as picking out "fair" odds. Of course, this is something that no rational bookie will do, but there one is.[1]

The long and short of it is: degrees of belief, on this view, are construed *behavioristically* and *globally*. Behaviorism isn't altogether unproblematic, and we may well find other ways of *measuring* degrees of belief, but *what* we are measuring on the Bayesian view is exactly the agent's willingness to bet on an uncertain outcome.

The result is a characterization of *coherence*. According to Ramsey (1931, p. 184), this is as far as "logic" takes us. L. J. Savage (1954, p. 59; 1966, p. 597) puts it this way: Probability theory can alert us to an incoherence, but it can no more be expected to tell us how to repair an incoherence than deductive logic can tell us how to repair an inconsistency in our beliefs.

To the best of my knowledge, all this is still Bayesian doctrine. Probabilities are coherent degrees of belief. And beliefs are construed behavioristically in terms of choices. It follows that maximizing expected utility is built in. To many this is the strongest possible recommendation for the Bayesian view.

3. Acts and Outcomes

Before we break out the champagne, however, let us take a closer look. Let us suppose we are considering the choice between a number of acts. Both probabilities and utilities must be relativized to acts: P_{A_i} and U_{A_i} are the probability and utility functions associated with act A_i. That is, $P_{A_i}(O_k)$ is the probability of outcome O_k given that act A_i has been chosen, and the utility of that outcome, under that assumption, is $U_{A_i}(O_k)$.

We must also consider the possible outcomes of these acts. We take the outcomes to be exclusive, since we can always arrange for this to be the case. Now let us atomize the outcomes: that is, let us find basic formulae $f_1, \ldots, f_t$ such that every outcome O_k can be found in the algebra whose atoms are conjunctions of the formulae f_i or their negations. Note that these need not be atoms in any deep metaphysical sense. They are just the atoms of an algebra in which the exclusive outcome events can be found. The outcome O_k can be expressed in Disjunctive Normal Form, $a_1 \vee a_2 \ldots \vee a_m$ where each of the a_i is a conjunction of atomic formulae f_i or negations of these formulae—what are often called *ground formulas.*

Probabilities, given act A_i, are global: that is, they are defined over the full field defined on the atoms f_i. Thus we are taking as known the probabilities of the conjunctions in the Disjunctive Normal Form of any outcome O_k. This is a reduction carried out already by Carnap (1950). The probability of O_k is the sum of the probabilities of these conjunctions of basic formulas.

We are now prepared for a theorem:

THEOREM: The expectation of act A_i is just the expected value of a collection of bets on the disjunction of events comprising O_k:

$$Exp(A_i) = \sum_{k=1}^{n} P_{A_i}(O_k) U_{A_i}(O_k)$$

$$P_{A_i}(O_k) = \sum_{h=1}^{m} P(a_h)$$

$$Exp(A_i) = \sum_{k=1}^{n} \sum_{h=1}^{m} P(a_h) U_{A_i}(O_k)$$

where and $a_h = f_{j_1} \wedge \ldots \wedge f_{j_s}$ and $O_k \equiv a_{h_1} \vee \ldots \vee a_{h_m}$

We can reduce the expectation of any action over a set of outcomes to the sum of the expectations of the action over the set of *atomic* outcomes whose disjunction is the normal form of each outcome O_k. The principle of maximizing expected utility becomes: Choose the act having the greatest expected return over the atomic outcomes. But it was just such choices that gave us the coherent probability functions P_{A_i} in the first place. There is thus a certain circularity in invoking the principle of maximizing expected utility.

We expect circularity in deductively valid arguments: what is in the conclusion had better, in some sense, be "in" the premises. But if you get the feeling that there is some sleight of hand going on here, you are probably correct.

How has probability served as a "guide in life"? Only as deduction serves. We have learned nothing from the probabilistic analysis that was not *given* in the original probability functions P_{A_i}, which represented our choices concerning the atomic outcomes.

We get guidance from probability (in Butler's sense) just in case probability shows us a way out of some perplexity or confusion. Probability must give us something we don't have to start with. In this case we start with choices equivalent to a transformation of the choice we face.

Well, circularity and validity are good friends; maybe what I'm inclined to call Ramsey's circularity is as benign as the fact that the conclusion of a valid argument is "contained in" the premises. But there is more to be said.

4. Rectifying Incoherence

The Bayesian view of the world is an idealization. It is natural to say that we have taken the assumptions—viz., that we have a coherent probability defined (by our dispositional choices) over all the relevant atomic events—too literally. Abandon this unrealistic assumption, and we can have some genuine perplexity over the choice among actions. Since we are taking the utility functions $U_{A_i}(O_k)$ to be unproblematic, this means that we are unsure of some of the probabilities.

Either some of the terms $P_{A_i}(a_j)$ are unknown, or there is an underlying incoherence. To say that such a term is unknown only means that it hasn't been evaluated. It's easy to fix that: Having performed act A_i, how much would you pay for a ticket that returns $1.00 if A_j turns out to be true? That is the value of $P_{A_i}(a_j)$.

Frail vessels that we are, it is the second possibility that most concerns us. My degrees of belief are incoherent—*that's why I don't know what to do!* Now is when I need guidance! But this is exactly what both Ramsey and Savage warn us probability theory can't give us: *It is not the business of probability theory to tell the agent how to repair an incoherence*, any more than it is the business of logic to tell an agent how to repair an inconsistency. The upshot is: *Either my complex choices follow deductively from my simple choices, in which case I need no guidance, or probability can give me no guidance.* One cannot be in error except by being incoherent, and probability provides no guidance as to how to get out of incoherence.

5. Back to Logic

If Bayesianism is Bankrupt, and Frequencies are Fantasies, where can we turn? Logic is all that is left. (What did Sherlock Holmes tell us?)

Carnap believed that if we could assign measures to sentences on logical grounds alone, we would be home free. Both "unknown" and "incoherent" probabilities are ruled out. We can get the guidance we seek from the logical measure. We are no longer trying to derive choices from choices, but choices from a combination of a utility function and a logical measure function. But as we already remarked, even Carnap lost his faith, or most of it. There is no agreement about what measure function to use. And there are technical problems even in defining such a function (as pointed out by Harman [1989] and others). One way out might be to be a little less demanding. We noted that C. A. B. Smith proposed to relax the requirement of closure under complementation for odds; perhaps there is hope for a logical interpretation along those lines.

In 1921 John Maynard Keynes published his *Treatise on Probability* (1952). In his view probability represented a logical relation like entailment (Salmon dubbed it "partial entailment") between evidence and hypothesis, but, unlike most writers on probability, Keynes took probability to be only partially ordered. We cannot always say of two propositions A and B that $P(A) > P(B)$ or that $P(A) < P(B)$, nor yet that $P(A) = P(B)$. The probabilities $P(A)$ and $P(B)$ may just be incomparable.

Perhaps when there is controversy about probability, we can shelter behind vagueness, and still somehow take the principle of maximizing expected utility to be justified.

Alas. For Keynes, probability is a logical relation, but you still have to "intuit" the basic probability relations, just as in deductive logic you were (in 1921) widely supposed to have to intuit the validity of *modus ponens.*

6. Evidential Probability

Here is another approach to logical probability that borrows fairly heavily from Keynes.[2] We do not suppose that we have a logical measure on the sentences of a formal language, but rather that all probabilities are based on known or reasonably believed relative frequencies. This is not a frequency view, since probabilities are not *identified* with frequencies, but only *based on* acceptable statements concerning frequencies, as well as other acceptable statements, all playing the role of evidence. The view depends on these assumptions, comprising an empirical dimension and a logical dimension:

1. Induction: we know some approximate long-run frequencies; this is the empirical dimension.
2. There are rules for picking out the right reference class; this is the logical dimension.[3]
3. The values of probabilities are given by the relevant imprecisely known long-run frequencies.

The upshot is that given a body of knowledge (taking it to include approximate empirical frequencies) the probability of any statement is given as an interval. Probability is a logical relation. It is not derived from choices, but from its relation to empirical evidence.

Since probability is not a real-valued function any more, we have to generalize the notion of expectation:

$$Exp(A_i) = \sum_k [P^l_{A_i}(O_k), P^u_{A_i}(O_k)]\, U_{A_i}(O_k) =$$
$$\left[\sum_k P^l_{A_i}(O_k)\, U_{A_i}(O_k), \sum_k P^u_{A_i}(O_k)]\, U_{A_i}(O_k)\right]$$

An action is thus characterized by an interval of utilities, corresponding to the probability intervals that enter into its mathematical expectation.

We can no longer order acts by their expected utility. Nevertheless it makes sense to *rule out* any act whose upper bound of expected utility is lower than the lower bound of expected utility of some other act. Let us call this principle the "Principle of Dominance in Mathematical Expectation."

Now the advice to maximize expected utility is substantive, if slightly incorrect. Given the evidence you have, and given the utilities you have (remember, we are leaving the analysis of utility to one side), we arrive at an (interval) value of expected utility for each alternative act. We can surely eliminate those acts whose upper utilities are less than the lower utilities of other possible acts.

To be sure, we are not left with a single admissible action. But we weren't left with a single admissible action before: we were left on the original analysis with a set of "undominated" acts. The difference is that in the Bayesian analysis these undominated acts all had exactly the same expected utility. Now the remaining acts may be characterized by various expected utility intervals.

Example: Suppose we are presented with a badly distorted die. We roll it many times, until we can be practically certain that the relative frequencies of the various outcomes are bounded by the tabulated intervals. These intervals determine a set of probability functions that we take to characterize what we know of the die.

1: [.2,.3]

2: [.1,.1]

3: [.2,.2]

4: [.2,.3]

5: [.1,.1]

6: [.0,.2]

The acts are to choose between receiving $1 if an odd number comes up, and receiving $3 if an even number comes up. The probabilities are:

Odd: [0.5,0.6]
Even: [0.3,0.5]

(Note that 0.6 is less than 1 minus the sum of the lower probabilities of Even, and that 0.5 is less than the sum of the upper probabilities of Even.) The expectations are:

Odd: [.5,.6]
Even: [.9,1.5]

It is clear that we should stake our winnings on an even outcome.

Now one might go further in developing principles: for example, if our choice was between receiving $1 if an odd number comes up and $2 if an even number comes up, the expectations would be [.5,.6] and [.6,1.0] respectively. It seems natural to strengthen our principle to allow a clear choice in this case, too, by rejecting any alternative whose upper bound is lower than *or equal to* the lower bound of another alternative.

But what do we do when the interval utilities simply overlap? We might say to choose the one with the highest upper bound; but it isn't clear that this is always the right thing to do. Suppose one utility interval includes another: should we reject the act corresponding to the broader interval, on the grounds that we will thereby be reducing (some kind of) uncertainty? A number of such principles suggest themselves, but I'm not sure that a compelling case can be made for them, though I am convinced of the value of the principle of dominance.

Of course, there are drawbacks to this approach.

1. We must make our background knowledge explicit.
2. Since probabilities are determined by background knowledge and evidence, we can only agree about probabilities if we can agree about the evidence.
3. Since expected utilities are intervals, the guidance we get is somewhat limited.

Nevertheless, this way of looking at probability does make sense of such principles as the principle of dominance (our version of the principle that we should maximize expectation). That becomes a substantive piece of advice to the perplexed. Even more important than that, to my mind, is the fact that this approach provides a framework within which to discuss choices constructively. If we are willing to share data, your body of knowledge and mine can be made similar, not because of Bayesian conditionalization, but because we come to accept the same approximate statistical generalizations. Since our probabilities are based on our empirical statistical knowledge, we will have similar (objective) probabilities. If we have similar probabilities and similar utilities, we can at least agree on some actions to be eschewed. And this represents progress in objectivity.

HENRY E. KYBURG, JR.
University of Rochester

NOTES

Research underlying this paper was supported by NSF grant SES-9906128.

1. An alternative is presented by C. A. B. Smith (1965; 1961). See also Walley 1991; Kyburg 1959; Good 1962; Suppes 1962. On this view you would let complementation go. In essence, degrees of belief are bounded above and below, but are not determined precisely.

2. This idea has appeared in a number of places and under a number of names; the main reference points are Kyburg 1961, Kyburg 1974, and Kyburg and Teng forthcoming.

3. Actually the rules are for rejecting the wrong reference classes; often this will leave only one relevant interval. Sometimes there will be more than one reference class not ruled out, and in such cases the probability in question is given by a covering interval.

REFERENCES

Butler, Joseph. 1736. *The Analogy of Religion, Natural and Revealed, to the Constitution and Course of Nature*. Philadelphia: Lippincott.

Carnap, Rudolf. 1950. *The Logical Foundations of Probability*. Chicago: University of Chicago Press.

de Finetti, Bruno. 1980. "Foresight: Its Logical Laws, Its Subjective Sources." In *Studies in Subjective Probability*, ed. Kyburg and Smokler, pages 53–118. Huntington, N.Y.: Krieger.

Earman, John. 1992. *Bayes or Bust?* Cambridge: MIT Press.

Good, I. J. 1962. "Subjective Probability as a Measure of a Nonmeasurable Set." In *Logic, Methodology and Philosophy of Science*, ed. Suppes, Nagel, and Tarski, pages 319–29. Berkeley: University of California Press.

Harman, Gilbert. 1989. *Change in View*. Cambridge, Mass.: Bradford Books.

Howson, Colin, and Peter Urbach. 1993. *Scientific Reasoning: The Bayesian Approach*. La Salle, Ill.: Open Court.

Jaynes, E. T. "Probability Theory in Science and Engineering." *Colloquium Lectures in Pure and Applied Science* 4: 152–87.

Jeffrey, Richard C. 1965. *The Logic of Decision*. New York: McGraw-Hill.

Jeffreys, Harold. 1930. *Scientific Inference*. Cambridge: Cambridge University Press.

Keynes, John Maynard. 1952. *A Treatise on Probability*. London: Macmillan and Co.

Kyburg, Henry E., Jr., and Choh Man Teng. Forthcoming. *Uncertain Inference*. Cambridge: Cambridge University Press.

Kyburg, Henry E., Jr. 1959. "Probability and Randomness." *Journal of Symbolic Logic* 24: 316–17.

———. 1961. *Probability and the Logic of Rational Belief*. Middletown: Wesleyan University Press.

———. 1974. *The Logical Foundations of Statistical Inference*. Dordrecht: Reidel.

Laplace, Pierre Simon Marquis de. 1951. *A Philosophical Essay on Probabilities*. New York: Dover Publications.

Mayo, Deborah. 1996. *Error and the Growth of Experimental Knowledge*. Chicago: University of Chicago Press.

Neyman, Jerzy. 1947. "Raisonment inductif ou comportement inductif." *Proceedings of the International Statistical Conference* 3: 423–33.

———. 1957. "'Inductive Behavior' as a Basic Concept of Philosophy of Science." *Review of the International Statistical Institute* 25: 5–22.

Reichenbach, Hans. 1949. *The Theory of Probability*. Berkeley and Los Angeles: University of California Press.

Savage, L. J. 1954. *Foundations of Statistics*. New York: John Wiley.

———. 1966. "Implications of Personal Probability for Induction." *Journal of Philosophy* 63: 593–607.

Skyrms, Brian. 1966. *Choice and Chance: An Introduction to Inductive Logic*. Belmont, Calif.: Dickenson.

Smith, C.A.B. 1961. "Consistency in Statistical Inference and Decision." *The Journal of the Royal Statistical Society A*, 128: 469–99.

Suppes, Patrick. 1962. "Subjective Probability as a Measure of a Nonmeasurable Set." in *Logic, Methodology, and Philosophy of Science*, ed. Suppes, Nagel, and Tarski, pages 319–29. Berkeley: University of California Press.

Walley, Peter. 1991. *Statistical Reasoning with Imprecise Probabilities*. London: Chapman and Hall.

PART II

Probability and Decision

7

A Dilemma for Objective Chance

PHIL DOWE

One attractive approach to decision theory asserts that knowledge of objective propensities makes appropriate degrees of partial belief rational. The essence of this approach is to identify the rational degree of partial belief with objective single-case chance. What makes this attractive is that it overcomes a difficulty, inherent in other conceptions of probability, in making application of probability to individual decisions nonarbitrary.[1]

The aim of this paper is to show that this approach does not make sense of the role chance plays in everyday decision making. I shall argue that there is a dilemma: when chance is irreducible (in a sense to be defined) it is inapplicable to most of the situations to which we want to apply it, but on the other hand, when chance is reducible it is not objective and cannot play the appropriate role in rational decision. In considering the relevance of this dilemma for the work of Salmon, Mellor, and Lewis, I shall argue in particular that the dilemma presents an acute difficulty for Salmon and Mellor.

—P. D.

* * *

Irreducibility, Objectivity, and Indeterminism

As John Earman points out, 'reducibility' is a weasel word, with two distinct meanings.[2] One sense concerns whether chance supervenes on something else, such as particular matters of fact, or if it is an unanalyzable primitive. The present work does not address that sense. I am concerned, rather, with Earman's other sense of 'reducibility', a sense of the word that has also been used by Krips, Batterman, Gisin, and Butterfield.[3]

The relevant notion of reducibility is close to something F. P. Ramsey thought was a necessary feature of objective chance:

> What we mean by objective chance is not merely our having in our system a chance $\frac{\phi(x)}{\psi(x)}$, but our having no hope of modifying our system into a pair of laws $\alpha x.\psi x \supset \phi x : \beta x.\psi x \supset \sim\phi x$, etc., where αx, βx are disjunctions of readily observable properties.[4]

Having "no hope of modifying our system" is close to what I mean by 'irreducibility'. However, the phrase "readily observable properties" suggests that Ramsey allows as objective cases where a system might in fact be modifiable in terms of properties like initial velocity and rate of rotation of a coin, since these are not properties that ordinary gamblers can utilize. But this is unacceptably epistemic as an account of objective chance. Following van Fraassen,[5] in calling a chance 'objective' I mean to say that it is a fact about the world that is true independently of human knowers. This is in contradistinction to 'epistemic' chance, which I take to be a judgement relative to some knowledge, in other words a 'measure of ignorance'. If 'objective' is not understood this way, it cannot warrant partial beliefs in the required way, as I shall argue.

An account of reducibility not epistemic in this way is suggested by John Earman in his book *A Primer on Determinism*. Earman suggests that we compare the notion to the reducibility of the probabilities in statistical mechanics.[6] Classical statistical mechanics employs probabilities representing our ignorance or partial knowledge of a system, in terms of properties such as the mean kinetic energy of an ensemble of particles, while the development of the underlying microstate is deterministic. These probabilities have an ignorance interpretation, that is, they are reducible.

This entails an important and controversial relation between objective chance and determinism: a deterministic system contains no irreducible chances, while an indeterministic system necessarily does. To put it another way, in a deterministic world, all chance is reducible, and hence epistemic. It also follows that the only objective chances are irreducible chances.

The Dilemma Identified: Salmon's Dynamic Rationality

The dilemma in question is perhaps most clearly a problem for the approach to decision theory taken by Wesley Salmon in his 1988 paper, "Dynamic Rationality: Propensity, Probability, and Credence."[7] In that paper Salmon argues that there are two types of probability, personal probabilities, which are subjective degrees of belief subject to coherence requirements; and physical probabilities, which are long-run frequencies. Salmon also allows propensities, not as an adequate interpretation of the probability calculus, but as 'probabilistic causes', as dispositional properties of particular objects or processes. (It is not entirely clear how Salmon intends to use the word 'chance'. There is some warrant for thinking that Salmon equates chance with propensities, at least in some cases.[8])

Salmon intends his theory to account for everyday decision making. In "Dynamic Rationality" he quotes Butler four or five times: "probability is the very guide of life." This is realized in the fact that personal probabilities form the basis of our decision making. The question Salmon addresses is, what is the link between personal probabilities, frequencies, and propensities?

The sense in which personal probabilities derive from propensities is that propensities are said to 'generate' (some) single-case personal probabilities. So, when we know the propensity, we base our personal probability on that knowledge. How do we know about propensities? One way is that frequency data provides evidence for the value of the propensity. The way this works is that the propensity is identified with the 'weight',[9] which in this case is the value of the probability taken from the broadest objectively homogeneous reference class; an objectively homogeneous reference class is one in which no statistically relevant partition can be made. This throws light on the application of objective probability to the single case, Salmon claims.

The way that this works seems to be as follows. A major problem facing the frequency theory of probability, applicability to the single case, can be avoided if we acknowledge propensities, which are properties of particular objects or processes. We know of propensities from our knowledge of frequencies (and from other sources), but propensities are not to be taken as just oblique references to frequencies. Then, our degrees of belief are rational when we match our personal probability to the propensity, or chance. This is 'dynamic' rationality because personal probabilities are 'propensity driven'.

This approach to rationality faces a dilemma. On the one hand, where we have frequency data, the propensity will be the frequency in the broadest objectively homogeneous reference class. This is equivalent to saying that objective chance or propensity is irreducible, for having an objectively homogeneous reference class means there is no way to determine a more accurate value. In fact, the only weights drawn from objectively homogeneous reference classes besides those equal to 0 or 1 will be cases of irreducible chance.[10]

On the other hand, propensities are supposed to generate probabilities so as to be the 'very guide of life'. Salmon is very explicit on this requirement (it is one of the three essential desiderata of a theory of probability,[11] and Salmon's criticism of Mellor is that his notion of chance rules out much of everyday chances[12]). Indeed, all of Salmon's examples of propensity are everyday cases: "There is . . . a propensity of a tossed die to come to rest with side 6 uppermost, a propensity of a child to misbehave, a propensity of a plant sprayed with herbicide to die, etc."[13] Furthermore, widespread applicability is a necessary requisite if the dynamic rationality theory is to be a general account of what makes rational our personal probabilities.

But if propensities are irreducible then it is clear that they don't generate much of everyday chance; yet if propensities guide typical everyday choices then it is clear that they are not irreducible. Take Salmon's example of the lottery, where numbers are drawn from a machine containing numbered ping-pong balls. Salmon says, "In cases such as the present—where we have a causal or stochastic process generating the outcomes—if the class is objectively homogeneous, I would consider the weight assigned to the outcome as the *propensity* or *objective chance* of that mechanism (chance setup) to produce that outcome."[14]

But in such cases the reference class is patently *not* objectively homogeneous. For, if in a particular instance we knew precisely the initial conditions of the balls, and the details of the 'shuffling' and drawing mechanisms, and the relevant laws, then we could give a more precise value for the propensity. Certainly, we should not assume determinism, but this does not by itself entail that a given epistemically homogeneous reference class is objective. In such everyday cases we surely think it is not. Thus the dynamic rationality model is a long-odds gamble that everyday cases involve objectively homogeneous reference classes. The stakes are worth having but the chances are but faint.

So either propensities are restricted to the weights from objectively homogeneous classes, in which case they have little applicability to everyday decisions; or we admit as propensities weights from merely pragmatically or epistemically homogeneous classes, in which case propensity is not objective and so cannot play the designated role in the dynamic rationality model. Either horn seems fatal to Salmon's model of dynamic rationality.

The First Horn: Where's Chance When You Need It?

In this section and the next I will look at three accounts of objective chance; one given by Lewis[15] and two given by Hugh Mellor: the account in his book *The Matter of Chance*[16] (call that theory 'Mellor$_1$') and a revised version given in a later paper[17] (call that theory 'Mellor$_2$'). I will show how each account is placed with respect to the dilemma discussed above.

In *The Matter of Chance* Mellor attempts an account of objective chance (Mellor$_1$) intended to yield what 'the professionals' take to be true of chance, namely that it is objective, empirical, nonrelational, and single case.[18] Being explicitly about objective single-case chance, Mellor's account is a good test case for my claim. However, Mellor$_1$ is also a 'personalist' since he seeks to characterize chance in terms of rational partial belief.[19] The stated reason for this approach is, in the words of Kneale, "that knowledge of probability is important chiefly for its bearing on action."[20] Mellor's idea is that connecting agency and objective chance in this way solves the problem that frequentists such as Reichenbach and Salmon have in applying probability to the single case.[21] But we need to bear in mind that the chances (which make partial belief rational) are objective, and that is what makes the partial belief rational. Some beliefs are more reasonable than others on account of the way things are in the world.

Mellor$_1$ is committed to the view that objective chance is irreducible. For on his account if determinism is true then there are no chances.[22] Mellor takes determinism to be the view that no true laws are statistical, which he takes to be false as a contingent, empirical fact.

Salmon has argued that this result "flies in the face of virtually universal common and scientific usage."[23] Salmon's point is that the truth of our everyday and scientific talk about chance is not dependent on the truth of determinism, and therefore Mellor$_1$ fails as an account of objective chance.

I would express the point as follows. Mellor must face the same dilemma that Salmon's dynamic rationality theory faces. Mellor's chances are to be objective, hence irreducible. Everyday examples, such as the toss of an unbiased coin, are reducible; therefore Mellor's account does not apply to such cases. Perhaps there are not very many objective chances around; at least, not ones that interact with human affairs and which constrain our partial beliefs so as to be the guide of life.

Yet everyday chances are Mellor's stock-in-trade examples. Throughout his book he regularly resorts to coins and dice as examples of objective chance.[24] Other examples include deaths and diseases, the yields of crops, and genetic characteristics of the offspring of biological species.[25] All of these are most likely reducible, and so ruled out by Mellor's theory. Thus the consequence is that chance is virtually banished from the world of everyday decision.

David Lewis[26] offers an account similar in important respects to Mellor$_1$. Lewis is a subjectivist who allows for the existence of objective chance, and his particular concern is to spell out the connection between credence and objective chance. This he does via his 'Principal Principle'[27]:

> Let C be any reasonable initial credence function. Let t be any time. Let x be any real number in the unit interval. Let X be the proposition that the chance, at time t, of A's holding equals x. Let E be any proposition compatible with X that is admissible at time t. Then $C(A|XE) = x$

The point of interest here is that, like Mellor_1, Lewis insists that the existence of objective chance is incompatible with determinism. "There is no chance without chance," as Lewis puts it. "If our world is deterministic there are no chances in it."[28] So it would seem that for Lewis objective chance is irreducible. What I call reducible chance Lewis calls "counterfeit chance":

> Counterfeit chances will be relative to partitions; and relative therefore to standards of feasibility and naturalness; and therefore indeterminate unless the standards are somehow settled. . . . Counterfeit chances are therefore not the sort of thing we would want to find in our fundamental physical theories . . . . But they will do to serve the conversational needs of determinist gamblers.[29]

Where does this leave the everyday cases, such as coin tosses, which Lewis uses as illustrations? Issac Levi[30] has offered a criticism of Lewis that parallels Salmon's criticism of Mellor_1. Levi urges that Lewis should deny that a coin has a chance of 1/2 of landing heads, and say rather that such chances do not stray too far from 0 or 1. The claim is that coin tosses are pretty well deterministic systems. Lewis's answer is interesting.[31] He clearly holds the view that all objective chance is irreducible (and so grasps the first horn of the dilemma), and that if coin tosses are deterministic then they don't display objective chances. But he holds that it is most likely that coin tosses are influenced by external microscopic factors that are indeterministic and so he believes that coin tosses do exhibit chances. He gives only a small credence to the hypothesis that the chance of heads on a given toss would be zero or one. He suggests the possibility that a coin's sensitivity to such processes as the influences of air molecules in fact completely dominates the minuteness of those effects, in which case the objective chance of heads is 1/2. But he gives only a small credence to that possibility.[32]

So Lewis accepts the consequence that what we normally think of as chances are most likely not objective chances; and that there is no guarantee of the kind of connection that Mellor_1 hopes for, between what we call chance and genuine objective chance. This means that, like Mellor_1, Lewis is forced onto the horn of the dilemma where objective chance is virtually banished from the world of everyday decision.

This is not a problem for Lewis in the way it is for Salmon, since the latter wants chance or propensity to be directly tied to everyday decision as the means for warranting reasonable degrees of belief, whereas the Principal Principle doesn't require that there be much, or indeed any, objective chance, but merely shows how to accommodate beliefs about objective chance in a subjectivist framework. If in fact there are no relevant objective chances, Lewis still has an intact theory of rational decision where probability is the very guide to life. Thus our dilemma does not pose a problem for Lewis in the way it does for Salmon and Mellor_1.

Would Mellor be happy to grasp the first horn of the dilemma? I think not, although there is some warrant for the view that this is the logical implication of the positions outlined in *A Matter of Chance*. Mellor does insist that the extent of actual objective chance in the world is a purely contingent matter, and so it is not for philosophical theory to predetermine that issue. But there are also reasons to think that Mellor would be very uncomfortable with the first horn. Firstly, we noted above that everyday chances are Mellor's stock-in-trade examples. These would have to all be taken as purely illustrative of a more elusive phenomenon. Secondly, Mellor's position on decision theory has always been objectivist.[33] But thirdly, and most persuasively, Mellor changed his position in response to Salmon's criticism. We now turn to that revised account of chance.

The Second Horn: Not Any Chance Will Do

In his 1982 paper, "Chance and Degrees of Belief," Mellor offers a revised account of chance,[34] which I am calling Mellor_2. In response to the argument of Salmon, Mellor_2 holds that a world with chances may or may not be deterministic. Chances, he now holds, are relative to human perceptual limits. They can count as knowledge because knowledge is relative to the same limitations. Thus a coin toss displays an objective chance of 1/2 because relative to beings with our perceptual apparatus the facts justify that chance. The degree of belief is rationally warranted: we would break even in the long run if we consistently accept bets based on that chance. Provided, that is, our opponents share the same limitations. As Mellor says, it would be very foolish to accept bets with God. So for Mellor_2 objective chances may be reducible.

The advantage of $Mellor_2$ is that it safely secures the connection between objective chance and everyday decision. Objective chances are the ones people in practice can't reduce, while those with obvious reductions don't warrant partial beliefs in the same way. So there are many instances of objective chance, all the sorts that Mellor refers to in *The Matter of Chance.*

However, the solution has a cost. The cost of insisting that chance refers to everyday chance is that 'objective' chance is not objective at all, but merely epistemic. If chance is relative to perceptual limitations then chance is relative to perceivers. For example, the chance of a coin landing heads is different for me, for God, for someone with telepathy and for a physicist with appropriate equipment. It varies for the physicist depending on whether her equipment is working or not. In short, chance is relative to our knowledge of the prior state: it takes different values for different epistemic states. The rationality constraint that our betting partner share our limitations begs the question, for the reason we wouldn't want to bet with God or some physicist is that such people have access to more accurate values of the chance. Bets with such people expose our false degrees of belief. It's because of the epistemic character of this notion of chance that we need such a requirement.

But if this notion of chance is epistemic, then $Mellor_2$ has not provided us with an account of objective chance at all. In fact, in application to the single case $Mellor_2$ faces essentially the same problem as other theories of probability—it will be arbitrary which reference class or amount of background knowledge one takes to warrant partial beliefs. Thus if chance is construed in an essentially epistemic fashion, then Mellor's approach to decision theory loses its central advantage, for we need a nonarbitrary definition of the probability value in the single case.

Thus Mellor is caught in the dilemma of objective chance. If he insists that chance is objective (as he does) then he must accept that its applicability is limited. If he insists that chance is a feature of everyday decision (as he seems to) then he must accept that chance is not objective.

Some Objections Answered

I now consider three possible objections to the above argument. Firstly, one may object by pointing to chaos theory: doesn't modern chaos theory show that many everyday processes are actually chaotic in nature, and so might there not be plenty of chance at the everyday level? But the inference from chaos to objective single-case chance just doesn't work. The case has been well argued by Hunt, Stone, and Batterman.[35] Chaos gives us a problem with predicting results, but the dynamics are deterministic, giving a unique, determinate result for all times. So there's no indeterminism or objective chance necessarily involved in chaotic systems. (Although Prigogine, Ford, and Jones[36] all persist in this view, although Suppes[37] has repented.)

Secondly, one may claim that there is genuine indeterminism in macrosystems, because, for example, quantum indeterminisms are magnified by chaotic effects. Coin tosses, for example, may be so affected.[38] Someone may argue (although Lewis doesn't): Coin tosses are most likely indeterministic, therefore the chance p = 1/2 that an unbiased coin will land heads is most likely due to indeterministic processes (here the strength of 'most likely' is subversively the same in the premise as in the conclusion). Therefore objective chance plays an important role in everyday decision. The fallacy in this reasoning is to jump from the idea of a mechanical process being influenced by random elements (in which case its evolution is not entirely deterministic, but would be governed by probabilistic laws) to the idea of a completely random mechanical process (whose evolution would be completely unpredictable). The jump is not warranted.

Thirdly and finally, one may accept that the result of a coin toss is determined by its prior state or distribution of initial conditions, but claim that the prior state is itself the result of a chance event perhaps somewhere back in its history, and so maintain that coin tosses are chancy, after all. This idea is suggested by the writings of Gillies, Kyburg, von Plato, and Krips.[39] But, following Lewis and Mellor, I take it that objective chances are time-indexical. Suppose I rig up a geiger counter and a tritium source to a reliable mechanical coin tosser, and starting at 12:00, if a decay is registered before five past, then the tosser will toss the coin at 12:05 beginning with heads up, which almost certainly produces a result of heads. If there is no decay by five past then the tosser tosses the coin beginning in a tails up position, which almost certainly produces a result of tails. Suppose the chance of a decay in a period of five minutes is 1/2. Then it is true that at 12:00 the objective irreducible chance of getting heads on that toss is 1/2. But at 12:05, just before the toss, the chance of heads is either 1 or 0. So the fact that at 12:00 the coin has an objective chance of 1/2 for heads can only be used as a response to the dilemma by virtue of an equivocation on different time indexed chances. (I do, of course, admit *some* decisions may be based on objective chance.) Those who do not take chance to be time-indexical probably take it to be conditional in a standard sense. In that case appeal to the past history of the coin will only work as an answer to my dilemma by virtue of an equivocation on what is being conditionalized on.

Conclusion

Any approach to rational decision which identifies the rational degree of belief with objective single-case chance is fatally flawed. I have shown, via an explication of the notion of reducibility, that the approach faces a dilemma. The chance to be identified with the rational degree of belief must be either reducible or irreducible. If it is reducible then it is not objective and not uniquely given, and the requirement of an arbitrary assumption as to which probability warrants the rational degree of partial belief returns. On the other hand, if the chance is irreducible, then it does not have much applicability to everyday decision.[40]

PHIL DOWE
University of Tasmania

NOTES

1. The problem is, for frequentists, which reference class applies to single-case probability; and for logical relationists, how much evidence should be invoked in the case of plainly nonrelational probability statements. See D. Mellor, *The Matter of Chance* (Cambridge: Cambridge University Press, 1971), p. 53.

2. J. Earman, *A Primer on Determinism* (Dordrecht: Reidel, 1986), p. 231.

3. H. Krips, "Irreducible Probabilities and Indeterminism," *Journal of Philosophical Logic* 18 (1989): 155–72; R. Batterman, "Randomness and Probability in Dynamical Theories: On the Proposals of the Prigogine School," *Philosophy of Science* 58 (1991): 241–63; N. Gisin, "Propensities in a Non-Deterministic Physics," *Synthese* 89 (1991): 287–97; and J. Butterfield, "Bell's Theorem: What it Takes," *British Journal for the Philosophy of Science* 43 (1992) 58–83.

4. F. P. Ramsey, *Philosophical Papers* (Cambridge: Cambridge University Press, 1990), p. 105.

5. B. Van Fraassen, *The Scientific Image* (Oxford: Clarendon Press, 1980).

6. Op. cit., note 2, p. 232.

7. W. Salmon, "Dynamic Rationality: Propensity, Probability and Credence," *Probability and Causality: Essays in Honor of Wesley C. Salmon*, ed. J. Fetzer (Dordrecht: Reidel, 1988), pp. 3–40.

8. Op. cit., note 7, p. 22.

9. Op. cit., note 7, p. 24.

10. W. Salmon, "Propensities: A Discussion Review," *Erkenntnis* 14 (1979): 198–99.

11. W. Salmon, *The Foundations of Scientific Inference* (Pittsburgh: University of Pittsburgh Press, 1967), p. 64.

12. Op. cit., note 10, p. 199.

13. Op. cit., note 7, p. 14.

14. Op. cit., note 7, p. 24.

15. D. Lewis, *Philosophical Papers,* Vol. II (New York: Oxford University Press, 1986), ch. 21.

16. Op. cit., note 1.

17. D. Mellor, "Chances and Degrees of Belief," *What? Where? When? Why?*, ed. R. McLaughlin (Dordrecht: Reidel, 1982), pp. 49–68. This view is expanded in *The Facts of Causation,* (London: Routledge, 1995) especially chapter 5, but here for simplicity I will focus on the 1982 paper. For my critique of the relevant point in Mellor's 1995, see P. Dowe, "Critical Notice: D.H. Mellor, 'The Facts of Causation'," *Philosophy of Science* 65 (1998): 162–70.

18. Op. cit., note 1, p. xi.

19. Op. cit., note 1, p. xii.

20. Op. cit., note 1, p. 3.

21. Op. cit., note 1, p. 54.

22. Op. cit., note 1, ch. 8.

23. Op. cit., note 10, p. 199.

24. Op. cit., note 1, pp. 4, 27, 29, 31.

25. Op. cit., note 1, p. 31.

26. Op. cit., note 15.

27. Op. cit., note 15, p. 87.

28. Op. cit., note 15, p. 120.

29. Op. cit., note 15, p. 121.

30. Levi, "Review of Studies in Inductive Logic and Probability," *Philosophical Review* 92 (1983): 121.

31. Op. cit., note 15, pp. 117–21.

32. Op. cit., note 15, p. 118.

33. D. Mellor, "Objective Decision Making," *Social Theory and Practice* 9 (1983): 289–309.

34. Op. cit., note 17.

35. G. Hunt, "Determinism, Predictability and Chaos," *Analysis* 47 (1987): 129–33; M. Stone, "Chaos, Prediction and Laplacean Determinism," *American Philosophical Quarterly* 26 (1989): 123–31; and op. cit., note 3.

36. I. Prigogine and I. Stengers, *Order out of Chaos* (Toronto: Bantam, 1984); J. Ford, "How Random is a Coin Toss?," *Physics Today* 36 (1983): 40–47; and R. Jones, "Determinism in Deterministic Chaos," *PSA 1990,* Vol. 2, ed. A. Fine, M. Forbes, and L. Wessel (East Lansing: Philosophy of Science Association, 1991), pp. 537–49.

37. P. Suppes, "Indeterminism or Instability, Does it Matter?," *Causality, Method and Modality,* ed. G. Brittan Jr. (Dordrecht: Kluwer, 1991), pp. 5–22.

38. Cf. Lewis's discussion in op. cit., note 15, p. 118.

39. D. Gillies, *An Objective Theory of Probability* (London: Methuen, 1973); H. Kyburg, "Propensities and Probabilities," *British Journal for the Philosophy of Science* 25 (1974): 359–75; J. von Plato, "The Method of Arbitrary Functions," *British Journal for the Philosophy of Science* 34 (1983): 37–47; and op. cit., note 3.

40. I would like to thank Huw Price and James Franklin for helpful discussions on this topic.

8

Simpson's Paradox: A Logically Benign, Empirically Treacherous Hydra

GARY MALINAS

Nancy Cartwright and Brian Skyrms drew attention to problems that Simpson's Paradox poses for probabilistic analyses of causation and for inferences from probabilistic relations to causal relations. C. R. Blyth and Judea Pearl drew attention to apparent counter-models to the Sure Thing Principle of Decision Theory and to argument forms that are valid in the Propositional Calculus that are based on paradoxical data. My essay disarms the apparent countermodels and it explains their apparent force. As the title advertises, the paradox is logically benign. However, it is also empirically treacherous. The boundary conditions for reversals of probability relations that characterize the paradox entail that Reichenbach's proposal for identifying common causes can be trivially satisfied. The essay concludes with a brief discussion of Elliot Sober's proposal that paradoxical setups can help to explain how traits such as altruism that disadvantage their bearers can evolve and become a stable feature of populations. If such causal structures can explain altruism, they might also explain how other traits that disadvantage their bearers, for example, ignorance, could become a stable feature of a population. It is an empirical question how widely (or narrowly) such structures are distributed.

—*G. M.*

* * *

1. Introduction

If the term 'paradox' is understood to refer to arguments that have premises that are taken to be true that entail conclusions which are false, then Simpson's paradox is mislabeled. On a broader understanding of the term 'paradox', a set of sentences that appear to be collectively incompatible can count as paradoxical if the incompatibility is only apparent. Simpson's paradox belongs to this second category. The statistician G. U. Yule is credited with first pointing it out in 1903, it was introduced into the philosophical literature by M. R. Cohen and E. Nagel in 1934, and it was the topic of a brief, witty article by the statistician E. H. Simpson in 1951.[1] Cohen and Nagel used it to set a problem as an exercise; Nancy Cartwright (1979) and Brian Skyrms (1980) resurrected it from philosophical dormancy.[2] The paradox has been alleged to provide counterexamples to argument forms which are valid in the propositional calculus and counterexamples to the Sure Thing Principle of decision theory.[3] The alleged counterexamples are spurious, however, and the paradox is benign for valid inference and rational choice. Nevertheless, the basis of the paradox poses genuine problems for inferences from data to probability assignments to hypotheses, for models of causal inference, and for probabilistic analyses of causation. These problems persist when actual and possible empirical setups that manifest paradoxical structures are analyzed. Coming to grips with them can help to explain the otherwise perplexing features of such setups.

2. An Example of the Paradox[4]

Suppose that a new drug is under test to determine whether it provides an effective treatment for an illness. In order to find out whether it is effective, a percentage of patients are treated with the drug and a control group is given a placebo. When the results of the trial are tabulated, the drug appears to be an effective treatment. Fifty-four percent of the treated patients recover and only 44% of the patients who were given placebos recover. Now suppose that testosterone is one of the components of the new drug, and the question arises whether the drug is more effective for males or more effective for females or whether its effects are independent of gender. When the populations of treated and untreated patients are partitioned by gender, however, it turns out that the recovery rates for both males and females who are given placebos are higher than the recovery rates of those who were given the new drug. For example, it is consistent with the recovery rates for the total population that 33% of the untreated males recover and only 27% of the treated males recover, and that 66% of the untreated females recover and only 64% of the treated females recover. So the drug appears to be effective when the total population is taken into account, but it does not appear to be effective for the male members of the population and it does not appear to be effective for the female members of the population. The following tables verify these relationships.

TOTAL POPULATION

	Recover	*Do Not Recover*
Received Treatment	105	90
Did Not Receive Treatment	40	50

MALES

	Recover	*Do Not Recover*
Received Treatment	15	40
Did Not Receive Treatment	20	40

FEMALES

	Recover	*Do Not Recover*
Received Treatment	90	50
Did Not Receive Treatment	20	10

3. Percentages and Probabilities

The example used to illustrate Simpson's paradox was given in terms of patients, treatments, genders, and recovery rates. An urn model can be provided which has the same arithmetical properties as the example, but instead of patients there are balls in the urn, and each ball is inscribed with three symbols, one from each of the sets {T, ~T}, {R, ~R}, {M, ~M}. For example, a given ball might carry the inscription [R, ~T, M]. The distribution of inscriptions on the balls is stipulated to conform to the tables above. Now the percentages of distributions of inscriptions on the balls can be represented as probabilities; the expression 'Prob(R/T)' is read as 'The probability that a ball is inscribed with an R given that it is inscribed with a T'. The model exhibits the following probability relationships.

Prob(R/T) > Prob(R/~T)
Prob(R/TM) < Prob(R/~TM)
Prob(R/T~M) < Prob(R/~T~M)

The feeling that these inequalities are paradoxical is assuaged when it is recalled that probabilities can be represented as weighted averages. For example,

$$\mathrm{Prob}(R/T) = \mathrm{Prob}(R/TM)\mathrm{Prob}(M/T) + \mathrm{Prob}(R/T{\sim}M)\mathrm{Prob}({\sim}M/T)$$

If the weights are sufficiently skewed, as they are in the above tables, a reversal of probability relations holds in the subsets of R under the further partitions of T and ~T by M and ~M. The following diagram illustrates the setup described by the tables above. The set of M's is represented by {a,b,c,d} and the ~M's by {e,f,g,h}.

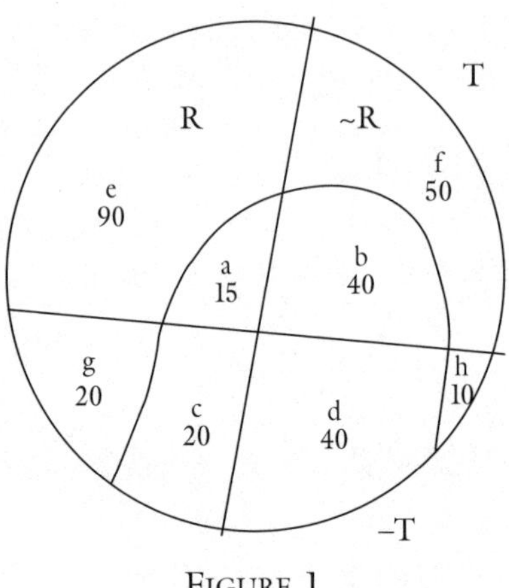

FIGURE 1

Figure 1 illustrates the consistency of the triad

a/a+b < c/c+d, and
e/e+f < g/g+h, but
a+e/a+b+e+f > c+g/c+d+g+h

where the last inequality represents the consolidated data for the total population in the example.

4. Boundary Conditions for Simpson Setups

The inequalities in the above example are preserved when the data are uniformly multiplied by any positive number. That suffices to show that there are infinitely many such setups. More generally, it is possible to have Prob(A/B) ≈ zero and Prob(A/~B) ≈ 1/n, with n = 1, and

Prob(A/BC) ≥ nProb(A/~BC), and
Prob(A/B~C) ≥ nProb(A/~B~C).

Hence, it is not only inequalities that can be reversed in repartitions of a sample space, but also equalities can be perturbed when data are repartitioned or consolidated.[5] This latter fact has bearing upon the reliability of causal inferences which aim to "screen off" spurious correlations by locating common causes for them. This is discussed below in section 6.2.

The diagnosis of Simpson's paradox in its probabilistic form showed that the reversal effects were due to skewed weights. Such skewing can be arithmetically countered by normalizing the data that represent proportions before they are used to represent percentages or probabilities. The effect of normalizing data is to provide constant denominators for the ratios that are used to represent percentages and to compute weights in the representation of probabilities as weighted averages. In the example of the trial for the new drug, there is a difference in the percentages of patients who received the placebos and those who received the drug amongst both the males and females. The aim of normalizing the data on treatments is to set up one-to-one correlations between the representation of treated males and untreated males, and similarly for females. Normalizing data to provide constant denominators is a sufficient condition for the alignment of inequalities which are exhibited by consolidated data and are represented in 2 x 2 tables to agree with the alignments of inequalities which are exhibited by the 2 x 2 x 2 tables from which the 2 x 2 tables are derived.[6] For instance, when the data from the drug trial are normalized on treatments, the drug does not appear to be effective for males, for females, nor for the total population. However, while normalizing data may be sufficient to block the reversals that characterize the paradoxical cases, it does not always lead to the right conclusion as to what the actual probability relationships are. This is illustrated by the fact that there is more than one partition which "cross grains" the partition of recoveries by treatments in the example, and different patterns of probability relations will be exhibited by subsets of the data under different repartitions. For example, keeping the figures for treatments and recoveries constant, a repartition by age might show positive correlations between recoveries for patients who are treated and are under fifty years of age, and similarly for those who are fifty years of age or older. Normalizing the data on treatments can then show a positive correlation between treatments and recoveries for those under fifty, those fifty or over, and for the combined populations. The following tables based on the same figures for recoveries in the total population illustrates this possibility. Let 'U' represent the property of being under fifty years of age, and '~U' the property of being fifty or older.

	RU	~RU	R~U	~R~U
T	20	15	85	75
~T	10	20	30	30

Here, treatment appears more favorable for recovery in both members of the partition {U, ~U}. If we "normalize" the tables to put the T's in one-to-one correspondence with the ~T's, we obtain the following tables:

	RU	~RU	R~U	~R~U
T	20	15	85	75
~T	12	23	80	80

Again treatment appears favorable for recovery in both tables and the combined table taken from them. While normalizing data is sufficient to prevent reversals of relations between percentages and probabilities when data are consolidated, it is insufficient for deciding what the correct relations are. Normalized data from different partitions of the same raw data can imply incompatible conclusions.

5. Two Spurious Problems

It has been mooted that Simpson's paradox provides counterexamples to classically valid arguments and to the Sure Thing Principle in decision theory. While the alleged counterexamples are fallacious, they do illustrate how easy it is to fall into the traps which paradoxical data facilitate.

5.1. Classically Valid Arguments

Arguments of the following form are valid in the propositional calculus. Premises: If p then r. If q then r. Conclusion: If p or q then r. Now consider the following dictionary.

p = A male patient takes the drug.
q = A female patient takes the drug.
r = Taking the drug is less favorable for recovery than not taking the drug.

It can appear on the basis of the tables and probabilities given in the examples of the drug trial and the urn model that this dictionary provides a countermodel to the PC-valid argument form.[7] A closer look at the structure of the alleged countermodel and the data dispels this appearance.

A plausible reading of the suggested counterargument assigns it the following form with (1) and (2) true but (3) false.

(1) If x is male, then Prob(Rx/Tx) < Prob(Rx/~Tx)

(2) If x is female, then Prob(Rx/Tx) < Prob(Rx/~Tx)

(3) If x if male or x is female, then Prob(Rx/Tx) < Prob(Rx/~Tx)

Is this, taken in conjunction with the tables provided, an instance of and a countermodel to the form that is classically valid? No. That it is not a countermodel is apparent when the probability values from the model are explicitly provided. The ratios to which the conditional probabilities are equivalent can be represented as percentages. Then we have the following:

If x is male, then .27 < .33.
If x if female, then .64 < .66.
But, if x is male or x is female, then .54 > .44.

The contents of the consequents are determined by the sets selected by the restrictive clauses of the antecedents and the rules governing the function Prob(../—). The propositional variable *r* does not have a univocal interpretation under the readings proposed for 'Taking the drug is less favorable for recovery than not taking the drug'. As *r* does not have a univocal interpretation on the proposed reading, the informal formulation of the argument is not an instance of the valid argument form.

Nonetheless, the argument does *appear* to be an instance of a valid form, and for many, it is intuitively *surprising* that the premises can be true and the conclusion can be false. A possible explanation for this is that within a broad, though limited, range of cases, the probability relations posited in the premises do entail a like alignment of the probability relations in the conclusion where data are consolidated. For example, as noted in section 4, when data are normalized, reversals of probability relations cannot occur. The case where data are "normal" is a special instance of a more inclusive class of arithmetical constraints on data which, if satisfied, are sufficient for the preservation of probability relations when data are consolidated.[8] If data that feature in setups where probabilistic inferences are intuitively drawn often or typically do fall within those arithmetical constraints, the inferences from probability relations that are supported by data from elements of partitions to like-probability relations when data are consolidated in conclusions will be truth-preserving (for those cases). In these cases, the weights that feature in the representations of the relevant conditional probabilities as weighted averages are not sufficiently skewed to reverse the probability alignments when data are consolidated. The general case, however, includes the cases that fall within the boundary conditions for reversals of probability relations when data are consolidated or repartitioned. This explains the intuition that the data from the example support a countermodel to a valid argument form by taking the intuition to be based upon a disposition to overgeneralize from cases where the weights do not perturb probability relations to the many cases where they do perturb them. Of course, it is an empirical matter whether the correct explanation of the apparent counterexample is due to an overgeneralization or some other quirk of intuitive reasoning in which useful but rough heuristic rules can lead to untoward conclusions.[9]

5.2. *The Sure Thing Principle*

The Sure Thing Principle (hereafter, STP) asserts that

> If you would definitely prefer *g* to *f*, either knowing that the event C obtained, or knowing that the event C did not obtain, then you definitely prefer *g* to *f*.[10]

Now consider the urn model described above and the following two player zero-sum game. Players select one of two options. Player 1 goes first and makes choices on the basis of STP, if it is applicable. Player 2 is required to take whichever option remains open. Balls are returned to the urn after they are drawn. The options are as follows:

> Option 1: Draw balls at random from the urn until you get one that contains a ~T. Bet one unit that it contains an R.
> Option 2: Draw balls at random from the urn until you get one that contains a T. Bet one unit that it contains an R.
>
> Before you exercise either option, you are told whether the selected ball contains an M or a ~M.

On a given round of the game, if both players turn up balls which have an R, or which have a ~R, the round is cancelled and another round with bets in place is played. A player gains a win when his selected ball contains an R and the other player's ball contains a ~R. The players' aim is to adopt the option that maximizes their chances of drawing balls that are inscribed with R's. Player 1 reasons as follows. Suppose he is told a given ball has an M. Then Option 1 gives him a .33 chance of it having an R compared with Option 2's .27 chance of its having an R. Next, suppose he is told that a selected ball has a ~M. Then Option 1 gives him a .66 chance of it having an R compared with Option 2's .64 chance of it having an R. Accordingly, STP appears to apply, and Player 1 selects Option 1. Player 2 is thus required to take Option 2. However, STP appears to give Player 1 bad advice. Fifty-four percent of the balls inscribed with a T are inscribed with an R, and only 44% of those inscribed with a ~T are inscribed with an R. Playing Option 1, Player 1 is more likely to have his Rs matched by Player 2, thereby cancelling the round, and is less likely to match Player 2's Rs, thereby losing the round. This remains the case despite the correlations of R's with M's and with ~M's. Has STP given Player 1 bad advice, or has he applied STP inadvisably?

For STP to be applicable to his preferences, Player 1 needs to prefer Option 1 given M and given ~M. His reasoning adopts these preferences on the basis of the probability relations

Prob(R/TM) < Prob(R/~TM)
Prob(R/T~M) < Prob(R/~T~M).

Do these rationally support a preference for Option 1 on being told that M, or ~M, in the setting of the game? No. It will help to see why the probability relations do not support these preferences if we consider a different setup than the one the players actually occupy in which Player 1's reasoning would be sound. Then, this will be contrasted with a variant of the setup the players actually occupy that is equivalent to it. The fallacy in Player 1's reasoning that leads him to adopt the preferences that are required for STP to be applicable will emerge from the contrast between these two setups.

Let balls from our model be placed in two urns. The first, Urn(M), has all and only balls that are inscribed with an M. The second, Urn(~M), has all and only balls that are inscribed with a ~M. The tables that describe this setup merely relabel the tables from the medical example in section 2 when data are partitioned by gender.

URN(M)			URN(~M)		
	R	~R		R	~R
T	15	40	T	90	50
~T	20	40	~T	20	10

Players' options and the criteria for winning and losing are unchanged. The information that M, or ~M, indicates the urn from which a ball originates. However, that information is not relevant to the players' choices. In this game, Option 1 (the ~T option) does dominate Option 2, and it has a positive expectation of showing a profit regardless of the urn from which a selected ball originates. The ratio of ~T's to R's is greater than the ratio of T's to R's in each urn. It is significant that this is not the setup that the players actually occupy and it is a different game from the one that they are playing.

Next, consider a setup where balls from our model are again sorted into two urns. The first, Urn(T), contains all and only balls inscribed with a T, and the second, Urn(~T), contains all and only balls inscribed with a ~T. Criteria for winning and losing are unchanged. Players' options are to play the game with balls drawn from Urn(~T), Option 1, or from Urn(T), Option 2. This game is equivalent to the one the players actually are playing. In it, 54% of the balls in Urn(T) have R's, and 44% of the balls in Urn(~T) have R's. Unlike the game where urns are homogenous with respect to M's and ~M's, the urns in this setup have a mixture of M's and ~M's. The relevance of that mixture is displayed by the representations of Prob(R/T) and Prob(R/~T) as weighted averages. The information that a ball has an M, or a ~M, does not perturb these ratios, and they are different ratios than those that feature in the setup with Urn(M) and Urn(~M).

The error in Player 1's reasoning was to suppose that the information concerning M's prior to each play of the game placed him in a situation analogous to the game where drawings are from Urn(M) and Urn(~M). The contents of these two urns preserve the skewed distributions that support a dominance argument for Option 1. In that game, STP applies, and it gives good advice. In the game where drawings are from Urn(T) and Urn(~T), however, there is no sound dominance argument for Option 1 given M or given ~M. The mixtures in the redistribution correspond to different ratios of R's to T's and ~T's than the ratios that feature in the game with Urn(M) and Urn(~M). These ratios are not perturbed by the "news" that a selected ball has an M (or ~M). So, this setup does not support a preference for Option 1 on being told that M or that ~M. STP is not applicable because rational players will not have the preferences that its applicability requires, that is, in the game where balls are drawn from Urn(T) and Urn(~T), a preference for Option 1 over Option 2 given M, and given ~M.

6. Statistical Inference, Causal Inference, and Probabilistic Analyses of Causation

Data sets that have the structure of Simpson's paradox have turned up in actual studies and experiments in the empirical sciences, in accountancy, in legal cases, and even in negotiations for salaries for baseball players in which their batting averages are relevant to the salaries they get.[11] For example, one player had a higher batting average than another in each of two years, but the latter had a higher batting average over the combined two-year period. Such data sets, as well as merely hypothetical data sets which share their structure, are relevant to testing theories of statistical inference, theories of causal inference, and analyses of causation which crucially rely on probability relationships.

6.1. Statistical Inference

Theories of statistical inference aim to formulate rules for drawing inferences from data about the frequencies of kinds of events or attributes to conclusions concerning their probabilities. A core issue for such theories is to determine which reference classes support such inferences and which do not support them. In the example of the drug trial, the negative associations between the rates of recovery for treated males and for treated females would seem to support an inference that the probability of recovery for a patient is higher if he or she is left untreated. Above it was noted that a partition of patients by age group could suggest the opposite conclusion. Alternately, if recovery rates for patients were probabilistically independent of both age and gender, and the association between treatments and recoveries was otherwise resilient, the appropriate frequency data to use as basis for inference would be the positive association between treatments and recoveries. This is brought out by the urn model described above. There, the association between R's and T's is independent of any other letters inscribed on the balls. The probability of a ball which is inscribed with a T also being inscribed with an R is uniquely fixed by the ratio of balls inscribed with [T R] and [~T R]. This suggests the following constraint for the plausibility of statistical inferences from data to probability assignments: Inferences from proportions exhibited by data concerning A's and B's to conditional probability assignments that correspond to those proportions, for example, Prob(A/B), are plausible with respect to a set of factors F, only if Prob(A/B) = Prob(A/B&Fi), for all Fi in F. This condition is met by the urn example concerning distributions of letters on balls; there is insufficient data in the example from the drug trial to tell whether or not it is met with respect to gender and/or with respect to the patients' ages. The underlying problem of which reference class or classes to use as a basis for inference from data to probability assignments persists even if the partition by age *and* gender is taken as a relevant alternative to either alone. Taking partitions which are fine grained or "maximally specific" as a basis for inference from data to probability assignments is no less secure from error than relying on partitions which are too coarse grained and which mask relevant information. When a reversal of probability relations under one partition of a body of data is not matched by a different partition of the data (the typical case) the question arises as to whether to take the weighted average across the data to determine probabilities or whether to normalize the data for the purposes of inference, thereby blocking the reversal. In the urn model described above, taking the weighted average gives the right answer for finding the probability of an R on a ball given that it is inscribed with a T. In other cases, normalizing the data gives the right answer. Whether it does will often turn on contingent background information which sometimes is, and often is not, available to inquirers.

6.2. Causal Inference

When kinds of events or properties are probabilistically relevant to each other, we have *prima facie* reasons to think that they are causally relevant to each other. Simpson's paradox serves as a piquant reminder of how difficult it can be to reliably infer and work out causal connections from probabilistic relationships. One example of this difficulty is provided by Reichenbach's attempt to identify common causes of events which are correlated but are causally independent of each other.[12] His proposal is that correlated events are causally independent of each other provided that there is some event which "screens off" the correlation. Assume that B is positively probabilistically relevant to A, that is, Prob(A/B) > Prob(A/~B). He says that C "screens off" B from A and is a common cause of them both just in case Prob(A/BC) = Prob(A/~BC). Recall that conditional probabilities can be represented as weighted averages. Accordingly, if the weights, Prob(B/C) and Prob(~B/C), are appropriately skewed, the screening off condition can be fulfilled without C serving as a common cause of A and B. To find an appropriate skewing, it is sufficient to provide models which satisfy the following formulae:

> Let terms take only positive values in the interval [0, 1]. Let Prob(A/BC) = x, and Prob(A/~BC) = y. On Reichenbach's proposal,
>
> C screens off A from B (and B from A, as independence is symmetrical) if and only if Prob(A/B) > Prob(A/~B) and x = y.
>
> Representing Prob(A/B) and Prob(A/~B) as weighted averages, the screening-off condition has the following form:

$$x(a) + b(c) > y(d) + e(f), \text{ and } x = y.$$

The probabilistic constraints on the values for {a,b,c,d,e,f} are insufficient to guarantee uniqueness for the screening-off factor C. For example, C's obtaining could be necessary and sufficient for D's obtaining so that C screens off A from B if and only if D does so as well. This allows for spurious screening-off conditions or, unlikely, for multiple common causes. It also has the consequence that from an arithmetical perspective, any positive correlation between A and B can be associated with some condition C which "screens off" A from B. This follows from the boundary conditions described above. The moral to draw is not that screening off is trivial or arbitrary, but that one needs to specify which conditions that fulfill the screening-off condition will, if they exist, count as relevant to establishing causal independence. The screening-off condition requires supplementation if it is to be taken as sufficient for identifying common causes of correlations of causally independent events or attributes.

6.3. Probabilistic Analyses of Causation

Reichenbach's screening-off condition is a special case of more general analyses of causation in terms of probabilistic relations. The intuition that such analyses of causation share is that causes increase the probability of their effects. Simpson's paradox poses a problem for this basic intuition since it shows that probabilistic relevance can be due to the effects of averaging in which causal information is lost. For example, if smokers attempt to counter the cardiovascular effects of their habit by taking regular exercise, and nonsmokers are blasé about exercising, there can be a negative correlation between smoking and heart disease, even if the incidence of heart disease is greater amongst the smokers who exercise compared with the nonsmokers who exercise, and similarly for the smokers who do not exercise compared with the nonsmokers who do not exercise. Such examples suggest that probabilistic relevance relative to background factors can better serve as the basis for extrapolating causal relevance. For example, B is causally relevant to A if and only if Prob(A/B and Fi) is greater than Prob(A/~B and Fi) for all relevant Fi. However, this proposal falls afoul in cases like that described by the urn model above. Suppose that a ball's being inscribed with an M or a ~M is taken to be the only potentially relevant background factor for the probabilities of its being inscribed with other symbols. Then we have the following:

Prob(R/TM) < Prob(R/~TM)
Prob(R/T~M) < Prob(R/~T~M)

But it would be an error to infer either that ~T or T is causally relevant to R, or that Prob(R/~T) > Prob(R/T). Even if further constraints concerning the discreteness of causes and effects and their temporal order are provided to supplement the probabilistic relations, examples which have the structure of the urn model can be provided to meet these as well. Sometimes the correlations in the cells of relevant partitions are the correct basis for inferring causal relations, and sometimes they are spurious correlations that should be ignored. It remains an outstanding problem for probabilistic analyses of causation to formulate supplementary conditions on probabilistic relations for the purpose of using the latter to infer causal connections.

7. Simpson's Paradox in Dynamic Settings

In the previous section I noted that paradoxical setups have occurred in a wide range of actual settings. Further, I noted that when they do occur, causal relationships can be masked by probability relationships and other correlations. For some cases, when these are disentangled, phenomena that are deeply puzzling or that even seem impossible (but for the fact that they occur) can become transparent. An example of phenomena that have puzzled biologists as well as ethicists is the occurrence of altruistic behaviors in species. It is a matter of definition that altruistic behavior disadvantages the individuals who engage in it while others reap its benefits. How, then, could it become a stable trait of the behavior of a group in a setup that evolves across time where the course of evolution punishes organisms that are less fit than those with whom they compete? Even if altruistic behavior did emerge, wouldn't it be an unstable characteristic of the group that exhibited it? Wouldn't they, or their behavior, be exploited by competitors and then driven to extinction or near extinction? Simpson setups provide models that allow for the evolution of altruism. Moreover, if some further conditions are imposed on those setups, altruism can become a stable feature of them. Elliott Sober describes a simplified model for the evolution of altruism in a biological setting. Once such models are at hand, it is a small matter to reinterpret them as models of possible social systems, for example, economic or political systems. Mapping social phenomena onto such models or variants them might be useful for explaining some social phenomena; also, they may be useful for institutional design.

Sober describes a highly simplified and extreme case for illustrative purposes.[13] Assume a total system which consists of equally numerous selfish elements (S's) and altruistic elements (A's) that form two distinct groups with initially skewed distributions of the two kinds of elements. Suppose that the average fitness of a population of elements declines as the percentage of its selfish members increases. The decline is experienced by both the S's and the A's. The S's gain a benefit from their interactions with A's, and the A's absorb the costs of their interactions with S's. The gains and losses of the S's in their interactions with each other tend to cancel out, and as fewer A's are available to be exploited as the percentage of S's increases in a group, their fitness level declines as well. Let a single selfish element in a population of 99 A's have a fitness level of 4, and the 99 A's a fitness level of 3, where fitness is narrowly interpreted to represent the expected number of offspring in that arrangement (say the elements propagate uniparentally). In an arrangement in which there are 99 S's and only 1 A, the S's level of fitness is 2, and the A's level of fitness is 1. As the percentage of S's increases, the level of fitness for A's declines continuously from 3 (with 1% S's) to 1 (with 99% S's), and there is a corresponding decline in the level of fitness for S's from 4 to 2. The average level of fitness for the total population declines from just over 3 to just under two as the ratio of S's to A's changes from 1:99 to 99:1. Now consider two groups, the first of which has just one S and 99 A's, and the second of which has one A and 99 S's. Let *w* represent the average fitness for elements in the two groups. The following table summarizes this arrangement.

Group 1	Group 2	Global Average
1S; w = 4	99S; w = 2	100S; w = 2.02
99A; w = 3	1A; w = 1	100A; w = 2.98

In this arrangement, the fitness level of S's is greater than that of A's in both groups, but it is lower than A's in the global average. Now suppose that parents die after reproducing, and that their reproduction exactly correlates with their levels of fitness. The census for offspring and their frequencies compared with frequencies for their parents are provided in the following table.

	Group 1	Group 2	Global Ensemble
Parent Frequency	1%S; 99%A	99%S; 1%A	50%S; 50%A
Offspring Census	4S; 297A	198S; 1A	202S; 298A
Offspring Frequency	1.3%S; 98.7%A	99.5%S; .5%A	40%S; 60%A

After one reproductive cycle, the frequency of A's has declined in each group, but it has increased in the global ensemble. What will happen after a succession of reproductive cycles? The reproduction rule limits the lonely A in group 2 to simply replacing itself while S's double with each generation. The hold of the A's on frequency declines, approximately halving, with each successive generation. The frequency of S's in Group 1 also rises with each successive generation, and this is bad news for the A's in Group 1. They are ineluctably driven to a fixation point where their population will stabilize at replacement while S's population continues to double in size with each generation. In this setup, the early global bloom of altruism is nipped by the local and global winter of selfishness, never to bloom again.

In order for reversal effects due to an initial skewing of elements to be sustained in a system, a skewing comparable to the skewing of the initial setup has to be sustained as the system evolves. In a system in which S's have an advantage over A's and they are equally distributed, S's will quickly become dominant and drive the A's to extinction or near extinction. However, if the system is structured so that there is an imbalance in the distribution and S's are clustered together with only a few A's amongst them, and A's are clustered together with few S's amongst them, it will be in the interest of the S's clustered with A's to keep other S's at bay, and this is an interest which they will share with the A's. Of course, even if they are successful at keeping other S's at bay, if their local numbers increase at a rate in excess of the increase for A's, as in the above tables for A's and S's, their comparative advantage over other S's will decline unless they redress the balance by expelling some of their numbers to form more clusters of S's. Alternately, S's might kill the offspring of other S's who are competitors in a biparental setup, thereby preserving a skewing effect. A variety of possible mechanisms are able to preserve the skewing. Sober observes that, "The groups must form new colonies rapidly enough to offset the within-group process that serves to displace the altruistic trait. Given favorable parameter values, altruism may come to exist at some stable intermediate frequency." He continues,

> Also crucial is the question of how new colonies are established. If groups are founded by individuals who are alike, this will enhance and preserve intergroup variation and allow group selection to exert a more powerful influence on the advancement of altruism. If, on the other hand, migrants from different groups mix together and then found new groups, between-group variance will be diminished and the evolution of altruism will be more difficult.[14]

Biological examples provide natural settings for exploring the effects of reproduction and replacement. Economic setups in which there is competition also have counterparts of extinction, reproduction, and replacement. Simpson setups might occur in them; independently of whether they are found to occur in them, it may be possible (and desirable) to design systems to exploit such possibilities and to secure stable pockets of altruism in a largely open-market system. However, if such setups can promote altruism despite evolutionary pressure against it, they have a structure that can also promote other (less desirable) traits against which there is evolutionary pressure, for example, stupidity and ignorance. They also suggest how a minority political party might gain maximum effectiveness in competition with other parties.

It is an empirical question whether Simpson setups occur in nature or society, and if they do, whether they are dynamically stable. Inquiry into whether they occur in large biological, social, or economic systems is in its infancy. One difficulty such inquiries face is intrinsic to Simpson setups: any body of data which is rich enough to support inferences to probability assignments can be repartitioned so that relations between proportions in the cells of the partition are reversed when the data are consolidated. This trivial arithmetical fact poses some deep difficulties for empirical inquiry and it exacerbates some already familiar difficulties. When a reversal is observed under partitions of data, it is apt to ask whether they are an artefact of the arithmetic or a stable feature of the kinds that are represented by the partitions. At this juncture applied problems of selecting the right reference classes for statistical inferences, extrapolating causal relations from statistical data, and the classical problem of induction join hands to make the inquirer's job a high risk occupation.

GARY MALINAS
University of Queensland

NOTES

1. G. U. Yule, "Notes on the Theory of Association of Attributes in Statistics," *Biometrika* 2 (1903): 121–34. M. R. Cohen and E. Nagel, *An Introduction to Logic and Scientific Method* (New York: Harcourt, Brace and Co., 1934). E. H. Simpson, "The Interpretation of Interaction in Contingency Tables," *Journal of the Royal Statistical Society* B 13 (1951): 238–41.

2. Nancy Cartwright, "Causal Laws and Effective Strategies," *Nous* 13 (1979): 419–37. Brian Skyrms, *Causal Necessity* (New Haven: Yale University Press, 1980).

3. Judea Pearl raises the issue of whether Simpson's Paradox provides counterexamples to argument forms which are valid in the propositional calculus in *Probabilistic Reasoning in Intelligent Systems* (San Mateo, CA: Morgan Kaufman, 1988). C. R. Blyth takes paradoxical data sets to provide counterexamples to the Sure Thing Principle in "On Simpson's Paradox and the Sure-Thing Principle," *Journal of the American Statistical Association* 67 (1972): [Theory and Methods Section] 364–66.

4. This and the following section recycle the tables and diagram used in Gary Malinas, "Simpson's Paradox and the Wayward Researcher," *Australasian Journal of Philosophy* 75 (1997): 343–59.

5. The boundary conditions for Simpson setups are given in Blyth, op. cit., and Y. Mittal, "Homogeneity of Subpopulations and Simpson's Paradox," *Journal of the American Statistical Association* 86 (1991): [Theory and Methods Section] 167–72.

6. Mittal, op. cit., provides a proof that data which are normalized do not give rise to the kinds of reversals which characterize Simpson's Paradox.

7. C.f. Pearl, op. cit.

8. C.f. Mittal, op. cit.

9. There is the further possibility that the proposed dictionary does provide a countermodel to the PC-valid form, and the proposed reading and interpretation of the argument as a case of equivocation does not correctly represent its form. While my analysis of the proposed countermodel and the explanation of why it intuitively appears to be a countermodel does not preclude this possibility, it does shift the onus to the provision of reasons that finesse the analysis.

10. L. J. Savage, *The Foundations of Statistics* (New York: John Wiley and Sons, 1954), pp. 21–22.

11. For examples, see S. Sunder, "Simpson's Reversal Paradox and Cost Allocations," *Journal of Accounting Research* 21 (1983): 222–33. R. J. Thornton and J. T. Innes, "On Simpson's Paradox in Economic Statistics," *Oxford Bulletin of Economics and Statistics* 47 (1985): 387–94. J. E. Cohen, "An Uncertainty Principle in Demography and the Unisex Issue," *The American Statistician* 40 (1986): 32–39. References from Mittal, op. cit.

12. Hans Reichenbach, *The Direction of Time* (Berkeley and Los Angeles: University of California Press, 1971), ch. 4.

13. Elliott Sober, *Philosophy of Biology* (Oxford: Oxford University Press, 1993), pp. 98–102. The tables below are recycled from Sober's discussion.

14. Elliott Sober, *The Nature of Selection* (Chicago: University of Chicago Press, 1993), p. 329.

9

Conditional Probability Is the Very Guide of Life

ALAN HÁJEK

I was a student of mathematics and statistics at Melbourne University before I became a philosopher. I was puzzled by the way in which orthodox Kolmogorov probability theory defines conditional probability, almost as an afterthought, via the usual ratio formula: $P(A|B) = P(A \cap B)/P(B)$, provided $P(B) > 0$. The proviso struck me as coy, and perhaps even worrisome, especially since my professors drummed into me that probability zero events can happen! At the University of Western Ontario, Bill Harper introduced me to Popper functions, primitive conditional probability functions. I liked them. My concerns about conditional probability deepened at Princeton University when I wrote my dissertation on probabilities of conditionals under the direction of Bas van Fraassen and David Lewis. I came to have further misgivings about the ratio formula, and went on to campaign against it and in favor of Popper functions.

Meanwhile, I became fascinated by the various 'interpretations' of probability. The reference-class problem is traditionally presented as a problem for the frequentist interpretations: all frequentist probabilities are explicitly or tacitly relativized to a reference class. But it seemed to me that if conditional probability is the fundamental notion of probability theory, then all probabilities must be tacitly relativized, however they are interpreted. Suddenly I saw the reference-class problem everywhere.

My two obsessions converged. The ubiquity of the reference-class problem across all the interpretations of probability gave me further grounds for rejecting the Kolmogorov orthodoxy in favor of primitive conditional probability functions. Vive la révolution!

—A. H.

* * *

Everyone knows that the reference-class problem is a problem for the frequentist interpretation of probability—everyone, that is, who worries about such things in the first place. What is not well known is that, suitably qualified, it is a problem for everyone. My first goal in this paper is to convince you of this by giving a general statement of the problem, and then systematically showing how it arises for all the leading interpretations of probability: the frequentist interpretation, of course, in its various guises, but also the classical, logical, propensity, and subjectivist interpretations.

But there is a sense in which a problem for everyone is a problem for no one. That is, the reference-class problem does not give us grounds for favoring some interpretations over others, since it besets them all indiscriminately. And given its seeming inevitability, perhaps we were wrong to think of it as a problem for the interpretation of probability at all. Perhaps, rather, it reveals a fundamental fact about the nature of probability. I contend that probability is essentially a two-place notion: all probability statements of any interest should be thought of as being at least tacitly relativized, tacitly conditional. This turns the tables on the traditional approach to probability, enshrined in Kolmogorov's axiomatization, that sees unconditional probability as fundamental, and that analyzes conditional probability in terms of the usual ratio formula. I have argued elsewhere (forthcoming) that we should reject the ratio analysis of conditional probability and take conditional probability as the proper primitive of probability theory. My second goal here, then, is to show how the ubiquity of the reference-class problem only reinforces these conclusions: to the extent that it is a problem at all, it is one for the ratio analysis of conditional probability, and indeed for any attempt to reduce conditional probability to unconditional probability.

1. What Is the Reference-Class Problem?

As far as I am aware, recognition of the reference-class problem originates with Venn (1876), and as usual his remarks on it are years ahead of his time. He begins by noting: "It is obvious that every individual thing or event has an indefinite number of properties or attributes observable in it, and might therefore be considered as belonging to an indefinite number of different classes of things . . ." (p. 194). Then, he canvasses how this leads to a problem in assigning probabilities to individuals, such as the probability that John Smith, a consumptive Englishman aged fifty, will live to sixty-one, and he concludes: "This variety of classes to which the individual may be referred owing to his possession of a multiplicity of attributes, has an important bearing on the process of inference . . ." (p. 196).

The reference-class problem has traditionally been regarded as a problem for *frequentism*; I think it is fair to say, moreover, that it is taken to be pretty much the most serious problem for frequentism. Surprisingly, however, it is generally unacknowledged that something akin to the reference-class problem besets *all* of the other leading interpretations of probability.[1]

Before defending this claim, I first need to state the reference-class problem in a general form. It arises when we wish to assign a probability to a single event E. We may suppose that E can be regarded as a token of various event-types. The reference-class problem is that the probability of E can change, depending on how it is typed. *Qua* event of type 1, its probability is p_1; *qua* event of type 2, its probability is p_2, where $p_1 \neq p_2$; and so on. Stated this way, the problem can be regarded as metaphysical: what, then, is *the* probability of E? For E remains the same, irrespective of how it is typed, and it surely has only one (unconditional) probability.[2] This quickly turns into an epistemological problem when we are wondering how confident we should be of E's occurrence. Depending on how we classify E, it seems that different degrees of confidence are justified.[3]

This is really a special case of a more general problem that one might still call 'the reference-class problem'. Let E be a proposition—it might correspond to an event-token, or an event-type, or statement in some language, or a set of possible worlds. What we want is the unconditional probability of E; but what we have are a host of unequal conditional probabilities of the form P(E, given A), P(E, given B), P(E, given C), and so on; moreover, we lack unconditional probabilities for A, B, C, etc. Relativized to the condition A, E has one probability; relativized to the condition B, it has another; and so on. What, then, is *the* probability of E?

2. The Reference-Class Problem and the Leading Interpretations of Probability

Frequentism

Let us return to frequentism for the moment. Since it comes in a number of flavors, it is worth quickly reviewing how the reference-class problem arises for some of the most important ones.

Frequentists, as I have said, identify probability with relative frequency—it's the exact nature of this identification that distinguishes among them. But the word 'relative' is already a tip-off that they will all face a reference-class problem. *Actual frequentists* (who are found more among scientists than among philosophers these days) identify the probability of an event-token of the form 'individual X has property Y' with a ratio of two frequencies: the denominator is the frequency of individuals of

X's type in the actual world, while the numerator is the frequency of such individuals who also have property Y. Thus, using an example of Venn's (p. 147), consider the probability of a given infant (this is the individual) living to be eighty years of age (this is the property). According to Venn, the denominator is the number of "all men"; the numerator is the number of men who live to age eighty. He assumes this ratio is 1/10. This, then, is the desired probability according to an actual frequentist.

Or is it? Venn does not specify whether the infant in question is male or not. He does specifically speak of "all men," although it's not clear whether this is just a quaint and politically incorrect way of saying "all people," or literally "all human males." I suspect it's the former. No matter—it's problematic either way, and it only drives home the reference-class problem. If it's the former, then the reference class is surely too broad, for the sex of the infant is surely relevant to its longevity. If it's the latter, then we had better go back and specify that the infant is male, or else it won't even be a member of the reference class. Be that as it may, the problem is clear: we will get one probability for the infant's reaching eighty, *qua* human; another for its probability of reaching eighty, *qua* human male. And obviously this is just the beginning, for our infant has countless further properties, many of which will make a difference to the desired relative frequency. What, then, is its probability of reaching eighty, *sans qualification*?

Limiting relative frequentists identify probability with the limit of a relative frequency sequence. Von Mises (1957) offers a sophisticated formulation of limiting frequentism based on the notion of a *collective*, rendered precise by Church: a hypothetical infinite sequence of 'attributes' (possible outcomes) of a specified experiment, for which the limiting relative frequency of any attribute exists, and is the same in any recursively specified subsequence. The probability of an attribute A, relative to a collective ω, is then defined as the limiting relative frequency of A in ω. Changing the collective will in general change the probability of A. This is how something akin to the reference-class problem, or again the reference *sequence* problem, arises for von Mises. Something akin—I choose my words carefully, since A is not here an event-token. Indeed, von Mises makes a point of eschewing the assignment of probabilities to single events. For example: "We can say nothing about the probability of death of an individual even if we know his condition of life and health in detail. The phrase 'probability of death', when it refers to a single person, has no meaning at all for us" (p. 11). Also: "It is utter nonsense to say, for instance, that Mr. X, now aged forty, has the probability 0.011 of dying in the course of the next year" (pp. 17–18).

So von Mises has a simple answer to the reference-class problem: deny that there is a problem. By refusing to assign probabilities to any single case event E, he deftly evades the problem of assigning E a probability *qua* member of this or that reference class. By dismissing talk of single-case probabilities as having "no meaning at all for us," and as "utter nonsense," the problem simply goes away. It goes away, that is, if you share von Mises's viewpoint; if you don't, the problem is simply ignored.

Venn's approach lies at the opposite end of the spectrum from von Mises's. Venn at this point seems to be committed to there being *many* probabilities of a given event-token, each relativized to a suitable choice of reference class, while von Mises is committed to there being *none*.[4] As we will see, my own proposal lies at the Venn end of the spectrum.

Classical Probability

The classical interpretation purports to determine probability assignments in the face of no evidence at all, or symmetrically balanced evidence. Its guiding idea is to give equal weight to each member of a certain set of events. As such, it actually bears certain structural similarities to frequentism (which gives equal weight to each member of a certain sequence of events). The classical probability of an event is again a ratio of two frequencies; again, the denominator counts all the cases of a certain type, and the numerator counts among them all the cases in which the event occurs—thus, it is again a *relative frequency* of a certain kind. And here again is our tip-off that a reference-class problem looms. This time it is *possible events,* rather than actual events, that are the cases counted: frequentism gone modal, if you will. It is assumed that we can partition the space of possible events into a set of 'equipossibilities', events for which we have no evidence, or symmetrically balanced evidence. Now there is no definitional obstacle to determining the probability of an event-token E. The probability of E is simply the fraction of the total number of these possibilities in which E occurs. (While E occurs at most once, the *possibilities* of its occurring may be manifold.) Classical probabilities thus must be relativized to a specification of the equipossibilities. Said in more modern-sounding terms: we must first specify a certain sort of symmetry in our probability space, a respect of uniformity of our probability assignment. Classical probabilities thus must be relativized to a specification of such a uniformity. This is the reference-class problem for them. *Qua* member of one such specification, we get one probability for an event E; *qua* member of another such specification, we get another.

Bertrand provided some of the earliest and most famous paradoxes of probability theory as problems specifically for the classical theory of probability. I regard them as making vivid the reference-class problem for classical probabilities. The following example (adapted from van Fraassen 1989, who in turn adapts it from Nagel) nicely illustrates how Bertrandstyle paradoxes work. A factory produces cubes with side-length between 0 and 1 foot; what is the probability that a randomly chosen cube has side-length between 0 and 1/2 a foot? The tempting answer is 1/2, as we imagine a process of production that is uniformly distributed over side-length. But the question could have been given an equivalent restatement: A factory produces cubes with face-area between 0 and 1 square-feet; what is the probability that a randomly chosen cube has face-area between 0 and 1/4 square-feet? Now the tempting answer is 1/4, as we imagine a process of production that is uniformly distributed over face-area. And it could have been restated equivalently again: A factory produces cubes with volume between 0 and 1 cubic feet; what is the probability that a randomly chosen cube has volume between 0 and 1/8 cubic-feet? Now the tempting answer is 1/8, as we imagine a process of production that is uniformly distributed over volume. What, then, is *the* probability of the event in question?

Logical Probability

The logical interpretation generalizes the notion that probability is determined in the absence of evidence, or in the face of symmetrically balanced evidence, to allow probability to be determined by the evidence, whatever it may be. Its most notable proponent, Carnap (for example, 1950) thought of probability theory as an elaboration of deductive logic. Specifically, he sought to explicate 'the degree to which hypothesis h is confirmed by evidence e', with the 'correct' conditional probability c(h, e) its explication. Statements of logical probability such as 'c(h, e) = x' were then to be thought of as logical truths.

Again, there is no special difficulty in assigning logical probabilities to single-case events. If our language is rich enough, we can always formulate a statement to the effect that a given event E occurs. However, logical probability is assigned not simply to such a statement, but to such a statement relativized to another (evidence) statement. Thus, we can determine the logical probability that the next raven observed is black, *given* the evidence that ten (observed) ravens were all black, the probability that the next raven is black, given the evidence that three (observed) ravens were purple and one was orange, and so on. Moreover, all such conditional probability statements are sensitive to the choice of language in which such statements are formulated: change the language, and the c function changes. *Qua* event described in one language, and relativized to a certain evidence statement, 'the next raven observed is black' has one probability; *qua* event described in some other language, and relativized to some other evidence statement, it has another probability.[5]

But what about the probability that the next raven is black, *simpliciter*? Isn't that simply the probability that the next raven is black, conditional on a tautology? Things are not that simple. I address the points in increasing order of importance.

Firstly, and least importantly, we will have to make a decision: is it to be a tautology of *classical* logic? It is not obvious that it should. Carnap at one stage favored a 'rational betting odds' view of logical probabilities: roughly, any ideally rational agent would agree to bet on a proposition at odds dictated by its logical probability (I ignore here complications about what the agent's evidence is). But as Weatherson (1998) argues, the appropriate logic for this interpretation is *intuitionistic*. His idea is that a bet on a proposition does not pay off until that proposition is verified, and intuitionistic logic is the one appropriate for a verificationist notion of truth.

Secondly, and far more importantly, our tautology will have to be formulated in some language or other, and once again our probabilities will in general be sensitive to this choice. So we do not get a single probability for the next raven being black, conditional on a tautology, but rather many such probabilities. To be sure, we could fix our language once and for all, thereby fixing our probabilities once and for all. But at this point logic seems to give way to arbitrariness: why should one language be chosen rather than another?

Now *perhaps* Carnap could appeal to a strong form of antinominalism, according to which some predicates correspond to 'natural' properties and relations, and others don't. He could perhaps hope to find a 'canonical' language, whose predicates consist of all and only such 'natural' predicates. But perhaps not. For naturalness comes in degrees. 'Green' is supposed to be a natural predicate, and 'grue' not. But really 'grue' is by no means the bottom of the barrel (simply tack on further disjuncts to its definition to create 'gruellow', 'gruellowurple', and still worse monstrosities); and 'green' is by no means the top of the ladder (it being itself a disjunction corresponding to many different wavelengths with a vague and somewhat arbitrary cut-off point, and applying heterogeneously to surfaces, radiant lights, after-images, images in dreams, and so on). Furthermore, even if we could somehow give a 'naturalness' ordering of predicates, and only admit those above a certain threshold, it would be ambitious to say the least to try to put together an exhaustive list of them. Clearly, the creator of a 'canonical' language has his work cut out for him. And for what it's worth, I would say he has that he has left 'logic' far behind.

But worst of all, recalling Bertrand's paradoxes for the classical interpretation, this proposal should strike one as quite ill-conceived. While logical probability generalizes classical probability, it retains its guiding idea that *symmetries among possibilities* should somehow determine *probabilities*. It thus retains its chief problem that where there are multiple respects of symmetry, probabilities have to be relativized to a particular choice among them. Recall the cube problem. *Logic* cannot tell us what procedures a given factory adopts in making cubes, nor which of the various competing respects of symmetry should be assumed. So even if we could find a canonical language, and agree on which sorts of tautologies in that language to conditionalize on, we should still be suspicious of any claim that it is then a matter of logic which of the possible symmetries is the 'right' one. Indeed, how could it be a *logical truth* that the factory adopts a procedure that is uniform, rather than biased, with respect to any of the possible parameterizations of the problem? Far more reasonable, though, is the thought that the probability of a cube having side-length between 0 and 1/2 can be determined *given* the nontautological evidence that the factory uses a procedure that is uniform according to one particular parametrization.

Here is an analogy. *Logic* cannot tell us which premises are true and which false in a given argument (setting aside those that are logically true or logically false).[6] All it can tell us is that certain conclusions are entailed by certain (sets of) premises, and others are not—it can only adjudicate the truth of the conclusions *relative to* the truth of those premises. Deductive logic can as it were make pronouncements on *conditional* truth, but not on unconditional truth. Logical probability purports to give us a notion of partial entailment. At best, it can only deliver probabilities of statements *relative to* the truth of other statements. It cannot make pronouncements on unconditional probabilities—be they of event-tokens, or otherwise.

The Propensity Interpretation

Propensity theorists think of probability as a physical 'propensity', or disposition, or tendency of a given type of physical situation to yield an outcome of a certain kind, or to yield a long-run relative frequency of such an outcome. For example, according to Popper (1959a), a probability p of an outcome of a certain type is a propensity of a repeatable experiment to produce outcomes of that type with limiting relative frequency p. The propensity interpretation is explicitly intended to make sense of probabilities of single events. However, for Popper, such an event does not have a propensity *simpliciter*; it only has a propensity insofar as it is generated by some "experimental arrangement." Or consider Giere's (1973) formulation, which takes as given a chance setup, CSU. He interprets the statement "P(E) = r" as follows: "The strength of the propensity of CSU to produce outcome E on trial L is r" (p. 471). Any assignment of propensities, then, must be relativized to a chance setup. This is typical of propensity theorists.[7] The result is a schema that by now should look familiar. *Qua* event generated by such-and-such physical situation, E has one propensity; *qua* event generated by another physical situation, it has a different propensity. We face this even in simple setups, such as coin tossing—for example, certain magicians can create an 'experimental arrangement' in which a given coin always land heads. All the more we face it in highly complex and large scale setups. Consider the propensity that the next space shuttle launch will end in disaster; it is quite unclear exactly what we should take to be the experimental arrangement, yet the arrangement makes a difference to the propensity.

Subjectivism

Subjectivists such as Ramsey and de Finetti regard probabilities as degrees of belief of suitable agents. It would seem that a reference-class problem of sorts arises immediately: where different agents have different degrees of belief in event-token E, there is no such thing as *the* probability of E; rather, we have to relativize its probability to this or that agent. A reference-class problem *of sorts*—for so far this one seems rather tame to me, even if it deserves the name. In a sense, subjectivists do not so much endorse one interpretation of probability, as a host of interpretations. We have Aaron's degrees of belief, Abel's degrees of belief, Abigail's degrees of belief, and so on—or better still, Aaron's degrees of belief-at-time-t_1, Aaron's degrees of belief-at-time-t_2, . . . , Abel's degrees of belief-at-time-t_1, Abel's degrees of belief-at-time-t_2, . . . , and so on. That is, there are as many legitimate interpretations of the probability calculus for the subjectivist as there are legitimate sets of degrees of belief. Moreover, a radical subjectivist such as de Finetti recognizes no constraints on assignments of subjective probabilities beyond their conformity to the probability calculus (with finite additivity). So it is hard to see how a reference-class problem could arise for such a subjectivist: Aaron-at-t_1's assignment to E is whatever it happens to be, Abel-at-t_2's is whatever it happens to be, and so on. *Qua* nothing.

I did say at the outset that, *suitably qualified*, the reference-class problem is a problem for everyone. I did not want to pause then to add the qualification, but now I should. The radical subjectivist's probability assignments are so unconstrained that there is no interesting reference-class problem for them. But if this is supposed to be a virtue of radical subjectivism, it is won all too cheaply. With so little constraining subjective probabilities, they can be can be totally insensitive to the way the world is. What probability do you assign, right now, to John Smith's living to age 61? Say 0.12345, or 0, or 1, or $1/\pi$ or whatever you like. It doesn't matter—as long as you stay coherent, you are supposedly beyond reproach. Thus, Hild (forthcoming) cogently lampoons the radical subjectivist for offering a "no-theory theory" (p. 27).

Interesting versions of the reference-class problem do arise, however, for certain less radical subjectivists, which I would say includes most subjectivists today—namely those who endorse certain further constraints on an agent's degrees of belief. As well they should.

Expert Functions, and Further Constraints. We often let our subjective probability assignments be guided by external sources. In particular, we may want to recognize the role that certain objective facts, or that experts about a subject matter of interest to us, may play in constraining those assignments. Call probability function Q an *expert function for* P if the following condition holds:

$$(*)\quad P(X|Q(X) = x) = x \quad \text{for all X such that } P(Q(X) = x) > 0.$$[8]

The idea is that the agent whose credence function is P strives to 'track' the assignments of Q, so that if the agent were certain of a particular Q-assignment, she would follow suit, making it her own. We might restrict the domain of X's for which (*) holds—perhaps to the domain of expertise of an expert on a particular subject matter. For example, if your favorite weather forecaster assigns probability 0.1 to its raining tomorrow, and you treat him as an expert on metereological matters, then you will assign probability 0.1 to its raining tomorrow; however, you may not place the same trust in his assignments at the race track. Be that as it may, there could be an interesting class of propositions for which the equation in (*) holds, for an agent with probability function P, with Q playing the role of an 'expert'.

The so-called Principle of Direct Probability bids one to treat relative frequency information as just such an 'expert'. For example, it may be reasonable for you to assign:

> P(heads on this coin toss | 95 out of 100 tosses of the coin landed heads) = 0.95.

A related principle, made famous to philosophers by Lewis (1980) asserts such a connection between a rational agent's beliefs about the *objective chance* of an event at a time, and her subjective probabilities. Lewis calls it the "Principal Principle" because he believes it is constitutive of chances to play this constraining role on credences:

$$P(E|\text{ch}(E) = p \;\&\; A) = p$$

where ch is the objective single-case chance function (perhaps relativized to a time), and A is any 'admissible' proposition—roughly, one that does not yield any extra information about whether E is the case or not. Thus, the probability that you should give to the coin landing heads on the next toss, given that it is fair and thus has a chance of half of doing so, is 1/2. A frequentist who thinks that chances just *are* relative frequencies would presumably think that the Principal Principle just *is* the Principle of Direct Probability; but Lewis's principle may well appeal to those who have a very different view about chances (e.g., propensity theorists).

Van Fraassen (1984 and 1995), following Goldstein (1983), contends that the probability assignments of your *future selves* should place certain constraints on your current probability assignments. He encapsulates this idea in his Reflection Principle, which we may write as follows:

$$P_{t_0}(E|P_{t_1}(E) = p) = p.$$

Here, P_{t_0} is your probability function at some time t_0, and P_{t_1} is your function at some later time t_1. Thus, for example, if you are now certain that tomorrow you will give probability 1/3 to its raining the day after tomorrow, then you should now give probability 1/3 to its raining that day. Van Fraassen defends the Reflection Principle with a diachronic Dutch Book argument (1984), and by analogizing violations of it to the sort of pragmatic inconsistency that one finds in Moore's paradox (1995).

Finally, if there really is such a thing as logical probability, then presumably it too has a claim on your credences. As I said, Carnap at one point regarded logical probabilities as subjective probabilities of an ideally rational agent. The logical probability that it will rain tomorrow, given all the evidence at your disposal, is presumably the probability that you should assign to its raining tomorrow if you were ideally rational. In this sense, logical probability is yet another expert function—perhaps the ultimate one, if Carnap is to be believed.

With various expert functions now in place, the reference-class problem is poised to strike. In fact, it can now strike in two different, though closely related, ways: firstly, if the expert functions disagree with one another; secondly, if the expert functions themselves are susceptible to a reference-class problem. Let's take these points in order.

All is well if all your experts speak in unison—as it might be, 10% of days 'like' tomorrow were rainy days, your favorite weather forecaster assigns a probability of 0.1 to its raining tomorrow, your own research convinces you that the chance of rain is 0.1, your current probability assignments to your future probability assignments concur, and (somewhat fancifully) it turns out that the logical probability of rain tomorrow, given your evidence, is the same again. But what if all is not well? Suppose you hear conflicting weather reports, none of which aligns with the frequency data at your disposal, nor again with your best estimate of the objective chance, which in turn differs from your best projections as to what your future selves will believe, which is also at odds with the logical probability. You can't serve all your masters at once, so you have to play favorites. But who trumps whom, which trumps which? You have no difficulty forming a series of conditional probabilities, each of the form (*), with different functions playing the role of Q in each case. Your difficulty arises in combining them to arrive at a single unconditional probability assignment.

Now, of course, you can simply weight your various experts' assignments, and use the law of total probability to mix them in order to come up with such an assignment. But what are the weights to be? If they are totally unconstrained, then we risk collapsing into radical subjectivism, and its 'no-theory theory': make the weights 0.12345, or 0, or 1, or $1/\pi$ or whatever you like. But if the weights are constrained by something external—some *expert*—then we find ourselves with further conditional probabilities, and no respite. Moreover, Simpson's paradox teaches us of the perils we can face when we mix probability assignments in this way: correlations that all of the experts see can be washed out or even reversed. Worse still, these correlations can be reversed again when we partition our probability space more finely—which is to say, when we refine our reference classes. Enter the reference-class problem again.

A further, related problem arises when the expert functions themselves are susceptible to a reference-class problem—and it seems to me that *they invariably are*. Consider again the Principle of Direct Probability: given its dependence on relative frequencies, it immediately inherits frequentism's reference-class problem. When I imagined above that 10% of days 'like' tomorrow were rainy days, my conscience forced me to use scare quotes—for what do we mean by days 'like' tomorrow? There are as many ways of answering this question as there are respects of similarity between days—which is to say, as many ways as there are reference classes to which tomorrow belongs. *Qua* one choice of reference class, the Principle of Direct Probability directs me one way; *qua* another choice of reference class, it directs me another way. This point carries over to the Principal Principle, for any account of 'chance' that is susceptible to the reference-class problem (e.g., the propensity account). Then depending on how we type E, we will get different values for ch(E), and this will carry over to P. As for human 'experts' (weather forecasters, your future selves) and their subjective probabilities: either they are constrained by something external to *them* or they are not. In the former case, the reference-class problem looms, for something else is playing the role of 'expert' for *them*. In the latter case it is dubious whether they have earned their title as 'experts'—we would be left with a 'no-theory theory' of expertise.

The two problems just discussed—the problem of conflicting experts, and the problem of inheriting the reference-class problem from your experts—are closely related. In a sense, the reference-class problem just *is* the problem of conflicting experts. When an event is typed one way, or relativized to one background assumption, any one of your experts—relative frequency information, chance, your weather forecaster, your future self, logical probability—assigns it one probability; when it is typed another way, or relativized to another background assumption, the same expert assigns it another probability. A single expert is conflicted with itself. Or looked at another way, any given expert fissions into many experts, one for each reference class. For each way of typing tomorrow, we have a relative frequency 'expert', a chance 'expert', and so on. The problem of conflicting experts is far worse than we might have thought, because we have so *many* of them. And this means that the reference-class problem for the non-radical subjectivist is far worse than we might have thought.

3. Conditional Probability as Primitive

Once we realize that the reference-class problem is seemingly inescapable, perhaps we should stop trying to escape it. Where we seek unconditional, single-case probabilities we keep finding conditional probabilities instead. Maybe there's a hint there to be taken.

Against the Ratio Analysis of Conditional Probability

Kolmogorov began by axiomatizing unconditional probability; for him, conditional probability was a derivative notion, defined in terms of unconditional probability by the familiar ratio formula:

$$\text{(RATIO)} \qquad P(A|B) = \frac{P(A \cap B)}{P(B)} \quad (P(B) > 0)$$

In "What Conditional Probability Could Not Be" (Hájek forthcoming), I argue that far from being a stipulative definition of our familiar concept of conditional probability, (RATIO) is not even an adequate analysis of that concept. One cannot merely stipulate that conditional probability is defined by this formula, even if one is as influential a figure as Kolmogorov, any more than one can stipulate that 'if A, then B' is defined by the material conditional $A \supset B$, even if one is as influential a figure as Russell. Of course, one can introduce a technical term and stipulate it to be whatever one likes. But the name "conditional probability," unlike "schmonditional probability" (say), is supposed to have a familiar ring to it. It is meant to capture the notion of the probability of A, qualified by or informed by some condition B: call it *P(A, given B)* for short. That notion may or may not be identified with a certain ratio of unconditional probabilities, but if it may, that just means that it is a good piece of conceptual analysis.

But I argue that it is not even that. It has been said many times before that (RATIO) falters when the condition B is possible, but has probability 0—but since the point remains important, I say it again, and for some new reasons. Call a probability function *regular* iff it assigns probability 1 only to logical truths (and hence 0 only to logical contradictions). I argue that rationality does not require one to have a regular probability function. Consider, then, some logically possible proposition Z that a rational agent assigns probability 0. Plausibly, for this agent, P(Z, given Z) = 1, P(¬Z, given Z) = 0, P(T, given Z) = 1, where T is a necessary proposition, and P(F, given Z) = 0, where F is an impossible proposition. However, (RATIO) can deliver none of these results, since P(Z) = 0. There are also more interesting conditional probabilities that cannot be identified with the corresponding ratio of unconditional probabilities. To take a familiar case, imagine a uniform probability measure over the Earth's surface. What is the probability that a randomly chosen point lies in the western hemisphere, given that it lies on the equator? 1/2, surely. But the probability that the point lies on the equator is 0, since the equator has no area.

Next, I argue that conditional probabilities can be sharp, while the corresponding unconditional probabilities are vague, and that (RATIO) cannot respect this fact. What is your probability that the Lakers win the next NBA championship? If you are like me, your probability is vague. (If you are even more like me, it will also be high, but let's ignore that.) But various conditional probabilities of yours are sharp: P(Lakers win, given Lakers win) = 1, and so on; and more interestingly, P(a fair coin lands heads, given Lakers win) = 1/2.

Next, we have what I consider to be the most important class of problem cases for (RATIO). They arise when neither P(A ∩ B) nor P(B) is defined, and yet P(A, given B) is defined. I adduce two main examples. The first involves a coin that you believe to be fair. What is the probability that it lands heads (H), given that I toss it fairly (T)? 1/2, of course. According to the ratio analysis, it is P(H|T), that is:

$$\frac{\text{P(the coin lands heads} \cap \text{I toss the coin fairly)}}{\text{P(I toss the coin fairly)}}.$$

However, I was careful not to give you any information on which to base these unconditional probabilities. I argue that this ratio may well remain undefined, and I rebut various proposals for how it might be defined after all. The second main example involves nonmeasurable sets. Imagine choosing a point at random from the [0, 1] interval. We would like to model this with a uniform probability distribution, one that assigns the same probability to a given set as it does to any translation (modulo 1) of that set. Assuming the axiom of choice and countable additivity, it can be shown that for any such distribution P there must be sets that receive no probability assignment at all from P—so called 'nonmeasurable sets'. Let N be such a set. Then P(N) is undefined. Nonetheless, I claim that P(N, given N) = 1, P(not N, given N) = 0, and so on. The ratio analysis cannot deliver these results.

The coin toss case may strike you as contentious, and the nonmeasurable case as pathological, although I defend them against these charges. In any case, I then turn to a host of examples taken from actual scientific and philosophical practice. I submit that we find instances of well-defined conditional probabilities yet undefined unconditional probabilities in:

- Born's rule in quantum mechanics for calculating the probability of a particular measurement outcome, given the performance of an appropriate measurement.
- Various central concepts in classical statistical significance testing, such as size, power, and p-value.
- Various analyses that have been offered of probabilistic causation.
- Adams's Thesis that the assertability of the indicative conditional 'if A, then B' goes by the conditional probability of A given B.
- Evidential decision theory's formula for the expected utility, or desirability, of an action.

I argue that collectively these examples span any interpretation of probability that you might consider.

This brings me back to *this* paper's discussion of the reference-class problem as it arises for the various interpretations of probability. We can regard the many examples that we have looked at as further instances of conditional probabilities that cannot be identified with corresponding ratios of unconditional probabilities.

Various frequentists could tell us the conditional probability that John Smith will live to age sixty-one, *given* that he is a consumptive Englishman aged fifty; but they could not tell us the unconditional probability that he is such a person. They would identify the probability of his being such a person with another relative frequency. But there's the rub: another *relative* frequency. The reference-class problem strikes again! *Qua* one way of classifying him, we get one relative frequency for his being a consumptive Englishman aged fifty; *qua* another way of classifying him, we get another relative frequency. As I would prefer to put it, we get further conditional probabilities. And the conditions, in turn, have various relative frequencies, but yet again, relative to still further reference classes. And so the regress goes. The process never 'bottoms out' with unconditional probabilities. To paraphrase an old joke, it's conditional probabilities all the way down.

And so it goes for the other interpretations as well. Proponents of the classical interpretation could tell us the conditional probability of a randomly chosen cube having side length between 0 and 1/2, *given* that a suitable uniformity assumption holds of the factory's manufacturing procedure; but they could not tell us the unconditional probability that this assumption holds. Advocates of the logical interpretation could tell us the probability that the next raven is black, *given* the evidence that ten black ravens have been observed; but they could not tell us the unconditional probability that such an observation is made. Propensity theorists may be able to tell us the chance that this die will land 6 on its next toss, *given* that it is tossed according to such-and-such specifications; but they could not tell us the unconditional probability that the die is tossed according to those specifications, and indeed would regard that as being meaningless. And nonradical subjectivists who recognize the constraints imposed by an external 'expert' could give us various conditional probabilities—that it will rain tomorrow, *given* that the weather forecaster assigns that probability 0.1, that this coin will land heads, *given* that it has a chance of 1/2 of doing so, and so on. But if they claim to give *unconditional* probabilities to conditions such as these, then their subjectivism becomes radical, a 'no-theory' theory; if these assignments are themselves constrained, then we only have further conditional probabilities. And so on.

It's All Relative

And so I conclude that the 'reference-class problem' only gives us more reason to question the hegemony of Kolmogorov's axiomatization. Now while the ratio formula does not provide an analysis of conditional probability, I do concede that it does provide a *constraint* on rational opinion and on chance. It tells us that whenever $P(A \cap B)$ and $P(B)$ are sharply defined, and $P(B)$ is nonzero, then the probability of A, given B, is constrained to be their ratio. My attack on the ratio, seen as an analysis, exploited examples in which these conditions failed to be met. Thus, it is not a necessary condition for a conditional probability to equal a particular value that the corresponding ratio equals that value.

How, then, should conditional probability be analyzed? Answer: *it shouldn't*. We should regard conditional probability to be the fundamental notion of probability theory.

Popper made two important contributions to the foundations of probability. The first is the propensity interpretation; the second is his theory of primitive conditional probability functions, so-called 'Popper functions' (1959b).[9] I think it is underappreciated how well the latter serves the former. Rather than defining conditional probability in terms of previously axiomatized unconditional probabilities, as is the Kolmogorovian orthodoxy, Popper lays down axioms for conditional probability functions directly.[10] Now, he offers no advice on how to assign unconditional probabilities to single-case events, but then we wouldn't expect him to. For him, it makes no sense to ask what the chance is that this die lands 6 on its next toss; it only makes sense to ask that *given* a specification of the experimental set-up—say, that it is tossed a certain height above a flat surface, with such-and-such angular velocity, and so on. Popper functions are well-suited to codify this information, being conditional probabilities of the form P(A, B): we simply let A be the event that the die lands 6 on its next toss, and B be a specification of the experimental arrangement.

All of the leading interpretations of probability face the reference-class problem. Popper functions, I contend, provide us a way to solve it—or as philosophers are fond of saying, *dissolve* it. The reference-class problem serves as another reminder that all probability statements are (at least tacitly) conditional. For each of the interpretations that we have surveyed, we found difficulty, or the outright impossibility, in assigning unconditional probability to a single-case event—doing so required a relativization to some reference class or other, some condition or other. But this reference class, this condition itself was not assigned an unconditional probability. Indeed, for many of the cases we considered, it couldn't be. On the other hand, there was no difficulty assigning two-place *conditional* probabilities throughout.

The reference-class problem began as a putatively serious problem for frequentism. I have endeavored to show that it is just as serious a problem for all the other leading interpretations of probability. Or just as unserious. It appears serious when one is gripped by the thought that conditional probabilities must somehow be reduced to unconditional probabilities. Kolmogorov offered such a reduction, and I have argued at length against his proposal. The reference-class problem turns out, then, not to be a problem for these various interpretations; rather, it is yet another problem for the ratio formula for conditional probability. Moreover, it is a problem for any attempt to reduce conditional probabilities to unconditional probabilities, for setting aside uninteresting cases, unconditional probabilities are simply not there to be had. It is a problem for any attempt to turn what is essentially a two-place concept into a one-place concept.

Let me end with two analogies. Consider the concept of an *average*—specifically, consider the concept 'average height'. John Stockton of the Utah Jazz is about 6 feet 1 inch tall; is his height average, above average, or below average? Of course, we could reasonably say that it's above average. *Qua* human being, and even *qua* human adult male, Stockton is considerably taller than average. Then how can we say in the same breath that he is a remarkable basketball player, considering how short he is? That's easy: he is a considerably shorter than average *qua* NBA basketball player. So Stockton turns out to be taller than average relative to one reference class, shorter than average relative to another one; and we could easily place him in still another reference class, relative to which his height is no more and no less than average. There is nothing mysterious about this, and we would hardly worry about a special 'reference-class problem' for the notion of average height. We simply accept that 'being of average height' is a *two-place* relation that someone bears or does not bear to a reference class to which they belong. To be sure, one reference class might be especially salient—as it might be, that of NBA basketball players—and could be assumed without explicit mention by all parties to a discussion. But that is a matter of pragmatics. At base, the notion of average height must still be relativized to a reference class.

A second analogy. It is natural to think that there is such a thing as *the* distance between two points, or *the* time interval between two events. But Einstein taught us that distance and time are reference frame–dependent notions. *Qua* points seen from one reference frame, they are a certain distance apart; *qua* points seen from another reference frame, they are another distance apart; *qua* events seen from one reference frame, they are separated by a certain time interval; *qua* events seen from another reference frame, they are separated by another time interval. To be sure, one reference frame might be especially salient—as it might be, that of the speaker, or that of the Earth, or that of our galaxy—and could be assumed without explicit mention by all parties to a discussion. But that is a matter of pragmatics. At base, the notions of distance and time must be relativized to a reference frame. No surprise that Einstein's theory is called *relativity*!

The reference-class problem drives home analogous points about probability. It is natural to think that there is such a thing as the probability of a proposition. But it turns out that probability is a reference class–dependent notion. To be sure, one reference class might be especially salient—as it might be, that of consumptive Englishmen aged fifty, or of cubes produced by a process that is uniform over side length, or of coins tossed under certain conditions, and so on—and could be assumed without explicit mention by all parties to a discussion. But that is a matter of the pragmatics of our probability discourse and practice. At base, probability assignments must be relativized to a reference class. This is the essential *relativity* of probability theory.[11]

ALAN HÁJEK
California Institute of Technology

NOTES

1. An important exception is Hild (forthcoming). He does a fine job of arguing that the reference-class problem arises for the propensity theorist and for the subjectivist who is constrained by the Principle of Direct Probability (see below). My discussion of those interpretations is inspired by and indebted to him; so too my dividing the reference-class problem into a metaphysical problem and an epistemological problem.

2. We might put the problem more generally still if we allow for probability gaps, as I would want to. Then, depending on how it is typed, E might also fail to have a probability at all—*qua* event typed a certain way, it might be a probability gap.

3. Cf. Mellor 1971, Fetzer 1977. I should note a caveat immediately. If E is necessary/logically true, then its probability is 1, and if it is impossible/a contradiction, then its probability is 0, and these probabilities are not sensitive to the choice of reference class. But this hardly blunts the reference-class problem, for it is unclear what it would even mean to 'type' such events. So let us set such events aside. After all, they are hardly the life-blood of probability theory.

4. To be sure, Venn goes on to give a prescription for choosing a privileged reference class, and thus a privileged probability. Reichenbach (1949) famously puts the prescription this way: "We then proceed by considering the narrowest class for which reliable statistics can be compiled" (374). But this prescription is patently inadequate. When are statistics "reliable"? This suggests more than just sufficiently large sample size (for example, unbiasedness)—and even that notion is all too vague. Worse than that, there may be many equally narrow classes for which reliable statistics can be compiled. Suppose that there are reliable statistics on the deaths of Englishmen who visit Madeira, and of consumptives who visit Madeira, but not on consumptive Englishmen who visit Madeira. John Smith is a consumptive Englishman visiting Madeira. In which class should we place him?

5. In fact, as Chris Hitchcock has reminded me, things are still more complicated for the later Carnap (e.g., 1963). He introduces a continuum of confirmation functions c_λ, each of which gives the weighted average (weighted according to a positive real number λ) of an a priori value of the probability in question, and that calculated in the light of evidence. So the probability that the next raven is black is further relativized: it is now dependent also on the value of λ.

6. Cf. note 3 above, in which I noted that the reference-class problem does not arise for necessary propositions/logical truths or impossible propositions/ contradictions.

7. See also Mellor 1971.

8. The term 'expert' in this context comes from Gaifman 1988.

9. William Harper coined the term 'Popper functions.'

10. Axiomatizations that take conditional probability as primitive are also given by Renyi 1970, Spohn 1986, and others.

11. I thank Fiona Cowie, Ralph Miles, Dominic Murphy, Peter Vranas, and especially Matthias Hild, Chris Hitchcock, and Jim Woodward for extremely helpful discussions.

REFERENCES

Carnap, Rudolf. 1950. *Logical Foundations of Probability.* Chicago: University of Chicago Press.

———. 1963. "Replies and Systematic Expositions." In *The Philosophy of Rudolf Carnap,* ed. P. A. Schilpp, pp. 966–98. La Salle, Ill.: Open Court.

Fetzer, James. 1977. "Reichenbach, Reference Classes, and Single Case 'Probabilities.'" *Synthese* 34: 185–217; Errata, 37: 113–14.

Gaifman, Haim. 1988. "A Theory of Higher Order Probabilities." In *Causation, Chance, and Credence,* ed. Brian Skyrms and William L. Harper. Dordrecht and Boston: Kluwer.

Giere, R. N. 1973. "Objective Single-Case Probabilities and the Foundations of Statistics." In *Logic, Methodology and Philosophy of Science* IV, ed. P. Suppes et al. Amsterdam: North-Holland, pp. 467–83.

Goldstein, Michael. 1983. "The Prevision of a Prevision." *Journal of the American Statistical Association* 77: 822–30.

Hájek, Alan. Forthcoming. "What Conditional Probability Could Not Be." *Synthese.*

Hild, Matthias. Forthcoming. "Introduction." *The Concept of Probability: A Reader.* Cambridge: MIT Press.

Lewis, David. 1980. "A Subjectivist's Guide to Objective Chance." In *Studies in Inductive Logic and Probability,* Vol. II, ed. R. C. Jeffrey. Berkeley: University of California Press, pp. 263–93; reprinted in *Philosophical Papers,* Vol. II, Oxford: Oxford University Press.

Mellor, D. H. 1971. *The Matter of Chance.* Cambridge: Cambridge University Press.

Popper, Karl. 1959a. "The Propensity Interpretation of Probability." *British Journal of Philosophy of Science* 10: 25–42.

———. 1959b. *The Logic of Scientific Discovery.* New York: Basic Books.

Reichenbach, Hans. 1949. *The Theory of Probability.* Berkeley: University of California Press.

Renyi, Alfred. 1970. *Foundations of Probability.* San Francisco: Holden-Day, Inc.

Spohn, Wolfgang. 1986. "The Representation of Popper Measures." *Topoi* 5: 69–74.

van Fraassen, Bas. 1984. "Belief and the Will." *Journal of Philosophy* 81: 235–256.

———. 1989. *Laws and Symmetry.* Oxford: Clarendon Press.

———. 1995. "Belief and the Problem of Ulysses and the Sirens." *Philosophical Studies* 77: 7–37.

Venn, John. 1876. *The Logic of Chance.* 2nd ed. New York: Macmillan and Co.

von Mises, Richard. 1957. *Probability, Statistics and Truth.* Rev. English ed. New York: Dover.

Weatherson, Brian. 1998. "On Uncertainty." Ph.D. Dissertation, Monash University.

10

Causal Generalizations and Good Advice*

CHRISTOPHER HITCHCOCK

In this essay, I focus on the convergence of two problems. The first is our old nemesis, the reference-class problem. The second is the problem of interpreting causal generalizations such as 'smoking causes lung cancer'. This problem has been with us since the time of Hume. Within the framework of the probabilistic theory of causation (which I have been exploring since the early '90s), this problem takes on a very precise form. All parties to the dispute agree that the truth of such a generalization depends upon certain conditional probabilities; they disagree about the configuration of these probabilities that must obtain in order for the claim to be true. The key to solving this second problem rests in the observation that causal generalizations can serve as guides to life: if I know that smoking causes lung cancer, that gives me a good reason not to smoke. Here is where the two problems converge. One way to formulate the reference-class problem is as follows: which objective, conditional probabilities should guide my decisions? I answer that one should be (partly) guided by the conditional probabilities that figure in the probabilistic theory of causation. This, in turn, helps us to solve the second problem. 'Smoking causes lung cancer' describes a configuration of objective, conditional probabilities, such that if the agent were guided by those probabilities, it would be rational for her to refrain from smoking. Like Hume, I conclude that the truth of a causal generalization is partly a subjective matter.

—*C. H.*

* * *

1. Introduction

The aim of this paper is to explicate causal generalizations such as:

G: Smoking causes lung cancer.

Such a claim might mean different things in different contexts. Causal generalizations such as **G** are relatively unproblematic when they are applied to a single individual or to a homogeneous population. In saying that they are 'relatively unproblematic' I do not mean that they are unproblematic on an absolute scale: the analysis of causation remains a vexing philosophical problem. But the problem takes on an added layer of complexity when **G** is asserted in the context of a heterogeneous population. Perhaps some individuals in the population are protected from the harmful effects of smoking; perhaps some are such that smoking even reduces the risk of lung cancer. Just how many such individuals can there be in a population before **G** ceases to accurately characterize it? It is just these sorts of problems that I address in the present essay.

Debate on this topic has cast more heat than light. This is due in part to the failure to make some key distinctions, and in part to the failure to articulate a clear desideratum for a successful account. In section 2 I will introduce some distinctions to help clarify what the problem is, and what it is not. In sections 3 through 5 I will formulate the question more precisely within the framework of a probabilistic theory of causation, and canvass some of the solutions that have been offered.

I will take as my central desideratum that an account capture one important aspect of the use of causal generalizations such as **G**: causal generalizations serve as *good advice*. After all, health officials issue statements such as G with the intention of dissuading people from smoking. I take this to imply the following principle:

GL A rational agent whose overwhelming desire is to avoid lung cancer ought to refrain from smoking just in case she believes **G** to be true.

The letters 'GL' stand for 'guide to life', an homage to Bishop Butler who famously wrote that "probability is the very guide to life" (1736, Preface). This may seem odd: Butler's aphorism is about what we would today call subjective probability, and not about causal generalizations. But my strategy will be to establish a link between the two guides to life. In section 6, I will present one formulation of causal decision theory, which codifies Butler's maxim about the directive role of subjective probability. In section 8, I use causal decision theory to show what an agent's degrees of belief would have to be like in order for it to be rational for her to refrain from smoking. In sections 9 and 10, I use this result to show just what the agent believes when she takes to heart the good advice encapsulated in **G**.

My argument will require that **GL** be sharpened; in particular, it will be necessary to spell out the idealizing assumptions that are to be built into the notion of a 'rational agent'. This is done in section 7. Different sets of idealizations lead to different precisifications of **GL**, which lead in turn to different analyses of **G**. This will leave the door open for defenders of different analyses to craft arguments of their own driven by **GL**, and I invite them to do so.

Beyond **GL** there may be other important and interesting features about the way in which causal generalizations like **G** are used, and it may be that a philosophical account that succeeds in capturing one of these features will do a poor job of capturing others. I will not try to articulate rival desiderata for a theory of causal generalizations, nor will I try to argue that my own account provides the best compromise among conflicting desiderata. Likewise, I will not attempt to refute those[1] who might argue that my account does not give *truth conditions* for causal claims such as **G**, but only assertability conditions, or conditions under which **G** can act as an action-guiding principle.

2. Causal Generalizations

It has been common in the philosophical literature to distinguish between *singular* or *token* causation and *general* or *type-level* causation. **G**, for example, would be construed as a claim about general causation, and would be contrasted with:

> **S**: David's smoking caused him to develop lung cancer.

Some authors, such as Sober (1985) and Eells (1991, Introduction and ch. 6) argue that claims like **S** and **G** describe different species of causal relation, calling for quite different theories of causation. Singular causal claims report singular causal relations holding between particular events, while general causal claims report type-level causal relationships holding between properties or event-types. Other authors, such as Carroll (1991) and Hitchcock (1995) have rejected this multiplication of causal concepts.

I now believe that the distinction between singular and general causation actually conflates (at least) two separate distinctions, and that this conflation has greatly impeded progress in the understanding of causal generalizations.[2] The first distinction is between *actual* causation and causal *tendencies*.[3] **S** is a claim about actual causation—it asserts that one event did, in fact, cause another. When used in a claim of actual causation, 'cause' is a success verb: such claims entail that the named events—in this case David's smoking and his developing lung cancer—occur. By contrast, claims about causal tendencies carry no such implications. Consider, for example:

> **T**: David is the sort of person for whom smoking tends to cause lung cancer.

T asserts that David is not one of those people who, through constitution or circumstance, are protected from the carcinogenic effects of smoking. It says nothing about whether David actually does smoke, or whether he actually does develop lung cancer; only that smoking would tend to promote that effect in him.

Despite this difference, there is an important respect in which **S** and **T** are similar: neither makes any claim about individuals other than David. Perhaps **T** might be construed as claiming that smoking tends to cause lung cancer in other individuals (if there are any) who are just like David in all relevant respects; but even so, the scope of application of **T** is very narrowly circumscribed. Let us say that such causal claims are *narrow*: they describe a causal relationship that holds within a single individual or a homogeneous population. By contrast, a *wide* causal claim is more general in the sense that it describes a causal relationship that holds within a broader, more heterogeneous population. Consider, for example:

> **W**: Every year, there are thousands of new cases of lung cancer that are caused by smoking.

W is *wide*: it does not apply only to a single individual or narrowly circumscribed type of individual. **W** is also a claim of *actual* causation: it implies that a certain number ("thousands") of cases of lung cancer and smoking did, in fact, occur.

It should be apparent by now that these two distinctions cross-classify: we have seen examples of narrow actual causation, narrow causal tendency, and wide actual causation. That leaves one category left, wide causal tendency, and it is to this category that causal generalizations such as **G** belong. This is not to deny that in the appropriate sort of context **G** might be used to make a different sort of causal claim, but typically **G** would be understood as reporting a wide causal tendency, and it is the content of just such a claim that I will attempt to unpack. These distinctions and the examples that illustrate each category are collected in table 1.

	actual causation	causal tendency
narrow	**S**: David's smoking caused him to develop lung cancer	**T**: David is the sort of person for whom smoking tends to cause lung cancer
wide	**W**: Every year, there are thousands of new cases of lung cancer that are caused by smoking	**G**: Smoking causes lung cancer

TABLE 1

3. Probabilistic Causation

Much recent philosophical work on causation—particularly work in the counterfactual approach pioneered by Lewis (1973)—has focused on analyzing claims of narrow actual causation, claims such as **S**. It turns out to be easier, however, to analyze claims of narrow causal tendency such as **T**. It may be that David is the sort of person for whom smoking tends to cause lung cancer, that David smokes, and David has lung cancer; and yet it may nonetheless be the case that David's lung cancer was actually caused by something *other than* his smoking. In cases such as this, our best theories of causation often get the claim of causal tendency right, while getting the claim of actual causation wrong (see Hitchcock, forthcoming). In particular, probabilistic theories of causation do a good job with narrow causal tendency claims. Proponents of probabilistic theories of causation have typically put them forward as theories about *wide* causal tendency claims, when in fact they are better understood as theories about narrow causal tendencies. Indeed, I think much confusion has resulted from a failure to recognize the distinction between the two types of tendency claim. I will formulate a probabilistic theory of narrow causal tendencies, and will then reformulate the problem of how to understand causal generalizations as the problem of how to extend this theory to a theory of wide causal tendencies.

According to a probabilistic theory of causation, **T** will be true just in case smoking raises the probability of lung cancer for people like David. This can be expressed in terms of conditional probabilities: $P_0(L|SB) > P_0(L|{\sim}SB)$; where *S* and *L* represent the 'factors' smoking and lung cancer, respectively; and *B* represents a conjunction of other factors that pertain to

David, the *causal background condition*. In conditioning on B, the factors corresponding to the conjuncts of B are 'held fixed'.[4] A *factor* is either an event-type or a property that can be instantiated by the appropriate sort of individual; factors, unlike particular events, are repeatable and may be instantiated on multiple occasions. The function P_0 is a measure of *objective* probability: causal claims such as **T** are not true merely in virtue of the opinions of agents.[5] I will adopt the convention of using 'P_0' for objective probability and 'P_s' for subjective probability or rational degree of belief. P_0 must represent the sort of objective probability that attaches to repeatable properties or event types, rather than to propositions or concrete occurrences. We do not suppose that values of P_0 simply hang in the air: $P_0(A)$ represents the probability of property or event-type A in some broadly characterized type of trial. For example, the probability of lung cancer may be the probability that an arbitrarily chosen human being has lung cancer, or that a hypothetical human being resulting from a human-generating process (such as evolution by natural selection, starting from some near-human ancestor two million years ago) has lung cancer.[6] Hypothetical limiting relative frequencies have the requisite features, although I will not commit myself here to any one interpretation of objective probability.

What must be held fixed when comparing the probability of lung cancer conditional upon smoking and its absence? We may address this question by considering what would go wrong if we were to hold *no* further factors fixed when evaluating whether one factor causes another. Suppose, for example, that we wanted to know whether coughing (C) causes lung cancer (for people like David). Since smokers are both more likely to cough and to develop lung cancer, we might well find that $P_0(L|C) > P_0(L|{\sim}C)$. But coughing does not cause lung cancer: the correlation between coughing and lung cancer is *spurious*. We can see this by holding fixed whether or not an individual smokes: among smokers, those who cough are no more likely to develop lung cancer than those who do not; and analogously for nonsmokers. In the terminology of Reichenbach (1956), smoking and nonsmoking *screen off* coughing from lung cancer: we have $P_0(L|CS) = P_0(L|{\sim}CS)$ and $P_0(L|C{\sim}S) = P_0(L|{\sim}C{\sim}S)$.

At this point, let us introduce the primitive relation of 'causal relevance' between factors. This primitive relation is essentially a type of wide causal tendency. Note, however, that causal relevance is *not* the relation that is asserted to hold between smoking and lung cancer by claim **G**: I will elaborate on this point below. The moral of the previous paragraph is that in order to evaluate whether factor C is a cause of factor E, we need to hold fixed other factors that are causally relevant to C or E. But we do not want to hold fixed *all* other factors that are causally relevant to C or E. For suppose that smoking causes lung cancer exclusively by causing the presence of tar deposits in the lungs (T). Then smoking will be a cause of lung cancer, even though $P_0(L|ST) = P_0(L|{\sim}ST)$ and $P_0(L|S{\sim}T) = P_0(L|{\sim}S{\sim}T)$. What is needed, then, is to hold fixed the presence or absence of factors that are causally relevant to C or E but are not themselves caused by C.

This recipe for constructing the causal background B that pertains to some particular case may be generalized to construct a *partition* $\{B_1, \ldots, B_n\}$ of *possible* background conditions relevant to the determination of whether C causes E. First identify those factors $C_1, \ldots, C_m$ that are causally relevant to C or E but are not themselves caused by C. Then the partition $\{B_1, \ldots, B_n\}$ will consist of maximal conjunctions of the C_i's and their negations; that is, each B_j will be of the form $\pm\ C_1\ \&\ \ldots\ \&\ \pm\ C_m$, where $\pm\ C_i$ is replaced by either C_i or its negation. Constructions of this sort are carried out in Cartwright 1979, 1989, Skyrms 1980, and in greatest detail in Eells 1991; I refer the reader to these sources for more detailed presentations.

Returning to our analysis of **T**, suppose that $\{B_1, \ldots, B_n\}$ is the partition into causal background conditions that is relevant to the determination of whether smoking causes lung cancer. Then **T** will be true just in case $P_0(L|SB_i) > P_0(L|{\sim}SB_i)$; where B_i is the member of the partition that characterizes David's situation. Other individuals are relevantly like David with respect to **T** if the same member of the partition characterizes their background situations. The problem of analyzing causal generalizations, then, can be recast as the problem of how to extend this account of narrow causal tendency claims to an account of wide causal tendency claims. The strategy of constructing a partition into causal background conditions suggests a natural approach to this problem: regard **G** as true just in case the relevant inequality $P_0(L|SB_j) > P_0(L|{\sim}SB_j)$ holds in 'enough' background conditions B_j. The trick, of course, will be to say just how many background conditions are 'enough'.

Before canvassing some proposed answers to this question, let us return to the primitive relation of causal relevance. Although this relation is a primitive within the probabilistic theory of causation sketched above, the theory itself imposes probabilistic constraints upon this relation: C is *causally relevant* for E if and only if there is at least one background condition B_i in the relevant partition such that $P_0(E|CB_i) \neq P_0(E|{\sim}CB_i)$. When we ask whether **G** is true, however, we are not merely asking whether smoking is causally relevant to lung cancer in this sense: we are asking whether smoking is a 'promoting', 'contributing', or 'positive' cause of lung cancer. If, by contrast, smoking 'prevents', 'inhibits', or is a 'negative cause' of lung cancer, then **G** will be false although smoking would still be causally relevant to lung cancer. The word 'cause' as it appears in **G** picks out a particular species of causal relevance. Indeed, it must do so if **G** is to act as advice to refrain from smoking: if **G** asserts only that smoking is causally relevant to lung cancer in some way (perhaps even preventing it), **G** would not recommend abstinence. This helps us to see that the circularity inherent in probabilistic analyses of causation need not be vicious. In determining whether *C* is a cause of *E*, we must construct a partition of possible background conditions, and the recipe for carrying out this construction appeals to causal notions. Therefore, the probabilistic theory of causation sketched above will not provide a reductive analysis of causation. Nonetheless, it may establish an interesting set of constraints connecting causal and probabilistic relationships. More to the point in the present essay, probabilistic theories of causation can be used to provide a reductive *taxonomy* of causal relevance; that is, they show us how to define new categories such as 'promoting' causes and 'preventing' causes in terms of probabilities and the primitive relation of causal relevance.

4. Contextual Unanimity, Pareto Dominance, and Fair Samples

Smoking causes lung cancer just in case $P_0(L|SB_i) > P_0(L|{\sim}SB_i)$ for 'enough' background conditions B_i. We turn now to the question: how many is 'enough'? Proposed answers to this question can be compared by expressing them all within the same general framework. The members of the partition into background conditions $\{B_1, \ldots, B_n\}$ are each given real-valued 'weights'; then $P_0(L|SB_i) > P_0(L|{\sim}SB_i)$ for 'enough' B_i just in case the total 'weight' of background conditions in which this inequality holds exceeds the 'weight' of background conditions in which it does not hold.[7]

The simplest proposal, endorsed in slightly different forms by Cartwright (1979, 1989), Eells and Sober (1983), Humphreys (1989), and Eells (1991), is that in order for *C* to count as a (positive or promoting) cause of *E*, *C* must raise the probability of *E* in *all* background conditions. Dupré (1984) has dubbed this requirement the 'contextual unanimity' condition, since the probabilistic impact of *C* on *E* must be unanimous across causal contexts. This proposal amounts to an assignment of finite weight—say one—to any background condition B_i such that $P_0(E|CB_i) > P_0(E|{\sim}CB_i)$, and of infinite weight to any background condition B_j such that $P_0(E|CB_j) \leq P_0(E|{\sim}CB_j)$.

Eells's (1991) version of the contextual unanimity requirement is particularly subtle and interesting. According to Eells, causal generalizations such as **G** are only true or false relative to a population *p*.[8] It may be the case that factor *C* fails to cause *E* in population *p* because there is some background condition B_j such that $P(E|CB_j) \leq P(E|{\sim}CB_j)$, while *C* causes *E* in the more restricted population *p'* in which this background condition does not (or cannot) occur.

Weaker than the requirement of contextual unanimity is that of 'Pareto dominance'. According to this proposal, advanced by Skyrms (1980) and Sober (1984), a cause must raise the probability of its effect in at least one background condition and lower it in none. This proposal translates into the following weighting scheme: background conditions B_i such that $P_0(E|CB_i) > P_0(E|\sim CB_i)$ are assigned a weight of one; those such that $P_0(E|CB_i) = P_0(E|\sim CB_i)$ receive zero weight; and those such that $P_0(E|CB_i) < P_0(E|\sim CB_i)$) are assigned an infinite weight.

Dupré (1984) criticizes the contextual unanimity and Pareto dominance requirements. Suppose that there is a rare gene *g*, such that those who possess *g* are *less* likely to develop lung cancer when they smoke. According to the contextual unanimity and Pareto dominance requirements, the existence (perhaps even the mere possibility) of such a gene would force us to deny that smoking causes lung cancer (in the overall population). This seems to fly in the face of ordinary usage: most of us would accept the claim that smoking causes lung cancer, despite the existence of such a gene. Although Dupré does not explicitly do so, this objection can easily be formulated so as to appeal to **GL** rather than ordinary usage. Suppose that an agent knows herself to belong to a population in which the gene *g* is very rare, but does not know for certain that she lacks the gene. In such a case, it would still be rational for her to refrain from smoking. Therefore, according to **GL**, this ought to be a situation in which the agent believes **G** to be true.

Dupré proposes that we replace the requirements of contextual unanimity and Pareto dominance with the requirement that a cause must raise the probability of an effect *in a fair sample*, where "[t]he crucial respect of fairness required is lack of bias with respect to independent causally relevant factors" (Dupré 1984, p. 173). Dupré's proposal has been misunderstood by some of its critics; Eells (1991, pp. 102–3), for example, argues that it threatens to reduce causation to "mere correlation."

In order to see just what Dupré's proposal amounts to, consider a controlled experiment designed to test **G**. Ethical qualms aside, the standard protocol is to randomly assign individuals to two groups, called the 'treatment' group and the 'control' group. Members of the treatment group are forced to smoke, whereas members of the control group are prevented from doing so. If the incidence of lung cancer is higher in the treatment group than in the control group, that provides prima facie evidence that smoking causes lung cancer. The purpose of randomization is to create fair samples in just Dupré's sense: if B_i represents some conjunction of factors that are causally relevant to lung cancer independently of smoking, we would expect B_i to be equally well represented in both the treatment groups and control groups. Assume that in this experiment, all frequencies are representative in the sense that they reflect the underlying probabilities.

What will be the frequency of lung cancer in both the treatment and control groups? If $\{B_1, B_2, \ldots, B_n\}$ is the relevant partition into background conditions, then the effect of randomization should be an equitable distribution of these conditions in both the treatment and control groups. That is, the frequency of condition B_i in each group should be the same, and represent the probability of this condition in the population as a whole, namely $P_0(B_i)$. Within the treatment group, individuals of type B_i will suffer from lung cancer at a rate of $P_0(L|SB_i)$. Thus the overall frequency of lung cancer in the treatment group will be $\Sigma_i P_0(L|SB_i)P(B_i)$. Likewise, the frequency of lung cancer in the control group will be $\Sigma_i P_0(L|{\sim}SB_i)P(B_i)$. Thus, smoking increases the probability of lung cancer in a fair sample just in case:

FS: $\Sigma_i P_0(L|SB_i)P_0(B_i) > \Sigma_i P_0(L|{\sim}B_i)P_0(B_i)$.[9]

In the special case where L is probabilistically independent of each B_i,the two terms reduce to $P_0(L|S)$ and $P_0(L|{\sim}S)$ respectively, and **FS** will hold just in case L and S are positively correlated. **FS** is not equivalent to mere correlation in general, however; in particular, the two are not equivalent in the sorts of cases that originally motivated us to hold background conditions fixed. In general, the proposal is that C causes E just in case $\Sigma_i P_0(E|CB_i)P_0(B_i) > \Sigma_i P_0(E|{\sim}CB_i)P_0(B_i)$. Since all terms in the summations are nonnegative, this inequality will hold just in case $\Sigma_i \{P_0(E|CB_i) - P_0(E|{\sim}CB_i)\}P_0(B_i) > 0$. This is equivalent to weighting each background condition B_i by $|P_0(E|CB_i) - P_0(E|{\sim}CB_i)|P(B_i)$, and requiring that the total weight of the background conditions B_i in which $P_0(E|CB_i) > P_0(E|{\sim}CB_i)$ exceeds the total weight of the background conditions in which this inequality does not hold.

Eells raises a number of objections to Dupré's proposal. One of them will be of particular interest to us, because it tacitly invokes a principle similar to **GL**: "a person contemplating becoming a smoker, and trying to assess the health risks, should not be so concerned with the population frequency of that condition [possession of the protective gene *g*], but with whether or not *he* has the condition" (Eells 1991, pp. 103–4). Suppose, specifically, that this person has very good reason to think that *he* possesses the gene *g* (perhaps on the basis of a genetic test), despite that rarity of this gene in the population as a whole. Then it would be rational for him to smoke, indicating his rejection of **G**. Dupré's fair sample account wrongly judges **G** to be true in this situation.

Our review of the three proposals makes plain the reasoning behind a claim made in the previous section: that it is easier to provide a probabilistic account of narrow causal tendency claims than of wide causal tendency claims. For suppose we restrict our attention to one particular background condition B_i, then all accounts agree that C causes E within this background condition just in case $P_0(E|CB_i) > P_0(E|{\sim}CB_i)$. The accounts come apart only when we try to analyze causal generalizations that pertain to a heterogeneous population. Our critique of the three proposals also illustrates roughly what a solution to our problem should look like: a successful account of causal generalizations should tell us how to weight the background conditions in such a way that causal generalizations can adequately function as guides to life.

5. Causal Generalizations and Generic Sentences

Carroll (1991) offers quite a different approach to the understanding of causal generalizations. In effect, Carroll denies one of the two distinctions described above in section 2: he thinks that there are no causal tendency claims. Rather, causal generalizations such as **G** are wide claims of actual causation like **W**. But whereas **W** explicitly states how many instances of singular causation must take place ("thousands") in order for it to be true, it is not at all clear how many instances of singular causation would have to be occur in order for **G** to be true. For example, **G** does not unambiguously mean any of the following:

(a) For some instance of smoking *s* and some episode of lung cancer *l*, *s* causes *l*.

(b) For every episode of lung cancer *l*, there is some instance of smoking *s* such that *s* causes *l*.

(c) For every instance of smoking *s*, there is some episode of lung cancer *l* such that *s* causes *l*.[10]

From the inability to explicate **G** precisely along the lines of (a) through (c), Carroll does *not* infer that **G** describes a distinct type of causal relation, one that holds between event-types rather than particular events. Rather, he argues that causal generalizations like **G** are *generic* sentences.

An example of a noncausal generic sentence is:

R: Rabbits have tails.

Paralleling our comments above, we note that (**R**) does not unambiguously mean any of:

R (a): For some rabbit *r*, and some tail *t*, *r* has *t*.
R (b): For every tail *t*, there is some rabbit *r* such that *r* has *t*.

R (c): For every rabbit *r*, there is some tail *t* such that *r* has *t*.

Perhaps **R**(c) comes closest, but we would hardly retract **R** upon discovering a tailless rabbit. Despite these difficulties in analyzing claim **R**, we are in no way tempted to conclude that there are two independent 'having' relations, one holding between *individuals* (e.g., individual rabbits and individual tails), the other holding between *types*.

According to Carroll, then, there is no *special* problem of analyzing causal generalizations; there are only the problems of analyzing singular causal claims like **S** and of analyzing generic sentences, whether causal or not. Carroll (1991) has nothing to say regarding the first problem, but he does offer a suggestion regarding the second: a generic sentence will be true just in case the relevant relative frequency is *high*. For example, **R** will be true if the relative frequency of creatures with tails among rabbits is high—that is, if the proportion of rabbits who have tails is large. Likewise, **G** will be true if a large proportion of cases of smoking do indeed cause episodes of lung cancer. How high is high enough? Carroll argues that the cutoff is both vague and context-dependent. There is no sharp cutoff: no precise ratio **r** such that **R** will be true just in case the ratio of rabbits with tails to rabbits is at least **r**. Moreover, what loose cutoff points do exist may vary with context: some contexts may impose very stringent high frequency requirements, while others are more forgiving. Carroll suggests that this vagueness and context-dependence tracks the vagueness and context-dependence inherent in generic sentences.

Note that on Carroll's view, causal generalizations carry no modal force—they are reports of actual frequencies. For this reason, Carroll's account violates **GL**. Suppose, for example, that by sheer coincidence only those who possess the protective gene *g* actually take up smoking. Then, on Carroll's view, **G** will be false; perhaps it would even be true that smoking *prevents* lung cancer. Suppose that an agent knows these facts, yet has good reason (perhaps based on frequencies) to think that she does not possess the protective gene *g*. Then it would be irrational for her to take up smoking, in violation of **GL**. In the majority of actual cases, smoking prevented instances of lung cancer rather than causing them; but this has no bearing on what would be likely to happen were our agent to commence smoking.[11]

Note that I do not deny that there can be generic causal sentences, nor even that causal generalizations such as **G** might, in an appropriate context, be interpreted as such. Indeed, I take it to be one of the advantages of the fourfold distinction of section 2 that it includes a category—wide claims about actual causation—into which the sentences of interest to Carroll naturally fall. I maintain only that there is a further type of claim that can be made by uttering **G** that does not merely report the frequency with which episodes of smoking actually do cause instances of lung cancer. It is the content of just this further type of claim that I seek to unpack.

Despite these objections, I think that Carroll's account has some attractive features that I wish to preserve in my own account. Carroll's mistake, I believe, lay in trying to understand a causal generalization such as **G** as a generalization over narrow claims of *actual* causation such as **S**. What I propose, instead, is to think of a causal generalizations such as **G** as generalizations over narrow claims of causal *tendency*, like **T**. **G** does not unambiguously mean either of the following:[12]

G(a) For some background condition B_i, smoking tends to cause lung cancer for those in condition B_i.

G(b) For every background condition B_i, smoking tends to cause lung cancer for those in condition B_i.

This suggests that I might modify Carroll's view and interpret **G** as a generic sentence asserting that smoking has a tendency to cause lung cancer—that is, raises the probability of lung cancer—in background contexts. This sentence would be true if the relative frequency of background contexts in which smoking tends to cause lung cancer is high, where the cutoff is both vague and context dependent. That is not too far off the mark, but my proposal will differ from this proposal slightly. First, it is not simply the *frequency* of background conditions in which smoking tends to cause lung cancer that matters: smoking must tend to cause lung cancer in a *weighted majority* of background conditions. In this regard, my proposal can be fit into the general framework sketched in section 4 above. Second, in my account, the cutoff point will be precise. This precision will be somewhat artificial, however, for the cutoff point will depend upon the subjective degrees of a belief of a certain type of rational agent, and the precision involved in assigning real numbers to degrees of belief is itself somewhat artificial. The cutoff point will be context-dependent, because it is determined in part by the beliefs of the intended audience.

The analogy with Carroll's view can be extended further. I think it is a mistake to think of **G** as describing some one causal tendency that smoking has for lung cancer in the human population as a whole. Something like this mistake sometimes lies behind the contextual unanimity view: for example, Eells and Sober (1983) write that if contextual unanimity fails, then "there will be no such thing as *the* causal role of smoking with respect to [lung cancer] in the population as a whole" (p. 37). But **G** does not describe some population-level causal tendency that is distinct from the various narrow causal tendencies described by claims like **T**. Rather, **G** is a generalization about the types of narrow causal tendencies that exist within heterogeneous populations.

6. Causal Decision Theory, Part I

In the twenty-first century, Bishop Butler's famous aphorism has been transformed into a formal theory of decision. Suppose an agent has a choice whether to perform an action *A*, or to refrain from doing so *(~A)*. The agent calculates an *expected utility* for each option, and then chooses the action that maximizes expected utility. The expected utility of an action is a function of the probabilities and utilities that the agent assigns to the various outcomes that might result from that action. Many philosophers now subscribe to some version of *causal decision theory;* in order to see why, we shall start by considering a rival: *evidential decision theory*.

The classic presentation of evidential decision theory is Jeffrey 1983. Assume that an agent is deliberating about whether or not to perform action *A*. Let $O_1, O_2, \ldots, O_m$ be the possible outcomes resulting from the agent's action (or inaction). *U* is the agent's utility function, which assigns utility values to various combinations of outcomes, according to how desirable the agent finds them. Finally, let P_s be the agent's subjective probability function; it represents the agent's degrees of belief that various possibilities will obtain. Then the (evidential) expected utility of action *A* is:

$$EEU(A) = \Sigma_j\, P_s(O_j|A)\, U(O_j\, A).$$

EEU(~A) is defined analogously. Evidential decision theory recommends that course of action which maximizes *EEU*.

Evidential decision theory leads to well-known difficulties in so-called 'Newcomb problems' originally described in Nozick 1969. Newcomb problems arise when an agent's action is known to be correlated with some outcome(s) because of a common cause, and the agent does not know for certain whether the common cause is present or not in the case at hand. The term $P_s(O_j|A)$ that figures in the formula for evidential expected utility reflects just such spurious correlations: it reflects the *evidential* relevance of *A* for O_j rather than the *causal* relevance of the former for the latter. Suppose for example, the agent believes that smoking does not cause lung cancer, but that they are correlated because some individuals have a genetic predisposition to lung cancer that also inclines them to smoke. Indeed, suppose that this is *true*, as was suggested by R. A. Fisher (1959). Suppose, finally, that the agent's utilities reflect an overwhelming desire to avoid lung cancer. Then evidential decision theory will recommend that the agent refrain from smoking, even though smoking is harmless (it does not cause lung cancer). By smoking, the agent provides herself with evidence she has the genetic predisposition to lung cancer; but it is irrational to arrange one's affairs to avoid receiving unwanted news.

Many responses to this sort of problem have been developed; the most promising involve attempts to formulate a decision theory that explicitly reflect relations of *causal* relevance. There are a number of different formulations of causal decision theory;[13] I will make use of the version developed in Skyrms 1980. Note that the problem raised by Newcomb cases is essentially the same as the problem of spurious correlations addressed by probabilistic theories of causation in section 3. This suggests that the two problems should have similar solutions. According to Skyrms's formulation of causal decision theory, the agent assesses the expected utility of A by constructing a partition of background states, $G_1, G_2, \ldots, G_r$. Each such background state holds fixed various factors, such as the presence or absence of a genetic predisposition to smoke. The agent then calculates the expected utility of A conditional upon each G_i, and takes the average using her subjective probability for each G_i. Thus the (causal) expected utility of A is

$$CEU(A) = \Sigma_i \Sigma_j P_s(O_j | AG_i) U(O_j AG_i) P_s(G_i).$$

The causal expected utility of $\sim A$ is defined analogously, and causal decision theory recommends the action that maximizes CEU.

Is the partition $\{G_1, G_2, \ldots, G_r\}$ used in the calculation of causal expected utility essentially the same as the partition $\{B_1, B_2, \ldots, B_n\}$ used in the probabilistic theory of causation? Skyrms, in a survey article, answers positively: "[t]he partition, $\{G_1, G_2, \ldots, G_m\}$ here [in causal decision theory] is just the partition relevant to saying whether and how much the act, A, has a causal tendency to produce the consequence, O_j, . . . according to the probabilistic theory of causation. . . ." (Skyrms 1988, p. 63, with minor changes in notation). As Skyrms himself must be aware, however, this statement is an oversimplification. The two partitions will be the same only if the agent knows what the appropriate partition $\{B_1, B_2, \ldots, B_n\}$ is for evaluating the causal relevance of the agent's actions for various outcomes. If the agent has false beliefs about other causes of those outcomes, or is uncertain about what else might cause those outcomes, then she must deliberate using a partition that reflects her imperfect causal beliefs. We will sidestep this problem by postulating an idealized agent, Ida, who *knows* that $\{B_1, B_2, \ldots, B_n\}$ is the partition appropriate to evaluating the causal relevance of smoking for lung cancer.

7. Ida and the Guide

With Ida's help, we will formulate the central principle **GL** more precisely. Ida knows that $\{B_1, B_2, \ldots, B_n\}$ is the partition appropriate to evaluating the causal relevance of smoking for lung cancer, although she does not yet know whether smoking does cause lung cancer. Before getting any information about this, Ida has subjective degrees of belief represented by the function P_s' . Above, we have used *S*, *L* and B_i to represent factors. Ida does not attach degrees of belief to these factors simpliciter, but rather to propositions to the effect that these factors are present or absent in particular cases. In particular, P_s' will be defined over propositions such as $S(I)$, $L(I)$, and $B_i(I)$—that Ida smokes, that Ida develops lung cancer, and that Ida is in background condition B_i. We also suppose that Ida's overwhelming desire is to avoid lung cancer. We may express this formally as follows: The only outcomes of interest are $L(I)$ and $\sim L(I)$. Ida's utility function *U* is such that for any B_i, $U(S(I)B_i(I)L(I)) = U(\sim S(I)B_i(I)L(I)) = m$ and $U(S(I)B_i(I)\sim L(I)) = U(\sim S(I)B_i(I)\sim L(I)) = n$, with $m < n$.

Ida is going to receive new information about the objective probabilities of *S*, *L*, and the B_i and revise her degrees of belief accordingly, yielding a new subjective probability function P_s. In order for her to do this, her subjective probability functions P_s' and P_s will also need to be defined on propositions about the values of objective probabilities: propositions such as $P_0(LSB_i) = p$. Upon gaining information about the values of such objective probabilities, she will conditionalize to arrive at a new subjective probability function.

We are now in a position to offer a precise statement of our guiding idea that causal generalizations such as **G** function as guides to life. Suppose Ida learns what the correct objective probability function P_0 is. Then:

> **IGL**: It will be rational for Ida to refrain from smoking just in case P_0 makes **G** true. If P_0 makes **G** false, then either it will be irrational to refrain, or she should be indifferent between smoking and refraining.

IGL (Ida's guide to life) is, I think, a plausible formulation of the idea that causal generalizations function as action-guiding principles. Our goal will be to use **IGL** to determine what P_0 would have to be like in order for it to make **G** true.

We could, of course, make a different set of idealizations. We could suppose that Ida does not know what the relevant partition of background hypotheses is, but rather assigns nonzero degrees of belief to a range of hypotheses. We could assume that Ida does not have degrees of belief about objective probabilities, but rather uses information about objective probabilities as a basis for Jeffrey conditionalization (Jeffrey 1983, ch. 11) on propositions that are not themselves about objective probability. We could suppose that Ida does not learn the exact values of P_0, but only learns whether or not they are in accordance with **G**. Or we could suppose that the intended audience of **G** is an epistemically heterogeneous population—they start with different subjective probability functions—and ask what would be required for a causal generalization to function as an effective action-guiding principle for the population as a whole. Each of these assumptions would substantially complicate the issue. I will leave to another occasion the question of how these idealizations would affect the answer to our central question. In each case, I think, the flavor of the answer will be the same: in order for **G** to be true, P_0 must satisfy a combination of objective and subjective constraints.

On the other hand, we could change the idealization so as to make it simpler. Perhaps Ida does not have subjective probabilities, but computes expected utilities using the objective probabilities that she learns. Perhaps she does not employ causal decision theory, but some type of dominance reasoning. In section 11 below I will show how the proposals canvassed in section 4 above emerge from different ways of simplifying the idealization described above.

8. Causal Decision Theory, Part II

Causal decision theory shows us what Ida's posterior degrees of belief P_s must look like in order for it to be rational for her to refrain from smoking: her expected utility for smoking, $S(I)$, must be lower than her expected utility for refraining, $\sim S(I)$. That is:

$$\begin{aligned}&\Sigma_i\, P_s(L(I)|S(I)B_i(I))\,U(L(I)S(I)B_i(I))P_s(B_i(I))\\&\quad+\Sigma_i\, P_s(\sim L(I)|S(I)B_i(I))\,U(\sim L(I)S(I)B_i(I))P_s(B_i(I))\\&<\Sigma_i\, P_s(L(I)|\sim S(I)B_i(I))\,U(L(I)\sim S(I)B_i(I))P_s(B_i(I))\\&\quad+\Sigma_i\, P_s(\sim L(I)|\sim S(I)B_i(I))\,U(\sim L(I)\sim S(I)B_i(I))P_s(B_i(I))\,.\end{aligned}$$

Because of our assumptions about Ida's utilities, $U(L(I)S(I)B_i(I)) = U(L(I)\sim S(I)B_i(I)) = m < n = U(\sim L(I)S(I)B_i(I)) = U(\sim L(I)\sim S(I)B_i(I))$. So the inequality is equivalent to:

$$\begin{aligned}&\Sigma_i P_s(L(I)|S(I)B_i(I))mP_s(B_i(I)) + \Sigma_i\, P_s(\sim L(I)|S(I)B_i(I))nP_s(B_i(I)) <\\&\quad\Sigma_i\, P_s(L(I)|\sim S(I)B_i(I))mP_s(B_i(I)) + \Sigma_i\, P_s(\sim L(I)|\sim S(I)B_i(I))nP_s(B_i(I))\\&\textit{iff}\ \Sigma_i P_s(L(I)|S(I)B_i(I))mP_s(B_i(I)) + \Sigma_i\,(1 - P_s(L(I)|S(I)B_i(I)))\,nP_s\\&\quad(B_i(I))) < \Sigma_i\, P_s(L(I)|\sim S(I)B_i(I))mP_s(B_i(I)) + \Sigma_i(1 - P_s(L(I)|\sim S(I)\\&\quad B_i(I)))nP_s(B_i(I)))\\&\textit{iff}\ \Sigma_i\, P_s(L(I)|S(I)B_i(I))mP_s(B_i(I)) + \Sigma_i\, nP(B_i(I)) -\\&\quad\Sigma_i P_s(L(I)|S(I)B_i(I))nP_s(B_i(I)) < \Sigma_i\, P_s(L(I)|\sim S(I)B_i(I))mP_s(B_i(I)) +\\&\quad\Sigma_i nP_s(B_i(I)) - \Sigma_i\, P_s(L(I)|\sim S(I)B_i(I))nP_s(B_i(I))\\&\textit{iff}\ (m-n)\Sigma_i P_s(L(I)|S(I)B_i(I))P_s(B_i(I)) <\\&\quad(m-n)\Sigma_i P_s(L(I)|\sim S(I)B_i(I))P_s(B_i(I))\\&\textit{iff}\\&\textbf{RR: }\Sigma_i\, P_s(L(I)|S(I)B_i(I))P_s(B_i(I)) > \Sigma_i\, P_s(L(I)|\sim S(I)\, B_i(I))P_s(B_i(I))\end{aligned}$$

The last inequality follows because $m - n$ is negative. Note that **RR** ('rational to refrain') has exactly the same form as **FS**, our formulation of Dupré's requirement that smoking must raise the probability of lung cancer in a fair sample in order for **G** to be true.

Does this mean that Dupré wins? No. *If* Ida's posterior degrees of belief P_s are identical to the objective probabilities given by P_0, then the structural similarity between **RR** and **FS** would show that it would be rational for Ida to refrain from smoking just in case smoking raises the probability of lung cancer in a fair sample. So *if* Ida sets her degrees of belief in accordance with what she learns the objective probabilities to be, Dupré's proposal would correctly rule that it would be rational for Ida to refrain from smoking just in case she believes that smoking causes lung cancer. But *should* Ida set her degrees of belief to what she believes the objective probabilities to be? In order to answer this question, we will need to explore the connection between subjective probabilities and beliefs about objective probabilities.

9. The Reference-Class Problem and the Principal Principle

Our problem is one of how to use knowledge of (or at any rate, true beliefs about) objective probabilities to guide our deliberations. It is not surprising, then, that our problem makes contact with that philosophical chestnut, the reference class problem. Suppose that P_0 is an objective probability function that assigns values to factors, or repeatable types of events, rather than to propositions or individual outcomes. The objective probability function that was used to formulate a probabilistic theory of causation in section 3 above has this character. Suppose that an agent knows that P_0 assigns correct probability values. He wants to bet on a coin toss at noon, and hence wants to know what the probability of heads *on that very coin toss* will be. The problem is that this very toss falls under many different generic descriptions or reference classes R_i, and $P_0(H|R_i)$ will take on different values for different R_i. So which value of $P_0(H|R_i)$ should the agent use to determine his betting odds for the coin toss at noon? The problem of the reference class is normally posed within the framework of a relative frequency interpretation of probability, but it arises in much the same form for any interpretation of objective probability that assigns values to types of outcome rather than to specific outcomes in specific trials.

Perhaps the solution is for the agent to let his deliberations be guided by his beliefs about *single-case chances*. One well-know proposal along these lines is David Lewis's (1980) 'Principal Principle'.[14] Suppose that *Ch* is a function that assigns single-case chances to particular outcomes, and let $H(n)$ be the proposition that the outcome of the coin toss at noon is heads. Assume that A is any 'admissible' proposition—we will have more to say about admissibility shortly. Then the Principal Principle states that a rational agent's subjective probability function should satisfy:

PP: $P_s(H(n)|Ch(H(n)) = p \;\&\; A) = p$.[15]

In words, the agent's degree of belief in the proposition that the coin will land heads when tossed at noon, given that the chance of heads on that toss is equal to p and given A, is equal to p. The agent's subjective degree of belief in heads should be set equal to what he believes the chance of heads to be.[16] Lewis does not give a detailed argument for **PP**, but defends it by an appeal to intuition.

PP requires that the additional information conditioned on, A, be 'admissible'. Note the if $P_s(A) = 1$, then $P_s(H(n)|Ch(H(n)) = p \;\&\; A) \equiv P_s(H(n)|Ch(H(n)) = p)$. Therefore, a conditional probability function might be incorporating inadmissible information even if that information is not explicitly represented on the right-hand side of the conditional probability stroke. Lewis gives no precise definition of admissibility, but offers several examples to illustrate the idea. Information about the composition of the coin, or about the frequency of heads in past tosses of this coin, would be admissible. Such information provides evidence about the outcome of the toss at noon only in virtue of providing evidence about the chance of heads at noon. Once the chance is specified, such further information is evidentially screened off. Inadmissible information would include the information that the coin will land heads at noon, or that the toss at noon will be one of a sequence of ten tosses, nine of which result in heads. Such information tells the agent about the outcome of the coin toss in a way that bypasses its chance of landing heads. Lewis claims that typically (barring clairvoyance, backward causation, and the like) purely historical information will be admissible. That is, if $Ch(H(n))$ reports the chance that the coin will land heads at noon as of some time t prior to noon, then if A describes matters of fact that occur entirely before t, A will be admissible.

Lewis proposed **PP** to show how a subjectivist might make sense of single-case objective chances.[17] I will not quarrel with this use here. I do want to argue, however, that **PP** does not give us what we are looking for in a solution to the reference-class problem. First, by replacing objective probability attaching to types of outcomes with single-case chances, Lewis makes knowledge of objective probability easier to use at the cost of making it harder to obtain. As originally posed, a solution to the reference class problem would provide us with information about what sort of frequency data would be relevant to our decision whether to bet on heads. Suppose we know that we should set our fair betting odds for heads to be equal to the objective probability $P_0(H|R_i)$. This expression makes explicit the frequency data that would be relevant: the frequency of heads in trials of type R_i. By contrast, if our decision about how to bet on the coin toss must be guided by single-case objective probabilities like $Ch(H(n))$, this tells us nothing about what sort of data we might gather in order to make a more informed decision.

Second, we cannot use **PP** unless we know whether the further information A that we have at our disposal is admissible or not. But this effectively presupposes a solution to the reference class problem: we need to know whether to take as our reference class tosses of coins where the chance of heads is p, or tosses of coins where the chance of heads is p and A holds.

Although **PP** does not therefore constitute a solution to the traditional problem of the reference class, it does provide us with a useful framework for thinking about the relationship between subjective probabilities and beliefs about objective probabilities. **PP** can be generalized to cover types of objective probability other than single-case chances by making suitable adjustments to our standards of admissibility. Suppose, for example, one knows that $P_0(H) = p$—the probability of heads in some very broadly specified type of trial (such as 'coin toss') is equal to p. Then, barring any further 'inadmissible' information, one should set one's subjective degree of belief that the toss of this coin at noon will result in heads to p. It certainly seems plausible that if one has *no* other information, then one might as well set one's degree of belief to p. This is a form of what is sometimes called 'direct inference'. And there is plenty of additional information—about the price of tea in China, the rules of accession to the British throne, and so on—which would not undermine this direct inference. On the other hand, information about the precise physical construction of the coin, about the precise manner in which it will be flipped, about its record in past tosses, and so on will all be *inadmissible*. The proposition that $P_0(H) = p$ differs from the proposition that $Ch(H(n)) = p$ in that propositions that are inadmissible with respect to the former are admissible with respect to the latter. To adapt the terminology of Skyrms (1980), degrees of belief conditional upon the latter are more *resilient* than degrees of belief conditional upon the former.

I wish now to bring this framework to bear on the sorts of probabilities that are relevant to **IGL**, namely objective probabilities of the form $P_0(B_i)$, $P_0(L|SB_i)$, and $P_0(L|{\sim}SB_i)$, and Ida's subjective probabilities of the form $P_s'(B_i(I))$, $P_s'(L(I)|S(I)B_i(I))$, and $P_s'(L(I)|{\sim}S(I)B_i(I))$. (It is Ida's *prior* probabilities P_i' that we are interested in, since it is constraints upon these that will, in conjunction with Ida's learning P_0, yield the posterior probabilities that figure in **RR**.) We may formulate two **PP**-like principles:

PP#: $P_s'(B_i(I)|P_0(B_i) = p \mathbin{\&} A) = p$ for admissible A.
PP*: $P_s'(\pm L(I)|\pm S(I)B_i(I) \mathbin{\&} P_0(\pm L|\pm SB_i) = p \mathbin{\&} A) = p$ for admissible A.[18]

Let us look at these two principles in turn. **PP#** is only a reasonable constraint on Ida's degrees of belief if a great many propositions A qualify as inadmissible. If our rational agent, Ida, has no further information about whether or not background condition B_i applies to her, she will set her new subjective probability $P_s(B_i(I))$ to what she learns the objective probability to be. But this degree of belief is not very resilient: it would be easy for her to have inadmissible information that would lead her to have a degree of belief in $B_i(I)$ that differs from the objective probability of B_i. It is just this point that Eells's critique of Dupré, described in section 4 above, exploits. Ida might know that the gene *g* which reverses the normal effect of smoking on lung cancer is rare, and hence that it has a low objective probability, while at the same time having good reason for thinking that *she* has this gene. Thus the connection between Ida's subjective probability $P_s(B_i(I))$ and her newfound knowledge about the objective probability $P_0(B_i)$ will be loose at best.

By contrast, objective probabilities of the form $P_0(L|SB_i)$, and $P_0(L|{\sim}SB_i)$ are chance-like in the sense that subjective degrees of belief based upon them will be highly resilient. That is, **PP*** will be true under a much more liberal classification of admissible propositions. Indeed, as an attempt to address the reference class problem, **PP*** has a number of advantages over the original **PP**. First, **PP*** makes explicit what sort of frequency information is relevant to the evaluation of the relevant objective probabilities: it is the frequencies of L among trials of type SB_i.

Second, because of the way in which B_i is constructed, **PP*** provides us with more detail about what is admissible and what is inadmissible. For example, information about the presence of causes of L that are held fixed in B_i will clearly be admissible, since adding it to the conjunction SB_i is redundant. By contrast, information about effects of S, and in particular about effects of S that are themselves causes of L (such as the presence of tar in the lungs) will not be admissible: they are not held fixed in B_i. Likewise, information about the presence of factors that share a common cause with L will be admissible if the common cause is held fixed in B_i, but will not be if the common cause is itself caused by S. Eells 1991 (ch. 4) contains a discussion of factors that *cannot* be held fixed as part of the background conditions; information about the presence or absence of such factors will not be admissible in general.

Third, given this characterization of inadmissible information, it is clear why agents typically don't have any: inadmissible information will be information about the presence or absence of factors that are causally downstream of *S*, and hence information that will be unavailable to the agent before deciding whether or not to perform action *S*. In most normal circumstances (barring backwards causation, clairvoyance, and the like), **PP*** implies it would be rational for an agent to set $P_s(\pm L(I)|\pm S(I)B_i(I))$ equal to $P_0(\pm L|\pm SB_i)$ once the latter is learned.

Finally, the form of **PP*** makes it easier to provide informal arguments that **PP*** is true. B_i is explicitly constructed to include all factors that are causally relevant to *L*, except for those that are themselves caused by smoking. It is also explicitly constructed so as to screen off spurious correlations with factors that are not themselves causally relevant to *L*. Thus, if Ida knows that $\{B_1, B_2, \ldots\}$ is the partition that has these features, then any proposition *A* that could bear evidentially on *L(I)* should either: (i) be included in $\pm S(I)B_i(I)$; (ii) be screened off by $\pm S(I)B_i(I)$; or (iii) report the effects of Ida's choice to smoke or refrain, in which case it would be inadmissible.

10. Causal Generalizations and Good Advice

Suppose, then, that Ida begins with a subjective probability function P_s' and learns that P_0 correctly characterizes the objective probabilities of factors of interest. What will her new subjective probability function P_s look like? If she has no other information about which background context applies to her case, **PP#** applies; conditionalizing on the information that $P_0(B_i) = p$ she will arrive at a posterior probability $P_s(B_i(I)) = P_s'(B_i(I)| P_0(B_i) = p) = p = P_0(B_i)$. If she already has substantial evidence about which background context applies, then P_s' will be incorporating inadmissible information: she may retain $P_s(B_i(I)) = P_s'(B_i(I))$, or she may do something else. By contrast, she is bound to set $P_s(\pm L(I)|\pm S(I)B_i(I)) = P_s'(\pm L(I)|\pm S(I)B_i(I)\ \&\ P_0(\pm L|\pm SB_i) = q) = q = P_0(\pm L|\pm SB_i))$, even if P_s contains additional information that is not explicitly represented in this formula, for (barring clairvoyance, backward causation, and the like) whatever additional information she may have will be admissible with respect to $P_0(\pm L|\pm SB_i)$.

Causal decision theory showed us that after learning P_0, Ida will find it rational to refrain from smoking just in case:

RR: $\Sigma_i P_s(L(I)|S(I)B_i(I))P_s(B_i(I)) > \Sigma_i P_s(L(I)|{\sim}S(I)B_i(I))P_s(B_i(I))$.

By the argument of the previous paragraph, we may substitute objective probabilities for some of the terms in **RR**:

RR*: $\Sigma_i P_0(L|SB_i)P_s(B_i(I)) > \Sigma_i P_0(L|{\sim}SB_i)P_s(B_i(I))$.

By **IGL**, then, smoking will be a cause of lung cancer just in case **RR*** holds. That is, **G** will be true just in case smoking raises the probability of lung cancer—just in case $P_0(L|SB_i) > P_0(L|{\sim}SB_i)$—in a weighted majority of background contexts, where each background context is weighted by $|P_0(L|SB_i) - P_0(L|{\sim}SB_i)|P_s(B_i(I))$. Note that the weighting function combines elements of both objective and subjective probability: a background condition receives high weight to the extent that smoking makes a large difference for lung cancer in that condition, and to the extent that Ida believes that condition to be *her* condition. **G** advises her to refrain from smoking because it tells her that smoking greatly increases the probability of lung cancer in those circumstances she believes most likely to be hers.

Some readers will find this conclusion shocking: isn't it supposed to be a purely objective matter whether smoking causes lung cancer? The subjectivity involved in my account of causal generalizations is fairly harmless, however. Here the analogy with Carroll's proposal is helpful. It is a vague and context-dependent matter whether rabbits have tails, but this is not because it is a vague and context-dependent matter whether any given rabbit has a tail. Vagueness and context-dependence arise when we ask how many and what kinds of exceptions we are willing to tolerate before we reject the generalization as false. Analogously, it is a wholly objective matter whether smoking causes lung cancer in some specific background condition B_i: this relation will hold just in case $P_0(L|SB_i) > P_0(L|{\sim}SB_i)$.[19] Let us call a background condition B_i an *exception* just in case smoking does *not* cause lung cancer in that background condition. Subjectivity enters only when we ask how many and what kinds of exceptions we are willing to tolerate before we reject **G** as a claim about the population as a whole. **RR*** presents a precise answer to just this question.

We may use **RR*** to reformulate objections to the proposals canvassed in section 4 above. In the special case where $P_s(Bi(I)) = P_0(B_i)$ for each B_i—the case where P_s incorporates no information that is inadmissible with respect to any $P_0(B_i)$—**RR*** will hold just in case **FS** does. In this special case, Dupré's proposal is correct: it will be rational for Ida to refrain from smoking just in case smoking increases the probability of lung cancer in a fair sample. This is the grain of truth in Dupré's proposal. But this proposal will not yield the right answer in general, as Eells's critique reveals. Suppose, for example, that smoking increases the probability of lung cancer in every background context except for B_g, that $P_0(B_g)$ is very low, but $P_s(B_g(I))$ is very high; then it might well be that Dupré's proposal would rule that smoking causes lung cancer, even though **RR*** shows that it would be irrational for Ida to refrain from smoking. By the same token, if $P_s(B_g(I))$ is very low (either because $P_0(B_g)$ is very low or because Ida has independent reason to think B_g does not apply to her case), then **RR*** implies that it will be rational for Ida to refrain from smoking even though the contextual unanimity and Pareto-dominance proposals would rule that smoking does not cause lung cancer.

11. On the Possibility of Other Idealizations

The idealizing assumptions made in section 7 are, I believe, reasonable and appropriate. But I have made no attempt to argue that they are the *only* reasonable and appropriate assumptions that can be made. This leaves open the possibility of making different idealizations, leading ultimately to different analyses of causal generalizations. For example, if one were to add to the idealized scenario that Ida has no information of the sort that would count as inadmissible with respect to **PP#**, then **GL** would rule that Dupré's fair sample proposal is correct (for reasons discussed in the previous section).

More radically, some might object to the entire 'Butlerian' tradition, of which causal decision theory is just one recent example. Such a critic would object to *any* use of subjective degrees of belief in a theory of rationality; *ipso facto* he would object to the specifications of Ida in section 7. Perhaps the rationality of Ida's decision should be judged along broadly frequentist lines: instead of subjective degrees of belief, Ida employs idealized population frequencies in her probabilistic computations. It is quite plausible that such a proposal, suitably spelled out, could be used to defend Dupré's account.

Alternately, one might assume that Ida does not assign any probabilities to propositions of the form $B_g(I)$, be they subjective degrees of belief or objective frequencies. Perhaps she simply has no relevant information. Then the following decision rule is plausible: it is rational for her to refrain from smoking just in case abstinence *dominates* smoking, where abstinence dominates smoking if the utility of refraining is higher than the expected utility of smoking in some background context, and lower in none. The expected utilities in background context B_i are now computed using Ida's utilities and the objective probabilities $P_0(\pm L|\pm SB_i)$. In this sort of decision framework (suitably spelled out), **GL** entails that the Pareto-dominance theory is correct. A slightly different dominance notion might be used to defend the contextual unanimity account.

These observations do not leave us back where we started. The predominant method of argument on this issue has been that of constructing hypothetical cases, and consulting our intuitions about whether we would accept a certain causal generalization in such cases. I have offered a rival methodology: derive an account of causal generalizations from **GL** in conjunction with suitable idealizing assumptions. There will still be arguments for rival proposals, but they will be precise arguments based on explicit premises, rather than appeals to intuition. Moreover, these arguments will make explicit the connections between competing views about the analysis of causal generalizations and broader debates within philosophy, in particular with debates about appropriate methods of reasoning under uncertainty. That is philosophical progress.

CHRISTOPHER HITCHCOCK
California Institute of Technology

NOTES

*This paper develops an argument originally sketched in Hitchcock 1998 (§ 2). Readers will also recognize that the argument is similar in spirit, albeit different in detail, from arguments presented in Mellor 1988 and 1995 (ch. 7).

1. Such as Carroll (see his 1991, pp. 264–65).

2. A similar claim is made by Woodward (1993), who argues that type-level causal claims actually include two distinct types of claim, *causal capacity* claims and *causal role* claims. I believe that Woodward's causal capacity claims are similar to what I will call narrow causal tendency claims, while causal role claims are similar to what I will call wide claims of actual causation. (See below.)

3. This terminology is based on terminology adopted by Good (1961/1962).

4. Note that I am following the standard approach of treating factors such as smoking and lung cancer as binary variables: they are either present or absent. In reality, of course, such factors come in varieties and degrees: they are variables with many values. In a number of other publications (e.g. Hitchcock 1993, 1996), I have argued that exclusive attention to the binary case has given rise to unnecessary problems in the theory of causation. I put these concerns aside for the present essay. An account similar to the one I give for **G**, where I assume smoking to be a binary variable, could be given for a more careful analog of **G** such as: smoking 20-pack-years in contrast to not smoking at all causes lung cancer. Simply replace *S* and *~S* with the appropriate values of the new variable. Hitchcock (1993) shows how to construct the partition of background conditions using nonbinary variables.

5. Although as I will argue below, causal generalizations such as **G** are at least partially true in virtue of subjective degrees of belief.

6. This means that our causal claims may have to be relativized to the type of trial we have in mind. This seems to be Eells's view: see note 8 below. On the other hand, we may hope that the relevant *conditional* probabilities will not be sensitive to how the *unconditional* probabilities are conceived.

7. I assume here that there are finitely or countably many possible background conditions. If there are uncountably many, discrete weights will need to be replaced with density functions.

8. More precisely, causal generalizations are made relative to a population and a population-type. A population-type may be thought of as a hypothetical process that generates populations, such as the actual population to which some individual like David belongs. An actual population will belong to many different population-types. It is a population-type, rather than the actual population, that determines the values of the objective probabilities of factors. See Eells 1991 (ch. 1) for details. For simplicity, I will continue to speak only of relativity to a population in what follows.

9. Note that this formula bears some similarity to the formula for the *basic assertability value* of a counterfactual in Skyrms 1980 (p. 98), and to the formula for the identification of *causal effects* in Pearl 2000 (pp. 79–80).

10. Note the similar remarks in Lewis (1973, cited from Lewis 1986, pp.161–62).

11. In fairness, this argument will not move Carroll, since he explicitly denies my guiding intuition that causal generalizations function as guides to life (1991, 264–65).

12. Note that there is no natural analog of (c) above.

13. See Lewis 1981 for an interesting discussion of the relations between them.

14. Related ideas are developed in Mellor 1971, and in Skyrms 1980, 1984.

15. See Lewis 1994 for a slight modification.

16. If the agent has no firm belief about what the chance of heads is, then his degree of belief in heads will be his *expectation* for the value of chance.

17. Mellor (1971) and Skyrms (1980, 1984) have similar agendas.

18. Note that we are to imagine that Ida learns *all* of the values of P_O, and not only those that are conditioned on in **PP#** and **PP***. I will assume that the additional information about the values of P_0 is admissible.

19. Contextual factors may play a role in determining how this claim is *made precise*. For example, they may provide answers to the following sorts of questions: How much must someone smoke before we take them to be 'smoking'? Do inhalers of second-hand smoke qualify? And so on. Contextual factors may also determine the implicit contrastive structure of such a claim; see note 4 above.

REFERENCES

Butler, J. 1736. *The Analogy of Religion*.

Carroll, J. 1991. "Property-Level Causation?" *Philosophical Studies* 63: 245–70.

Cartwright, N. 1979. "Causal Laws and Effective Strategies." *Noûs* 13: 419–37.

———. 1989. *Nature's Capacities and Their Measurement*. Oxford: Oxford University Press.

Dupré, J. 1984. "Probabilistic Causality Emancipated." In *Midwest Studies in Philosophy* IX, ed. P. French, T. Uehling Jr., and H. Wettstein, pp. 169–75. Minneapolis: University of Minnesota Press.

Eells, E. 1991. *Probabilistic Causality*. Cambridge, U.K.: Cambridge University Press.

Eells, E., and E. Sober. 1983. "Probabilistic Causality and the Question of Transitivity." *Philosophy of Science* 50: 35–57.

Fisher, R. A. 1959. *Smoking: The Cancer Controversy.* Edinburgh and London: Oliver and Boyd.

Good, I. J. 1961/1962. "A Causal Calculus I–II." *British Journal for the Philosophy of Science* 11: 305–18; 12: 43–51.

Hitchcock, C. 1993. "A Generalized Probabilistic Theory of Causal Relevance." *Synthese* 97: 335–64.

———. 1995. "The Mishap at Reichenbach Fall: Singular vs. General Causation." *Philosophical Studies* 78: 257–91.

———. 1996. "Farewell to Binary Causation." *Canadian Journal of Philosophy* 26: 267–82.

———. 1998. "Causal Knowledge: That Great Guide of Human Life." *Communication and Cognition* 31.

———. Forthcoming. "Do All and Only Causes Raise the Probabilities of Effects?" In *Causation and Counterfactuals,* ed. J. Collins, N. Hall, and L. Paul. Cambridge, Mass.: M.I.T. Press.

Humphreys, P. 1989. *The Chances of Explanation.* Princeton: Princeton University Press.

Jeffrey, R. 1983. *The Logic of Decision.* 2nd ed. Chicago: University of Chicago Press.

Lewis, D. 1973. "Causation." *Journal of Philosophy* 70: 556–67. Reprinted in Lewis 1986.

———. 1980. "A Subjectivist's Guide to Objective Chance." In *Studies in Inductive Logic and Probability,* vol. II, ed. R. Jeffrey, pp. 263–94. Berkeley: University of California Press. Reprinted in Lewis 1986.

———. 1981. "Causal Decision Theory." *Australasian Journal of Philosophy* 59: 5–30. Reprinted in Lewis 1986.

———. 1986. *Philosophical Papers,* vol. II. Oxford: Oxford University Press.

Lewis, D. 1994. "Humean Supervenience Debugged." *Mind* 103: 473–90.

Mellor, D. H. 1971. *The Matter of Chance.* Cambridge, U.K.: Cambridge University Press.

———. 1988. "On Raising the Chances of Effects." In *Probability and Causality: Essays in Honor of Wesley C. Salmon,* ed. J. Fetzer. Dordrecht: Kluwer, pp. 227–39.

———. 1995. *The Facts of Causation.* Cambridge, U.K.: Cambridge University Press.

Nozick, R. 1969. "Newcomb's Problem and Two Principles of Choice." In *Essays in Honor of Carl G. Hempel,* ed. N. Rescher. Dordrecht: Reidel, pp. 114–46.

Pearl, J. 2000. *Causality: Models, Reasoning, and Inference.* Cambridge: Cambridge University Press.

Reichenbach, H. 1956. *The Direction of Time.* Berkeley and Los Angeles: University of California Press.

Skyrms, B. 1980. *Causal Necessity.* New Haven: Yale University Press.

———. 1984. *Pragmatics and Empiricism.* New Haven: Yale University Press.

———. 1988. "Probability and Causation." *Journal of Econometrics* 39: 53–68.

Sober, E. 1984. *The Nature of Selection.* Cambridge, Mass.: M.I.T. Press.

———. 1985. "Two Concepts of Cause." In *PSA 1984*, vol. II, ed. P. Asquith and P. Kitcher, pp. 405–24. East Lansing: Philosophy of Science Association.

Woodward, J. 1993. "Capacities and Invariance." In *Philosophical Problems of the Internal and External Worlds*, ed. J. Earman et al., pp. 283–328. Pittsburgh: University of Pittsburgh Press.

PART III

Probability and Causation

11

Instrumental Probability

CLARK GLYMOUR

Thirty-five years ago, I learned of various philosophical accounts of the meaning of probability from Wesley Salmon. I found none of them convincing, and when, fifteen years later, I began actually to read and do statistics, I found the philosophical accounts remote from practice, and the practitioners' philosophical descriptions of what they were doing and why they were doing it equally at variance with their practice. This essay, which I think is only the second I have ever written on the interpretation of probability, arose from that work and reading, from many years of instruction from Teddy Seidenfeld, from conversations with Kevin Kelly, from a joint seminar in statistics given with Jay Kadane at Carnegie Mellon in 1985, and from a seminar on the history of probability given with John Norton at the University of Pittsburgh in the early 1990s. One of the critical ideas came directly from reading Stephen Stigler's History of Statistics. *The essay that follows was written shortly after the seminar with Norton and has rested unused ever since, but I still believe it. So far as I know, the account I give of the meaning and use of probability is original, but related views can be found in the work of Richard Braithewaite and Henry Kyburg.*

—C. G.

* * *

Prefatory Note: Probability as a Guide in My Life

The essay you may next read was written several years ago, after a seminar I taught with John Norton at the University of Pittsburgh. It was occasioned by reading some of the history of statistics and by many years of effort in melding statistics and computation, but its real source, almost surely, is in the many ways probability and utility have informed my life.

My earliest acquaintance with probability came in contests in Avon, Utah, around 1944, between my dog Curly and the neighbor's boar, from which Curly was my assigned protector. The boar, fixated on the prospect of eating me, would snuffle my way each morning when I was set out in the yard, and with equal reliability Curly would interpose himself, ready to bite at snout, trotter, tail or knee. The boar had learned his own vulnerable points and, in a calculated way, sought to protect whichever of them he guessed Curly would go for, tucking his snout down, or raising his tail, turning sideways, whatever pig maneuver seemed likeliest to protect the point to be attacked. Curly, perhaps less intelligent than the boar, seemed to choose his targets at random, and no policy the pig could hatch reliably avoided Curly's bite. So I learned early that randomness defeats intelligence. (Eventually, my father shot the neighbor's boar for ravaging our garden, which Curly was not assigned to protect, and thereby taught me quite another lesson.)

When my father went broke cowboying in Utah, we moved to south-central Los Angeles, where my education in probability continued. I learned that steelies would more probably knock marbles out of a circle than would glassies, that bigger kids would probably beat smaller kids in fights, that the men who delivered blocks of ice to our neighborhood each week would probably not notice if we climbed into the back of their truck to steal shards of summer ice. I learned about the occurrence of rare events, most memorably the Saturday afternoon when the girls in the neighborhood rounded up all the boys under seven years of age, sat us against the wall on the floor of an empty garage, and entertained us with a strip tease. That singular event also began my inquiries into the theory of utility, leading to the conclusion that despite the overwhelming interest of adults in paper money, something else must be the best thing in the world, although I was not sure exactly what.

When I was seven the family moved to east Los Angeles and after elementary school I attended Eastmont Junior High where I learned more about probability under the tutelage of two gangs, known respectively as the Anglos and the Mexicans. I learned that you would probably be hospitalized if a gang-member's girlfriend flirted with you, or vice-versa, or if you put a gang bully in his place, or stepped into a cross-fire. Rather more gently, I learned that a supposedly deterministic game, chess, does not feel the least bit deterministic when you are playing against a human opponent, and there was no other kind in 1954. (Later, when I played against machines, the game did feel more deterministic: I always lost.) Summer days on California porches, I learned while playing blackjack and poker that my lesson from Curly and the Utah pig had to be qualified, that chances are conditional and if you take advantage of the conditions you can win more often than you lose. My inquiries into the theory of utility continued, helped enormously by a girl named Jane Trent. I hope she is well.

Improbably (unless you know my father—you should be so lucky), we moved to Butte, Montana the summer I was thirteen and amid the certainties of forty-below winters and dirty ice in the face when I put the chains on the rear tires of the car, I learned more about conditional probability. Evenings, after football practice, I put on a cheap suit and worked the town as a Fuller Brush Man, leaving sales brochures at every house in a neighborhood one night and retrieving them the next, this time with my black briefcase of demonstration goods in hand. The probability of a sale was low, but increased considerably if I acted on the conditions presented by the customer. I learned that speaking English I could sell nothing to the deaf family that lived in the Flats, but they became regular customers once I learned to sign. I learned that the enormously fat lady who lived in a single, dark room separated in two by a hanging blanket would almost certainly buy nothing except the canned foot spray that she could apply to the feet she could not reach. I learned more from other jobs. I worked for a while assisting the only doctor in town who performed vasectomies, standing at the head of his examination table behind the patient, while he worked at the business end. I learned that, with very high probability, the patients, all men in their forties with too many children and unwilling wives in a Catholic town without contraceptives, would come up swinging when the scalpel came out. My job, for which I earned a handsome five bucks an operation, was to slam them back down, and keep them there. Saturdays, I delivered groceries around town for Milo's Main Street Market, driving a Ford stationwagon through the Flats and up on the Hill, making friends. I learning nothing of probability, but my deliveries to the brothel on Mercury street (ceased operation in 1987 and now a National Historical Site, no kidding, you can go there and see the brass plaque) furthered my studies of utility.

There is more, much more, but even an advertisement should stop.

C. G.
Pittsburgh, June 2001

1. The Science of Nothing

The claims of science and the claims of probability combine in two ways. In one, probability is part of the content of science, as in statistical mechanics and quantum theory and an enormous range of "models" developed in applied statistics. In the other, probability is the tool used to explain and to justify methods of inference from records of observations, as in every science from psychiatry to physics. These intimacies between science and probability are logical sports, for while we think science aims to say what happens, what has happened, what will happen, what would happen if other things were to happen, what could and could not happen, what will nearly happen, or what will approximate what will happen, probability claims say none of these things, or at least none of them about the phenomena with which science is concerned. On that, at least, almost all philosophical interpreters of probability since DeMoivre agree, with whatever reluctance. Consider some examples.

According to Hume and to many moderns, probability is a measure of opinion, of credence or degree of belief. But measures of opinion are not statements about what happens in nature or society, what has happened, what will happen, what would happen if other things were to happen, and so forth. They are at most statements about the mental state of the opinion holder, or about what the opinion holder will do if offered wagers. To press the obvious, from "Hume's degree of belief that the sun will rise tomorrow is .9999" it does not follow that the sun will rise tomorrow, or that it will not. Thomas Bayes, along with a smaller group of our contemporaries, defined probability as a norm of belief, a measure of what one ought to believe. Norms of belief are as remote from empirical claims about nature as is Hume's simpler subjectivism. Propensity theories of probability propose a physical property that cannot be recorded and does not necessitate or preclude any occurrence. Limiting frequency accounts parse probability claims as statements about the limiting relative frequency of a property in an (ill-specified) infinite sequence, but any limiting frequency claim is consistent with any claim about any finite collection of events, and so entails nothing about what will happen at any time. Provided some way to fix their reference, limiting frequency probability claims would at least say something about limiting properties of sequences, which is more than the alternative interpretations offer but rather less than what we hope for from science.

2. Probabilistic Theories and Their Content: The Example of the Rasch Model

Theories whose content consists entirely of probability claims were once rare and now abound. Consider psychometrics, where until about 1960 theories of mental abilities typically assumed that there is a linear relation between how an individual performs on a psychometric test and values of various unmeasured factors, some of which also influence how that individual performs on other tests and some of which are peculiar to a single test. It was generally assumed that all factors operate in the same way for all individuals, although the values of the latent traits, and in some cases the values of the linear coefficients, may differ from individual to individual. Psychometric theories of this kind had a definite nonprobabilistic content. Probability entered only in the form of assumptions about how values of the unobserved causal variables are distributed. The distributional claims—normality, for example—were essential in order to use statistical methods to make inferences about the values of linear coefficients, the number of unobserved causes, and other matters, but they were ancillary to the content of the theories. Models of this kind are still common.

In 1960 Georg Rasch published a remarkable and influential book that changed the form, and the content, of many psychometric theories. Rasch says he drew his inspiration from statistical mechanics and quantum mechanics, although his theory is more thoroughly probabilistic than either. Rasch supposed that two parameters are associated with a psychometric battery of tests and a population of people who take, or might take, the battery. One parameter varies from test item to test item and measures the difficulty of each; for each test item, that parameter has the same value for all persons. The other parameter varies from person to person and, for each person, measures the ability of that person; for each person the parameter is constant across all test items.

Rasch's framework is used in related ways to produce "models" of several kinds of tests. For a reading test that is essentially a battery in which a subject may make any number up to n errors in n items the Rasch model says that the probability a person makes k errors is given by a Poisson distribution whose single parameter is the ratio of the difficulty and ability parameters. That is the entire content of the theory. There are no underlying functional dependencies postulated, only probability relations. This, presumably, is the kind of theory philosophers of science who write of "probabilistic causality" have in mind. Although Rasch himself described orthodox estimation and test statistics for his models, the Rasch model has been given Bayesian extensions by postulating prior distributions on the Rasch parameters and letting the Rasch model describe the likelihoods.

Rasch's theory says that within the variation allowed by a psychometric battery, a person's ability is not relative to test item and the difficulty of a test item is not relative to persons. Beyond that, the theory seems to say nothing about what happens when people take a psychometric test. If we interpret the probabilities of the Rasch models as limiting relative frequencies, the theory says nothing, literally nothing, about any observed population, no matter how large. If we interpret the probabilities of the Rasch models as subjective, then such a model is only strange and implausible autobiography. The theorist is then saying that if she knew the values of the Rasch parameters were such and such, she would have a particular distribution of degrees of belief about the errors a test subject would make. The theory says absolutely nothing about why the theorist should have those degrees of belief, about the grounds or reasons for them, nothing about the tests or the subjects or their relations that make those degrees of belief plausible, only that they are what they are. Whatever kind of theory this is, it is not science.

3. Instrumental Probability

The logical oddity of Rasch's theory suggests that probability has some instrumental role, and that the real content of the theory is hidden in methods of data analysis that use probabilities. Instrumentalism about some part of language is the doctrine that sentences formulated within it are not claims but linguistic devices used to make inferences about real claims formulated in other parts of language. Skepticism about atoms, for example, was initially epistemic—facts about atoms could not be obtained from a kind of evidence relative to a vague but fixed set of assumptions. Implausible attempts were made to turn that epistemic problem into a semantic difficulty, but the transition never worked. A case has been made for instrumental mathematics, on the grounds that mathematics is a separable addition to the rest of science, which for philosophical purposes can be formulated without using mathematical terminology. The case for instrumental probability is more robust and more semantic; it rests on the fact that probability claims say nothing about what happens or could happen in the domain under scientific study, not just on the fact that they say nothing about what could be observed to happen. How, then, can probability claims be an instrument for inferences from data?

Mathematical statistics has in some measure answered this question and avoided the foundational perplexities of probability with a kind of semi-instrumentalism that uses two ingenious bridges permitting traffic only in opposite directions, one from nature to probability and the other from probability to judgments about nature. The bridge in one direction is the theory of estimation, whether in its Fisherian or Bayesian form, which provides rules connecting what happens with probability claims (either by calculating posterior distributions or through the sampling theory of estimators). The other direction is bridged by the theory of decision making which specifies rules for action (including deciding what to believe) as a function of the subjective (or other) probabilities and the utilities of the actor. Probability and utility can be used to calculate what to say about what will happen, what would happen if . . . , and so on.

Mathematical statistics and decision theory leave opaque the claims of probability in the content of science, but they clarify immensely the role of probability in the analysis of data. There is a price. The justification for the circuitous route is that given the evidence, given the supposition that the reasoner was rational before acquiring the evidence, and given the utilities of the reasoner, the judgments that result are required by rationality. The clarification requires a change in the primary goal of inquiry from the pursuit of truth to the pursuit of rationality.

These remarks, which contain nothing novel, suggest a number of questions: The first is historical: why and how did the goal of rationality displace the goal of informative truth in the analysis of data? I will offer what can only be a conjecture, but I hope a conjecture that while at first surprising becomes plausible after reflection. The second question is philosophical: Besides the detour through decision theory, is there an alternative that explains how the mathematics of probability can be used to analyze data and that keeps foremost the goal of truth rather than the goal of rationality? And the third is interpretive: can applied statistical practice be understood as part of such an enterprise? I will offer answers to each of these questions.

4. Computation and the Probabilistic Revolution in Data Analysis

We are so accustomed to treating variation in observations by statistical methods that it is hard to imagine any other way of proceeding, but it was not always so, and how it came to be is something of a puzzle. Modern methods of data analysis are usually traced to Legendre's introduction of least squares in the appendix to his essay from 1805 on the orbits of comets. Within ten years of its appearance, the method of least squares was used in astronomy and geodesy throughout Europe. Stephen Stigler's excellent history of statistics begins with a discussion of the emergence of least squares methods for parameter estimation and the probabilistic justification of those methods through the theory of the normal distribution. Stigler asks: "What were the characteristics of the problems faced by eighteenth-century astronomers and geodesists that led to the method's introduction and easy acceptance?" Stigler answers his own question in an historian's way, by describing the variety of other methods that emerged in the eighteenth century at the hands of people such as Cotes, Euler, and Mayer. Stigler's implicit answer is that in view of these precedents the emergence and acceptance of least squares is less surprising. I think a more specific answer may occur to anyone who reads Stigler's history alert to issues of computational complexity. That answer, which I will develop here, is different in emphasis from Stigler's, although not in any way incompatible with what he says. My analysis makes no pretense to original scholarship.

More than half a century before Legendre wrote, Jacques Cassini and Roger Boscovitch had used a nonprobabilistic method to test hypotheses against inconsistent observations, the method now sometimes called in engineering texts "uncertain but bounded error." Their methods could in principle also have been used for parameter estimation. The idea is simple: in using a set of measurements either to test hypotheses or to estimate parameters, the investigator believes that the errors in the measurements are within some specific bound. That is, when a value x of variable X is recorded in measurement, the true value of X on that occasion is within F(x) of x, where F is some explicit function assumed known, most often, but not necessarily, a constant. The measured values of variables then determine necessary bounds on parameters to be estimated, and may exclude a hypothesis when no values of its parameters exist that are consistent with both the measurements and the error bounds assumed.

To be more definite, suppose two measurements give values Q1 and Q2, with Q1 < Q2. Then if e is the error bound for both measurements, we know the following things about the true value of Q:

$$Q1 - e < Q < Q1 + e$$
$$Q2 - e < Q < Q2 + e$$

But since Q1 < Q2, it follows that $Q2 - e < Q < Q1 + e$, which determines the interval ΔQ of possible values of Q.

Uncertain but bounded errors propagate through calculations. Consider the "ideal gas law": pressure (P), volume (V) and temperature (T) of any sample of any gas are related by

$$P\,V = K\,T$$

where K is a real number that is the same for all time for any one sample of gas, but which may differ for different samples of gases. Suppose we want to use the ideal gas law to calculate the pressure of a sample of gas at a particular time, t2. We can measure T and V at that time, but we can't use the measurements and the ideal gas law to calculate P unless we have a value for K. We measure T and V and P at some other array of values (say at time t1) for that same sample of gas and calculate K by

$$K = P_1\,V_1\,/\,T_1$$

Since K is constant, this value of K can be used to calculate P at time t2 from measured values of V and T for that time. In other words, we calculate:

$$P_2 = (P_1 V_1 T_2)/(T_1 V_2)$$

Suppose there are uncertainties in the other measurements are. What is the bound on the uncertainty of P_2 if we calculate P_2 from these measurements? Let's suppose all quantities are positive (so we're measuring temperature on the Kelvin scale), and to make the arithmetic easy, suppose that all measurements have numerical value 100 and all error bounds have numerical value 1. Then the most we can say is that for certain,

$$95.118 < P_2 < 105.122$$

Uncertainties of one part in a hundred become uncertainties of one part in ten! We can reduce the uncertainty of calculated quantities by repeated measurements of the quantities they are calculated from. Consider determining the value of K for a gas sample. We can calculate K from measurements of P, V, and T. Any one such calculation will give us error bounds on K: $K_{1min} < K < K_{1max}$. Now suppose a second set of measurements of P, V, and T are taken. Since the measurements are not perfectly accurate, PV/T will generally not be exactly equal for the two sets of measurements. Suppose, for example, that $P_2V_2/T_2 < P_1V_1/T_1$. Then if the error bounds are constant, $K_{2min} < K_{1min}$ and $K_{2max} < K_{1max}$. If $K_{2max} < K_{1min}$ the ideal gas law is refuted. Otherwise, $K_{1min} < K < K_{2max}$ is a narrower bound on K than either single set of measurements provides. In fact it is easy to see that repeated measurements can give arbitrarily accurate estimates of computed quantities provided (1) the law used to do the computation is true, and (2) the error bounds of each individual measurement are the best possible—that is, errors as large as those allowed do occur, but no larger errors occur.

The method illustrated above is similar to methods that antedate least squares. In 1755, Father Boscovitch analyzed 5 data points on the length of meridian arc at various latitudes, taken with the purpose of testing the Newtonian hypothesis of an ellipsoidal Earth. Boscovitch in effect had a linear equation (see Stigler, p. 42) in 2 unknowns and 5 data points, allowing 10 determinations of the unknown parameters. He in fact computed all 10 values, and also computed the average value (1/198) of one of the parameters, the ellipticity, and argued that the difference between the individual values of the ellipticity (ranging from 1/78 to –1.486) and the average was too large to be due to measurement error. He concluded that the elliptical hypothesis must be rejected.

Boscovitch's argument is valid if we accept his bounds on the errors of measurement. Stigler claims that Boscovitch's error bounds were unreasonable at the time, and using a more reasonable error bound (100 toises) he finds that the least squares line is within the error interval for all five observations. But that is only to deny Boscovitch's premise, not the validity of Boscovitch's argument. Had Boscovitch used the larger error value he could have used his procedure to estimate an interval of values for the ellipticity of the figure of the Earth.

Boscovitch's procedure is sensible, simple in description, informative about the truth or falsity of hypotheses of interest, and requires only an elementary kind of prior belief that could readily be elicited from scientific practitioners. It corresponds to an interval estimation procedure that is, if the assumptions about error bounds are correct, logically guaranteed to give an interval estimate containing the true value if one exists. Moreover, in most realistic cases, the interval estimates obtained from a number of measures would be very informative, narrowly circumscribing the true value. Boscovitch himself later abandoned the method for a procedure that minimized the sum of absolute values of differences between estimate and observations. And after the turn of the century uncertain but bounded error methods such as Boscovitch's were rapidly displaced by least squares, a method that had no guarantee of truth at all. Why?

Part of the reason is, of course, that within fifteen years of the appearance of Legendre's book, Gauss and Laplace gave least squares what remains the standard justification for its use: the expected value of least squares estimates is the true value for normally distributed variables, and minimizes the expected squared error of the estimate—in modern terms least squares is the minimum variance unbiased estimator. I don't know just when it was realized that least squares is also the maximum likelihood estimator for normal distributions, but maximum likelihood ideas had already been introduced, after a fashion, by Daniel Bernoulli. The central limit theorems justified the normal distribution: normal distributions are the limits of binomial distributions, or more substantively, the normal distribution results in the limit from summing appropriately small, unrelated causes.

Despite these arguments, some further motive seems required to explain the rapid adoption of least squares, for despite its elegance and mathematical pedigree, this justification for least squares sidestepped the question of how most reliably to infer the true value of an unmeasured parameter from inconsistent premises consisting of an equation containing the parameter and multiple observed values of other quantities in the equation. Then as now, probability had no evident connection with truth, and while least squares had an evident connection with minimizing expected squared loss, it had a less evident connection with estimating the truth. Probability could not be reduced to any natural property that could be determined from observation; despite Bayes's and Laplace's efforts no logical connections had been established between probability as a measure of credence and truth; and the limiting connections between truth, probability and frequency were not only in the limit, they were circular. Bernoulli's theorem, for example, did not say that a binomial probability could be determined in the limit from a sequence of trials; the theorem was twice circular, requiring that the trials be independent and giving convergence only in probability. In contrast, under assumptions investigators were disposed to make, the method of uncertain but bounded error could be applied directly to measurements rather than to distributions, and elements of that application were used—especially to test hypotheses—until the appearance of least squares.

I suggest that besides having a justification that called forth the great mathematics and mathematicians of the age, and besides giving intuitive results, least squares had an essential virtue that uncertain but bounded error did not: least squares is *computationally tractable.* The complexity of least squares computations is linear in the number of data points and bounded above by the cube of the number of unknowns. With k unknowns, Boscovitch's procedure requires solving all possible sets of k equations that can be formed from n data points, or n choose k cases. So the number of computations required by Boscovitch's method is on the order of 2k to the n choose k power. There may, of course, be more efficient methods of estimation or of testing by uncertain but bounded error than Boscovitch's, methods that reduce the time complexity to a polynomial in the number of observations. If so, the methods are not obvious. I guess, to the contrary, that uncertain but bounded estimation of (rational) values of k coefficients in a linear equation with r > k variables from n > k observations of (rational) values is NP hard (in n) for all k > 2, although I have no reduction to offer. (Even if my guess is true for the most informative uncertain but bounded estimate, it is obviously not true for estimates that are less informative—that produce wider estimates of the possible values of the parameters of interest. Indeed any set of k measurements will produce bounds on the parameter estimates that include the best bounds produced by a more informative procedure.)

In general, there is little to be said in favor of arbitrarily throwing away information, but in particular cases it may be evident that certain sets of measured values will produce the tightest estimated bounds on specific parameters, while other estimated values will produce the tightest bounds on other parameters, and so on. Where this is so, heuristic selection of the subsets to be used for estimating specific parameters may produce estimated sets of values for parameters that are reasonably close to those that would be produced by a full procedure such as Boscovitch's, and, indeed, may be small enough that a point estimate reasonably conveys the information about estimated values of parameters. Some of the proposals Stigler describes that intermediate between uncertain but bounded error and least squares involve just such heuristic selection of subsets of measurements, or other devices that reduce the complexity of the calculation by neglecting information. Avoiding computational complexity appears to have been the principal motivation for these innovations. Thus Euler, for example, tried to estimate 8 free parameters of unknown but constant values in a linear equation with 7 measured variables for which 75 observations were available. Although from various passages it seems likely that Euler thought of the problem in terms of uncertain but bounded error, for complexity reasons he obviously could not follow Boscovitch's example. Instead he determined values for 2 of the 8 unknown parameters by noting that the coefficients of the other 6 parameters were periodic with a period of 59 years. Subtracting values for 2 pairs of observations, one element of each pair taken a multiple of 59 years from the other observation of the pair, he obtained 2 equations in the 2 unknown parameters, which he solved. The result was not sensitive to the pairs chosen. That left 6 unknowns. Euler tried the same strategy for the other unknowns but found inconsistent values because there were no periodicities that exactly separated the other parameters. Stigler reports that Euler essentially gave up on the problem. Euler's chief idea appears to have been to combine estimation with induction: by finding additional independent constraints in the data, values for parameters can be determined and the complexity of the estimation problem exponentially reduced. That is a good but perhaps not often applicable idea.

A year after Euler's work appeared, in addressing a problem from lunar theory, Johann Mayer obtained a linear equation in three unknown parameters—I will refer to them as a, b, and c—and 3 measured variables for which he had 27 observations. Again, Boscovitch's method is infeasible. Instead, substituting each observation into the equation, Mayer formed 27 equations in 3 unknowns. He divided the 27 into 3 groups of 9 equations each, putting in one group the equations with the largest positive values for the coefficient of b, putting in a second group the equations with the 9 largest negative values for the coefficient of b, and putting the remaining equations in a third group, which Mayer claimed (incorrectly) had the largest values for the coefficient of c. Mayer then summed the equations in the respective groups to obtain 3 equations in the 3 unknowns, which he then solved.

Replacing a set of equations in the same variables by the equation of their sums evidently decreases the complexity of the problem exponentially, but it can and typically will lead to errors in the estimate, and from the perspective of uncertain but bounded error one would like to know the bounds on those errors. Mayer himself seems to have endorsed this perspective, and, giving error bounds on individual observations, proposed that bounds on the errors of his estimates could be calculated by following them through his procedure, although he did not give the calculation, which would require a good deal of work.

The structure of complexity for estimation and for testing need not be the same. In testing a linear hypothesis, for example, we need only consider the family of lines passing within the error bounds of the most extreme observations, and determine whether at least one of those lines intersects the error region around every other observation. If so, the hypothesis is consistent with the observations, and otherwise not. The procedure is polynomial in the number of observations, and generalizes to more dimensions. Boscovitch's procedure, which may be necessary for estimation, is unnecessarily complex for hypothesis testing. That had in effect been discovered by Jacques Cassini prior to Boscovitch's work.

In 1740, Cassini discussed 16 observations of the obliquity of the ecliptic over a span of nearly 2,000 years. Cassini was interested in the hypotheses that the obliquity changes linearly with time. He analyzed the data by fitting a straight line to the first and last observations, and then computing the interpolated values for each recorded time of measurement. Cassini claimed that the observed and interpolated values were too great to be due to measurement error, objecting especially to the difference between interpolated values and those given by Ptolemy and Pappus. Goldstein has shown that, to the contrary, Ptolemy's value was influenced by those of his predecessors and was in error by about 10'. That aside, Cassini's argument appears to have an interesting structure. He believed that none of the observations could be in error by more than a specific interval e, and he showed that some of the observations are more than that interval away from the unique line determined by the two observations that are most extreme in their values for both variables. He concluded that no line can account for the observations.

The defect I have conjectured our predecessors found in uncertain but bounded error is computational. Of course, I do not claim that anyone in the eighteenth or nineteenth century did an explicit complexity analysis. No one had to do so in order to recognize that uncertain but bounded error estimation could not be carried out in practice, and least squares could be. In judging the plausibility of an historical explanation that places so much weight on computational considerations, one might usefully keep in mind that in more recent times computational considerations have had a strong influence on the forms of probabilistic data analysis. Guilford's *Psychometric Methods* examines both Thurstone's factor analysis and a competing procedure due to Spearman. Thurstone provided an algorithm for generating linear theories that used unobserved common causes to account for rank constraints exhibited in the covariances among measured variables. Spearman had a technique for theory generation based on accounting for rank one constraints. Guilford recommended Thurstone's method over Spearman's on the grounds that Spearman's procedures were computationally intractable. More recently, with the computer and computer algorithms, the argument has been reversed, yielding claims that iterative fitting of covariance models is so computationally demanding that it limits search, and adaptations of Spearman's methods are actually more feasible. Again, Bayesian methods have been slow to be adapted partly for philosophical reasons, but perhaps more importantly because the circumstances in which posterior distributions can be computed from prior distributions and data have been very limited. Very recently there has been a lively interest in an adaptation of ergodic theorems to produce posterior distributions by simulation.

Before we leave uncertain but bounded error, there is a last, irresistible confusion to consider: that assertions of uncertain but bounded error are limiting cases of assertions of a probability that a quantity lies in some specified set of values. The idea is that simple uncertain but bounded error claims are really claims of probabilistic certainty, probability 1 claims. The more general form, according to this idea, is "the probability is p that the value of X lies within epsilon of x." The idea is wrong. The assertion "X lies within epsilon of x" does not entail, nor is it entailed by, "the limiting relative frequency of cases in which X lies within epsilon of x is one," nor by "my degree of belief is one that X lies within epsilon of x." The sentence "X lies within epsilon of x" has no logical connection with any interesting probability claim.

5. Approximation, Distributional Forms, and Finite Frequencies

In contrast to the philosophical accounts of probability, there is an unphilosophical account often advanced by practitioners and teachers that does connect probability claims directly with claims about what happens, and that connection may explain the popularity of the proposal. The "long-run frequency" interpretation of probability, popular in textbooks, says the probability of an outcome in a trial is approximately the relative frequency of the outcome in a "long" sequence of trials. A nonsequential version of the same idea is that probability claims are about the approximate relative frequency distribution of values of features of individuals in large populations (of whatever). For apparently good reasons, the finite frequency account is short on philosophical champions: it is twice vague, since it does not specify the meaning of "approximate" or of "long"; for any way of making the finite frequency claim precise, typical literal probability claims (e.g., the claim that a distribution is normal) are false; and the finite frequency interpretation seems committed to the Gambler's Fallacy, for if "the probability of heads is 1/2" means something like "in a sequence of 1000 tosses or more the frequency of heads will be nearly 1/2" then the gambler who finds that a coin he believes to be fair has turned up heads in 500 consecutive tosses can reasonably infer that tails are due: unless almost all of the remaining tosses are tails the probability claim, under the finite frequency interpretation, will be false.

I recommend charity to gamblers and to practitioners. I suggest that the finite frequency story is something else besides a definition of "probability," that it is a compressed account of how inferences from data may be made with the aid of the mathematics of probability, but without the obscure thing itself. I think we are more faithful to practice if we understand the finite frequency interpretation as a proposal to use the language and mathematics of probability to approximately describe actual or potential finite populations, and as a means of generating definite, nonprobabilistic hypotheses. Thus, to illustrate the first point, the claim that "adult human male height has a normal probability distribution" is a way of saying that a histogram of the relative frequencies of such heights would be approximated by the curve of the normal density function. The claim may be compared to "this sample of gas approximately satisfies the ideal gas law." Both have an unspecified parameter—the degree of approximation—and both are properties of a collective, the entire population in the case of probability and pairs of P,V,T states in the case of the gas law. To the objection that informed people do not behave as though they were committing the distributional analogue of the gambler's fallacy, I say that so far as that is true it is so because in such cases informed people reject the distributional assumption. When the sample is large but the distribution wants a tail, we reject the proposition that in a still larger sample the distribution will be normal. And when we are not allowed to reject the distributional assumption and we are dealing with inferences about a finite population from samples taken without replacement from that population, the gambler's fallacy is no fallacy at all, only good logic.

One might reasonably wonder whether there is any gain in content in moving from claims about probability to claims about the "approximate" form of distribution of an unspecifiedly large sample. Unlike the probability claim itself, the degree of approximation in an approximate empirical frequency claim can be made explicit and empirical in various ways. Analytic measures of approximation can be used to generate claims that are perfectly definite and perfectly empirical, even though they may be clothed in the language of probability. For example, one may say that the sum of squared vertical distances from bar heights on a frequency histogram and points on some normal distribution is less than some specific number, or that for each point in the histogram the distance to the normal curve is less than a percentage of the height of histogram, and so on. Again, uncertain but bounded error in measurements will create uncertain but bounded errors in the points on the histogram, and thus a family of normals that might, within any measure of approximation, describe the histogram. When made explicit in these or other ways, "probability" claims become assertions about bounds on arrangements of values of quantities in finite populations. They become an especially interesting variety of claims, not about probabilities, but about uncertain but bounded errors in finite frequency distributions. Entirely explicit versions of finite frequency claims of probability, on my analysis, are claims about the uncertain but bounded error of some function of the empirical distribution of a quantity (or quantities) in an actual or potential finite population.

The Rasch models and other theories whose claims appear to be probabilistic have some content if we understand the probabilities involved to be hypotheses about the approximate distributions of values in large finite samples. That interpretation may make the content of theories vague, but vagueness is better than vacuity. The interpretation may violate the mathematics of probability, but that is essential to the very idea of probability theory as an instrument.

One scientific value of approximate distributional hypotheses lies in the fact that variables in systems that satisfy approximately no informative restriction on n arbitrary observed values, for small n, may nonetheless have useful approximations that satisfy distributional hypotheses for large n. The claim that a finite population of values is distributed approximately as some probability density sometimes conveys important extra information that could not be given by saying that some quantity or quantities have specific values, approximately. Independence hypotheses provide one important example, fundamental to experimental design, where approximate distributions can be much more informative about parameters of interest than can uncertain but bounded error claims about the values of quantities whose distribution is described.

Consider an experiment to test a simple linear hypothesis:

$$Y = aX + e$$

The object is to estimate the parameter a. We will suppose that values of X are determined deliberately by some mechanism that is believed to distribute x approximately independently of e. Suppose we assume that X and Y are measured perfectly. With uncertain but bounded error nothing can be inferred about the value of parameter a because e is unknown. We can only estimate a if we assume some definite, finite set of possible values for e without the help of any measurement of that quantity.

The treatment with approximate distributions is quite different. Because X is a treatment variable under experimental control, all experimental design assumes that e and X are (approximately) independently distributed. Then a can be estimated in various ways, for example from estimates of the variances and covariances related to the parameter a by the familiar derivation:

$$
\begin{aligned}
&\mathrm{Exp}(X,Y) = a\ \mathrm{Exp}(X,X) + \mathrm{Exp}(X,e) = \\
&a\ \mathrm{EXP}(X,X) + \mathrm{COV}(X,e) + \mathrm{Exp}(X)\mathrm{Exp}(e) = \\
&a\ \mathrm{Exp}(X,X) + \mathrm{Exp}(X)\mathrm{Exp}(e) = \\
&a\ \mathrm{Exp}(X,X) + \mathrm{Exp}(X)\mathrm{Exp}(Y) - a\mathrm{Exp2}(X) \\
&(\text{Because } \mathrm{Exp}(X)\mathrm{Exp}(Y) = a\mathrm{Exp2}(X) + \mathrm{Exp}(X)\mathrm{Exp}(e)) \\
&\mathrm{Exp}(X,Y) - \mathrm{Exp}(X)\mathrm{Exp}(Y) = a\ (\mathrm{Exp}(X,X) - \mathrm{Exp2}(X)) \\
&\mathrm{COV}(X,Y) = a\ \mathrm{Var}(X)
\end{aligned}
$$

Once one thinks of approximate descriptions of real or potential finite frequency distributions, the relation between the absence of causal connection and approximate independence or conditional independence, opens a huge space of applications unavailable without distributions.

6. Concluding Remarks

I have tried to say how the theory of probability, which, much as Locke's substance, is about something we know not what, has provided and can provide instruments for making valid inferences about the values of quantities and the truth or falsity of hypotheses, rather than valid inferences as to which decision has the highest expected utility. The sometimes bitter debates between those who describe themselves as frequentists and those who describe themselves as subjective Bayesians has often turned on charges by the former than the latter abandon the "objectivity" of science and by the latter that the former dissemble about the "subjectivity" of their probability judgments. My belief is that, among statisticians anyway, the dispute often confuses content with justification. The "objectivity" of the frequentists is in the content of their probability judgments, which while usually stated as about an unempirical probability are often really vague empirical claims about finite frequencies. That sort of objectivity is genuinely lost in subjective Bayesian interpretations. The "subjectivity" kept hidden by frequentists is that there is often no explicit justification beyond their own opinion for aspects of their empirical claims. That subjectivity can be made entirely explicit without sacrificing the objective—that is, empirical—content of frequency claims, and its recognition does not require, or even invite, recourse to subjective probability. Bayesian criticisms do address a confused and uncertain frequentist statistical practice, in which the point of making empirical claims is often forgotten or fudged. Data analysis might look somewhat different, and from a logical perspective, better, if "orthodox" or "frequentist" or "objectivist" statisticians were candid and consistent about the instrumental use they would make of probability, and if probability were understood as a tool for idealization and approximation rather than a normative scold.

CLARK GLYMOUR
Carnegie Mellon University
Institute for Human and Machine Cognition, University of West Florida

REFERENCES

Guilford, J. 1936. *Psychometric Methods.* New York: McGraw-Hill.
Rasch, G. 1960. *Probabilistic Models for Some Intelligence and Attainment Tests.* Copenhagen: Studies in Mathematical Psychology.
Stigler, S. 1986. *The History of Statistics.* Cambridge: Harvard University Press.

12

What Is Wrong with Bayes Nets?

NANCY CARTWRIGHT

If probability is a guide to life, that is in part because it is a guide to causality. My contribution suggests that the metaphor of the guide is apt: guides can give advice about getting around, but they cannot provide a surefire recipe. I defend this claim by looking at what is probably the currently most popular way of connecting causes and probabilities, via Bayes nets. I argue that the assumptions about the relations between causes and probabilities that justify Bayes-nets methods hold in certain kinds of circumstances—but not in others. These methods are not special in that respect, however; there are no universal connections between causes and probabilities. Methodologists look for necessary and sufficient conditions to link the two, but the relation between them, I argue, is far more like that of a disease to its symptoms.

—N. C.

* * *

1. The Basic Question: Can We Get to Causality via Bayes Nets?

Probability is a guide to life partly because it is a guide to causality. Work over the last two decades using Bayes nets supposes that probability is a very sure guide to causality. I think not, and I shall argue that here. Almost all the objections I list are well known. But I have come to see them in a different light by reflecting again on the original work in this area by Wolfgang Spohn and his recent defense of it in a paper titled "Bayesian Nets Are All There Is to Causality."[1]

Bayes nets are directed acyclic graphs that represent probabilistic independencies among an ordered set of variables. The parents of a variable X are the minimal set of predecessors that render X independent of all its other predecessors. If the variables are temporally (or causally) ordered, we can read the very same graph as a graph of the (generic-level) causal relations among the quantities represented, it is maintained. This commits us to the *causal Markov condition* described below, which is a relative of Reichenbach's claim that conditioning on common causes will render joint effects independent of each other. It is also usual to add an assumption called *faithfulness* or *stability* as well as to assume that all underlying systems of causal laws are deterministic (plus the *causal minimality condition*, which I will not discuss). With these assumptions in hand there are a variety of algorithms for inferring causal relations from independencies. These I will loosely call "Bayes-nets methods."

In criticizing the inference of causes from Bayes nets it is usual to list the objections I note. Is this just an arbitrary list? And why should one have expected any connection between the two to begin with? After all, Bayes nets encode information about probabilistic independencies. Causality, if it has any connection with probability, would seem to be related to probabilistic dependence.

The answers to the two questions are related. When we see why there might be a connection between causality and independence, we see why there will be a list of objections. The answer to why is not one that will sound surprising, but I want to focus on it because working through the argument will show that we have been looking at probability and causality in the wrong way. Probabilities may be a guide to causes, but they are, I shall argue, like symptoms of a disease: there is no general formula to get from the symptom to the disease.

2. The Call for Explanation

It is usual to suppose that once the right set of assumptions are made about the causal systems under study, we can read information about causes from a Bayes net that satisfies those assumptions. Wolfgang Spohn maintains that if there is a tight connection like this between Bayes nets and an independent notion of causation, there should be a general reason for this. He cannot find one; so he proposes that the notion of causation at stake is not independent. The probabilistic patterns of a Bayes net is our concept of causation: "it is the structure of suitably refined Bayesian nets which decides about how the causal dependencies run."[2]

I agree with Spohn that if there is a tight connection, there should be a reason for it. The alternative is what Gerd Buchdahl called a "brute force" connection,[3] one which holds in nature but has no "deeper" explanation. There are such brute-force connections between concepts we use in science. These are what we record in fundamental laws. And some of them involve relational concepts like " . . . causes. . . ." For instance, if the allowed energy configuration for a system in relation to its environment is represented by a specific Hamiltonian, say H, then whatever the system's current state (say Φ), the system will evolve in time according to $-i/h\ \partial\ \Phi\ /\partial t = H\ \Phi$.

But I do not think there is a brute-force connection in the case of Bayes nets and causation. That is primarily because there is a reason for the connection, a good reason. The problem is that the reason does not justify a *tight* connection. The reason lets us see why the connection will hold when it does, but it also allows us to see how loose the connection between the two is:

1. It only holds in special populations in special circumstances.
2. We cannot give good direct characterizations of what these populations are.[4]
3. The populations really are special—we rarely come across them in our investigations.
4. And there are other connections that can provide us with sound casual inferences in other kinds of populations governed by different kinds of systems of causal laws.

For simplicity I will stick to yes-no causes and effects in the subsequent discussion. We are looking for an equivalence between causal connections and Bayes nets. I will start with causation and see first how—and when—we can get from causation to the probability relations pictured in Bayes nets.

3. From Causation to Probabilistic Dependence

3a. Where Have All the Caveats Gone?

Causes produce their effects; they make them happen.[5] So, in the right kind of population we can expect that there will be a higher frequency of the effect (E) when the cause (C) is present than when it is absent; and conversely for preventatives. What kind of populations are "the right kinds"? Here are some of the conditions that we know need to be satisfied:

- C should not be correlated with preventatives of E
- Nor with requisite triggers or auxiliary factors for these

- Nor anti-correlated with other causes
- Nor with requisite triggers or auxiliary factors for these
- Nor anti-correlated with triggers or auxiliary factors necessary for its own operation
- Nor should these be anti-correlated with each other
- Nor with other causes
- Nor with requisite triggers or auxiliary factors for these
- Nor corrlated with preventatives
- Nor with requisite triggers or auxiliary factors for these
- *C* should not also be a preventative of *E*
- Nor a trigger nor an auxiliary factor for a preventative

The trouble with Bayes nets is that they ignore all these caveats. When Bayes nets are used as causal graphs, effects are probabilistically dependent upon each of their causes. That's it. Nothing can mask this. The assumptions about causality made by the Bayes-net approach go all the way back to the first, then ground-breaking, probabilistic analysis of causality by Patrick Suppes.[6] Suppes begins with *prima facie* causation: any earlier factor that is correlated with an effect is a *prima facie* cause of that effect. Real causes are ones that survive the same independence tests that are required in the Bayes net. But nothing gets to be a candidate for a cause unless it is correlated with the putative effect.

Twenty to thirty years later we have the Bayes-net approach, in all essentials equivalent to the original formulation proposed by Suppes when the subject first began. It is as if Simpson's paradox and causal decision theory never existed. Nor decades of practice by econometricians and other social scientists, who plot not simple regressions but *partial* regressions. Nor the widely deployed definition proposed by Granger in 1969, which looks for probabilistic dependence only after conditioning on the entire past history of the cause—which ensures that all the other causes up to the time of the putative cause will be held fixed.

The demand that effects always be probabilistically dependent on each cause follows in the Bayes-net approach from the assumption that Peter Spirtes, Clark Glymour, and Richard Scheines call *faithfulness*.[7] Judea Pearl calls it *stability*.[8] The assumption is necessary to the approach. Without it the procedures developed by Pearl and by Spirtes et al. cannot get very far with the discovery of causal connections; and the proofs that assure us that they will not make mistakes if sample sizes are large enough will not go through. For Spohn it matters because he argues that causal connections *are* the connections marked out on God's big Bayes net once the variables have been temporally ordered. With the faithfulness/stability assumption, the causal connections are unique; but they are seldom unique otherwise.

For those readers who are not already deeply into this discussion let me rehearse the standard objections to the assumption that all genuine causes are *prima facie* causes. First there is *Simpson's Paradox*: facts about probabilistic dependency can be reversed in moving from populations to subpopulations. For example, factor X may be positively dependent or negatively dependent or independent of Y in a population, but still be any of these three in all partitions of the population along the values of a third factor Z, if Z is itself probabilistically dependent on X and Y. Z may, for instance, be a preventative of Y; because of its correlation with X, the presence of X does not, after all, increase the frequency of Y's in the population as my opening argument suggests.

It is typical in social science to sidestep this problem by looking for probabilistic dependence between a putative cause and its effect only in subpopulations in which all possible confounding factors are held fixed. This is apparent in the econometrics concept of Granger causality, where X Granger causes Y if X and Y are probabilistically dependent holding fixed *everything* that has occurred up to the time of the putative cause.

The same strategy was at the heart of various versions of causal decision theory two decades ago. What is the probability that if I were to do C, E would occur? The conditional probability P(E/C) gives the wrong answer. It could be either way too big or way too small because of the operation of confounding factors; relevant here—it could be zero even though my doing C could have a substantial impact on whether E occurs. One standard proposal (the one I urged[9]) is to set $P(C \rightarrow E) = P(E/C\&K)$, where K is a state description over the values of a full set of "other" causal factors for E that obtain (or will obtain) in the decision situation.[10] Where we do not know the values of the factors in K we should average over all possible values using our best estimate of the probability that they will occur: $\Sigma P(E/C\&K_j)P(K_j)$.

Exactly the same formula has reappeared among the Bayes-nets causal theorists. Judea Pearl has recently produced a very fine and detailed account of counterfactuals and their probabilities, based on Bayes nets. According to Pearl, the probability of y if we were to "set" $X = x_j$ is $\Sigma P(y/x_j$ & parents of X)P(parents of X).[11] Despite Pearl's endorsement of stability, from this formula it looks as if a factor can have a high degree of causal efficacy even though on his account it is not really a cause at all because it is not *prima facie* a cause. I take it that Pearl does not take this to be a problem because he thinks cases where "stability" is violated involve "'pathological' parameterizations"[12] and are not in the range he will address.

The second kind of case usually cited in which genuine causes are not *prima facie* causes is when one and the same cause has different kinds of influence on the effect. The different influences may cancel each other. The easiest version of this to handle is when a given factor acts as both cause and preventative of the effect, by different routes. G. Hesslow's birth-control pills[13] are the canonical philosophical example. The pills are a positive cause of thrombosis. On the other hand, they prevent pregnancy, which is itself a cause of thrombosis. Given the right weights for the three processes, the net effect of the pills on the frequency of thrombosis can be zero.

If we suspect that cancellations of this kind are occurring, we can confirm our suspicions by looking at the probabilities of thrombosis, given the pills in populations in which factors from the separate causal routes between pills and thrombosis are held fixed. But this is no comfort to the Bayes-nets theorist.

Even this strategy is not available where there are no routes between the cause and its effects. We have two kinds of trouble with routes. The first is a worry that I share with Glenn Shafer.[14] Let us accept that in every case of singular causation there is a temporally continuous process connecting the cause with the effect. That does not guarantee that there will always be a vertex between any two other vertices in God's great causal graph. That is because the graphs are graphs of causal laws that hold between event-types. Every token of the cause-type may in actuality be connected by a continuous process with the effect token without there being some chain of laws in between: C_1 causes C_2, . . . , C_n causes E. For instance, the signal from the cause to the effect may piggyback on causal processes that the cause in question does not initiate. This is particularly likely where there are a lot of processes with the necessary spatio-temporal relations already available for use in conveying the influence from the cause to the effect.[15]

Roman Frigg offers a number of examples.[16] He explains that what is wanted are cases for which there is

> **A generic law without contiguity:** On the generic level cause and effect do *not* exhibit contiguity, neither in space nor in time.
>
> **No unique causal chain:** There is no unique causal chain that connects cause and effect. That is, on the *concrete level* the connection between the two can be realised in many different ways.

One of Frigg's examples involves as cause Person B getting an HIV virus from another person and as effect, that B dies later on. He tells us

> 1. The infection with the HIV virus leads in most cases to death. But a long period of time elapses between these two events.

2. The infection with the HIV virus leads (in most cases) to the outbreak of AIDS, i.e., the destruction of the immune system. This in turn can lead to death by a variety of different routes. To mention just a few:

    (1) Diarrhoea (various pathogens possible)

    (2) Encephalitis with brain atrophy

    (3) Neuropathy

    (4) Pneumonia

    (5) Ringworm (various types)

    (6) Meningitis

    (7) Herpes simplex

    (8) Tuberculosis

    (9) Fever.[17]

Frigg also offers examples of death by malaria and from exposure to strong radiation, and of the democratic election of an individual as president of a country resulting in that person's becoming president, the receipt of a court order causing someone to appear in court, and the ordering of a plane ticket causing a person to receive a ticket.

The other is a problem we all sweep under the rug: the representations in a causal graph are discrete; for every vertex there is always a predecessor and a successor. Is causality really like that? If it is then we can have cases of causes with mixed influences on the effect, directly, not by different routes. That is, the same factor both causes and prevents a given effect, as in the example of the birth-control pills; but does so directly, not via any routes.

For example, an atom in an excited state can either cause or prevent photons by, in the first case, spontaneous emission or in the second, spontaneous absorption; and we think that nothing happens in between the event of the atom's being in the excited state and the event of it being de-excited with photons present or more excited with photons having disappeared. In cases like this it is not possible to hold fixed vertices along the various routes since there aren't any such vertices. So we will not have available our usual methods that look for probabilistic dependence between cause and effect holding fixed factors first on one putative causal route and then the other to test whether a factor is really causally inefficacious for the given effect or instead rather has mixed influences that just cancel each other.

3b. Can the Caveats Be Ignored?

What justification do Bayes-nets theorists give for ignoring all these caveats and insisting that all causes must appear as causes at the first crude look? Spirtes, Glymour, and Scheines discuss Simpson's Paradox at length. They present two graphs, the first embodying Simpson's paradox; the second is a graph that by contrast is "faithful" to all the independencies assumed in the paradoxical case—that is, as in Suppes's original formulation, all causes are *prima facie* causes:[18]

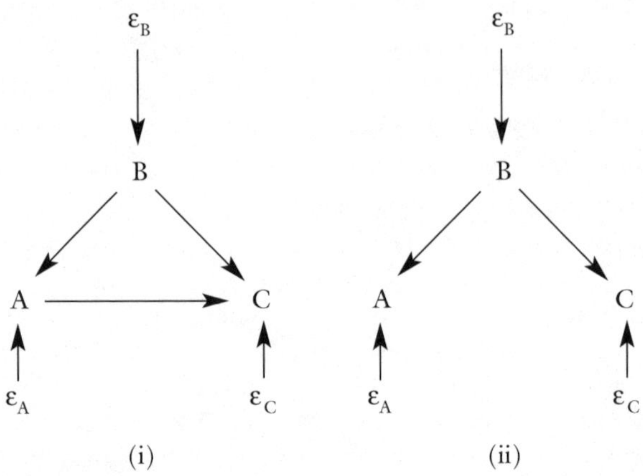

They then invite us to

> [s]uppose for a moment that we ignore the interpretation that Simpson gave to the variables in his example. . . . Were we to find A and C are independent but dependent conditional on B, the Faithfulness Condition requires that if any causal structure obtains, it is structure (ii). Still, structure (i) is logically possible,[19] and if the variables had the significance Simpson gives them we would of course prefer it. But if prior knowledge does not require structure (i), what do we lose by applying the Faithfulness Condition; what, in other words, do we lose by excluding causal structures that are not faithful to the distribution [i.e., that allow genuine causes that do not appear as causes *prima facie*]?[20]

I assume that this passage is meant as a defense of the faithfulness condition since it appears at the end of the long exposition of Simpson's Paradox in the section in which they introduce faithfulness as an axiom[21] and just before the only other remark that could be construed as a defense of this axiom in the face of Simpson's Paradox. But what is the defense? The answer to their question is obviously: What we lose is getting the causal structure right.

Perhaps they mean to suggest that when we do not know anything, it is more reasonable to plump for structure (ii) than for structure (i). But what is the argument for that? I respond with a truism: when you don't know, you don't know; and it is often dangerous to speculate. If we have no idea what the variables stand for, let alone how they operate, we are not in a position to make a bet with any degree of credibility. "Ah yes," I am sometimes told, "but what if you *had* to bet?" Well, tell me more about the context in which I am forced to bet—a psychological experiment perhaps?—and I may be able to tell you which bet I would plump for.

Perhaps, however, Spirtes, Glymour, and Scheines are speaking sloppily. They did not mean "*what* do we lose?" but rather "*how often* will we lose?" For immediately after this they report that "[i]n the linear case, the parameter values—of the linear coefficients and exogenous variances of a structure—form a real space, and the set of points in this space that create vanishing partial correlations not implied by the Markov condition [i.e., that violate faithfulness] have Lebesgue measure zero."[22]

This is surely intended as an argument in favor of faithfulness—and it is frequently cited as being so intended—though I am not sure exactly what the conclusion is that it is supposed to support. I gather we are to conclude that it is unlikely that any causal system to which we consider applying our probabilistic methods will involve genuine causes that are not *prima facie* causes as well.

But this conclusion would follow only if there were some plausible way to connect a Lebesgue measure over a space of ordered n-tuples of real numbers with the way in which parameters are chosen or arise naturally for the causal systems that we will be studying. I have never seen such a connection proposed; that, I think, is because there is no possible, plausible story to be told. Moreover, were some connection mooted, we should keep in mind that it could not bear directly on the question of how any actual parameter value is chosen because, as we all know, any specific point in the space will have measure zero. So we not only need a story that connects a Lebesgue measure over a space of n-tuples of real numbers with how real parameter values arise, but we need a method that selects as a question to be addressed before values are chosen: shall values occur that satisfy faithfulness or not?

Judea Pearl argues somewhat differently about the choice of parameter values. He uses the term *stability* for the condition that insists that effects be probabilistically dependent on their causes even before confounding factors are conditioned on. Here is what he says in its entirety:

> Some structures may admit peculiar parameterizations that would render them indistinguishable from many other minimal models that have totally disparate structures. For example, consider a binary variable C that takes the value 1

> whenever the outcomes of two fair coins (*A* and *B*) are the same and takes the value 0 otherwise. In the trivariate distribution generated by this parameterization, each pair of variables is marginally independent yet is dependent conditioning on the third variable. Such a dependence pattern may in fact be generated by three minimal causal structures, each depicting one of the variables as causally dependent on the other two, but there is no way to decide among the three. In order to rule out such "pathological" parameterizations, we impose a restriction on the distribution called stability. . . . This restriction conveys the assumption that all the independencies imbedded in [the probability distribution] P are stable; that is, they are implied by the structure of the model *D* and hence remain invariant to any changes in the parameters [of *D*]. In our example only the correct structure (namely, A → C ← B) will retain its independence pattern in the face of changing parameterizations—say, when one of the coins becomes slightly biased.[23]

We can see here two points of view that Pearl takes that make stability seem plausible to him. First, Pearl thinks causal systems should be decidable. It is clearly a criticism of the systems described that "there is no way to decide among the three." This attitude is revealed in discussions of other topics as well. For instance, as we shall see below, I reject the causal Markov condition. Pearl objects that by so doing I make questions about the causal structure and about the truth of certain counterfactuals unanswerable.[24]

Unanswerable given what information? Immediately after the section defining "stability" Pearl tells us, "With the added assumption of stability, every distribution has a unique minimal causal structure . . . , as long as there are no hidden variables."[25] Clearly he intends that the questions he is concerned about should be answerable given an order for the full set of causally relevant variables and the probability distribution over them. But so far as I can see, once we have given up the idea that there is something wrong with the notion of *cause* so that it has to be reduced away, there is no good reason to suppose that probabilities should be able to answer all questions about causality for us. (Nor am I sure that Pearl insists they should; for it is unclear whether he thinks *all* causal systems are stable or takes the more modest line that his methods are capable of providing answers to all his questions only for systems that are stable.)

The other point of view that matters for Pearl's claims about stability is the point of view of the engineer—which he is. It is apparent from the passage that Pearl thinks of causal structures as in some sense coming first: they get fixed, but then the parameter values can vary. But, of course, a causal system comes with both its structure and its parameters—you can't have one without the other.

I think the way to put the issue that makes sense of the idea of "structure first" is in terms of the kinds of operation we typically perform on the kinds of engineered devices Pearl generally has in mind. Think of a toaster. Its parts and their arrangement are fixed. We may bend the position of the trip plate a little, or of the expanding metal strip which it will meet, in order to keep the brownness of the toast calibrated with the settings on the brownness control. The values of the parameters do not matter so long as the basic causal structure does not break down; indeed the values are just the kind of thing we expect to drift over time. But we would have a legitimate cause of complaint if the same were true of the structure within the first year we owned the toaster.

That is fine for a toaster. But for other situations the parameters may matter equally with the structure, or more so. If birth-control pills do cause thrombosis we may work very hard to weaken the strength with which they do so, at least to the point where people who take the pills are no worse off than those who do not. Indeed we may take this as an important aim—we are more obliged to get the effects to cancel out than we are to continue to spend money and research time to reduce the risk of thrombosis among pill-takers below that of non-pill-takers. Getting the cancellation that stability/faithfulness prohibits is important to us.

This brings us to what seems to me a real oddity in the whole idea of stability/faithfulness. Probabilities and causal structures constrain each other. If the probability is fixed, then nature—and we—are not allowed to build certain kinds of causal structures. For instance, if we have the three binary variables, A, B, and C, as in Pearl's example, with a probability in which they are pairwise independent and have to create a causal arrangement (or lack of!) among the three, we are prevented from building just the one Pearl describes. Or, to think of it with causal structure first, as Pearl generally seems to, if C is to take value 1 or 0 depending on whether the outcome of the flip of two coins is the same or not, we are prevented from using fair coins and must introduce at least a little bias.

I come, finally, to the question of whether we should in fact expect to see a lot of causes that are not causes *prima facie*. A good many of the systems to which we think of applying the methods advocated by Bayes-nets theorists are constructed systems. Either highly designed, like a toaster or an army admissions test, or a mix of intentional design, historical influence, and unintended consequences, as in various socio-economic examples. In these cases cancellation of the effects of a given cause, either by encouraging the action of other factors or by encouraging the contrary operation of the cause itself, can be an important aim, particularly where the effect is deleterious. It will often be a lot easier to design for, or encourage the emergence of, cancellation than it is to eliminate the cause of the unwanted effect, or less costly or more beneficial overall (as in my discussion of birth-control pills). There is no good reason to assume that our aims are almost always frustrated.[26]

This is a view that Kevin Hoover also stresses in his work on causality in macroeconomics. He considers a macroeconomic example in which "agency can result in constraints appearing in the data that [violate faithfulness]."[27] He concludes

> Spirtes et al. . . . acknowledge the possibility that particular parameter values might result in violations of faithfulness, but they dismiss their importance as having "measure zero." But this will not do for macroeconomics. It fails to account for the fact that in macroeconomic and other control contexts, the policymaker aims to set parameter values in just such a way as to make this supposedly measure-zero situation occur. To the degree that policy is successful, such situations are common, not infinitely rare.[28]

Consider some homely examples with which we are all familiar. Parents who worry about their young children being hassled or attacked walking home from school are often surprised to learn that the reported incidences are no higher now than they used to be. But it is not a puzzle: there is no correlation between the presence of bullies and criminals on the street and the harrassment of children because the parents drive the children back and forth to school. They have engineered an anticorrelation between the presence of bullies and the presence of children. Or think about nondrowsy decongestants. There is no correlation between ingesting the principal chemical in them that relieves congestion and getting sleepy, even though the chemical produces drowsiness. That's because the chemical comes in the same pill as a stimulant.

This last kind of example is an important one to notice. I remarked that cancellations are often just what we want, for political, social, commercial, or medical ends. The decongestants remind us, moreover, that it is often fairly exact cancellation that we demand. The pills are supposed to decongest. They are no more supposed to hype you up than they are supposed to put you to sleep. Getting the balance right matters.

Perhaps, however, the issue will be made: can we ever really expect *exactly* exact cancellation? After all, to get an arrow in a Bayes-net causal graph, any degree of dependence between cause and effect will do. After we have the arrow in, we need not be misled by the smallness of the dependence to think the influence is small. For we can then insist on measuring degree of efficacy by the formula above that I and other causal-decision theorists proposed and that Pearl endorses for $P(C \rightarrow E)$.

One reason we may think exact cancellations are rare is that actually getting any really precise value we aim for is rare. In a recent discussion of instrumentalism, Elliott Sober talks about a comparison of the heights of corn plants in two populations. One thing we know, he claims, is that they are not really equal. Still, that is the working hypothesis. I take it that one of the reasons he thinks we know this is that "exactly equal" is very precise; and any very precise prediction is very likely to be wrong in an imprecise discipline.

This raises some very difficult issues about modelling and reality, especially for probabilities. We design a device to set the difference between two quantities at zero; tests for quality-control show that, within bounds of experimental error, we succeeded; and we model the difference as zero. Should we think it "really" is zero? It is not certain the question makes sense, even when we are thinking of, say, a difference between the length of two strips in a single designated device. It becomes particularly problematic when we are thinking about a difference of two probabilities in a population. Is the increase in probability of thrombosis on taking birth-control pills exactly offset by the decrease via pregnancy prevention in British women between the ages of 20 and 35 in the period from 1980 to 1990? All the conventional issues about what we intend by talking about the true probability become especially acute here.

Exactly exact cancellations are not really the issue, though, at least when we are thinking about the application of the Bayes-nets approach to causality as opposed to the philosophical issue about substitutability raised by Spohn. For we are going to be using these methods in doing real social, medical, and engineering science, using real data.[29] And here it is not unusual for our best estimates from the data to render two quantities probabilistically independent where estimates of appropriate partial conditional probabilities—as well perhaps as our background knowledge or even other kinds of tests we have conducted for the relevant causal connections—suggest the result is due to cancellation. In this case we either have to insist that the probabilities are not those our best estimates indicate or forsake the commitment to faithfulness.

Before leaving this section I should repeat an old point, for completeness. Sometimes it is argued that Bayes-nets methods should *supplement* what we know. So if we do have independent evidence of cancellation, we should use it and not insist on faithfulness. But where we do not have such information we should assume faithfulness. As I indicated earlier, this strategy is ill-founded; indeed, I think irresponsible. Where we don't know, we don't know. When we have to proceed with little information we should make the best evaluation we can for the case at hand—and hedge our bets heavily; we should not proceed with false confidence having plumped either for or against some specific hypothesis—like faithfulness—for how the given system works when we really have no idea.

4. From Probabilistic Dependence to Causality

If we have a hypothesis that C causes E, we can use what we have just reviewed to test it, via the hypothetico-deductive method. But that is a method that we know to be more accurate at rejecting hypotheses than confirming them. Bayes-nets methods promise more: they will bootstrap from facts about dependencies and independencies to causal hypotheses—and, claim the advocates, never get it wrong.

Again, as Spohn argues, if there really is this tight connection, there ought to be an argument for why it obtains. And there is. Again, we can see from looking at the argument why the inference from dependencies and independencies sometimes works, and why it will not work all the time. As with the other direction of inference, there is an argument for the connection and the argument itself makes clear that the connection is not tight.

What kinds of circumstances can be responsible for a probabilistic dependence between A and B? Lots of things. The fact that A causes B is among them: *Causes produce their effects; they make them happen*. So, in the right kind of population we can expect that there will be a higher frequency of the effect (*E*) when the cause (*C*) is present than when it is absent; and conversely for preventatives. With caveats.

What else? Here are a number of well-known things:

- A and B may have a common cause or a common preventative or correlated causes or correlated preventatives.
- A and B may cooperate to produce an effect. In populations where the effect is either heavily present or heavily absent, A and B may be dependent on each other.
- A and B may be produced as product and by-product from a probabilistic cause.
- When two populations governed by different systems of causal laws or exhibiting different probability distributions are mixed together, the resulting population may not satisfy the causal Markov condition even though each of the sub-populations do. So A and B may be correlated conditional on the parents of A without A causing B.
- A and B may be quantities with the same kind of temporal evolution, both monotonically increasing, say. Then the value of A at t will be correlated with the value of B at t.

Let us look at each in turn and at what the defenders of Bayes nets have to say about them. I begin with the first which is the case that advocates of Bayes-nets methods acknowledge and try to deal with squarely—assuming the underlying system is deterministic.

4a. Why Factors May Be Dependent

(1) Common causes (where nature is deterministic). Following Judea Pearl,[30] let us call the total effect of all those causes of X that are omitted from V and which combine with the direct causes in V of X to form a set of causes sufficient to fix the value of X, a *random disturbance factor* for X.[31] Bayes-net methods are applied only to special sets of variables: sets V such that for each X in V, the random disturbance factor for X is probabilistically independent of that for every other variable in V. In such a variable set we can prove that the causal Markov condition will be satisfied.[32]

The causal Markov condition, along with the assumption that all causes are *prima facie* causes, lies at the heart of the Bayes-net methods. It tells us that a variable will be probabilistically independent of every other variable except its own effects once all of its direct causes have been conditioned on. So we eliminate cases where a dependence between A and B is due to reason (1) by requiring that the dependence persist once we have conditioned on the parents of A.

Everyone acknowledges that some constraint like this is necessary. You cannot get directly from dependence to causation; you at least have to first hold fixed the causal parents or something equivalent, then look for dependence. So in the remaining sections when I talk about the route from dependence to causation, I mean dependence conditional on a set of causal parents. To claim that this is enough to ensure a causal connection is to maintain the causal Markov condition.

My description of the restriction on the variable set V is rather longwinded. The first reason is to avoid a small problem of characterization. What I have called "random disturbance factors" are sometimes called "exogenous" factors. There are various concepts of exogeneity. This usage obviously refers to the one in which exogenous factors are not caused by any variables in the system. Pearl clearly assumes that is true of random disturbance factors. But the proof requires more, for it is possible for all exogenous causes of one variable to be independent of those for another without the disturbance terms themselves being independent. That's because it is possible for a function of X and Y to be dependent on Z even if the three factors are pairwise independent. So it is not enough that the exogenous causes for a variable be independent of those for other variables: the proof needs their *net effects* to be independent.

The second reason is that some of the other terminology used in the discussion is unclear. Often we are told, as by Spirtes, Glymour, and Scheines,[33] that the methods will be applied only to sets that are causally sufficient, adding the bold assumption that as a matter of empirical fact, this will ensure the necessary independencies among the disturbance factors. But what is *causal sufficiency*? Spirtes, Glymour, and Scheines tell us, "We require for causal sufficiency of V for a population that if X is not in V and is a common cause of two or more variables in V, that the joint probability of all variables in V be the same on each value of X that occurs in the population."[34]

Let us assume that C is a common cause of A and B if C is a cause of A and a cause of B. The problem then is that this definition is too demanding. Every cause of a common cause is itself a common cause. These could go back in time *ad infinitum*. And for any system for which there is a temporally continuous process connecting a cause with an effect at the type-level, between each common cause and an earlier one there will be infinitely more. If we apply the methods only to variable sets that get them all in, we will not apply them at all. What we want to get in are all the *last* ones—the ones as close to both effects as possible.[35] But it will take some effort to formulate that properly. Spirtes, Glymour, and Scheines are particularly hampered here because they restrict their definitions to facts about *causally correct representations* rather than talking about causal relations in the world.

Spirtes, Glymour, and Scheines avoid this problem by offering a different characterization. They define *common cause:* "We say that a variable X is a common cause of variables Y and Z if and only if X is a direct cause of Y relative to {X,Y,Z} and a direct cause of Z relative to {X,Y,Z}."[36] And for *direct cause*: "C is a direct cause of A relative to V just in case C is a member of some set **C** included in V/{A} such that (i) the events in **C** are causes of A, (ii) the events in **C**, were they to occur, would cause A no matter whether the events in V/({A} ∪ **C**} were or were not to occur, and (iii) no proper subset of **C** satisfies (i) and (ii)."[37]

The variables in V are seldom sufficient to fix the value of an effect. So how can fixing whether the events in **C** occur or not ensure that A occurs? So let us add into the set **C** the random disturbance factor for A. But in fact, it looks as if we have to assume as fixed all exogenous causes, or at least the "last" one if that makes sense, since it will not help to fix one but allow temporally subsequent ones to vary. We also need to add that quantities occurring between **C** and A in nature's objective graph must be assumed to take on the values dictated by C. And so forth.

I do not know how to formulate all this correctly. But it needs to be done if the notion of causal sufficiency is to be used. Quite reasonably the advertisements for Bayes-nets methods make much of the fact that the subject is formal and precise: we can prove theorems about manipulation, abut efficient conditioning sets for measuring the size of a causal effect, about the certainty of the results of the algorithms when applied to systems satisfying specific conditions, and so on. But this is all pseudo-rationalism if we do not provide coherent characterizations of the concepts we are using.

The trouble with the characterization of "causal sufficiency" arises from the fact that for Spirtes, Glymour, and Scheines the notion of *direct cause* is relative to the choice of a particular variable set. Spohn's talk of the set of "all variables needed for a complete description of empirical reality,"[38] temporally ordered, avoids this; Pearl, too, because he supposes that the underlying system is a set of deterministic causal laws on a finite set of causally ordered variables. No one to my knowledge has a good account of causal sufficiency for dense sets of effects, for instance, for the kinds of systems studied by time-series analysis. As I remarked, Spirtes, Glymour, and Scheines talk only of correct causal representations.[39] That not only allows them to appear to avoid metaphysics, as Spohn and Pearl clearly do not, but also leaves an opening for supposing that the underlying metaphysics is continuous. But the advantages are illusory if we cannot produce adequate definitions.

Before proceeding to look at the list of factors that undermine the causal Markov condition, I should comment on one recent defense of it. Daniel Hausman and James Woodward[40] offer a proof of the condition alternative to the proof by Pearl and Verma. Central to their discussion is a concept they call *modularity*: each separate effect under study should be manipulable without disturbing any other. They claim that, given certain other conditions (such as the existence for each effect of a cause not in the variable set under consideration), the causal Markov condition is "the flip side of" modularity. This would be a good defense if it were true. For we need not agree with Hausman and Woodward that all causal systems must be modular; we could nevertheless (supposing their other conditions are met) assume the causal Markov condition whenever we assume modularity.

The trouble is that the proof does not bear the interpretation they put on it. For given their other conditions, both modularity and the causal Markov condition follow separately. One is not the flip side of the other, both are the result of the conditions they suppose at the start. And these conditions are at any rate strong enough to call the Pearl and Verma proof of the causal Markov condition into play.[41]

4b. Other Reasons Why Factors May Be Dependent

(2) When two causes cooperate to produce one effect, they will be mutually dependent in a population homogeneous with respect to that effect. These kinds of cases are common in practice. Data is hard to come by. We collect it for one reason, but need to utilize it for many others. Imagine for example that we have data on patients from a given hospital, where one disease, D, is especially prevalent. But we are interested in another condition, B.

Unbeknownst to us B cooperates with A in the production of D, so A and B are dependent in our population (even once we have conditioned on all the parents of A in a causally sufficient variable set). We erroneously infer that A causes B in this kind of population.

The problem here is not with the sample size. We can imagine that the sample is large and the frequencies are indicative of the "true" probabilities for the population involved. The problem for the causal Markov condition is with the choice of population. We all know that to study the relation between A and B we should not use populations like this. But how should we—properly—characterize populations "like this"?

(3) Mixing. Even if we assume the causal Markov condition for populations where the probabilities of the effect are fixed by the causal history, for mixed populations cooperating causes can still be correlated if the proportion of the effect is determined by some external factor rather than the causal history. Spirtes, Glymour, and Scheines tell us that there are no cases of mixing for causally sufficient variable sets: *"When a cause of membership in a sub-population is rightly regarded as a common cause of the variables in V, the Causal Markov Condition is not violated in a mixed population."*[42] I think this is a bad idea: the "variables" that are the "cause of membership in a sub-population" will often look nothing like variables—they don't vary in any reasonable way and there is no reason to think there is a probability distribution over them; and even if we did count them as variables, it looks as if we would have to count them as common causes of every variable in V to ensure restoration of the causal Markov condition.[43]

(4) Many quantities change in the same direction in time. There will thus be a probabilistic dependence between them. Social scientists solve this problem by detrending before they look for dependencies. Spirtes, Glymour, and Scheines maintain that there is no problem to solve. They use their previous solution to the problem of mixing plus a bold claim: "If we consider a series in which variable A increases with time, then A and B will be correlated in the population formed from all the units-at-times, even though A and B have no causal connection. Any such combined population is obviously a mixture of populations given by the time values."[44]

Like others[45] I find this claim ungrounded. Moreover it seems to me to be in tension with their commitment to determinism—which is important to them since in deterministic systems the causal Markov condition is bound to be true if only we add enough into the set of parents. Their idea I take it is that there will be different probability distributions across the causes operating at each time slice, hence mixing. But consider deterministic models in physics. These I take it are important for Spirtes, Glymour, and Scheines because these are what make many people sympathetic to their claim that all macroscopic processes are deterministic. Any two systems moving inertially will have their positions correlated, and they have exactly the same causes operating at each instant with the same probability distribution over them, namely—none.

(5) Products and by-products are mutually dependent, and when causes act purely probabilistically, no amount of conditioning on parents will eliminate the dependence. Perhaps then there isn't any purely probabilistic causation—that would save the causal Markov condition. But that is a big metaphysical gamble, especially in the face of the fact that for the kind of variables for which Bayes-nets methods are being sold, we seldom are able to formulate even a reasonable probabilistic model, let alone a deterministic one. We can, of course, stick to the metaphysical insistence that everything must be deterministic. Again, I think that this is not only unwarranted, but also irresponsible. But I will say no more about the matter here since I have written much about it elsewhere.[46]

5. Analysis

Dependence could be due to causation. But there are lots of other reasons for it as well. Bayes-nets methods stress one—the operation of common causes—and tell us how to deal with it when the underlying system is deterministic. The other four reasons standard in the philosophical literature are badly handled or made light of. And what about other reasons? Have we listed them all?

The reasons I listed are prevalent not only in the philosophical literature. They are standard fare in courses on social-science methodology, along with lots of other cautions about the use of probabilities to infer causes in even experimental or quasi-experimental contexts. And they are not handled so badly there. In part the failures in the philosophical discussion arise from the requirement that the connection, whatever it is, be tight. We look for a claim of the form: A causes B iff A and B are probabilistically dependent in populations satisfying X. Then X is hard to formulate in the kind of vocabulary we need for formal proofs and precise characterizations.

But why should we think the connection is tight? As Spohn says, if it is tight there ought to be a reason. There is, as I have argued, a reason for the connection between probabilistic dependence and causality, but the very reason shows that the connection is not tight. Causes *can* increase the probability of their effects; but they need not. And for the other way around: an increase in probability *can* be due to a causal connection; but lots of other things can be responsible as well.

I think we are still suffering under the presumptions of the old Hume program. First, we don't like modalities, especially strange ones.[47] My breakfast cereal box says: "Shredded Wheat can help maintain the Health of your Heart." In the same sense, causes can increase the probability of their effects. Distressed at this odd modality, we try to render this as a claim that causes *will* increase the probability of their effects, given X; then we struggle to formulate X. Second, we cannot get loose from the idea that causes need associations to make them legitimate. So we want some "if and only if" with probabilities on the right, even if we grudgingly have to use some causal concepts to get the right-hand side filled in properly. I think we are looking at the issue entirely the wrong way. The connection between causes and probabilities is not like that. It is, rather, like the connection between a disease and one of its symptoms. The disease can cause the symptom, but it need not; and the same symptom can result from a great many different diseases.

This is why the philosopher's strategy is bad. We believe there must be some "if and only if" and so are inclined to make light of cases that do not fit. The advice from my course on methods in the social sciences is better: "If you see a probabilistic dependence and are inclined to infer a causal connection from it, think hard. Consider the other possible reasons that that dependence might occur and eliminate them one by one. And when you are all done, remember—your conclusion is no more certain than your confidence that you have eliminated all the possible alternatives."

NANCY CARTWRIGHT
London School of Economics and
University of California, San Diego

NOTES

1. Spohn, forthcoming.
2. Spohn, forthcoming, p. 10.
3. Buchdahl 1969.
4. This is not meant to be a formal claim. But one example of a characterization that is not a good direct one is the one I shall be discussing here, which supports the application of Bayes-nets methods—the population is governed by deterministic laws; and it is a population for which the variables we are not using to study it are all probabilistically independent of each other; it is a population in which causes and effects are always probabilistically dependent. . . .
5. When we deal with quantities of more than two values, there are other possibilities; e.g., a cause may raise the level of the effect.
6. Suppes 1970.
7. Spirtes, Glymour, and Scheines 1993.
8. Pearl 1999.
9. Cartwright 1983, "Causal Laws and Effective Strategies."

10. What counts as a complete set of factors is not so easy to characterize for probabilistic causality. (For one definition, see Cartwright 1989, p. 112.) The task is easy if we are allowed to help ourselves to the notion of the objective system of causal laws governing a population, as Pearl and Spohn and I do (see Cartwright forthcoming). In that case K ranges over all the parents of E, barring C, relative to God's great causal graph for the population.

11. Pearl 2000, p. 73.

12. Pearl 2000, p. 48.

13. Hesslow 1976.

14. Shafer 1996.

15. For further discussion, see Cartwright 1999, chs. 5 and 7.

16. Frigg 2000.

17. Frigg 2000, p. 1.

18. Spirtes, Glymour, and Scheines 1993, p. 68.

19. I suppose they mean by "logically" possible that it is consistent with the other assumptions they wish to make about causal laws and probabilities.

20. Spirtes, Glymour, and Scheines 1993, pp. 67–68.

21. In fact this is not literally true since the section, though headed "Axioms," only introduces a definition of faithfulness and does not make any claims about it. It is clear from the various sales pitches they make for their methods, however, that they take it to be a condition true of almost all causal systems.

22. Spirtes, Glymour, and Scheines 1993, p. 68.

23. Pearl 2000, p. 48.

24. UCSD Philosophy of Economics Seminar, May 1999.

25. Pearl 2000, p. 49.

26. For further discussion see Cartwright 1999, ch. 2, and 2000a.

27. Hoover forthcoming, pp. 7–33.

28. Hoover forthcoming, pp. 7–35.

29. For an example of an attempt to use the Spirtes, Glymour, and Scheines methods on real economic data in economics, see Swanson and Granger 1997. Their struggles there are particularly relevant to my point in this paragraph. Which of the low partial correlations observed in their data should be taken to indicate that the "true" partial correlation is zero? They consider various alternatives among the lowest observed partial correlations that one might suppose are "really" zero and show the different results that follow.

30. Pearl 2000, p. 44.

31. These are often designated u_x when variables in V are designated $x, y, \ldots$

32. Cf. Verma and Pearl 1991 or Pearl 2000, p. 30.

33. Cf. Spirtes, Glymour, and Scheines 1993, p. 54.

34. Spirtes, Glymour, and Scheines 1993, p. 45.

35. Note that where A c⟶ B and B c⟶ C and B c⟶ D, if C and D are independent conditioning on B, they need not be independent conditioning on A if $P(B/A) \neq 1$. So B must be included if the causal Markov condition is to be satisfied.

36. Spirtes, Glymour, and Scheines 1993, p. 44.

37. Spirtes, Glymour, and Scheines 1993, p. 43.

38. Spohn forthcoming, p. 11.

39. This is my account. They do not say what they do. For instance, in their section "Axioms," they provide no axioms but only definitions (of the causal minimality condition, the faithfulness condition, and the causal Markov condition). But I take it their claims are: every correct causal graph over a causally sufficient set of variables satisfies these conditions.

40. Hausman and Woodward 1999.

41. For a full discussion see Cartwright 2002.

42. Spirites, Glymour, and Scheines 1993, p. 60, ital. orig.

43. For details see Cartwright 1999, ch. 5, and Cartwright 2000a.

44. Spirtes, Glymour, and Scheines 1993, p. 63.

45. Cf. Berkovitz forthcoming and Hoover forthcoming, ch. 7, and Sober 1988, pp. 161–62, and 2000.

46. See Cartwright 1997; 1999, ch. 5; and 2000a.

47. I offer a treatment—though not yet really satisfactory—of these kinds of modality in Cartwright 1999.

REFERENCES

Berkovitz, J. Forthcoming. "The Many Principles of the Common Cause." In *Reports on Philosophy,* Issue on the Common Cause Principle.

Buchdahl, G. 1969. *Metaphysics and the Philosophy of Science.* Oxford: Blackwell.

Cartwright, N. 1983. *How the Laws of Physics Lie.* Oxford: Oxford University Press.

———.1989. *Nature's Capacities and Their Measurement.* Oxford: Clarendon Press.

———. 1997. "What Is the Causal Structure?" In *Causality in Crisis? Statistical Methods and the Search for Causal Knowledge in the Social Sciences,* ed. Vaughn R. McKim and Stephen P. Turner. Notre Dame, IN: University of Notre Dame Press.

———. 1999. *The Dappled World: A Study of the Boundaries of Science.* Cambridge: Cambridge University Press.

———. 2002. "Against Modularity, the Causal Markov Condition and Any Link Between the Two." *British Journal for the Philosophy of Science* 53: 411–53.

———. 2000a. "Causal Diversity and the Markov Condition." *Synthese* 121: 3–27.

———. 2000b. *Measuring Causes: Invariance, Modularity and the Causal Markov Condition.* London: CPNSS Discussion Paper Series: Measurement in Physics and Economics, London School of Economics.

———. Forthcoming. "Two Concepts of Invariance, Two Concepts of Intervention and Two Concept of What It Is to Be Causally Correct." *Philosophy of Science.* (Also appears as ch. 3 in Cartwright 2000b.)

Frigg, R. 2000. *Examples of Multiple Routes.* MS. CPNSS, London School of Economics.

Granger, C. 1969. "Investigating Causal Relations by Econometric Models and Cross-Special Methods." *Econometrica* 37: 424–38.

Hausman, D., and J. Woodward. 1999. "Independence, Invariance and the Causal Markov Condition." *British Journal for the Philosophy of Science* 50: 521–83.

Hesslow, G. 1976. "Discussion: Two Notes on the Probabilistic Approach to Causality." *Philosophy of Science* 43: 290–92.

Hoover, K. 2002. *Causality in Macroeconomics.* Cambridge: Cambridge University Press.

Pearl, J. 1999. *Causality.* Cambridge: Cambridge University Press.

Pearl, J., and T. Verma. 1991. "A Theory of Inferred Causation." In *Principles of Knowledge, Representation, and Reasoning,* ed. J. A. Allen, R. Fikes, and E. Sandewall, pp. 441–52. San Mateo: Morgan Kaufmanns.

Shafer, G. 1996. *The Art of Causal Conjecture.* Cambridge: MIT Press.

Sober, E. 1988. *Reconstructing the Past.* Cambridge: MIT Press.

———. 2000. "Venetian Sea Levels, British Bread Pieces, and the Principle of the Common Cause." MS, Dept. of Philosophy, Logic and Scientific Method, London School of Economics.

Spirtes, P., C. Glymour, and R. Scheines. 1993. *Causation, Prediction, and Search.* New York: Springer-Verlag.

Spohn, W. 2001. "Bayesian Nets Are All There Is to Causality." In *Stochastic Dependence and Causality,* ed. D. Constantini, M. C. Galavotti, and P. Suppes. Stanford: CSLI Publications.

Suppes, P. 1970. *A Probabilistic Theory of Causality.* Amsterdam: North-Holland.

Swanson, N., and C. Granger. 1997. "Impulse Response Functions Based on Causal Approach to Residual Orthogonalization in Vector Autoregressions." *Journal of the American Statistical Association* 92: 357–67.

13

Don't Take Unnecessary Chances!

HENRY E. KYBURG, JR.

The dominant motivation for introducing such abstract objects as "propensities" and "chances" seems to be the difficulty of otherwise accounting for single-case probabilities in an objective way. It has long seemed to me that most single-case probabilities can be accounted for by the judicious selection of a reference class. For example, while the relative frequency of heads exhibited by a coin, newly minted, tossed, and then destroyed must be either 0 or 1, its single toss is also a member of many classes of tosses in which the relative frequency is one-half. Why not select one of those classes as the reference class for heads on the toss of that coin? One needs rules, of course, that lead to the right reference class.

Given the set of epistemic rules that will lead an agent with a given body of knowledge to an appropriate reference class: (a) Can the relevant parameter of that class always be interpreted as an actual finite frequency? (b) If there is no actual finite frequency that can serve to ground the parameter, is it generally possible to provide a hypothetical finite frequency? (c) Are there cases in which actual or hypothetical infinite sequences are required—for example, in attributing normality to the distribution of errors of measurement. (d) Are there instances in which the parameter that becomes a probability in the right epistemic circumstances must be interpreted as a "propensity" or a "chance"?

The conclusion we come to is that actual finite relative frequencies and hypothetical finite relative frequencies are required, but that in "ordinary" cases nothing else, nothing of a fancier metaphysical category, is required. By "ordinary" I mean to exclude such theoretical phenomena as are discussed, for example, in quantum mechanics. In these rarefied domains there may be a case for propensities and chances; but the case will have to be made within the discipline, and not on the basis of probabilistic considerations.

—*H. E. K.*

* * *

ABSTRACT

The dominant argument for the introduction of propensities or chances as an interpretation of probability depends on the difficulty of accounting for single-case probabilities. We argue that in almost all cases, the "single-case" application of probability can be accounted for otherwise. "Propensities" are needed only in theoretical contexts, and even there applications of probability need only depend on propensities indirectly.

1. Introduction

Donald Gillies, in *Philosophical Theories of Probability* (2000), attributes the introduction of the propensity theory of probability to Karl Popper in 1957. The motivation was the need of quantum mechanics to have "single-case" probabilities—that is, probabilities that could be assigned to unique events, such as the disintegration of a particular radioactive atom. James Fetzer (1981) also finds in quantum mechanics a knockdown argument for propensities. Ron Giere (1988) would *like* to regard quantum mechanics as the only source of propensities, but reluctantly stands back from endorsing unreservedly the absolute claim that propensities are ontological features of the natural world.

A careful analysis of these various kinds of propensity theories is to be found in Ellery Eells's penetrating article (1983). All of these approaches, however, suppose that all instances of "objective probabilities" should be given the same treatment. Furthermore, they are all motivated, at least in part, by the desire to account for the objectivity of some ascriptions of probability to specific events or occurrences or the sentences describing them.

We shall argue that there are two quite distinct objective bases for probability, each appropriate to a different domain. In particular, we shall say that a simplified finite frequency basis serves for almost all ordinary probability assertions. But we must allow for some probabilities—those based on quantum mechanics, for example—to be based on some kind of irreducible chance. Our main point, however, will be that the demand for propensities or chances is rarely warranted.

The framework I'll use will be my own evidential probability. That will not undermine our inquiry, since evidential probability has two dimensions: an empirical dimension and a logical dimension, and the empirical dimension clearly makes use of what can be called "objective empirical probabilities." These are just the things that have been construed as finite frequencies or limiting frequencies or chances or propensities or dispositions or measures.

In the following section, I shall give the bare bones of my theory of evidential probability—enough that we may see the relevance and importance of objective empirical probabilities. I will then examine several different kinds of circumstances that may be thought to call for some kind of chance statement to serve as background for probability.

2. Probabilities

My own preference is to take "probability" to be univocal, and to stand for a function that measures as an interval, (possibly degenerate) the evidential relation between a *statement* (possibly indefinite) and a *body of knowledge* (possibly hypothetical), all expressed in a formal language. Let me unpack (some of) this.

I assume that our actual bodies of knowledge contain statistical knowledge concerning frequencies or chances. It is this that will be the focus of our concerns. I will follow Carnap (1950) and refer to the concept central to these statements as "probability_2."

Evidential probability is a form of logical probability, or probability_1. The value of the probability of a statement *S* for an agent is determined by two things: what he has rational grounds for accepting concerning some probability_2 (for example, that the proportion of blue counters in a certain bag lies between 0.6 and 0.8), *and* that this is the right reference class (and target class) for determining the agent's rational degree of belief in *S*. The view is "logical" because the probability_1 is determined, not by the state of the world, but by what the agent has rational grounds for accepting. It is also tied to objective empirical probability_2 because it is that that determines the value of the agent's probability_1.

In the full theory we must ensure that if the agent accepts the biconditional $S \equiv T$, then he assigns the same (interval) probability to *S* and to *T*. We need not be concerned with such refinements here. We may assume, for simplicity, that the form of the statement is membership: "the next toss $\in$ the set of heads," "the fifteenth card in the deck $\in$ the set of clubs," and so on.

There is one special case that will concern us corresponding to the use of the indefinite article in English: we often speak of the probability that *a* toss of a coin will land heads, or that a birth will be the birth of a male. It would be possible to introduce a "mere instance" operator to have these locutions correspond to our basic membership locutions, but for present purposes we can as comfortably construe them as ways of asserting probability$_2$ statements.

What we need to think about are the conditions for "selecting the right reference class" or determining the probability$_2$ statement relevant to a particular statement *S*. First of all, we must restrict our considerations to something like Fetzer's "permissible predicates" (Fetzer 1981; Fetzer 1977). Fetzer is more generous than I in characterizing these predicates, but for present purposes I think we can simply suppose that there is an enumeration of predicates or open formulas in our language that are "permissible." These predicates are (in my framework) dependent on the primitive predicates and functions of our language.

Once we have the permissible predicates of the language, there are three principles that I call on to determine the right reference class. Two of them are easy to name and describe; the third is a little more complicated.

The *principle of precision* advises us to use that reference class about which we have the most precise knowledge, *other things being equal.* Our knowledge about the reference class R_1 is "more precise" than our knowledge about the reference class R_2 just in case the interval associated with R_1 is properly included in the interval associated with R_2.

What does "other things being equal" come to? That there is no reason to eschew R_1 as a reference class. Thus if our knowledge about R_3 is even more precise, we might prefer R_3; or if another potential reference class R_4 were characterized by an interval that *conflicts* with R_1 in the sense that it is characterized by an interval that neither contains nor is contained in the interval characterizing R_1, we might prefer R_4.

To illustrate this principle, consider the case of a gambler planning to bet on the toss of a quarter. We have here a compulsive and conscientious gambler, who has assembled evidence concerning the frequency of heads in various classes of coin tosses. Since there are many more tosses of coins in general than there are of tosses of quarters, it is reasonable to suppose that his body of knowledge might contain "the proportion of tosses of coins in general that yield heads is in [0.495,0.505]" and "the proportion of tosses of quarters that yield heads is in [0.490,0.510]." The reason that the former interval is narrower than the latter is that his sample of coins is larger than his sample of quarters. He (and we) have no reason to suppose that tosses of quarters are weird, and there is thus no reason not to use the smaller interval.

This principle does not correspond to anything traditional in discussions of chance or propensity, since these theories focus on what is *true* rather than on what is known or reasonably believed. All frequencies, or chances, are assumed to be *given* with perfect precision. Of course, what is *true* is of interest to us mainly because we might know or reasonably believe something *approximating* it.

The principle of specificity directs us to use the contained rather than the containing reference class if there is a conflict between them, *other things being equal.* "Conflict" is construed as meaning that neither interval is a subset of the other. Put otherwise: R_1 and R_2 conflict in our body of knowledge just in case the interval we take to be characteristic of R_1 contains points that are not in the interval we take to be characteristic of R_2 *and* the latter interval also contains points not contained in the former.

To illustrate this principle, consider issuing theft insurance on an economy vehicle. Clearly an important factor in our calculations will be the probability that the vehicle will be stolen. On the basis of voluminous records, we may have reason to believe that the probability$_2$ that a vehicle will be stolen in the space of a year is in the interval [0.015, 0.025]. But we may also know that economy and luxury vehicles are stolen at different rates: for economy cars [0.017, 0.028]; for luxury vehicles [0.010, 0.018]. Under these circumstances, we would compute the premium based on the probability$_2$ interval [0.017, 0.028], other things being equal.

It is interesting to compare what we are led to by these two principles alone with the conclusion to which Fetzer is led by the principle that one should seek the smallest homogeneous reference class. Eells (1983) takes Fetzer as defining "an ontically homogeneous reference class with respect to an attribute A and a trial (single event) x (roughly) as a class B such that $x \in B$ and for all $B' \subseteq B$, $P(A|B) = P(A|B')$. In terms of probability$_2$ intervals, a natural replacement for the final clause is: for all $B' \subseteq B$, $P(A|B) \subseteq P(A|B')$. Though there is a world of difference between an objective empirical constraint concerning *all* sets B' and an objective *logical* constraint concerning our *knowledge* of the existence of such a set, it is the latter that seems to come closest to Reichenbach's stipulation that "further narrowing will no longer result in noticeable improvement" (Reichenbach 1949, pp. 375–76).

The third and last condition on the choice of a reference class requires us to go beyond the simple model of an object x and a set of sets, partially ordered by inclusion, to which it belongs. This is the principle of *richness.* The idea involved has not, so far as I know, played a large role in discussions of chance, so it will be best to introduce it by means of an example.

Consider a two-stage experiment: first we choose one of three urns, and then we choose a ball from the selected urn. What do we know? Well, the choice of the urn is made with the help of a well tested die, so that the probability$_2$ of selecting each urn may be taken to be very close to 1/3. We know that in one urn there are nine black balls and one white ball; in each of the other two urns there are ninety white balls and ten black balls. The process of selecting balls is similarly regimented by a randomizing device, so that the probability$_2$ of getting a black ball from the first urn is 0.9, and of getting a black ball from each of the other two urns is 0.1.

Now "the next ball to be drawn"—let us denote it by *a*—is one of the 210 balls in the three urns, of which 27 are black, corresponding to a relative frequency of about 0.129. This is clearly not the right probability$_1$ to attribute to the ball's being black. What we want to say is that the probability$_1$ that *a* is black is $1/3*9/10 + 2/3*10/100 \approx 0.367$.

There are a number of ways in which this result can be brought about. The principle of *richness* is one: it requires that if a potential reference class can be construed as the cross product of two reference classes , and the probability$_2$ of the target property in $R_1 \times R_2$ *conflicts* with its probability$_2$ in R_2, then it is the cross product $R_1 \times R_2$ that takes precedence.

In the example, the probability$_2$ of being a black ball in R_2 is about 0.129; the probability$_2$ of being a black ball among outcomes of the experiment is about 0.367. It is the two-dimensional set that is the right reference class, and generates the appropriate probability$_2$. If, of course, other things are equal!

The application of these three principles yields, not a unique reference class, since there may be any number of epistemically equivalent reference classes[1], but a unique interval-valued probability$_1$. This is determined by the probability$_2$ characteristic of the set of permissible reference classes that are undefeated by any of the three principles just spelled out informally. The unique interval-valued probability is the minimal cover of the intervals determined by these reference classes.[2]

This discussion of evidential probability is relevant to the evaluation of the propensity interpretation of probability$_2$ for two reasons. First, evidential probability is parasitic on probability$_2$, or, speaking more carefully, on what we can justifiably believe (or know, or claim to know) of such probabilities. How probability$_2$ statements are interpreted certainly makes a difference to the conditions under which we can justifiably assert them.

Second, and to my mind even more important, what we want from an interpretation of probability$_2$ statements depends on what we are going to do with them. On my view, there are two roles that probability$_2$ statements play in our intellectual economy. For one thing, as we just noted, single-case probabilities are parasitic on them. By "single-case" of course we also mean to include statements concerning a fixed number of instances of the *kind* of thing that might exhibit a propensity: the next pair of coin tosses; the next hundred coin tosses, the next thousand coin tosses. We shall argue that there are also circumstances in which we might well want to apply the probability$_2$ value to the *last* toss, or the *last* 1000 tosses.

The other important role that probability$_2$ statements play concerns our general knowledge of the world. Much of what we know about the world, at present, can be codified only in probability$_2$ statements. We know that roughly half of coin tosses land heads, that errors of measurement of a certain sort are distributed approximately normally, that smoking decreases life expectancy. We may ask: Does the propensity interpretation of probability$_2$ serve these functions better than or less well than the finite frequency view, better than, or less well than, the limiting frequency view?

3. Propensities

According to Gillies (2000, p. 113), Popper took the main drawback of the frequency theory to be its failure to provide objective probabilities for single events. Much of *Scientific Knowledge* (Fetzer 1981) is dependent on the effort to regard propensities as causal in character, and therefore to be tied to both prediction and explanation of single cases, as well as, preeminently, to understanding.

On the view of Miller (1994) and (according to Gilles) the later Popper, as well as Fetzer, propensities are displayed in each single case: "Propensities depend on the situation today, not on other situations, however similar. Only in this way do we attain the specificity required to resolve the problem of the single case" (Miller 1994, p. 186). Fetzer writes (1981, p. 46): "The difference [between universal laws and statistical laws], therefore, is not a matter of the proportion of members of a reference class which possess the appropriate attribute, but rather of how strong the dispositional tendency is that is possessed by every member of that reference class."

An alternative, explored in Kyburg 1978, due in essence to the early Popper (1957) and Hacking (1965) is to assign the propensity to the *experimental setup* itself, in the case of experiments, or, by extension, to the experiment of drawing an item from a population. On this view, propensities can be defined in terms of actual or *hypothetical* long-run relative frequencies.

The difference between the two approaches is metaphysical. The former view attributes a *causal power* to the circumstances surrounding the individual toss of the coin. According to Miller, these circumstances may comprise the whole state of the universe; according to Fetzer, the circumstances are to be construed as *repeatable.* In either case, however, it is the individual event that embodies the (to me) mystical Power to exhibit one or another outcome in a manner that can be modeled by statistical distributions. On the long-run view, it is the whole sequence of trials, whether actual or hypothetical, that embodies the propensity; but here, within a sequence, "propensity" comes to no more than long-run relative frequency—a pedestrian enough concept.

Later we will come back to this metaphysical question. First, however, we will argue that in almost all cases in which we use probability as a guide in life, or to express generalities about the world, we have no need to call on propensities of either sort to play a role in the probability$_2$ statements on which our probability$_1$ statements are based.

4. Insurance

The simplest and clearest use of probability as a guide in life is in insurance. From the point of view of the insurance company, every insurance contract is a single case, which is either won or lost. It is curious, since insurance so clearly involves the single case, that very little of the philosophical literature discusses insurance. Too crass?

Of course, an insurance company typically issues a great many insurance policies, and thus benefits from the law of large numbers. If one engages in a million gambles, each of which has a positive expectation, one is almost sure to gain. *But the collective gamble, though complex, is still a single case: the company either gains or loses.*

Furthermore, there are insurance companies who issue policies on blatantly "unique" objects or events: the legs of Betty Grable, the hands of Vladimir Horowitz. Lloyd's of London is typically thought of as willing to insure almost anything for the right premium. That the premium is high insures that their mathematical expectation, Premium – P(loss) × (face value), is high. But this does not keep P(loss) from being a single-case probability.

In insurance the values of probability$_2$ on which the company bases its premiums are in turn based on statistical knowledge. Consider the insurance of vehicles against theft by a hypothetical insurance company. There are extensive records from the past, concerning the annual frequency of theft of vehicles of various kinds, operated in various *places*, by various classifications of *operators*. This data concerns the past; it has only an inductive bearing on the premiums the insurance company will charge for insurance against theft *next* year.

What the insurance company needs is the probability$_2$ of theft of a vehicle of kind k, operated at place p, by an operator of type o.

Before this, of course, it needs to know that these are the three (most) relevant pieces of information germane to the theft of a vehicle, and that partitions of kinds, places, and operators preserves the distinctions important to determining the probabilities the insurance company is interested in. What this comes to is that if there is no statistical significance in rate of theft between kinds of vehicles k_1 and k_2, then the distinction is unimportant for the insurance company, while if the class of operator o_1 can be usefully divided into two subkinds o_{1_1} and o_{1_2} that is what should be done. We have here the classical (and largely unsolved) scientific problem of seeking "natural" kinds.

Note that there exists a classification $\{\langle k_i, p_j, o_n \rangle\}$ such that in the historical record each "kind" of triple suffers either 100% loss or 0% loss. This represents "overfitting," and results in samples so small that they cannot be reliably projected into the future. We need samples large enough to support (for example) confidence intervals at a high level of confidence that are relatively narrow.

The next stage (which, of course, is not independent of the first stage) is obtaining an approximate inferred distribution, at a high level of confidence, that yields interval-valued probability$_2$ projections for each "kind" of triple we have identified. These projections concern the future, not the past, though of course they are based on past data. How much of the future? The insurance company is aware that there are secular trends in vehicle theft, and may even work to identify them. Nevertheless, what is inferred is that the future (including any identified trends) will be *approximately* like the past (including any identified trends).

Here is where one *might* want to invoke propensities. Do the values of probability$_2$ that constitute the knowledge of the insurance company, and on which it bases its probabilities characterize a class of instances that is regarded as indefinitely large, compared to the database, or do they represent *propensities* of kinds of instances to be instances of theft?

To put the question this way sounds, even to my ear, a bit question-begging. Nevertheless, since the propensities useful to the insurance company at one stage in its history may well be different from the propensities useful to it at another stage, it is hard to see them as stable theoretical entities. The alternative, that the values of probability$_2$ characterize an indefinitely large class of instances "produced by the same forces as" the data also invokes something hypothetical. It does, however, have the virtue of pretending to be no more than it is: a useful hypothetical relative frequency.

This is all we need to determine the probabilities (in the sense of probability$_1$) we need to determine the premiums we need to charge to keep our expectations positive. Of course, since, properly speaking, these probabilities are interval valued, so are the expectations; we need to charge premiums that keep our *lower* expectations positive.

Insurance companies like long forms, and like to have all the blanks filled in. But even if they didn't insist on this, it would be possible to determine the probability$_1$ of theft on the basis of projective statistical knowledge by using the principles outlined above.

It is hard to attribute causal powers to the classes of autos and operators. But there are cases of insurance where there are clearly causes at work. For example, one expects there to be a cause of death. On most propensity theories, this means that the propensity for the death of an individual within a year is either 1 or 0. That doesn't bother the insurance company, though of course the company will be alert to the causes of death that can be identified early enough to have a bearing on who they insure. This is no different in principle than finding the "natural" classification of risks in the case of auto theft. The operation of the causes of death is not directly germane to the interests of the life insurance company. That company, like the company discussed above, is interested in projecting statistical data, including secular trends, from the observed past to the hypothetical future. It does so in the same way: by inferring probability distributions that give rise to the values of probability$_2$ that can be used as the basis for the values of probability$_1$ that it needs as a guide in life (insurance). There is a need for large hypothetical populations to carry these values, but there is no need for propensities.

5. Errors of Measurement

If insurance seems crass (surely it is no more crass than gambling apparatus, which we shall think about in the next section), let us look at pure science. Almost every science involves measurement. Every measurement involves error. Without a treatment of error, we cannot have quantitative science.

The full explanation of where our knowledge of the statistical distributions of error come from is complicated. For some fairly elementary considerations, see Kyburg 1984 and Kyburg 1987. For present purposes, it suffices to note that in the most important cases error itself is quantitative, and it is taken to be characterized by a probability density function. For example, in most cases the errors produced by a specific *method M* of measurement are taken to be distributed approximately normally, with a mean of about μ (generally close to 0) and a known standard deviation of about σ.

This statistical generalization that characterizes *M* is obtained by a statistical analysis of applications of *M*, or perhaps a comparison of the results of applying *M* to the results of applying another method, *M* * whose error distribution is known.

So far we have no occurrence of the word "probability" except as a modifier of the phrase "density function": we infer the probability density distribution (actually, a set of them, since we cannot claim to know such a function precisely) from the empirical statistical evidence. There may be a priori reasons to suppose that this probability density function is roughly normal—Gauss gave some—but even if we accept that the distribution is roughly normal, we must still estimate the mean and standard deviation.

Probability makes its appearance when we perform a measurement by method *M*, and obtain result *r*: We say, "It is overwhelmingly probable that the true value of the quantity measured is within 2σ of *r*." Obviously, since this is epistemic, this is a probability_1. If we have two (or *n*) measurements of the same quantity, what is overwhelmingly probable changes: it becomes the claim that the true value lies within $2 \times (1/\sqrt{2})\sigma$ of the average of the two measurements (or within $2 \times (1/\sqrt{2})\sigma$ of the average of the *n* measurements). It is not hard to show that these conventional results fall easily out of the principles previously given.

More interestingly, suppose we measure a quantity by several methods characterized by different distributions of error. If we suppose that the measurements are "independent," we can compute the distribution of error of the resulting compound method. (Incidentally what it *means* to say that the measurements are independent is that the *errors* of the measurements are independent.)

What concerns us in all these cases is not the well-understood problem of combining a number of measurements, but the issue of how we interpret the probability_2 statement on which the final probability_1 statement depends.

We have already seen what it is based on: at bottom the analysis of numerical data obtained from applications of the method or methods involved. We might think of saying that the probability_2 statement is to be understood in terms of propensities: as saying that the propensity of *M* to produce results within 2σ of the true value is overwhelming. But what can this mean? Surely it is odd to think of a method of measurement as *causing* errors. What can it mean but that in a large (possibly hypothetical) set of measurements, the frequency of errors that large is very rare? The introduction of propensities seems to add little but an analog of dormative power to the relevant piece of statistical knowledge.

6. The Melted Coin

The most frequently mentioned motivation for turning to a propensity conception of probability_2 is our desire to apply probabilities to "the single case." In gambling we are concerned with outcomes that have been designed, engineered, to yield each of a finite number of alternatives with equal frequency. Dice, cards, and coins may be imperfect; but no sooner does it become clear that they are imperfect—that the frequency of three deviates significantly from 1/7—than the die is withdrawn from the game (to mention the least melodramatic possible outcome).

We want to say that the *chance* of heads on the next toss of this coin is a half. Of course, the *frequency* of heads on the next toss is either 0 or 1, but we don't know which. The probability of heads on the next toss cannot be the frequency of heads on the next toss.

It is therefore suggested either that the next toss itself has a propensity to land heads (a single-case propensity) or that the chance setup of which the next toss is a member exhibits a (long-run) propensity of a half to yield heads. There are obvious difficulties with the latter view: what is the principle of individuation of chance setups? Is a coin toss performed by Jane an instance of a different chance setup than a coin toss performed by Tom? The problem of the reference class threatens in a form which requires a metaphysical solution. This is recognized by both Fetzer and Gillies. Gillies bites the bullet and concludes that the propensity interpretation of probability does not provide a solution to the problem of the single case. Fetzer, on the other hand, accepts a single-case propensity view of probability, and takes an ontological solution to the reference class problem (what repeatable matrix of causes generates the propensity in this single case?) to be central in his book *Scientific Knowledge*.

There is no need for us to look at the matter in either of these ways, however. Let us consider a particular coin toss, that performed by Jane at a certain place and time. Just to dispose of a few irrelevancies, let us suppose that it is a newly minted US quarter, that it has never been tossed, and that it will be destroyed immediately after Jane tosses it. For brevity let us call this toss *T*.

I claim that for the sake of using the probability that this toss yields heads as a guide in life, there is no need to invoke either a single-case propensity, or a long-run propensity, or even a long-run hypothetical frequency. Actual frequencies will do just fine.

It has been argued that this won't do, since the probability that the coin lands heads is either 0 or 1: it will only be tossed once. The relative frequency of heads among the set of all tosses of this coin is clearly uninformative.

But *T* is a member of many classes of tosses other than its unit set. It is a member of the set of all coin tosses, a member of the set of tosses performed by Jane, a member of the set of tosses of US quarters, and so on. In general, in the case of something like coin-tossing, the larger the sample, the more closely will the sample reflect the relative frequency in the parent population. Thus one would expect that our knowledge of the relative frequency of heads among coin tosses in general would be more precise than our knowledge concerning US quarters—though in either case the known frequency would be in a small interval around a half.

Of course, it is quite possible that we know something about Jane's propensity to throw heads with US quarters. Suppose, for example, we know (at an appropriately high level of acceptance) that Jane throws heads between 40% and 80% of the time. For example, she might have thrown heads 60 times out of a total of 100 tosses. In itself that would cut no ice, since what we know of coins in general does not *conflict* with that, but is merely more precise; the precision rule leads us back to coins in general.

Suppose we have a sample of a thousand of Jane's tosses, and that from that data we can infer that between .55 and .65 of the tosses she makes will result in heads. It is important to note that this inference proceeds on the assumption that there will be an indefinitely large sequence of tosses by Jane. The rule of specificity tells us to use the interval [0.55, 0.65], since in this case there *is* a conflict between our more general knowledge and our knowledge about Jane.

Note that what we infer from the sample of Jane's tosses is taken to concern a set of tosses that is "large" relative to the sample we have. If we observe 601 heads out of 999 tosses, and we know for sure that Jane will never toss a coin again after today's trial, we do not infer that the relative frequency of heads on tosses by Jane is between .601 and .602—at least not on statistical grounds, and not relevantly to the outcome of the thousandth toss.

On the other hand, suppose that *T* occurred yesterday, and that we know that Jane made 10 tosses yesterday, and that 7 of them yielded heads. In a suitable state of ignorance, specificity will again carry the day, and we will want to say the probability that *T* lands heads is [0.7, 0.7].

There is indeed a touch of hypotheticality associated with the inference from a sample, especially a sample of a temporally extended population drawn at a specific time, to a statistical characteristic of that population. Our inference is based on a supposition that the population extends well beyond the sample, and in fact concerns the unsampled part of the population. Such a supposition is far too weak to support talk of propensities.

Let us make two more observations about the coin toss. Most people regard the outcome of a coin toss to be completely determined by the force initially imparted to it, and by the coefficients of elasticity of both the coin and the surface on which it lands, and so on. Thus on the view that takes probability$_2$ to be a single-case propensity, it seems that its value must either be 1 or 0. (Eells makes this point in Eells 1983.) Surely this is no help as a guide in life.

On the other hand it is possible to argue that small difference in initial acceleration make all the difference between heads and tails, and that the accelerations imparted to tossed coins vary smoothly over quite a large range. It follows that approximately half of coin tosses yield heads. This, of course, is an *actual* frequency. Although it may support a propensity, no propensity need be invoked. This treatment of the coin toss is what has explanatory power; but the explanatory power clearly comes from the underlying physics, not from any derivative propensity of coins to land heads half the time.

Let us consider one final tossing case: tossing a dodecahedron with numbered sides. We may suppose (arrogantly!) that this dodecahedron is the only one that has ever been made, or ever will be made. It will be rolled just once, and destroyed in a great conflagration. The probability that it will land on side number 1 should be about 1/12.

What probability$_2$ can we invoke to get this result, and how can it be justified? The outcome of the roll of the dodecahedron is determined by the laws of mechanics, but as in the toss of the coin, we may infer from the circumstances of the roll that in any large set of rolls, the frequency with which the roll would land on any one side would be about 1/12. In addition we know that there will be no such large set of rolls. But if there were a large sequence of rolls, the first roll would land with the 1 down about one-twelfth of the time.

We must, of course, in statistics as in the rest of science, make sense of hypothetical and counterfactual arguments. But it seems no more difficult to do so in the case of statements concerning probability$_2$ than in the case of statements of mechanics. Propensities are needed neither as a guide in life nor for explanation at the level of coin tosses.

7. Conditional Probabilities

As is clear from the discussion of the relation of probability$_1$ to probability$_2$, probability$_2$ can serve as a basis for conditional probabilities. We can apply the usual "definition"[3] or take probability$_2$ to be conditional at the outset. Of course probability$_1$ is essentially conditional to start with: it represents a relation between a statement *S* and a body of knowledge *K*. But it is natural to introduce a hypothetically conditional form of probability$_1$, in which we consider the relation between *S* and the body of knowledge augmented by *T*: Probability$_1$ $(S|K \cup \{T\})$.

Where *S* and *T* are suitably related, it may be the case that probability$_1$ $(S(a)|K \cup \{T(b)\})$ = probability$_2$ $(S|T)$. For example, consider the relation between spots and measles. We may perfectly well know both $P_2(\mathit{measles})$ and $P_2(\mathit{spots}|\mathit{measles})$ quite precisely in some population *R*. And what we know about Tom may warrant $P_1(\mathit{measles}(\mathit{Tom})|K) = P_2(\mathit{measles})$ and $P_1(\mathit{spots}(\mathit{Tom})|K \cup \{\mathit{measles}(\mathit{Tom})\}) = P_2(\mathit{spots}|\mathit{measles})$. In this case it makes reasonably good sense to regard $P_2(\mathit{spots}|\mathit{measles})$ as providing a measure of the propensity of measles to produce spots.

On the other hand, if we reverse the role of *T* and *S*, this plausibility vanishes.[4] If we know the frequency of spots in the population *R*, we will know the approximate value of $P_2(\mathit{measles}|\mathit{spots})$ in *R*, and, if *K* is suitably constrained, we may even have $P_1(measles(Tom)|K \cup \{spots(Tom)\}) = P_2(measles|spots)$. But surely we cannot sensibly speak of the propensity of spots to cause measles. Notice, in fact, that this propensity would vary from population to population: it would have a different value in a population of teenage boys than it would have in a population of kindergarten girls, though conditional frequency of spots among measles victims might remain constant.

Thus we cannot in general take the values of probability$_2$ to represent causal propensities, even if in some particular cases it might make sense to do this. If causal propensities play a role in conditional probabilities, it will go the other way around: knowledge of a causal propensity *might* give us grounds for accepting a conditional statistical generalization. More naturally, however, the inference will go the other way around: reason to accept a conditional statistical generalization may, with other background knowledge, give us reason to accept a causal claim.

8. Probabilistic Theories

The strongest case that can be made for propensities, from a scientific point of view, is that made in connection with quantum mechanics. Only in quantum mechanics do we seem to encounter laws that are irreducibly probabilistic, and not merely consequences of statistical observation and statistical inference. It may be that in quantum mechanics, and perhaps in other areas of physics, propensities play an important foundational role.

However, even if propensities, with or without the qualifying "causal" play a fundamental role, it still appears that empirical probabilities cannot all be so construed. If $P(A|B)$ represents the propensity of B to "produce" A then in general there will be difficulty in interpreting $P(B|A)$ in the corresponding way.

Even more to the point, the laws of quantum mechanics are given, not in the form of sentences like "Probability$_2(A|B) = p$," but in the form of mathematical equations involving, among other things, probability *densities.* A "probability density" may of course give rise to expectations and probabilities, but what seems to be fundamental or foundational is the density itself. The proposal to regard the derived probability$_2$ statements as embodying propensities in a fundamental way seems gratuitous in the absence of a reason to construe the densities with which the theory actually deals as "propensity densities." (To be sure, "propensity density" has a nice ring to it.)

In short, I see no reason why the probability$_2$ statements derived from the quantum mechanical laws cannot be construed, like the statistical generalizations on which insurance depends, as statistical hypotheses concerning large hypothetical populations.

9. Conclusion

If we suppose, as I would like to have it, that a probability$_1$ is based on (a) a probability$_2$ and (b) a set of constraints on our body of knowledge that pick out that probability$_2$ statement as relevant, then we can go on to ask: what is the nature of probability$_2$? Is it an assertion about chance? Or propensity? Or limiting frequency? Or actual frequency? Or finite frequency? If we focus on the single case, which has been seen by many as the strongest reason for construing probability$_2$ as propensity, we can distinguish two functions served by these statements. First, they serve as a basis for probability$_1$ statements, and thus as a guide to life. Second, they represent a significant part of our knowledge about the world.

We examined the role of probability$_2$ statements in insurance. Primarily they serve as a foundation for the probability$_1$ statements that guide our decisions with regard to premiums. We saw that while there is no reason whatsoever to take these statements as statements of single-case propensities, there are good reasons to take probability$_2$ statements as making claims about frequencies in large hypothetical populations. Once we have the application problem taken care of, this is all we need and all that is warranted.

A more scientific use of single-case probabilities involves errors of measurement. Again the data on which the relevant probability$_2$ statements are based is frequency data; again, there seems to be no reason to take what we infer from this data—the statistical distributions that yield the relevant probability$_2$ statements—to involve reference to anything more than large finite populations.

The probabilities of the kinds of events that are designed as chance events are a little more complex, since in some cases the probability$_2$ statements on which they are based are in turn derivable from very general and very weak physical assumptions. Nevertheless we argue that these assumed distributions need not be taken to represent anything beyond frequencies in large finite populations. Even in this case, propensities seem to add nothing.

In the case of conditional probabilities, there are circumstances in which the condition of the probability (that is, measles in the claim that the probability$_2$ of spots conditional on measles is high) may plausibly depend on knowledge of the operation of a causal power. As has been pointed out, however, this in itself is a poor argument for *interpreting* probability$_2$ as a causal propensity, exactly because while we can say that measles has a propensity to produce spots, we cannot say that spots have a tendency to produce, or to have been produced by measles.

Perhaps the strongest case in favor of construing probability$_2$ statements as causal propensities concerns their theoretical role in such disciplines as quantum mechanics. But even in this case the attribution of causal propensities to the world seems gratuitous. All we need, to tie the mathematical apparatus of quantum mechanics to the world, are the derived probability_2 statements that can be construed as frequencies in hypothetical finite populations.

There thus appears to be no reason, once we have resolved the epistemic problem of applying statistical knowledge to particular cases, to invoke the mysteries of propensity. We cannot be simple-minded empiricists, to be sure, but we need stray no farther from that path than is required to talk of frequencies in hypothetical finite populations.

HENRY E. KYBURG, JR.
University of Rochester

NOTES

This work has been supported in part by the National Science Foundation program in Science and Technology Studies.

1. For example, the set of unit sets of the members of a class *R* will exhibit the same frequency of being a subset of the set of black things as the objects in *R* exhibit of being black.

2. For a detailed treatment of this notion of probability_1—there just called "probability"—see Kyburg and Teng 2001.

3. It isn't really a definition because it is conditional in form, and thus does not allow the general replacement of $P(A|B)$ by an expression involving only unconditional probabilities.

4. This phenomenon was first noticed by Paul Humphries, whose observation was first published by Wesley Salmon (1979). It has since been discussed by Fetzer (1981) and others.

REFERENCES

Carnap, Rudolf. 1950. *The Logical Foundations of Probability.* Chicago: University of Chicago Press.

Eells, Ellery. 1983. "On a Recent Theory of Rational Acceptance." *Philosophical Studies* 44: 331–44.

Fetzer, James H. 1977. "Reichenbach, Reference Classes, and Single Case 'Probabilities'." *Synthese* 34: 185–217.

———. 1981. *Scientific Knowledge.* Dordrecht: Reidel.

Giere, Ronald N. 1988. *Explaining Science.* Chicago: University of Chicago Press.

Gillies, Donald. 2000. *Philosophical Theories of Probability.* London and New York: Routledge.

Hacking, Ian. 1965. *Logic of Statistical Inference.* Cambridge: Cambridge University Press.

Kyburg, Henry E., Jr., and Choh Man Teng. 2001. *Uncertain Inference.* New York: Cambridge University Press.

Kyburg, Henry E., Jr. 1978. "Propensities and Probabilities." In *Dispositions*, ed. R. Tuomela, pages 277–301. Dordrecht: Reidel.

———. 1984. *Theory and Measurement.* Cambridge: Cambridge University Press.

———. 1997. "Quantities, Magnitudes, and Numbers." *Philosophy of Science* 64: 377–410.

Miller, David W. 1994. *Critical Rationalism: A Restatement and Defence.* La Salle, Ill.: Open Court.

Popper, Karl R. 1957. "The Propensity Interpretation of the Calculus of Probability, and the Quantum Theory." In *Observation and Interpretation,* ed. S. Korner, pages 65–70, 88–89. Butterworth's Scientific Publications.

Reichenbach, Hans. 1949. *The Theory of Probability.* Berkeley and Los Angeles: University of California Press.

Salmon, Wesley. 1979. "Propensities: A Discussion Review of D. H. Mellor, the Matter of Chance." *Erkenntnis* 14: 183–216.

14
The Reduction of Causation

MARIAM THALOS

Hume's problem of induction is taught routinely as a problem, possibly the most difficult, in the theory of knowledge. But it has never failed to impress me as different from any proposed by Descartes. One can view it simply as Descartes's problem repotted for philosophical display in the garden of modern science. There it simply takes the form of, "How can we be sure that the future will resemble the past, even if it has done so always up until this point in time?" Or we can view it as a problem specifically about knowledge of causal relations. If we do the latter, the problem takes on a different character. For here it becomes, "How do we make judgments about a category of reality for which the only prospects for evidence fall into a different category altogether?" Viewed this way, Hume's problem is more closely allied to the problem of understanding how we make moral judgments than it is related to Cartesian epistemological problems characterized very generally. What sort of facts are causal facts, and how come we to make such prodigious use of them, in light of the problems of evidence that Hume illuminates? And this raises too the question of just what sort of fact is referred to by a probability statement like, "If this torch is set down, the whole forest will probably go up in flames." It must be closely related to a causal fact (between fire in a torch and fire in the forest). Indeed an influential school of twentieth-century philosophy discerns an intimate relationship between the two types of fact: facts of causation are nothing other than one factor or event raising the probability of another. Taking this position makes us think quite differently about causation than we are naturally inclined to do. We are less tempted to follow the path marked out by Kant, where we are urged to view the facts of causation (among other things) as human constructions of one kind or another. Kant's path, I am persuaded, will lead to nothing but philosophical dead ends.

—*M. T.*

* * *

ABSTRACT

It is a perennial philosophical enterprise to propose the reduction of causal facts to facts of some other kind. Just as it is also a perennial enterprise to proclaim that certain such proposed reductions are doomed to failure. Here I shall champion a certain family of reductionist proposals—namely, those that quantify the notion of causality—referring to them as *quantitative reductions.* The opposition to quantitative reductionism proclaims that an antireductionist analysis of causation is to be preferred, because such an analysis of causal matters can code for either more information, or for information of a radically nonquantitative sort also. The charge is that purely quantitative models have no means of handling this surplus. I will undertake to show that it is not so.

1. The Reductive Enterprise and Its Milieu

Ever since Hume there has been enormous controversy over how, philosophically, to handle the matter of causation. Hume himself took for granted that philosophical handling of such things as cannot be directly observed (like, for example, the relation of cause and effect) is different from handling such things as leave a trace or signature upon the senses (like, for example, ordinary objects and their perceptible qualities). But certain of Hume's successors were of a different mind. Both Kant and Husserl, for example, on opposite ends of a certain epistemological spectrum, nonetheless agreed amongst themselves, but disagreed with Hume, on the question of whether the unobservable should be handled differently from the directly observable. They understood all skeptical challenges as continuous with Cartesian doubts, making no discriminations of kind amongst varieties of skepticism. And thus their respective treatments of skepticism have nothing special to say about cause and effect, as such. When they give account of our knowledge of cause and effect, this is in no interesting sense different from their account of our knowledge of ordinary workaday objects. This failure to differentiate is ill advised. For the category of cause and effect (for example) is substantively different from—among other things—the categories of object and observable quality. It demands special attention, for the very simple reason that we don't initially know what we're looking at, from the standpoint of metaphysics, when we are contemplating the relation of cause and effect. The category of relation under which the relation of cause and effect falls, is not a given. For is it given how the relation of cause and effect differs from the relation of larger than? From the relation of equidistant from point A? Since the answer is no, we cannot be certain that the treatment of skepticism that befits the case of everyday objects, or even persons, will apply to the case of cause and effect equally well.

The point needing emphasis is not the (obvious) one—that knowledge of the indirectly known is indirect, and hence more difficult, complex, or (if you prefer) impossible. That's already the point we wish to resist making at this stage. For making that point rests on having already accepted (groundlessly) the proposition that, as regards metaphysics anyway, the category of cause and effect is in no significant way different from the category of object—that cause and effect relations are just as out in the world, equally subject to evidence, equally subject to being known. But this might be false. It might be that the reason we do not have direct evidence of cause and effect is deeper: that cause and effect relations are different in kind from the relations of larger than or equidistant from. Handling the epistemology of cause and effect must therefore begin with a treatment of its metaphysics. And in this regard, the philosophical treatment of causality might be importantly different from the treatment of other relations. The philosophical handling of causation is, in substantive ways, more like the philosophical treatment of theological or moral matters than it is like handling the objects of everyday experience.

Today there prevail three quite distinct understandings of the enterprise of elucidating causation. The first and most visible is what may be termed the *semantic* understanding of the enterprise, and is preeminently exemplified by J. L. Mackie's book *The Cement of the Universe.* (Variants, but in the same school, are the accounts of David Lewis [1979, 1974] and D. H. Mellor [1988]). The semantic approach consists first and foremost in seeking a conceptual analysis of the term 'cause' and its cognates in everyday life. The second, and what I shall refer to as the *definitionalist* understanding of the enterprise of elucidating causation, looks to Hans Reichenbach as its hero. This approach seeks an elucidation of causation via an examination of the so-called "fundamental" physical theories of the universe. I call it definitionalist for the simple reason that on this approach physics, *by definition*, is engaged in the business of illuminating causes, and in such a way as ranks it a higher authority on the subject of causation than for example biology.

The semantic understanding presupposes a certain uniformity in our everyday uses of the term 'cause'—namely, that there is one unique, or at least one core, causal concept, or at least one primary focal point in the meaning of everyday applications of the term. And real-life deviations from this ostensibly singular usage, once having come to light, are typically legislated away as either metaphorical or peripheral usages, or even as downright misuses of language. The definitionalist understanding, on the other hand, presupposes that there is a certain fundamental relation amongst events, that this fundamental relation is what is meant by 'cause,' and that (furthermore) it is causal relations which are illuminated by fundamental physics. And evidence to the contrary of these presuppositions is never a matter of concern, less yet of discussion.

The third understanding—which gives rise to the reductionist enterprise—is subtly different from its two compatriots. This understanding resides in the reductionist's two-step project. First, the reductionist seeks to identify a core conception of cause, as the central function of the causal concept in the economy of human life, without necessarily seeking to identify it as a meaning focal point. For in the eyes of the reductionist, the fact that in everyday life, some or even all folks are disposed to accept or reject some statement couched in causal language, under specified conditions, is fundamentally insignificant, in itself, vis-à-vis the enterprise of accounting for causes. Neither does the reductionist seek corroboration of the central conception in fundamental physical theories or physical phenomena, for the reductionist does not—or at any rate *need* not—assume that physics aspires to describe the world in causal terms. In fact, the reductionist, as reductionist, takes no position of any kind on the physicist's professional occupation. One of the most resilient reductionist proposals can be traced back to Hume himself. It consists of the idea that causal facts are nothing more than configurations of certain facts about chances—specifically, facts about certain factors improving the chances of others. This is the proposal that lies behind all probabilistic accounts of causality.

After identifying a core conception of cause as the crystalizing notion around which causal language can be understood functionally, the reductionist subsequently seeks to demonstrate that all potential propositions, true or not, that are worth expressing in causal language, translate comfortably into language openly referring only to facts of the preferred kind—for example, facts about chances or chance-raising. (For example, that the proposition that smoking causes heart disease comes out true, and acceptable, only on condition that so-and-so facts hold about objective chances for each sort of event.) This, as the reductionist sees it, is a proposal concerning how to proceed with precisifying common parlance for the purposes of a particular discipline such as medicine or engineering. The reductionist then proposes to explain this remarkable fact, that causal formulae can be successfully and entirely replaced by formulae in a preferred language with well articulated rules of inference, by the metaphysical proposal that there is nothing more to causal facts—at least for the purposes of these disciplines concerned with precise formulation of them—than facts of the preferred kind. And if there's nothing more to causal facts for the purposes of engineering and medicine than this, then there is nothing more to causal facts, unconditionally.

The reductionist approach to causation, unlike the definitionalist approach, does not presuppose either that there is a unique fundamental (causal) relation amongst events, or that the most fundamental physics undertakes the illumination of that relation. It claims only that, where there is a causal fact, this is nothing over and above certain facts of the preferred kind. The point is simply that the reductionist is operating at the level of conceptions, and their economy in human life. To put the same point somewhat differently, the reductionist is concerned purely with the *metaphysics* of causal facts as such, not with the empirical question whether the world we live in is a causal one (a question that the friend of the definitionalist approach, true to name, answers definitionally).

Thus the reductionist is decidedly not concerned, as reductionist, with whether particular events in the world conform to the demands of causal regularity. So it serves the antireductionist badly, for example, to criticize the reductionist by drawing attention to the fact that her account does not accommodate the strange (Bell-type) phenomena of the quantum sphere.[1] For the reductionist, as reductionist, has no particular stake in being able to explain actual sequences of events in the world causally. Thus the reductionist strategy is (as I like to put it) empirically clean: it makes no undercorroborated linguistic assumptions about the nature of everyday usage of causal formulae; it makes no axiomatic statements about the aims of fundamental physics; and it endorses no sweeping empirical generalizations about the nature of the dependence relations manifested in our world. The reductionist enterprise is in the purest sense metaphysical. The reductionist proposes, perhaps in a revisionist spirit,[2] and certainly with an eye for clarity and precision, inference rules that take us from facts of the preferred kind to facts about causality and back, without there being a residue in either direction—and, significantly, without appealing to anyone's partialities on the subjects of physics' aims, the linguistic behaviors of typical human subjects vis-à-vis causal language, or the causal nature of the contingent world.

It is clear by now that I favor the reductionist approach. But there are many reductionist ways of proceeding. The one I favor proposes construing causes as chance-raisers. But why favor such a construal of causation? Why *not* view causation as the substratum of the universe revealed to us in scientific inquiry? I have offered one preliminary reason already: the definitionalist, true to name, provides no grounds for the proposition that physics elucidates causes or even has the means whereof to do so. Of course, it would cause no harm if we were prepared to accept, again definitionally, any results which physics might achieve as illumination of causes.

But we are not. The most important case in point is EPR-type correlations in the quantum regime. (It is a well-known fact that while quantum physics is quite capable of coping with these correlations via ordinary means available to physics from its inception, "common sense" decisively resists them as amenable to causal analysis, no matter how far we are willing to stretch our conception of cause, even in a revisionist spirit. The reason, as will become clear presently, is precisely the reason Einstein was disposed to give: that EPR-type phenomena violate the relativistic principle that no one thing can act on another at a distance, without going through intermediaries—that, effectively, there can be no causal action at a distance.) This particular case proves—decisively, to my mind—that we cannot simply be definitional about causation. That we simply cannot, definitionally, view physics as illuminating causes. The point, then, is that our conception of causation tells us, in advance, the sorts of correlations that cannot be subsumed under a causal construal of event patterns.

Now it does not follow from this datum alone that we must be reductionist about causation. But it does show that there is considerably more at stake for us—as denizens of the world—in the concept of causation than is let on by the idea that causes are just what physics illuminates. It implies that even before we do physics, we are dividing between the patterns of events that can and cannot be subsumed under a causal understanding of some event pattern. And this datum speaks quite decisively against the definitionalist answer to the question of elucidating causation.

So, against the definitionalist attitude towards elucidation of the notion of causation, we can say that our philosophical account of causation should leave it open as a genuine possibility that our world does not conform to causal expectations, whatever these happen to be. For it should be possible that our practical (by contrast with theoretical) concepts—the cognitive instruments that evolution has managed to instill in us—are incapable of subsuming every identifiable pattern of events in the world under the concept of causally explainable, if to be so capable would be more costly in the economy of human life. It should, in other words, be possible to discover that our ordinary, everyday cognitive tools are rough hewn, and not suited to absolutely every scientific endeavor—as contrasted with those endeavors that are imperative to survival. It should be possible to discover that our ordinary cognitive tools serve certain uses but not others. And so also it should be possible to discover that the proper aims of successful "fundamental" physical theories—which are decidedly not imperative to survival—are not the confirmation of our causal expectations about the world.

The reductionist proposal that I shall display throughout this essay, as the archetype of all such proposals, enshrines the principle that a cause functions to render its effects more likely. This (as I've already mentioned) is the insight behind all probabilistic accounts of causation. It is also a Humean approach. I shall, in due time, argue at some length that nothing is lost in reductionism that is gained by refraining from performing the reduction. And something quite substantial is gained—namely, a quite precise—even mechanical—means of locally assessing whether something should be counted as a cause. (Just the sort of thing that a statistics software package will in the future, I am persuaded, do brilliantly, possibly without oversight of any kind.) The reductionist maneuver gives no room for judgment or difference of opinion. There is a mechanical way of deciding the question. And this is an advantage that cannot be underestimated for engineering purposes. What is at stake, as I shall argue towards the end of this essay, is the fundamental function of the very conception of cause.

2. Preliminary Remarks

Everywhere one turns there are distractions to the project of illuminating causation. Consider for example the instance of so-called negative causation. A golfer hits a ball towards a cup (see Salmon n.d., Eells and Sober 1983, and Papineau 1993). The shot is a good one, very likely to carry the ball to its mark. But a pesky squirrel runs out into the path of the ball, and makes foot contact as it passes. The squirrel kick puts something of an undesirable spin on the ball. Even so, the ball comes through for the golfer. Does the kick help cause the ball's advantageous arrival? Everyone can agree (let's suppose) that the squirrel kick makes a negative contribution to the golf ball's chances of reaching the cup.[3] At issue is whether the kick is also a *cause* of the ball's making its mark. Does addition of the latter statement enlarge the tale of golf ball and squirrel? Or does it add nothing? Friends of the proposition that a cause functions to render its effects more likely—probabilists, as I shall call them—say that the statement adds nothing. Boosters of the probabilism propose to equate causes with their functions—with what crassly we may call the 'summable' or 'quantitative' roles they play in bringing about the patterns of events we observe—and thus (equivalently, as they see it) with the regularities purely that are manifested in nature. So it is a Humean approach to causes. But one can maintain, as Nancy Cartwright (1989) and Elliott Sober (1988) do, that a probabilistic theory of causation will not reduce causal relations to relations in terms of probabilities, but only illuminate the nature of the causal relations by showing how they are intertwined with probabilistic relations. Theirs is thus an antireductionist position on the question of the conceptual ties between cause and effect relations, on the one hand, and probability relations, on the other. What is at stake for them?

If, on the one hand, we incline towards squirrel kick being a cause of birdie, then we are entitled, or so it would seem, to the proposition that the ball enters into a *single, unbroken, causal process* from tee to cup. If, on the other hand, we say that lowering the probability of the ball's reaching its destination, counts against something's being a cause, then we seem to lose title to that proposition. For it seems we shall be compelled to say that the causal process inaugurated at the tee is broken when ball encounters squirrel, and possibly a new process begun then. The question, then, is whether the occurrence of a probability-lowering event terminates one process and inaugurates another.

Some of our company are prepared to say that the kick is a true cause, but nonetheless contributes *negatively* towards production of the effect. Thus that the squirrel kick is a *negative cause* of the ball's dropping into the cup. Friends of negative causes want to save causal *processes*. If we go along with them, we shall be in no position to discriminate between causal process and noncausal, on facts about chances alone, for we will in effect be embracing the idea that events in a causal process do not have to make a positive incremental contribution to the occurrence of succeeding events, in order properly to belong to it. And so we shall have to call on some *independent* notion, such as for example Salmon's mark criterion,[4] or something more elaborate like the transference theory or the conserved quantity theory,[5] to discriminate the causal process from the noncausal. Or we will simply, and even less satisfactorily, have to take the notion of causal process as a primitive one, *sui generis,* and subsequently rely on intuitions alone to make the discriminations. And, of course, we shall then have to abandon the enterprise of reducing the facts of causation to facts about objective chances.

But we might instead find that our philosophical taste runs to system, rather than to scrutiny of case-by-case intuitions about ball-and-squirrel examples, and that consequently we are more prepared to put faith in the guidance that objective probabilities provide in the hunt for cause-and-effect relations, than in whatever initial reactions are had, universally or not, to ball-and-squirrel stories. In that case we might be hostile to the very idea of a negative cause, as a kind of oxymoron. Ruling against the very notion of negative causation preserves the possibility of reducing causes to objective chances. But as Papineau (1989, pp. 344–46), who recommends this approach, points out, we shall also have to confess that there are fewer causal processes than initially supposed. Or, to put it more precisely, we shall have to confess that the causal processes we used to acknowledge as single and of an appreciable duration, are at best artificial concatenations we humans manufacture, of many truly causal processes of much shorter duration each. But the confession might be well worth our while.

Cases like ball-and-squirrel demonstrate that the Humean approach faces difficulties in accommodating common sense on the subject of causal *processes.* Elsewhere I have shown that probabilists are in a position to do no worse at accommodating causal processes than at accommodating simple two-term causal relations of the form: C causes E. In other words, if we simply assume that the probabilist's account of 'C causes E' is acceptable, we can show that probabilists can handle causal processes in an equally acceptable fashion. So that causal processes pose neither extra, nor special work, for probabilists, over and above what already they have to do to satisfy us on the subject of 'C causes E'. And that therefore focus upon processes as such, or the problem of negative causes and its relatives, simply diverts attention from the question whether the reductionist account of 'C causes E' should be accepted. The issue of processes is a red herring. It is now time to direct attention to whether the reductionist account should be accepted. A good deal hangs on our philosophical disposition vis-à-vis the reduction of causation. Much more than the friends of causal processes acknowledge. We need to turn away from the distraction of causal processes, and focus at some length upon the central case for reduction.

3. The Probabilist Strategy: Screening Off

Probabilists, like everybody else, have been suckled on the principle that a statistical correlation or covariation between two factors, such as for example smoking and heart disease, does not automatically, or all by itself, imply causation between them. But probabilists, no less than their fiercest opponents, are typically realists about causation: they typically adhere to the proposition that causes are manifested in the world of everyday experience, and that the cause-effect relation exhibits many of the central features we commonsensically attribute to it. Probabilists will thus be last to side with the lot who wish to do away with the notion of causation as philosophically disreputable. And for probabilists, just as for their opponents, doing justice to causal relations between factors or events has something in common with drawing arrows of sorts (of possibly different sizes) between them, to depict a certain asymmetrical relation of dependence. Probabilists depart from their opponents, however, in maintaining that we can achieve a complete understanding, as well as a full representation of these arrow-like dependence relations, by confining attentions exclusively to numerical probabilities, that these can in turn be worked out purely from relative frequencies. And all this is because they don't believe there's more to causal reality than a certain configuration of chancey and chance-raising relations, which is not (necessarily) immediately evident from limited information about correlations.

How do probabilists say the reduction works? For the sake of concreteness I will illustrate the project with David Papineau's scheme of reduction in Papineau 1989 and 1993. Other probabilist schemes differ in matters of detail or emphasis, but all remain true to the basic principle: causes raise the probabilities of their effects, and we can measure that incremental enhancement of an effect's chances of occurring, which is due to a certain one of its putative causes, by measuring the effect's elevated frequency in populations where (very roughly) everything but that putative cause is held fixed. Here now, for illustration, is (more or less) Papineau's formula for reduction.

First, we need to define the notion of screening off:

Definition 3.1. *S* screens off *E from C if* $P(E|C\&S) = P(E|S)$.[6]

This definition says that an event or factor S shall be said to screen off one factor E from a second C, exactly on condition that the second factor C's addition to S (the screen), as further qualification of the situation, makes no further contribution to the probability that must be attributed to the first factor's appearing. And now we use the following three axioms, to be invoked as they apply, in the process of inferring backwards, from relative frequencies to causal relations:

Axiom 1 (A1). Pairs A and B of events or factors that are unconnected (either directly or through a common causal ancestor) will be uncorrelated: they will cooccur at chance; so $P(A\&B) = P(A) \cdot P(B)$.

Axiom 2 (A2). Pairs A and B of events or factors that either have a common causal ancestor, or are such that one causes the other, are (at least partially) correlated: they will cooccur at better than chance: $P(A\&B) > P(A) \cdot P(B)$.

Axiom 3 (A3). Causal ancestors and causal intermediaries screen off the correlations we expect to see by (A2); so that if S is either a common cause of A and B, or a causal intermediary between them (for example, if A causes B *through* causing S which causes B), then it will be true that $P(A\&B) > P(A) \cdot P(B)$, but also that $P(A\&B|S) = P(A|S) \cdot P(B|S)$.

The basic idea, on this formula, is that of screening off, in terms of which the three axioms are intended to do their work. The notion of screening off is itself couched in probabilistic terms—and thus reducible to a structure of objective chances. A1 and A2, together, tell us that where there are no causes at work, there are no correlations, and also no screeners-off. And then A3—the primary reductionist insight—says that we must work backwards from the identification of screeners-off, to the identification of common causes and causal intermediaries. A3 is put purely in terms of screeners-off (everything that comes after the semi-colon is purely by way of explicating everything that comes before). This fact—that the central insight of probabilism can be captured in terms of a single fundamental notion, that can itself be spelled out purely in quantitative terms—is quite important, as we will discover. For it is the ground of the argument I shall make, to the effect that the quantitative account of causality can be transformed with no remainders into a qualitative account. This will provide a basis for arguing that the quantitative notion of causality suffers no deficiencies in a comparison with a qualitative notion.

Our particular way of framing the probabilist proposal (for which we have Papineau primarily to thank), in terms of a procedure of working backwards from correlations to causes—one that can be carried out recursively—also makes it absolutely transparent that there will be trouble. A3 reveals that we might run into difficulties when it comes to discerning, when we have a screener-off, whether it is a causal intermediary within a causal chain or a common cause of a number of joint effects. And we will have similar troubles when there are different and independent causal routes to a particular event. Thus the philosophical task reductionists undertake, for purposes of illuminating the precise and detailed causal relations between any two events, is to work out strategies for discriminating common causes, from intermediaries, from cases involving alternative routes. However, philosophical reductionists are not working in isolation on this task. They are not the only ones concerned with making these discriminations. There is an entire academic field, within mathematical statistics, devoted to working out strategies for making the discriminations reductionists want made, by cleverly designing experiments to produce the right correlational data for comparisons. The point of designing such experiments is to identify more and more causal detail, about intermediaries, alternative routes, and the like, so that the inference from frequency data to causes becomes, ultimately, indisputable. The strategies are discussed by Spirtes, Glymour, and Scheines (1992), and lightly sketched also by Papineau (1993).

4. A Fluid-Dynamic Model of Reduction: Causal Flow

The gist of the probabilist proposal is that causality is a quantitative matter. That therefore one can measure the strengths of causes in absolute fashion, and as a result can compare the relative strengths of one against another. The probabilistic idea is that causality is all about this figure which represents the strength of a causal contribution, for or against a certain outcome. And that it is about nothing else. If we extract this abstract idea from the probabilist proposal, we can characterize a certain family of reductionist proposals in a way that is not itself quantitative, but qualitative. The proposition I will advance in this section is that we can think of the reductionist proposal as in effect the idea that causation concerns the motion of a causal effluvium. I shall argue that the reductionist idea has at its core the notion that causation speaks of the flow of something that has all the distinguishing characteristics of a fluid—that, in other words, the laws of causation are in their form fluid-flow laws. Consequently, the laws of causation as acknowledged by quantitativists admit of being conceptualized as a set of laws governing a causal medium of which one can have any amount one wishes, and which flows in a continuous as contrasted with discontinuous way. The central law of any such set, is that there can be no action at a distance. The argument will proceed in three steps, as follows.

First, I invoke an argument that I have advanced elsewhere,[7] to the effect that the chance-enhancement notion, as encapsulated in A1 through A3, is *fully equivalent* to the principle according to which spatiotemporal separation is a barrier to causal interaction, which is the insight behind Einstein's Theory of Relativity. (This proposition is true, as I have argued in Thalos 2002b, because A1 through A3 are equivalent to axioms governing the notion of simple spatial separation. The argument goes through equally well for spatiotemporal separation.) This fact grounds the next step in the argument, in which we assert, on the strength of step 1, that the probabilist proposal (for example, as spelled out by Papineau) is tantamount to the idea that causation is a matter of a series of causal exchanges that occur by contact in space and time—that, in other words, causation between two spatiotemporally separated events must be seen as involving an unbroken sequence of space-time interactions that spans in an unbroken fashion the intervening spatiotemporal expanse. This insistence upon spatiotemporal continuities is, as we say at this stage of the argument, precisely the conception of fluid flow across a spatial boundary. Thus, the probabilist's quantitative conception stands behind the qualitative conception of causal flow or causal transmission. And equally, that the qualitative conception of flow stands behind the quantitative conception as articulated in A1 through A3. The quantitative and the qualitative come together. Steps 1 and 2 together thus bring us to the conclusion that the probabilist reduction of causation—and this will no doubt come as a surprise to many of its adherents as well as nearly all of its pioneers—is tantamount to the (qualitative) idea that causation is the flow of something in space and time. In the last stage of the argument, we shall consider extension of this conclusion for a larger class of reductionist proposals: we shall conclude that reductions that work in the same way as A1 through A3, in a way to be made precise shortly, are also tantamount to the qualitative idea that causation is flow. And we shall in the meantime review some ideas that ground the theory of relativity first proposed by Einstein.

The principle that causal action does not occur at a distance, but requires a contiguity, answers two important questions: (1) what are the *units* in which happenings in the world break down, if we care to give a causal account of relations between them? and (2) what sort of thing is causal influence, and how does it flow from the causing event to its effects? The answer to the first question is what may be referred to as a *space-time* answer: that for purposes of causal analysis events are localizable at unextended space-time points.[8] And the answer to the second question, according to the principle of no action at a distance, is quite simply that causal influence is transmitted or transferred via contact, as a parcel may be passed about: the flow of causal influence involves a continuous sequence of asymmetrical transactions among events. Hence causal influence is an all-but-palpable thing, according to Einstein's conception, which passes along space-time trajectories much as bodies themselves pass. One is even tempted to say of this conception that it comprehends causal influence as paradigmatically *exemplified* by bodies, and hence that it is a mechanistic conception of causation. Officially speaking, then, there can exist no finite spatiotemporal distance between a causing event and that which it brings about directly (that is, without going through intermediaries); but we may relax this restriction when it comes to causes and their *mediated* effects. Thus on this conception, if some event A has had causal impact on some event B separated from A by an expanse of space-time, then causal influence must have traveled across that expanse at an allowable speed. It follows that when no influence passes from A to B through the intervening expanse of space-time, possibly because an upper bound on speed of signal transmission prohibits it, then there can be no causal dependence between the two events.

We are now ready for the third step of the argument: so long as a given reductionist proposal is quantitative, in such a way as to admit of an axiomatic equivalence with Judea Pearl's axioms of spatial separation (and apply equally well to spatiotemporal separation), we can view that proposal as putting forward an account of causal flow. For it is in virtue of being equivalent to Pearl's axioms of spatial separation, that the axioms A1 through A3 have been put forward in steps 1 and 2 of this argument as being candidates for equivalence with the qualitative concept of flow. Everything I shall say from here on out will apply to each such reductionist proposal.

The "flow" model is now as follows. Think of events in the world as transpiring within a space-time structure. And think of processes occurring in that structure as potentially having a direction of movement. The model we shall develop will be based on A1 through A3, but will apply to all quantitative analyses of causation that admit of axiomatization that is equivalent with axioms of spatial separation. A1 through A3, as I've said, speak of the travels, along world lines, of something that we can call causal *influence*—that can be quantified in such a way that enables us to add or subtract contributions to a certain outcome, from this or that space-time point. We can thus model this causal influence being transmitted from one space-time point to another, as a fluid, the quantity of which at one place-time can be measured either absolutely or in relation to a base magnitude, referenced at a certain fixed point. (Either way, the result is a fully universal, fixed scale, perhaps a unit scale in the interval [0,1]. When interpreted as probabilities, it becomes a measure of absolute probabilities.) Or we can compare what's left over when contributions to the level of the stuff, flowing in from some third place-time, is subtracted away. (In probabilistic terms, this is a measure of conditional probabilities.) We can compute these additions and subtractions arbitrarily, between any two place-times, interpreted as nodes in the causal nexus. And we can leave it entirely open whether processes can intersect or overlap at such nodes, whether they can cross over one another, whether they can flow together, and whether they can flow along the same spatiotemporal worldlines against one another. All these possibilities can be left open, as far as the reductionist proposal is concerned (though, of course, a specific reductionist proposal may come down one way or another on these issues, and the answers one gives will determine whether the fluid modeling the flow is compressible or incompressible). The only thing that all reductionists must disallow, axiomatically, is the possibility of a cause directly lowering the level of causal flow to its effect.

In these terms, then, the gist of a reductionist proposal is (roughly) that the raw or absolute magnitude of "having been caused"—the absolute or unconditional probability, in probabilistic terms—of a given event at a particular place-time, is not in itself a good guide to the causal structure of the world. This raw quantity needs to be broken down, in the way of income, into parts according to source or provenance, and its subsequent movements tracked. So we require the capacity to compare the levels of the stuff (the elevation of the causal medium) when contributions flowing in from different points are subtracted away. This will reveal the *deep* structure of the flow. And this deep structure is what causality consists in. Causality is what *overlays* irreducible, stochastic reality—the baseline of pure, unmitigated chance, wherever there is pure, unmitigated chance—and gives rise to the regularities upon which we come to rely in ordinary life.

What is the dispute between reductionists and antireductionists in these terms? The reductionists claim that this deep structure is all there is to causality. The antireductionists claim that there is some *even deeper* structure to the world, which (at least partly) explains the deep structure at the first level of depth. What does this deeper structure consist in? Perhaps the antireductionist has it in mind that this deeper structure is something analogous to the topography of that certain terrain over which causal influence flows, which would exist whether the fluid exists or not—that is, whether or not any particular contingent events take place, or any events at all for that matter. This initial way of dividing between the reductionists and their opponents, couched in the terms of the modeling being developed here, is an attempt to explicate the idea that causal facts are not necessarily quantitative, and thus of a radically different nature from facts about chance raising.[9]

A distinct and separate way of dividing between reductionist and antireductionist is to say that the difference consists in the antireductionist holding to there being, not *deeper* structure, but structure of a *finer grain* than that which can be represented via dynamic fluid levels. The reductionist proposes that causal facts are just facts about the *total* contribution of influence flowing from one event to another. Causal modeling, on the other hand, is more refined: it allows us to discuss the structure of this total contribution, to analyze it into separate contributions from the *same* event along *different* causal paths. An example that Nancy Cartwright (1989, ch. 3) discusses at some length might help here. Figure 1 depicts a situation in which an event A brings about another event B by making contributions to two causal paths.

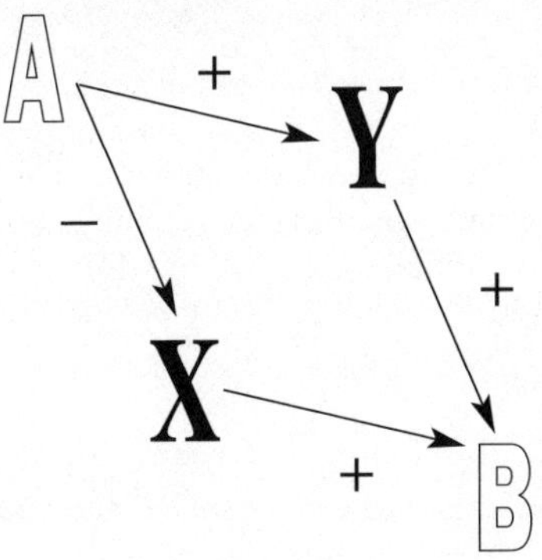

FIGURE 1

It is quite possible that when we sum the total contributions to each path, we get zero, since there is some negative contribution along one of the paths. The reductionist approach would paper over this fine structure, and might even declare there is no causal connection at all between A and B since the total contribution to B from A is zero. The reductionist's approach, so the argument might go, is incapable of discriminating fine structures like these.

I will examine each of these distinct antireductionist positions in turn, but first, a look at what these positions *cannot* achieve.

5. What Antireductionism Cannot Achieve

Some antireductionists object to a class of reductionist proposals because (as the complaint goes) they do not account for the asymmetry of cause and effect: the reductionists don't, according to these critics, give a proper account of asymmetry. The proposals under attack hold that the asymmetry between cause and effect lies in certain higher-order facts about the certain first-order fundamental facts they say constitute causation. Papineau (1993, pp. 239–40), for example, writes:

> Take any event C. Then among the events which are correlated with C will be some that are correlated with each other in such a way that the correlation is screened off by C—these are C's effects; and among the events which are correlated with C will also be some that are not correlated with each other—these will be C's causes.

The reductionist can subsequently embed the axioms of flow within a larger account of the asymmetry of causation. Papineau (1985, p. 280, emphasis added) does it as follows:

> I want to claim that the asymmetry of causation derives from the fact that the *background conditions* together with which causes determine their effects are independent of each other, whereas the same does not hold of the *background conditions* together with which effects 'determine' their causes. . . . [I]f we look at the probabilistic conditions satisfied at the different ends we get our asymmetry . . . : for the initial conditions satisfy independence requirements which do not hold of the final conditions.

On Papineau's account, the asymmetry rests in the fact that "joint effects" of a common cause are screened off by the common cause, but that "joint causes" of a common effect are not screened off by the common effect. And this, in turn, is due to the fact that the different sets of *background conditions* which must hold for each of the respective "joint causes" to be true causes of the common effect in isolation, must be negatively correlated with each other. On Papineau's account, asymmetry emerges as a *global* rather than *local* feature of probabilistic independence relations. Consequently the asymmetry entered into by cause and effect is not an *intrinsic* feature of a two-term relation between a single cause and a single effect. This account of asymmetry is therefore liable to be unsatisfying to those—and antireductionists are right at the center of the bunch—who believe that causal relations are, in the first instance, relations between individual events rather than relations among event populations or large event networks, and that these relations are intrinsic features of the relata.

It would be a mistake, however, to view the antireductionists as being generally in a better position vis-à-vis this issue than the reductionists. For example, the antireductionist who believes in deep, deep structure might, if nothing else will serve, need to draw attention to *global* properties of the deep, deep structure (in terms of the flow model we have been developing, to the underlying terrain over which causal influence flows) to explain why local deep structures (fluid depths, in our terms) are as they are. If Papineau's position on asymmetry is unsatisfying, for the reasons we are now surveying, its antithesis among the antireductionists fares no better.[10]

Now perhaps the antireductionist will wish to fire a different charge vis-à-vis asymmetry, to the effect that the reductionist strategy for diagnosing amongst the varieties of causes and effects will not be generally successful—that it will invariably get certain types of cases wrong. In other words, that the reductionist's strategy for making cause-effect discriminations—for drawing arrows from cause to effect—is in general flawed. This is a different, and more difficult charge to turn away, as there might be many different reasons for the antireductionists to make the accusation, and as each such reason will require a different response. These sorts of complaints concern the methodology of reductionism as an instrument for diagnosing causal relations.

Gurol Irzik (1996), for example, has made the claim that every principle in the reductionist's methodology for constructing effective strategies is flawed, because (roughly) the focus on comparisons between conditional and unconditional probabilities is still too coarse-grained to make the fine discriminations needed to distinguish between certain causal structures locally. And the reductionist's reply (offered by Papineau 1993) has been that the reductionist proposal can do the trick if applied sufficiently widely, and the information exists to be discriminated. Now methodological points are interesting and important, but their metaphysical force is not altogether clear. And it is ostensibly metaphysics, and not something more practical, dividing between the reductionists and their opponents.

Perhaps the force of the methodological criticisms is more epistemological than metaphysical. Perhaps the complaints are to the effect that the reductionist can never achieve knowledge of how to construct an effective strategy for bringing about certain events, since knowledge of correlations does not necessarily put one in possession of how to bring events about, and since the reductionist is willfully ignorant of the deeper or finer structure which does afford this knowledge. We cannot evaluate this criticism until we have a clearer account of what the reductionist is missing out on. For surely antireductionists do not have epistemological entitlements simply *as* antireductionists. We need to have some account of the type of knowledge a reductionist will be barred from achieving, and also an account of how the antireductionist is not so barred. We cannot make metaphysical hay out of methodological necessities, even if allowed to do so, if we cannot identify what these necessities are.

One type of antireductionist (with instances at Cartwright 1989 and Irzik 1996) claims, quite correctly in my view, that the only way to *deduce* facts about causation is to infer them from statements or premises about further causal facts. The methodology is called *bootstrapping*. An implicit argument is then built upon this true proposition: Since bootstrapping is the only way to draw causal inferences, and since we are obviously in possession of causal facts, it must follow that causal facts are not reducible to facts about chances alone. So bootstrapping, which is now serving to solve Hume's epistemological problem, can also be utilized as a means of rejecting Humean reductionism.

This argument is ostensibly about metaphysics, since the conclusion is a metaphysical doctrine. But if so, the argument is invalid. For it does not follow from the proposition that the only way to deduce facts about causality is to infer them from other statements about causality, that these *latter* statements aren't at bottom (as the reductionist would claim) statements *about* objective chances. In other words, the reductionist can embrace every step in this argument, and reject the conclusion, *simply* on grounds that everything referred to by the term 'causal fact' is simply a fact of the preferred kind.

Figure 1 is arguably the most difficult problem so far brought forward against reduction of causes to chances. It serves equally well as a general problem for a quantitative reductionist, for it is a problem insofar as those who bring such figures to our attention, are purporting that a quantitative analysis of the sort we have been entertaining will not always discriminate the causal structure correctly—that whether a quantitative analysis is successful is a matter of pure luck: if we are fortunate, positive and negative contributions do not cancel to zero, and we come away with a correct if somewhat coarse-grained understanding of the causal relationship between A and B. What does this complaint amount to, in terms of the issues as we have carved them up above?

6. Deeper Structure

What distinguishes the reductionist from the antireductionist? The antireductionist asserts the proposition that there's something which cannot be extracted from the structure of a set of quantitative facts that obey a generalized fluid dynamics. Of course, the *best* support for this proposition would be a tight argument to the effect that this surplus something is of a very radically different nature from that which is susceptible of a quantitative model such as we have displayed. For if this surplus for which antireductionists hope to make room, and allege that reductionists cannot discriminate, were simply more of the same kind of thing that reductionists *can* discriminate, in what sense would there be a failure of *reduction*? But the opponents of reduction have failed to produce convincing argumentation to the effect that reduction fails for such deep reasons. And indeed the argument above, asserting the equivalence of certain quantitative with qualitative features, under certain assumptions about the nature of these quantitative features (namely, that they must conform to A1 through A3), is really evidence to the contrary, which should itself make us reconsider the antireductionist position. For this equivalence is testimony favoring the proposition that the notion of cause can be subjected to a purely quantitative analysis.

I, for one, can't think how the dispute between friends of *deep* structure (among whom we find friends of causes-as-chance-raisers) and friends of *deeper* structure (among whom we might classify *some* antireductionists) is more than a verbal disagreement. True: the antireductionist's claim, to the effect that there is some deeper structure to the world, which is independent of the totality of contingent events, is quite a metaphysical claim. And on the face of it, this significant metaphysical claim would seem to separate the reductionists from the antireductionists. But what more does the antireductionist position amount to than the proposition that there *really* is deep structure?

One thing we should be quite clear about: it does *not* amount to the difference between regarding probabilities as propensities and regarding them merely as relative frequencies. For the reductionist I am envisioning will say that if propensities themselves are not the deep structures she has been at such pains to illuminate, then they can be of no service in illuminating the nature of causation. For the reductionist is not afraid of the metaphysics of propensities, as such. She is concerned, rather, that whatever we say about propensities, in the way of an analysis of causes, must ultimately illuminate how they render service as a guide to life.

And so one must ask quite pointedly at this juncture: just what separates reductionists from antireductionists? Are antireductionists, in their office as antireductionist, asserting that the laws governing (for example) physical interactions could *not* have been different from what they actually are? Why would antireductionists, as such, have a stake in so strong a metaphysical doctrine of necessity? I think that there is something rather different afoot here. I shall offer my conjecture in the way of a conclusion (in section 11) to this essay. But before I can reach that stage, I must consider other proposals.

7. Fine Structure: Is the Reductionist Position Adequate?

It would thus appear that the better way of dividing between reductionists and antireductionists is to say that the latter hold to the existence of finer-grained structure than is present in the structure of objective chances. The case of figure 1 can then be called upon as an example of the sort of case in which fine structure can be lost if we could not determine the magnitudes of contributions along each causal path. Such fine structure *could* in fact elude our gaze if we are sufficiently unlucky or careless in our experimentation. Reductionists quickly draw attention to this possibility of missing out on fine structure when they acknowledge that the causal *dependence* between any two event "nodes" in a space-time network is the net *sum* of negative and positive causal contributions along all the causal paths that connect them. But so long as reductionists can determine quantitatively the contribution between *any* nodes whatever, reductionists will miss out on no fine structure. In other words, so long as reductionists can make the intermediate assignments, such as between A and X and A and Y, they will miss out on nothing. But if there's a possibility that some of the intermediate connection strengths will elude them, then, of course, they may not end up with a representation of the true fine structure. And, of course, this will be true *whether or not* they admit to the possibility of there being finer structure. In other words, reductionists can admit to the possibility of fine structure (in their own quantitative terms), and still be unlucky or careless when diagnosing it. And the reason is that the reductionist's instrument for analysis is indirect: it works backwards from correlated effects to cause, *as well as from gross causal structure to fine causal structure.* For example, the indirect methodology of the probabilists will typically work by detecting the fact that smoking raises the chances of cancer first, before it can assess whether smoking achieves this effect primarily through the introduction of toxins, or through promoting a neurological condition, or through the toxins *despite* offering protection against cancer via promoting a neurological condition. And at any point in the process the investigator can be unlucky. The best reductionists (really, anybody) can do, is to assemble as much data bearing on the direct relations between A and B as resources will allow. If sufficient such data can be assembled, the complicating factors X and Y will show themselves. And application of A1 through A3 to a maximal body of such data will identify the correct node strengths A–X and A–Y, as well as X–B and Y–B.

Why should reductionists be troubled by the fact that they may not always be lucky? Presumably, because epistemology (or, more precisely, methodology) should be capable of leading where the metaphysics points. But this presumption is too presumptuous: it is presuming much too much on the kindness of nature. Knowledge, as every good empiricist acknowledges, is a conditional achievement, and not a right on which to lay claim.[11] More importantly, how does the antireductionist propose to lay claim to this knowledge? Ostensibly by bootstrapping. But is bootstrapped knowledge worthy of the name? If the reductionist's answer here is yes, then the reductionist-antireductionist dispute is not a dispute about metaphysics. It is a dispute about epistemology. And therefore not deserving of *its* name.

Therefore, here—in the direct determination of node strength—is precisely where the antireductionists have got to get a foothold against the reductionists: they have got to make a case for the stance that the reductionist cannot get at the direct causal relations through the avenue proposed—in other words, by applying something analogous to A1 through A3 in a diligent fashion. But is there an argument for that stance? Irzik (1996, p. 262) in a very dark passage, insists on a point that Papineau (1989, pp. 330–31), to my mind, has already answered to satisfaction—namely, that the reductionists' analysis will be viciously circular. The answer, of course, is that it is recursive, but that recursivity is not circularity. Cartwright, more recently, takes another tack.

Cartwright (1989, ch. 3) suggests there is a certain reason for the reductionist to be worried by the likes of figure 1. She says that all reductionist efforts will prove fruitless, if A's action to produce X is not independent of its action to produce Y. This is because our quantitative analysis simply assumes that the contribution to B by A is a *simple sum* of its contributions along each path: in other words that a common cause always screens off its effects. But what if this simply isn't true? She directs attention to the controversial EPR-type correlations.

This suggestion is quite sweeping. For once we allow that a cause may not act independently on each of its joint effects, the flow analysis of A1 through A3 is practically useless: for when it gets things right, it does so only by pure accident. Cartwright is *not* alleging that there might be a *further* link between X and Y, or that A brings about X purely through bringing about Y: this would simply be to replace figure 1 by some other figure, in which the actions from A to B *do* sum linearly. What Cartwright is suggesting is that the reductionist cannot in principle choose between the structure of figure 1, in which the actions do not sum linearly, and a different figure in which actions sum linearly, purely on relative strengths between nodes alone. But why not?

In point of fact the reductionist does in practice choose between figure 1 interpreted as having interacting branches, on the one hand, and another figure in which the branches are noninteracting, on the other: the reductionist simply appeals to flow analysis implicit in something like A1 through A3, which automatically decides the matter in favor of noninteracting branches. For it simply follows from A1 through A3 that a common cause always (and by definition) screens off its joint effects. (This is, in effect, how Papineau [1991] replies in his review of Cartwright [1989].) In other words, the probabilist solves Cartwright's decision problem on doctrinal grounds, thereby proving Cartwright wrong in saying the reductionist simply has no basis for choice.

But Cartwright will reply it isn't playing fair. After all, isn't figure 1, interpreted as having interacting branches, a distinct logical possibility? The reductionist says no—on reductionist flow logic. Who is right? It looks like the reductionist is appealing more to dogma than could be thought becoming. Thus the reductionist position appears to have all the advantages of theft over honest toil. I wish to argue that the appearance here is very deceiving.

In suggesting that figure 1, with interacting branches, is a genuine logical possibility, Cartwright (1989, p. 114) contrasts two different ways that we might model the operation of causes: one in which the cause brings about joint effects independently, and another in which this is not true:

> The simple case where a cause operates independently to produce its different effects can be modelled on independent drawings from separate urns. The urns contain black and white balls in the appropriate ratios. The cause [presumably modeled as a drawing by someone with instructions to draw out a black ball from each urn] operates to produce the first effect if and only if a black ball is drawn from the first urn; and the second, if and only if a black ball is drawn from the second. In the more general case, there is a single urn containing balls yoked together in pairs, where the four different kinds of pair appear in the appropriate ratios. A single drawing is made to determine simultaneously the production of the first effect and the production of the second.

Cartwright then suggests that many everyday examples operate in the second way. For example: you have 10 dollars weekly to spend at the grocery store (event E consists of money changing hands), to be divided between meat and vegetables. Once a week you come away with x dollars' worth of meat (X) and y dollars' worth of vegetables (Y), which sums to 10 dollars. The ratio of X to Y may be a matter of chance, on a specific occasion say, but not their sum. Thus, according to Cartwright, E is the common cause of X and Y jointly, but its action on X is not independent from its action on Y. To make the story more believable as an instance of a cause producing its effects in a dependent fashion, and so ruling out such rebuttals as that there is a direct causal influence propagating between X to Y, Cartwright should have said that there is a difference between selecting the ratio of meat to vegetables yourself, and pushing a cartful of meat and vegetables, worth considerably more than 10 dollars, through the lane, and telling the clerk to stop at 10 dollars. In the first instance, we might have a cause acting from X to Y directly, but surely we do not in the second instance.

Now Papineau will find this argument unconvincing, as do I. Because we can always construe the X and the Y, in these purported counterinstances, as one and the same event, described in two different ways. (And the yoked-balls model tellingly supports this interpretation: drawing a yoked pair is a single event.) The purchase of x dollars' worth of meat is at one and the same time the purchase of 10-x dollars' worth of vegetables, for example, if (as in the example) 10 dollars changes hands (together with instructions to the clerk) before the balance between meat and vegetables has been worked out in reality. So there's no sense in appealing to anything like a causal account of events to explain the correlation between such a pair of events: causal analysis does not apply to correlations between an event and itself!

Now Cartwright might complain that this is pure metaphysical prejudice, simply to declare all potential counterexamples to the common cause principle out of bounds on grounds that we can always reconceive of the events in question as one rather than two. But the decision to rule these out as nonthreatening cases is not by any means arbitrary. For the events in question all happen at the same space-time point. I can think of no case with the sort of structure Cartwright seeks (short of EPR) in which the events in question do not occur at the same place-time. This point is crucial. For, as we've discussed, it is a foundational principle of quantitative reasoning about causality, that events in question be individuated in terms of their place-times alone. Therefore Cartwright can't accuse her opponents of arbitrariness or prejudice: the very framework in terms of which reductionists conduct their causal analyses requires this answer. Thus it is by no means pure, unmitigated dogma to reject the proposition that common causes can fail to screen off their effects. It is, instead, dogma resting upon dogma, with the latter being very hard to quarrel with. And so the probabilist has a well-motivated strategy for dismissing any such everyday example alleging the failure of quantitative flow analysis.[12]

8. Means Too, Not Structures Purely

Perhaps what separates reductionists from their opponents has nothing at all to do with structure, but rather with "means." So that, after all, the fluid dynamical model is an inappropriate way to handle the representation of causes. At least, it is insufficient or inadequate. Here is what I mean.

Some people smoke (S), and get lung cancer (C) from A-type chemical interactions of smoke with lung cells. Other people get lung cancer, through smoking, via B-type chemical interactions of smoke with lung cells. (Let us not concern ourselves with details.) There are no intermediaries, let us suppose, in either case. And let us suppose further that there are no side effects of either A or B, besides lung cancer itself and whatever that malady entails. Then the structure of causes in each case is the same; it is: S $\rightarrow$ C. Neither A nor B (let us suppose) are themselves events—at least, they are not events on the level of events that we are dealing with.

Now, perhaps antireductionists want to say that there are two different causal stories to be told. A-afflicted people and B-afflicted people experience different causes. The reductionists, of course, have no way to accommodate such a statement. The difference is that reductionists are *consequentialist* (while their opponents are not) about causes—they identify causes purely with the strength of their contributions towards production of their effects. While the antireductionist I am now envisioning thinks that the causal story has got to be richer: it's got to tell us the *how* of causal action, not just the *how much*. The antireductionist position I have in mind maintains that analysis of causes has got to be both consequentialist and hence quantitative (and so ascertains *how much* a cause contributes towards production of its effect), and also taxonomic (and so ascertains also the *sort* of contribution being made). And perhaps this is what Cartwright has in mind when she insists on the possibility that common causes not be required to bring about their effects independently. Perhaps when we are required to draw different types of arrows between events, we will be more sensitive to the potential for different *combinations*, among the species of causal arrows, to be attended by different combinatoric "logics." So that, for example, figure 2 would be depicting a different causal picture from figure 3, even though they exhibit the same causal *structure*, and even though the strengths of the connections between nodes might be exactly the same.

When the antireductionist I am now envisioning says that someone gets lung cancer from smoking via process A, she is not saying that lung cancer is brought about by smoking *through* bringing about some other, intervening condition or event, when an A-type interaction takes place. This would just amount to saying that S brings about an A-type event, which in turn brings about C. And this would just play right into the hands of the reductionists, who could then retort that they are reducing "ways" to structures.

None of the reductionists' critics have taken a position like the one I am now describing, but they might. If they did, they would be claiming that the fluid model of causation I have been developing is too simple-minded, since its sole concern is quantifying contributions, not classifying them as well. Now the important question is this: would antireductionists

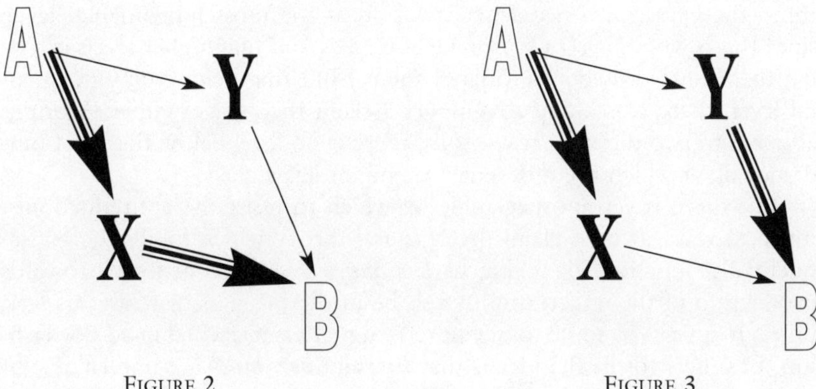

FIGURE 2 FIGURE 3

of this persuasion be entitled to insist that the two types of functions of a theory of causation—consequentialist on the one hand, and taxonomic on the other—are compatible? In other words, can they be entitled to a theory of causation fulfilling both types of function at the same time? There is no question that a theory of causation will be required to fulfill the consequentialist function. But can it fulfill the taxonomic one as well? I think not. Here is why.

9. Causal Theories and the How

Let's go back to the example of smoking causing cancer in two different ways, without bringing about intermediaries that (unassisted further, so to speak) bring about cancer. How can this be possible? The reductionists will wish to say that it cannot be; if smoking brings about cancer in two different ways, this is just another way of saying that smoking can cause cancer by way of two different causal paths, which differ in at least some of their intermediate nodes (intermediaries between initial cause and final effect). And I have argued that, if there is any substantive dispute between reductionists and their opponents, on the subject of metaphysical reduction itself, it's got to be here. Is there anything to choose between the following two positions: (1) two ways, no intermediaries; and (2) two paths, different intermediaries? Possibly.

I think that the only way that an antireductionist can maintain the two-ways-no-intermediaries position, is by sponsoring a metaphysics of levels of causation—so, for example, a macrolevel and a microlevel, and perhaps more in between. But, vis-à-vis the dispute about reduction, this will not help their case as much as they might wish. For the reductionists will simply reply that the level of causation they are concerned with lies at the bottom—they are concerned with causation at the most fundamental level, since this is where *real* causation takes place. (And that higher levels can be left to whomever happens to fancy them.) But that below the fundamental level, there is nothing to support a claim that, for example, A brings about B in two different ways, since there is no level below the most fundamental, at which the different ways might lie.

But there is yet another angle by which to resist the antireductionist move to ways. It is to claim that a causal theory which fulfills the consequentialist function, of telling us *how much* a cause contributes towards production of the effect, cannot also be in the business of telling us *how*, unless it appeals to some totally unrelated matters, attached in ad hoc fashion. In other words, the idea is that *how* and *how much* are unrelated subject matters, philosophically speaking. And since any acceptable account of causation has got to cover the *how much*, whatever else it might be inclined to do, it is hard to see how an acceptable account can cover also the *how*.

Here is how the case might go. Suppose antireductionists are right that there are different species of causal relation that two events can stand in towards each other, which nonetheless may not differ in strength, so that A could stand in two different causal relations to B, despite the fact that either way A would contribute the same amount (as measurable on a normalized scale, with magnitudes ranging, for example, between zero and one) towards production of B. In such a case, the reductionist will say they differ by intermediaries. And there may be no way to decide the matter, whether in favor of antireductionists or reductionists. But the two sides will agree on this much: that A causes B, that it does so by making a certain contribution towards production of B, and that this contribution can be measured against certain other contributions.

Suppose now we make the suggestion that what a theory of causality has to treat, are questions of the form "What caused E?" Such questions are not asking for identification of the shape of the causal arrow between E and its cause. Rather, they are asking for identification of the node causally upwind of E. Everyone can agree about this. Antireductionists, however, will insist that we should also treat the question asking after the shape of the causal arrow from C to E: how does E come about from C? They do not think it suffices to say that the shape of the arrow is "causal." As far as they are concerned, causal relations are not generic. They are branded. It matters, causally, whether it was Rolaids, or some Rolaids look-alike, slightly different in chemical composition, and imprinted with the local chain store name, but which makes the same numerical contributions towards alleviating indigestion and promoting tooth decay.

Now we might concede that it matters *to somebody* that it was Rolaids and not its look-alike. It matters, for example, to the pharmaceutical companies producing each. But why should it matter to the causal theorist?

The question whether it was Rolaids or the look-alike is a change of subject for the causal theorist. The causal theorist, after all, is not concerned with antacids, as such. The causal theorist does not automatically make the same discriminations as the chemist; she leaves chemistry to the chemists, just as she leaves physics to the physicists. The causal theorist abstracts from chemical structures to causal structures. If she did not do so, in what sense would she be offering something different from the chemist? Thus the causal theorist is concerned with antacids only under their causal aspects. For example, Rolaids might come in a variety of flavors, which differ from each other in chemical composition and hence in taste. The ones I happen to ingest today are minty rather than fruity. The causal theorist is right to be concerned with their capacity to alleviate my indigestion. But we would think her wrong if she were to take a professional interest in their flavor. So if the causal theorist is right to take no interest in flavor, why should it matter that it was the Rolaids, and not the slightly chemically different look-alike? It is hard to see why a difference in chemical composition, purely as such a difference, should matter more to the causal theorist, than a difference in taste. The antireductionist would have to provide us with a reason for grouping the relevances as they do. We reductionists have already given our story, having to do with the connection between the quantitative and the spatiotemporal, for grouping our concerns together as we have.

10. Trouble with the Quantitative?

There is one more effort on the part of antireductionists that we have yet to consider. When we have had a look, it shall be immediately clear that it should be a course of last resort. And the attention we give this effort will consolidate the reductionist motivations behind such strategies as exemplified in A1 through A3.

Suppose now that we have a common-causal structure, with C serving as the common cause of A and B as in figure 4a. The reductionist insists that for there to be a true common cause, causal flow from C to A must be noninteracting with causal flow from C to B. They say that if C is a true common cause, there can be no flow from A to B, so that C must screen each of A and B from the other. This is a precondition of being able to apply the likes of A1 through A3 in the endeavor to work backwards from effects to causes.

But now Cartwright has an argument that this quantitative picture of causality has got to be incorrect. It is quite possible, she suggests, to have a common cause which does not bring about its effects independently, so that A and B will not be screened off. She gives a number of examples.[13]

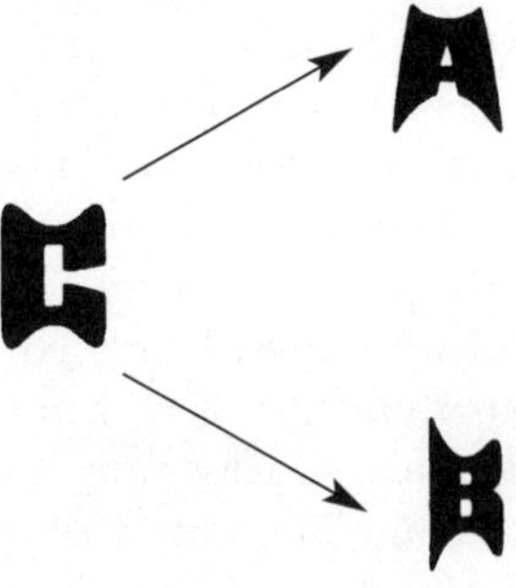

FIGURE 4A

The salient ingredient in these examples is that A and B are more perfectly coincident with each other than knowledge of their cause C only would lead one to predict. So, for a simple, nonrealistic example, suppose that smoking causes both cancer and heart disease, and that nothing else does. Suppose in addition that in an overwhelming proportion of those instances where smoking does cause cancer, it also causes heart disease, and that the reverse is true as well, but that not everyone who smokes gets both diseases. In such a world, smoking would not be a fail-safe predictor of heart disease, and cancer would be a better predictor, despite its being neither a cause nor an effect of heart disease.

For each such example the reductionist will insist that if indeed there is nothing but causality at work in these cases, then they cannot in fact be instances of a common-causal structure. For there must, in addition, be causal flow between A and B. The reductionist must reject the example as a genuinely live causal structure.

Cartwright explains the reductionist rejection of such examples by saying that reductionists attend only to intuitions schooled in purely deterministic settings. Only a determinist could deny the story about heart disease and cancer being perfectly coincident, but nonetheless stochastically (nondeterministically) produced joint effects of smoking, as a genuine causal possibility. In other words, Cartwright is charging reductionists with taking their causal arrows too literally, and consequently interpreting them as logical implications.

However, reductionists have very good reasons for insisting on identifying causal flow between the joint effects in the sorts of cases Cartwright brings forward as unproblematic instances of common-causal structure. Take the smoking case again. Suppose that the chances of cancer, with smoking, is fifty-fifty, and that the same holds true for heart disease. Now the story further has it that the cases of heart disease coincide with those of cancer more perfectly than fifty-fifty. For the sake of argument just suppose they coincide exactly. This will help us see why we must reject the example. For wouldn't it be simply magical for heart disease and cancer to be so perfectly coincident, as a matter of a causal law, without there being a direct causal connection? If we were to model the case on drawings from an urn, we would have to yoke balls together to achieve the right chance figures, exactly as Cartwright says. But the yoking of balls together is precisely the point at which the story turns magical. For it is precisely the point at which the model gives no explication of any kind for the correlation: it is put in purely by hand.

According to the story Cartwright would like us to accept as possible, that coincidence would be *a matter of the causal structure of the case,* and not just an accident. But that this coincidence would not, at the same time, be a matter of direct causal action. How can this be? We would be able to count on the perfect coincidence. But our reliance upon this regularity does not have so much as a single cause to ground it. It rests purely on the magic of yoked balls.

For Cartwright to reply (as she does) that such a regularity could hold as a matter of a causal law, without there being a direct and separate causal connection to uphold it, would be like suggesting that in any world governed entirely and unremittingly by causal laws, it can be reasonable for someone to expect to be dealt a queen whenever she is dealt an ace, from an ordinary deck of fifty-two playing cards, *while at the same time acknowledging that there is no direct and separate causal connection between being dealt an ace and being dealt a queen.* But under what possible circumstances could such an insistence be acceptable? None. At any rate it is not acceptable in the name of causality. Thus this challenge to quantitative causality is baseless.

Two fundamental ideas, according to the reductionist, belong in the center of mature causal reasoning. The first is that what is distinctive about the rates of coincidence between the effects of common causes, is that they admit of being screened off from each other: their rate of concurrence is explained entirely in terms of a common cause. And the second is that what is distinctive about causality is that it is diametrically opposed to pure randomness, but that it overlays it and so creates certain graspable patterns. Thus, according to the probabilist, we cannot, contrary to Cartwright's suggestion, sponsor any rate of coincidence whatsoever, between any two factors, and still name the name of causality: we cannot account for causal phenomena on the model of drawing yoked balls from an urn. By the same token we cannot sponsor the causal ordinariness of EPR-type rates of coincidence in the name of causality. The distinctiveness of EPR-type rates of coincidence is precisely that they transgress causal proprieties.

But Cartwright believes that she has a case to persuade us otherwise. She asks us to consider a chemical plant, which manufactures A for sale, and B as a by-product of the process producing A. The manufacture of A at this chemical plant is imperfect: we get A on only four out of five days in the week; and the same for B. But on each day that we get A, we also get B. Isn't this a perfectly acceptable causal scenario? Not if the causal structure we are to accept is figure 4a rather than figure 4b. All the reasoning we applied in the cancer-heart disease example applies here equally. Only the names have been changed, to protect our sensibilities.

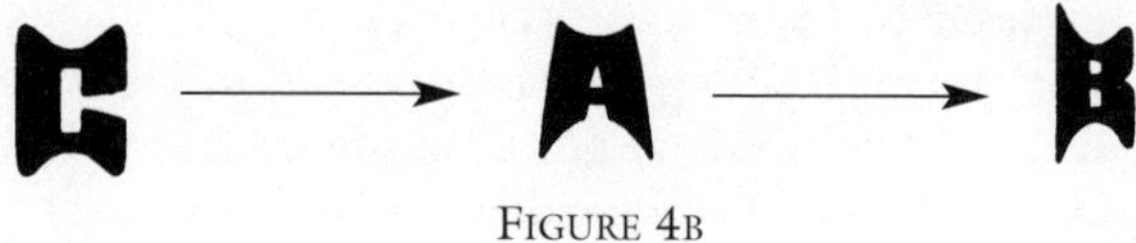

FIGURE 4B

It cannot be further from the truth to suggest that reductionist intuitions vis-à-vis the common cause have been schooled in a LaPlacean environment. To the contrary: they have been schooled in gaming halls. Furthermore, they have been schooled in those halls in which the drawings from urns occur amongst balls that are not magically yoked together. So it is indeed truly ironic that Cartwright should charge reductionists with deterministic sensibilities.

11. Paying the Piper

There is always a price to pay for reduction. After all, a reductionist proposal declares of two apparently different categories in the world, that they amount to the same category. It says that, whereas we might unreflectively have supposed that there are two categories at play, possibly because we have managed somehow to have generated two terms for it in our language, there really is only one. The bid for reduction is in some regards a wager, to the effect that we shall absolutely never encounter an occasion in which the (distinct) terms and concepts we called into play, when (earlier on) we supposed there to be two distinct categories, must be articulated in decisively different ways. In other words, the bid for reduction is a wager to the effect that a certain pair of concepts render fundamentally the same service in the economy of human affairs. The bid for reduction of causes to chance-raisers, is a wager to the effect that these ideas render fundamentally the same service in the economy of human life. What price must be paid by those who offer this wager? Here, finally, is where reductionists and antireductionists part company.

Reductionists proclaim that in the economy of human affairs the notion of cause renders a particular service—namely, that it serves as a guide to life. When one seeks answer to the question of causal relations amongst certain factors, they proclaim, one is seeking to learn whether a variation in one improves the chances of (and therefore affords a means to) altering the other. One seeks answer to the question whether, and the extent to which, one of these two factors can be controlled by manipulations of the other. Reductionists, in other words, view the notion of cause as fundamentally and irremediably an engineering notion, that would serve the beaver in dam-building precisely the way it renders service in the economy of human affairs. The notion of cause renders service as a guide to life. And there's nothing more to be said about it.

The antireductionist claims more for the notion of cause. The antireductionist claims that the notion renders us service in our bid for scientific knowledge, as such, whether or not it ever renders service as a guide to life. (As we've seen, antireductionists claim *also* that knowledge of causes always makes a practical difference, but these claims have gone unsubstantiated.) For antireductionists are convinced that the notion of cause and effect lies at the dead center of absolutely all scientific investigations. This is why—I am convinced—some antireductionists (like Cartwright 1989) proclaim that we require something besides the notion of chance-raising to make sense of quantum mechanics.[14] The point is that they have failed to show how this can be a matter of where reductionism goes wrong vis-à-vis the metaphysics of causation.

MARIAM THALOS
University of Utah

NOTES

1. The favorite example concerns the spins of particles in the so-called "singlet state." We measure the spins, in a variety of directions, of pairs of separated particles, originally produced together at a common site in the singlet state, and set in flight in opposite directions. Let S^L_θ represent the spin of the particle in the "left" wing of the setup, in the direction θ transverse to the particle's line of flight, and let and $S^R_{\theta'}$ represent the spin of the particle in the "right" wing of the setup, in the direction θ' transverse to that particle's line of flight. Experimentally we determine that:

1. each of S^L_θ and $S^R_{\theta'}$ can take on only one of two magnitudes; I will say either +1 or –1;
2. the relative frequencies of each of: (a) $S^L_\theta = +1$; (b) $S^L_\theta = -1$; (c) $S^R_{\theta'} = +1$; and (d) $S^R_{\theta'} = -1$; is ½;
3. the relative frequencies of (a) and (c) together, or (b) and (d) together, when $\theta = \theta'$, is zero; and, surprisingly, to those who adhere to the standards of causal explanation—

4. the relative frequencies of (a) and (c) together, or (b) and (d) together, when the angles are unrestricted, is $\frac{1}{2}\sin^2\left(\frac{\theta-\theta'}{2}\right)$; similarly the relative frequencies of (a) and (b) , or (b) and (c) together, is $\frac{1}{2}\cos^2\left(\frac{\theta-\theta'}{2}\right)$

J. S. Bell showed that these experimental facts are inconsistent with the proposal that there is a common-cause explanation of correlations between distant events. In particular, he showed that the only common-causal explanation of (3) above is inconsistent with (4). (This is because (4) is inconsistent with the common-causal assumption that $P[(a) \wedge (c)|\,\lambda] = P[(a)|\,\lambda] \times P[(c)|\,\lambda]$ —which states that S_θ^L and $S_{\theta'}^R$ are statistically independent once contributions from the (unknown) common factor λ has been accounted for—which is the only common-causal way of explaining (3). Details of this inconsistency are found in the introduction to Cushing and McMullin 1989, as well as in Hughes 1989.

2. The contrast is with "descriptivist metaphysics." For the *locus classicus* of this distinction see Strawson 1959.

3. This is as a matter of fact incorrect: not everyone will be prepared to grant this as a case of negative contribution, but some will make an effort to account for each event of the process as each one making a successor more likely. One might, as for example Christopher Hitchcock suggested in personal correspondence, follow Deborah Rosen's lead (as reported in Suppes 1959, p. 41) in suggesting that the squirrel kick raised the probability of a successor event, and that that successor raises the probability of the ball going into the cup. So suppose the golfer's putt sends the ball rolling, it is kicked by the squirrel in such a way as to encounter a rock, which changes its trajectory so that it falls into the cup. The initial putt increases the probability of the squirrel kicking it; the squirrel's kick raises the chances that it will encounter the rock just as it did; and the encounter with the rock, in just the fashion it did, raises its chances of making its mark. This strategy will not always be successful, as I argue in Thalos forthcoming (b).

4. Salmon (1984); see also the discussions of the mark criterion by Kitcher (1989) and Dowe (1992).

5. See the transference theories of Aronson (1971) and Fair (1967), criticized by Dowe (1995).

6. Papineau adds the following condition as well: $P(E\,|\,C\&\neg S) = P(E\,|\,\neg S)$. For our purposes Def. 3.1 will be sufficient.

7. (Thalos 2002b). The argument relies upon results achieved by Judea Pearl and co-workers, see Pearl 1988, Pearl and Paz 1985, and Geiger and Pearl 1988.

8. This was suggested to me by J. Butterfield (1989), although he does not spell out the matter as I do here.

9. Might this in fact be what Cartwright (1989) has in mind by "capacities"?

10. For another discussion of how antireductionist accounts are not generally free of this problem, see Dowe 1992.

11. I disagree with Papineau (1993) that we can, or even should, answer this criticism. His attempt to do so leads to a rather too strong statement about metaphysical possibilities, ruling out (for no reasons that an empiricist can justify) the possibility of cosmic conspiracies in which contributions can cancel out to zero in every actual case. He then writes: "A world in which no probabilistic dependencies

at all manifested some supposed causal structure would be a world in which that causal structure did not exist" (p. 246).

12. That is, all except cases of the EPR type. And when it comes to that, all the reductionist need do is simply confess that not everything admits of causal explanation, even if human beings are wont to demand it.

13. Which to the initiated have the same quantitative structure as EPR-type cases, in Cartwright 1993.

14. For what it's worth, I think they are mistaken: see Thalos 2002a and Thalos n.d.

REFERENCES

Aronson, J. 1971. "On the Grammar of 'Cause'." *Synthese* 22: 413–30.

Butterfield, Jeremey. 1989. "A Space-Time Approach to the Bell Inequality." In *Philosophical Consequences of Quantum Theory,* ed. James T. Cushing and Ernan McMullin, pages 114–44. Notre Dame, Indiana: University of Notre Dame Press.

Cartwright, Nancy. 1989. *Nature's Capacities and Their Measurement.* Oxford: Clarendon Press.

———. 1993. "Marks and Probabilities: Two Ways to Find Causal Structure." In *Scientific Philosophy: Origins and Developments,* pages 113–19. Dordrecht: Kluwer.

Cushing, James T., and Ernan McMullin, eds. 1989. *Philosophical Consequences of Quantum Theory.* Notre Dame, Indiana: University of Notre Dame Press.

Dowe, Phil. 1992. "Wesley Salmon's Process Theory of Causality and the Conserved Quantity Theory." *Philosophy of Science* 59: 195–216.

———. 1995. "What's Right and Wrong with Transference Theories." *Erkenntnis* 42: 363–74.

Eells, Ellery, and Elliott Sober. 1983. "Probabilistic Causality and the Question of Transitivity." *Philosophy of Science* 50: 35–57.

Fair, D. 1967. "Causation and the Flow of Energy." *Erkenntnis* 14: 219–50.

Geiger, D., and J. Pearl. 1988. "Logical and Algorithmic Properties of Conditional Independence." Technical report, Cognitive Systems Laboratory, UCLA.

Hughes, R. I. G. 1989. *The Structure and Interpretation of Quantum Mechanics.* Cambridge: Harvard University Press.

Irzik, Gurol. 1996. "Can Causes Be Reduced to Correlations?" *British Journal for the Philosophy of Science* 47: 249–70.

Kitcher, Philip. 1989. "Expanatory Unification and the Causal Structure of the World." In *Minnesota Studies in the Philosophy of Science,* ed. Philip Kitcher and Wesley Salmon. Minneapolis: University of Minnesota Press.

Lewis, David. 1973. "Causation." *Journal of Philosophy* 70: 556–70.

———. 1979. "Counterfactual Dependence and Time's Arrow." *Nous* 13: 455–76.

Mackie, J. L. 1974. *The Cement of the Universe.* Oxford: Clarendon Press.

Mellor, D. H. 1988. "On Raising the Chances of Effects." In *Probability and Causality,* ed. J. H. Fetzer, pages 229–39. Dordrecht: Kluwer.

Papineau, David. 1985. "Causal Symmetry." *British Journal for the Philosophy of Science* 36: 273–89.

———. 1989. "Pure, Mixed and Spurious Probabilities and Their Significance for a Reductionist Theory of Causation." In *Minnesota Studies in the Philosophy of Science,* ed. Philip Kitcher and Wesley Salmon, pages 347–88. Minneapolis: University of Minnesota Press.

———. 1991. "Correlations and Causes." *British Journal for the Philosophy of Science* 42: 397–412.

———. 1993. "Can We Reduce Causal Direction to Probabilities?" *Proceedings of the 1992 Biennial Meeting of the Philosophy of Science Association* 2: 238–52.

Pearl, J. 1988. *Probabilistic Reasoning in Intelligent Systems.* San Mateo: Morgan Kaufman.

Pearl, J., and A. Paz. 1985. "A Graph-Based Logic for Reasoning about Relevance Relations." In *Advances in Artificial Intelligence,* ed. D. Hogg, B. DuBoulay, and L. Steels. Amsterdam: North-Holland.

Salmon, W. C. 1984. *Scientific Explanation and the Causal Structure of the World.* Princeton: Princeton University Press.

———. N.d. "Probabilistic Causality."

Sober, Elliot. 1988. "The Principle of the Common Cause." In *Probability and Causality,* ed. J. H. Fetzer. Dordrecht: Kluwer.

Spirtes, P., C. Glymour, and R. Scheines. 1992. *Causation, Prediction, and Search.* New York: Springer-Verlag.

Strawson, P. F. 1959. *Individuals: An Essay in Descriptive Metaphysics.* London: Methuen.

Suppes, Patrick. 1959. *A Probabalistic Theory of Causality.* Amsterdam: North-Holland.

Thalos, Mariam. N.d. *The Enterprise of Explanation.* Manuscript in progress.

———. 2002a. "Explanation Is a Genus: On the Varieties of Scientific Explanation." *Synthese.*

———. 2002b. "The Reduction of Causal Processes." *Synthese.*

PART IV

Wider Applications of Probability

15

Is It a Crime to Belong to a Reference Class?

MARK COLYVAN, HELEN M. REGAN, AND SCOTT FERSON

We examine the statistical evidence presented in the legal case of United States versus Shonubi. This evidence, as we argue, is flawed in many ways. Perhaps of greatest interest is the fact that the data is subject to reference-class problems. This case is a wonderful illustration of the practical importance of the reference-class problem—whether Shonubi would be sentenced to extra time in prison or not, would hang on the acceptance or rejection of the statistical evidence. We came across the Shonubi case early in 2000 and our pretheoretic intuitions were that the statistical evidence in this case was not enough to justify the extended sentence that Shonubi was facing. It came as some surprise, then, to find that all the commentators on this case held the opposite view. This essay is thus an attempt to back up our pretheoretic intuitions with something more substantial. In doing so we draw attention to the wide-ranging practical significance of problems in the foundation of statistics.

—M. C., H. M. R., and S. F.

* * *

ABSTRACT

In this paper we examine the statistical evidence presented in the legal case of United States v. Shonubi. In drug smuggling cases such as this, the length of sentence is dependent on the total quantity of drugs imported. In this case it was

*This paper was first published in *The Journal of Political Philosophy* 9, no. 2 (June 2001): 168–81. We thank Blackwell Publishers for permission to reproduce it here.

determined that Shonubi was involved in seven prior drug-smuggling trips with the quantity of drugs imported on these trips unknown. In order to determine what the total quantity of drugs imported by Shonubi was, the prosecution relied heavily on statistical data gathered on other similar drug smugglers. Although this statistical evidence was ultimately rejected by the courts, many feel that the evidence should have been allowed and that the rejection of such evidence amounts to the wholesale rejection of statistical evidence in U.S. legal trials. We argue that the rejection of this statistical evidence was appropriate in this case. We present several arguments in defense of our claim. The most significant of which is that it should not be a crime to belong to a reference class—the quantities of drugs imported by other drug smugglers does not give us reliable information about the quantity of drugs smuggled by Shonubi. This is a classic case of the well-known reference-class problem in probability theory, and surely it would be a travesty if Shonubi were to suffer an extended jail sentence because U.S. courts failed to recognize such a longstanding statistical problem. Moreover, the determination of the appropriate sentence is a problem of decision theory; it cannot be determined purely on the basis of probabilities, we also need to take into consideration the relevant utilities. Finally, we argue that to reject the statistical data in this case does not amount to the wholesale rejection of statistical evidence from U.S. jurisprudence.

Introduction

On December 10th, 1991 Charles Shonubi, a Nigerian citizen but a resident of the U.S.A., was arrested at John F. Kennedy International Airport for the importation of heroin into the United States.[1] Shonubi's *modus operandi* was "balloon swallowing." That is, heroin was mixed with another substance to form a paste and this paste was sealed in balloons which were then swallowed. The idea was that once the illegal substance was safely inside the U.S.A., the smuggler would pass the balloons and recover the heroin. On the date of his arrest, Shonubi was found to have swallowed 103 balloons containing a total of 427.4 grams of heroin. There was little doubt about Shonubi's guilt. In fact, there was considerable evidence that he had made at least seven prior heroin-smuggling trips to the U.S.A. (although he was not tried for these). In October 1992 Shonubi was convicted in a United States District Court for possessing and importing heroin. Although the conviction was only for crimes associated with Shonubi's arrest date of December 10th, 1991, the sentencing judge, Jack B. Weinstein, also made a finding that Shonubi had indeed made seven prior drug-smuggling trips to the U.S.A.

The interesting part of this case was in the sentencing. According to the federal sentencing guidelines, the sentence in cases such as this should depend on the total quantity of heroin involved. This instruction was interpreted rather broadly in the Shonubi case so that the total quantity of drugs should include all eight of Shonubi's drug-smuggling episodes. It was estimated that the total quantity of heroin that Shonubi carried into the U.S.A. on his eight trips was $427.4 \times 8 = 3{,}419.2$ grams. This was above the crucial 3,000 gram threshold and so corresponded to a base offense level of 34 (which, in Shonubi's case, resulted in a sentence of 12 years and 7 months imprisonment). (Call this *Shonubi I.*)

Shonubi appealed this sentence and the Second Circuit Court of Appeals vacated the sentence because the total quantity of drugs smuggled by Shonubi had not been established by a preponderance of evidence.[2] This was in part because there was no "specific evidence" that Shonubi smuggled the quantity of drugs on which the sentencing was based. The case was sent back to Judge Weinstein in the District Court for resentencing. (*Shonubi II.*)

In response to the lack of specific evidence, the prosecution offered data collected by the U.S. Customs Service. This data consisted of the quantities of heroin seized from 117 Nigerian, balloon-swallowing drug smugglers arrested at JFK Airport between the dates of Shonubi's first- and last-known drug-smuggling trips: September 1st, 1990 and December 10th, 1991. The prosecution statistician used repeated sampling (with replacement) from the 117 data points and produced a Gaussian-like histogram for the quantity of drugs imported on Shonubi's seven prior trips. The statistician concluded that there was a 0.99 chance that on the seven previous trips Shonubi smuggled at least 2,090.2 grams of heroin. When this was added to the 427.4 grams found on Shonubi on his last trip, the total quantity of drugs imported by Shonubi was estimated to be about 2,500 grams. Based on this evidence, Judge Weinstein found that Shonubi smuggled between 1,000 and 3,000 grams of heroin in his 8 trips for a base offense level of 32 which (after an enhancement added for Shonubi's lies and obstruction of justice) resulted again in a sentence of 12 years and 7 months imprisonment. (Call this *Shonubi III.)*

Once again Shonubi appealed and once again the sentence was vacated by the Second Circuit. Two very interesting points were made by the appellate court at this stage. The first was to reiterate the requirement for "specific evidence" and to point out that the Customs Service data did not constitute such evidence. The second point was that preponderance of evidence was too low a standard of proof for sentencing matters relating to disputed aspects of relevant conduct. In particular, when a significantly enhanced sentence was at stake, a more rigorous standard of proof was necessary. The court then referred the case back to the District Court for resentencing with the additional instructions that the prosecution had had two previous opportunities to provide specific evidence of the total quantity of drugs imported by Shonubi and no further opportunity to provide such evidence would be allowed. (*Shonubi IV.*)

Back in the District Court, Judge Weinstein had no choice but to sentence Shonubi based only on the 427.4 grams found on him on his last trip. This resulted in a sentence of 8 years and one month imprisonment. (*Shonubi V.*) The trial then moved out of the court and into the academic arena where it continues to this day.

The general consensus amongst commentators on this case seems to be that the Second Circuit Court's decision at *Shonubi IV* to vacate the sentence of *Shonubi III* was a poor one. In particular, most commentators suggest that this poor decision was due to lack of understanding of statistical methods. Moreover, some suggest that the real importance of the Shonubi case is in the lessons it holds for statistical evidence generally. Here's what some of the commentators have said:

> The opinion of the court of appeals is interesting, important, and—above all—depressing because of what it suggests about the difficulties that many judges may have when they confront statistical methods and statistical evidence: it suggests that quite a few judges—including some very eminent and intelligent ones—still may not have a grasp of some basic characteristics of probabilistic and statistical methods and arguments. (Tillers 1998)

> [T]he opinion of the court of appeals in *Shonubi IV* is not a distinguished one. [. . .] [T]he Second Circuit's view that the statistical evidence relied upon by Weinstein was defective because it was not "specific" is most unfortunate. The notion that evidence of a person's actions must be somehow "specific", either to that person or to his [sic] behavior on a specific occasion, is at best otiose and, at worst, nonsensical. (Tillers 1998)

> The Shonubi case illustrates the legal system's failure to fully appreciate statistical evidence. (Gastwirth, Freidlin and Miao 2000, p. 405)

Judge Weinstein even suggested that the decision of *Shonubi IV* "represents a retrogressive step towards the practices relied upon from the Middle Ages to the late Nineteenth century" (quoted in Tillers 1998).

Now it seems that there is much more at issue here than the sentencing of Charles Shonubi. If we are to accept what some of the commentators are saying, the use of statistical evidence in U.S. courts is on trial. The concern is that the rejection of the statistical evidence in this case amounts to the wholesale rejection of statistical evidence (presumably because the statistical evidence here is as good as statistical evidence ever gets). We disagree with the commentators above on two counts. First, we believe that the Second Circuit Court's decision was not a poor one—the reasons given for the decision were perhaps not expressed as well as they might have been, but the idea was right. Second, we do not believe that the statistical evidence in this case was as good as statistical evidence gets, so there is no serious threat to the future of statistical evidence in U.S. jurisprudence.[3]

For the most part, we defend the Second Circuit's decision by criticizing the statistical evidence accepted at *Shonubi III*. Along the way, however, we say a little to defend the reasons given by the Second Circuit Court for rejecting this evidence. In the next section we discuss our main objection to the evidence presented at *Shonubi III*: the evidence founders on the well-known reference-class problem. In the following section we discuss the Shonubi case from a decision-theoretic angle and suggest that the close attention to the statistical evidence in this case has blinded many to the importance of the relevant utilities.

The Reference-Class Problem

There were several serious flaws in the methods employed by the District Court at *Shonubi III* in determining the quantity of drugs on which Shonubi's sentencing was based.[4] Perhaps the most serious of these flaws was that no estimates of measurement error or other uncertainties about the quantities of drugs recovered were recorded in either Shonubi's case or for the other points in the data sets. Moreover, these errors were likely to be rather significant once the methods of determination are considered.[5] Moreover, the fact that these errors were significant should have been obvious, given that 17 of an original 142 data points from the Drug Enforcement Administration contained inconsistent information (net weights greater than or equal to gross weights).[6] We shall not dwell on such matters here. Although these details are important, the real issue is whether Shonubi should have been sentenced based on evidence gathered from *other people*. That is, should he have been sentenced based on his membership in a particular reference class?[7]

First we note that although Shonubi was not *convicted* because of his membership in a reference class, this possibility is not ruled out. The only difference between the standards of evidence required for conviction and sentencing is that the former employs the beyond-reasonable-doubt standard, while the latter employs the preponderance-of-evidence standard. So, for instance, if the probability that Shonubi carried more than 2,000 grams of heroin into the U.S.A. was sufficiently high (0.99, say) then presumably this would suffice for a conviction.[8] That is, if this kind of evidence is to be accepted as Tillers and others suggest, we ought to accept it for conviction as well, in which case it *would* appear to be a crime to belong to a reference class. So, for example, let's suppose that 99% of people from a certain reference class cheat on their taxes. Does this mean that we're justified in charging and sentencing someone in this class with tax evasion, without further evidence? No, of course not; we require more evidence than simply their membership in the reference class in question. It is important to note that we require further evidence *not* because we wish to raise the probability from 0.99 to something higher (after all a probability of 0.99 seems a good candidate for beyond reasonable doubt). Rather, we require further evidence because the reference-class evidence is not specific to the individual in question.

The problem here is rather well known and it is somewhat surprising that the critics of *Shonubi IV* do not acknowledge this.[9] The problem is, of course, the reference-class problem. To appreciate the problem consider the following defense of Shonubi's innocence. Shonubi is a toll collector at the George Washington Bridge. Let's suppose that no other toll collectors at this bridge were engaged in drug smuggling. Now Shonubi could appeal to his membership in *this* reference class to protest his innocence (or to argue that he imported considerably less than 1,000 grams of heroin in his eight trips). The point is simply that Shonubi is a member of many (in fact infinitely many) reference classes; some of these classes consist largely of unsavory types while others consist largely of saints. Membership in reference classes, it seems, does little to establish anything about Shonubi's own behavior.[10]

We are not claiming that there is no solution to the reference-class problem, just that there is no straightforward solution, and until a satisfactory solution is provided, the difficulty we raise here is serious. As an illustration of how deep the reference-class problem is, we will discuss and put to rest a couple of possible candidates for solutions that might suggest themselves in the case at hand. The basic idea behind the following suggestions is that the reference class of Nigerian, balloon-swallowing, heroin smugglers is thought to be intuitively relevant, whereas the class of toll collectors, for instance, is not. We need to find an argument in support of this intuition, though.

The first suggestion for justifying the reference class of Nigerian, balloon-swallowing, heroin smugglers might be that it was Shonubi's membership in this class that landed him in court in the first place.[11] This, however, is simply not true. It was Shonubi's membership in the class of apprehended drug smugglers that landed him in court. The mode of transport, country of origin, and, indeed, the kind of illegal substance were not relevant—he would have ended up in court if he were caught smuggling cocaine from Australia in stuffed toys, say. Indeed, he would have ended up in court if he had been caught engaging in any illegal activity. We take it, however, that the reference class of apprehended criminals is not intuitively the appropriate one, so this justification of the reference class in question will not do.

Next consider the suggestion that the class of Nigerian, balloon-swallowing, heroin smugglers is more robust than others. That is, taking the intersection of this class with others (such as the class of toll collectors) will not significantly change the estimate of the quantity of drugs smuggled. If correct, this amounts to the claim that the reference class in question is homogeneous with respect to the quantity of drugs smuggled. The problem is that such homogeneity has not been established by any of the statistical evidence presented, and to simply assume homogeneity is to beg the question. Whether this reference class is homogeneous and, in particular, whether it delivers the correct answer for Shonubi, is precisely what is at issue. We cannot invoke such unsupported assumptions to justify the appropriateness of this reference class.

Finally, consider the suggestion that there is a causal story to be told here: there is a causal connection between Shonubi's membership in the reference class in question and his carrying the quantity of heroin with which the District Court sentenced him at *Shonubi III*. The story would, in fact, be a story about a common cause: perhaps all members of the reference class in question worked for the same drug lord, say, who ensured that all drug couriers carry, more or less, the same quantity of heroin on each trip. At the very least, you might believe there to be a counterfactual dependence between carrying a certain quantity of heroin and being a member of the reference class in question: had Shonubi not carried the quantity of drugs on which he was sentenced at *Shonubi III*, he would not have been a member of the reference class in question. The problem with these responses is that in the former variant, causal connections that have not been established are being assumed, and in the second variant, homogeneity of the reference class is again being illicitly invoked. It seems that this justification also fails.

We do not wish to turn this discussion into a survey of proposed solutions to the reference-class problem; we merely wish to note that (i) the problem is serious and (ii) the obvious "solutions" fail. Whether there are more sophisticated strategies that can be made to work, we leave as an interesting open question. It is worth noting, however, that no justifications, sophisticated or otherwise, were provided by critics of the Second Circuit Court's decision at *Shonubi IV*. The reference-class problem, for the most part, was simply ignored. We now turn to the question of whether the reference-class problem is a problem only for frequentist interpretations of probability.

What is at issue here is the probability that Shonubi carried between 1,000 and 3,000 grams of heroin. We are not interested in how many others (no matter how much they're like Shonubi) carried between 1,000 and 3,000 grams of heroin. That is, we are interested in a single-case probability, not a frequency relative to some reference class. Once put this way it sounds as though what is at issue is the notorious problem of the correct interpretation of probability. According to frequentists such as von

Mises (1957), we can't even make sense of single-case probabilities, for probabilities are simply ratios of frequencies of certain kinds. (This view should be contrasted with other interpretations such as the subjectivist interpretation or the propensity interpretation, where single-case probabilities are countenanced.[12]) Indeed, such a frequentist view seems to be lurking in the background of the criticisms of *Shonubi IV*.[13] It would take us too far afield to defend an interpretation of probability theory that countenances single-case probabilities. Suffice to say, however, that it is hard to see how any view that did not allow single-case probabilities could be of any use in decision theory (which is, after all, what we are talking about here—we have more to say on this in the next section). In any case, the critics of *Shonubi IV* should at least acknowledge that there is considerable debate over the interpretation of probability; they should not simply assume a naïve frequentist view without comment.[14]

There is another reason for not embarking on a defense of single-case probabilities here: single-case probabilities may not solve the problem at hand. It might be argued that the reference-class problem also has considerable bite on interpretations of probability that countenance single-case probability statements. After all, even subjectivist and propensity views of probability should be answerable to the frequencies. For example, subjective probability assignments should (at least roughly) coincide with relative frequencies, when such frequency data is available, otherwise huge epistemic problems loom for these interpretations of probability. The point is simply that while non-frequency interpretations of probability deny that probabilities should be *identified* with frequencies, they ought not deny that probabilities are at least in some sense answerable to frequencies.[15] But this is enough for the reference-class problem to be reinstated, because the frequencies to which the non-frequency interpretations must answer suffer from the reference-class problem. For example, let's suppose that an agent A assigns the subjective probability s to some event e occurring under circumstances c. Now this subjective assignment might need to be revised when new evidence comes to light. So, for instance, let's suppose that it is found that e occurs p percent of the time in circumstances like c and that $s \neq p/100$. It seems reasonable to suppose that A should revise s to something closer to $p/100$ (perhaps by Bayes's theorem). But the reference class used to determine p can be questioned. Had we used a different reference class we might have found that e occurs q percent of the time (where $q \neq p$) and A's revision of s would have been different. It thus seems that the reference-class problem arises whenever relative frequencies are used—it is not simply a problem for the frequency interpretations of probability.[16]

It is interesting to note that although the Second Circuit Court did not mention the reference-class problem in their rejection of the evidence presented at *Shonubi III*, nevertheless, it seems that their concerns were closely related to the reference-class problem (at least if it's thought of as a problem for the frequency interpretation of probability). But if what we have suggested above about the reference-class problem being a problem for single-case probabilities as well (at least for those that are answerable to frequencies), it might seem that we are committed to the wholesale rejection of statistics from legal evidence. This, however, is not the case. We now sketch a way of making sense of the Second Circuit's request for specific evidence that does not involve the rejection of all statistical evidence.

First, we note that no matter how you cash out the phrase "specific evidence," there is an obvious candidate for such evidence in the Shonubi case: Shonubi's previous behavior. This evidence might include previous convictions, records of financial dealings and so on. Now such evidence may not have actually been available in the Shonubi case but it is certainly not "nonsensical" (as Tillers [1998] suggests) to ask for such evidence. It is important to note that the reference-class problem arises in relation to such specific evidence as well but at least the events in any such reference class would all be events involving Shonubi; he would not be sentenced based on the behavior of others, but on his own previous behavior.

Second, it is useful to bear in mind the distinction between inductive reasoning (typically involving frequency data) and abductive reasoning or inference to the best explanation (which may involve probabilities interpreted subjectively or as propensities). For example, it seems that inference to the best explanation was employed to arrive at the conclusion that Shonubi was involved in seven previous drug-smuggling trips. That is, the best explanation for his multiple visits to Nigeria (and his multiple passports that presumably try to disguise this fact) on his relatively low income as a toll collector is that he was smuggling drugs on each of these occasions. Whatever problems inference to the best explanation may face,[17] it does seem to satisfy the constraint of specific evidence and that is all we're interested in here. (For example, the above argument for the conclusion that Shonubi was involved in seven prior drug-smuggling trips does not involve evidence pertaining to anyone other than Shonubi.) Now if we accept inference to the best explanation, we have another kind of evidence that might have been employed in the Shonubi case to support the prosecution's claims about the total quantity of drugs imported by Shonubi. This evidence might consist of economic considerations such as the minimum quantity of heroin needed to cover the costs involved in the smuggling operation.[18]

To sum up this section, we've argued that while the Second Circuit's reasons for rejecting the statistical evidence of *Shonubi III* might not have been expressed as clearly as one would like, their decision was correct. The statistical evidence presented at *Shonubi III* ignored the well-known reference-class problem—statistical data was presented that was based on a particular reference class as though doing so were uncontroversial. One cannot simply assume that the reference class used is privileged, especially when significant increases in prison penalty may result. Finally, we deny that rejecting the evidence of *Shonubi III* amounts to the wholesale rejection of statistical evidence in law and we provide two examples of statistical (broadly construed) evidence that should count as specific in this context.

A Decision-Theoretic Perspective

Another line of attack on the District Court's decision at *Shonubi III* is that we are not simply interested in the probability that Shonubi carried more than 1,000 grams of heroin into the U.S.A.; we wish to decide on some course of action and so we must also consider the utilities associated with the outcome of the proposed actions. When faced with a decision for which both the relevant probabilities and utilities are available, decision theory counsels us to choose the action that maximizes expected utility.[19] To ignore the importance (or even the existence) of utilities in any decision-making exercise is tantamount to accepting that all consequences have identical value—that we are indifferent to the outcomes of the proposed acts. To illustrate how utilities can make a difference to a decision, suppose we are asked to walk across a narrow beam placed a few inches above the ground. If we successfully cross the beam, we win a small sum of money; if we fall off, then we miss out on the cash. In this case the utilities are such that we would elect to cross the beam provided we have no specific objection to beam walking. Now suppose the beam is placed high across a ravine, below which are crocodile-infested waters. Even though the probability of successfully crossing the beam is identical to that of the previous scenario (our beam-walking skills have not altered) the utilities have changed to such an extent that we are no longer inclined to accept the challenge.

The importance of utilities in judicial decision making is recognized routinely. The option of a plea bargain in many criminal cases is based on maximizing expected utilities. The benefits to the prosecution and the courts aside, defendants often opt to plead guilty to crimes in order to receive a reduced sentence. In such cases, even though the probability of being found guilty has increased to (or, in some cases, remains at) a value of one, the expected utility, measured (inversely) in terms of jail time, is maximized with the act of pleading guilty. It is surprising then, that criticism of the appellate court's decision in *Shonubi IV* was leveled squarely at issues relating to probabilities, with no regard to the relevant utilities.

Tillers (1997; 1998), Izenman (2000; 2000a), and Gastwirth *et al.* (2000) all quite rightly emphasize the importance of probabilities in judicial decision making, but they completely overlook the role of utilities. In decisions under risk, the utilities are as important as the probabilities. In fact, in decisions under ignorance, where the probabilities are not known, we can base decisions purely on utilities via dominance reasoning, maximin rule or minimax regret (Resnik 1987; Jeffrey 1983). So it seems that the prosecution in *Shonubi III* and the critics of *Shonubi IV* have ignored the one thing that cannot be ignored.

In all such cases there is the significant issue of how to determine the relevant utilities. There are, in fact, two quite distinct issues here. The first is that of whose utilities we seek to maximize. After all, the defenses' utilities and the prosecutions' utilities are quite different. Moreover, the utilities of Justice or of society as a whole might be different again. For instance, it does not seem unreasonable to consider the defendant's utilities as being inversely proportional to the size of the sentence, whereas the prosecution's utilities might be thought of as being proportional to the size of the sentence. The second issue is that even once we agree upon whose utilities we wish to maximize, the matter of how we measure them is nontrivial. Do we measure them in terms of years in prison?; the natural logarithm of years in prison?; financial loss or gain? These two issues are very important and, so far as we can tell, without obvious resolutions. Fortunately we do not need to settle these matters for our purposes here. All we require is that from any reasonable point of view (for example, from the point of view of Justice) there is significant disutility in handing down a sentence longer than that which is justified.[20] We take it that there's nothing too controversial in this.

Issues relating to sentencing, and therefore to utilities, in the Shonubi case are complex. The sentencing guideline "allows punishment for conduct of which the defendant has not been convicted" if that conduct is deemed relevant to the conduct for which the defendant was convicted (*Shonubi IV*). While the sentencing judge is not required to take such conduct into account s/he is entitled to increase the punishment up to the maximum applicable sentence if appropriate. Furthermore, in the case of Shonubi, the degree of severity of the sentence for the previous seven drug-smuggling episodes, for which Shonubi was neither charged nor convicted, could be the same as for the crime for which he was convicted. Since sentencing for drug offenses is determined largely by the quantity of drugs involved, Judge Weinstein deemed it necessary to estimate the aggregate weight of heroin involved across the eight drug-smuggling trips.

Although the appellate court did not specifically appeal to utilities or couch their opinions in decision-theoretic terms, their ruling was clearly in this spirit. They found that:

> [a] guideline system that prescribes punishment for unconvicted conduct at the same level of severity as convicted conduct obviously obliges courts to proceed carefully in determining the standards for establishing whether the relevant conduct has been proven. We have recognized the need for such care with regard to the basic issue of the degree of the burden of proof. Thus, though the Sentencing Commission has favored the preponderance-of-the-evidence standard for resolving all disputed fact issues at sentencing, [. . .], we have ruled that a more rigorous standard should be used in determining disputed aspects of relevant conduct where such conduct, if proven, will significantly enhance a sentence. (*Shonubi IV*)

Hence the appellate court determined that "specific evidence," in the form of drug records, admissions, or live testimony, was what was necessary to meet the burden of proof requirements for sentencing Shonubi for the seven prior drug-smuggling trips.

There are two issues at play here. The first is the Second Circuit's concern that evidence that has not brought about a conviction beyond reasonable doubt, is used to determine a sentence for relevant conduct at the same level of severity as if the defendant had been convicted with that evidence. The second issue is that since the consequences of using untried evidence are so dire for the defendant (notwithstanding the consequences for legal precedence), the burden of proof relating to the quantities of heroin smuggled by Shonubi in the previous seven trips should be at a higher level than preponderance of evidence. In short, the Second Circuit ruled that since the associated utility plummets with a substantially enhanced sentence (from Shonubi's and the Second Circuit's point of view, in any case), a more rigorous standard of proof is required in the form of "specific evidence." (Particularly since doubt had been cast on the assumptions behind the statistical analysis.) Fortunately, the Second Circuit considered both utility *and* probability issues in their final decision.

It is interesting to note that the request by the Second Circuit for a higher standard of evidence was not a request for evidence that implied a higher probability that Shonubi carried over 2,000 grams of heroin. After all, according to the prosecution's statistical analysis, the probability of this was already very high: 0.99. Instead, the request for a higher standard of evidence arose out of concerns about the method employed to derive the figure of 0.99. Thus the Second Circuit was concerned by what we might think of as meta-uncertainty.[21] It is difficult to know how to even quantify such uncertainty let alone provide a convincing case that this uncertainty is low. (For example, how do we answer questions such as: what is the probability that the reference class in question was the appropriate one?) We take the thrust of the Second Circuit's point about utilities to be that in light of the potentially significantly increased sentence involved in this case, we need to be extremely confident that Shonubi carried more than 2,000 grams of heroin over his eight trips. In order to have the required degree of confidence we need both our statistical analysis to yield a high probability for the event in question *and* to have confidence in the method used to obtain that probability. It was the second of these that the Second Circuit was not satisfied with in the Shonubi case.[22]

In closing, we note that if the aggregate estimate of drug quantities for the previous seven occasions had not increased the base offense level of the trip for which Shonubi was actually convicted, there would be no cause for appeal (on the grounds of lack of specific evidence, in any case). It is precisely because of the utilities involved that the sentencing led to appeal.

Conclusion

We reject the claim that the Second Circuit Court's findings in *Shonubi IV* amount to a wholesale rejection of statistical evidence in law. Indeed, statistical evidence was used, and accepted by the Second Circuit Court, to estimate the quantity of heroin Shonubi smuggled on the trip for which he was convicted. Their objection to the statistical evidence presented for the seven prior trips was a cautious and carefully-considered reaction to the distinction between the crimes for which Shonubi had been charged and convicted (where there was direct evidence of the quantities involved) and crimes for which he had not been charged (where there was only evidence of the quantities others had smuggled). Moreover, the Second Circuit's rejection of the statistical evidence can be understood as a concern about reference classes, and their suggestion that the preponderance of evidence was too low a standard of evidence in this case can be understood as an appreciation of the importance that utilities play in the problem at hand. Once seen in this light, the Second Circuit's decision is not only, in our view, a fair and just one, but it is also theoretically well motivated.[23]

MARK COLYVAN
University of Tasmania, Australia

HELEN M. REGAN
San Diego State University

SCOTT FERSON
Applied Biomathematics, New York

NOTES

1. Our discussion here follows Izenman (2000). See that paper for further details of the Shonubi case.

2. There are three different standards of proof appealed to (in decreasing order): beyond reasonable doubt, clear and convincing evidence, and preponderance of evidence. While beyond reasonable doubt is required for conviction, sentencing requires only preponderance of evidence.

3. See Tribe 1971 for a somewhat more pessimistic view of the proper role of mathematics in the legal process.

4. Leaving aside the obviously flawed method of multiplication by 8 used in *Shonubi I*.

5. See Izenman 2000a for details of the various shortcomings in the estimate of the quantity of heroin found on Shonubi on December 10th, 1991—the date for which he was convicted.

6. Although this data was not used as evidence (it was the Custom Service data that was ultimately used as evidence), the Drug Enforcement Administration data was used in determining the relationship between gross and net weights in the Custom Service data.

7. There are in fact two issues here: the choice of reference class and the specificity of the evidence. These issues can, of course, come apart. For example, consider a case where the reference class in question consists of patterns of an individual's past behavior. Evidence obtained from such a reference class, we take it, would pass for specific evidence, but would still suffer from concerns about the choice of reference class. Evidence obtained from the reference class in the Shonubi case, however, was clearly nonspecific, since it arose from data collected from individuals other than Shonubi. For the most part, our discussion focuses on the reference-class issue although our concerns are motivated by the nonspecific nature of the class used at *Shonubi III*. (We discuss the specific evidence issue in more detail toward the end of this section.)

8. Of course the reference class used to derive the statistics at *Shonubi III* presupposed Shonubi's guilt and indeed his guilt seems beyond question. The point remains, however, that if we accept such statistical evidence and such evidence could be obtained without presupposing his guilt, that data would, it seems, suffice for a conviction.

9. Actually Tillers (1998) does discuss this issue briefly but he doesn't pursue it because he does not believe that this is the reason for the Second Circuit Court's rejection of the customs service data.

10. Note that it is not simply a question of getting the reference classes tight enough. That is, it's not just a question of specifying enough predicates to be jointly satisfied so that the reference class in question contains very few (but nonzero) members. The size of the reference class is irrelevant (unless it contains just Shonubi); we require homogeneity of the class and this, in general, has nothing to do with its size.

11. We thank an anonymous referee for this and the next suggestion.

12. See Resnik 1987 for a brief introduction to some of the different interpretations of probability.

13. For instance, recall Tiller's second passage above where he suggests that the request by the Second Circuit Court for specific evidence was "nonsensical" and that the rejection of the statistical evidence in this case may amount to "a blanket condemnation of statistics and statistical methods" (Tillers 1998).

14. See Hájek 1997, Jeffrey 1992, and Papineau 1995 for criticisms of frequency interpretations of probability. See Carnap 1945 for the suggestion that there are two distinct conceptions of probability.

15. See Beebee and Papineau 1997, Lewis 1986, Reichenbach 1949, Kyburg 1974, and Mellor 1971 for the related issue of how degrees of belief should be constrained by objective chance.

16. We owe this point to Phil Dowe (unpublished). See also Hájek forthcoming and Ayer 1972 (pp. 54–88).

17. See van Fraassen 1980 and Cartwright 1983 for some of these.

18. We should point out that economic evidence was also rejected as nonspecific by the Second Circuit Court. It is not clear what this evidence consisted of, but if it was the kind of evidence we are suggesting here, we would, in this instance, disagree with the Second Circuit Court's decision.

19. Of course, we may choose to use some other decision-theory rule such as maximin or minimax regret. We discuss these shortly. For the moment let's stick with maximizing expected utility.

20. Of course, the idea of Justice as an agent with a relevant utility function raises all sorts of issues: what is Justice?; can we really think of Justice as an agent?; how do we access Justice's utility function?

21. This uncertainty has a striking resemblance to what is often called "model uncertainty" in mathematical modelling. When one is using a mathematical model of a complex system to make predictions about that system, no matter how high the probabilities delivered by the model, there remain questions over the reliability of the model itself. More precisely, there is uncertainty surrounding the assumptions on which the model is based and it is notoriously difficult to quantify such uncertainties.

22. See Mayo (forthcoming) for more on the relationship between meta-uncertainty and decisions with a moral dimension.

23. This publication reflects discussions held while Mark Colyvan was visiting the United States for research supported in part by a University of Tasmania Industry Collaborative Research Grant and by a Small Business Innovation Research grant to Applied Biomathematics from the National Cancer Institute (9R44CA81741). Any opinions, findings, conclusions, or recommendations expressed in this publication are those of the authors and do not necessarily reflect the views of the National Cancer Institute. Earlier versions of this paper were presented to: the School of Philosophy at the University of Tasmania; the Philosophy Program of the Research School of Social Sciences at the Australian National University; the Department of Philosophy at Macquarie University; the Department of Statistics and Applied Probability at the University of California, Santa Barbara; and the Science, Ethics, and Public Policy Seminar Series at the California Institute of Technology. We would like to thank the participants in the subsequent discussions for their valuable contributions. We are also indebted to Phil Dowe, Alan Hájek, and Peter Menzies for useful conversations and corre-

spondence and to several anonymous referees for their insightful comments on an earlier draft of this paper.

REFERENCES

Ayer, A. J. 1972. *Probability and Evidence.* New York: Columbia University Press.

Beebee, H., and D. Papineau. 1997. "Probability as a Guide to Life." *Journal of Philosophy:* 217–43.

Carnap, R. 1945. "The Two Concepts of Probability." *Philosophy and Phenomenological Research* 5: 513–32.

Cartwright, N. 1983. *How the Laws of Physics Lie.* Oxford: Clarendon.

Dowe, P. Unpublished. "A Dilemma for Objective Chance." Paper read to the Australasian Association of Philosophy Conference at the University of Queensland, July 1992.

Gastwirth, J. L., B. Freidlin, and W. Miao. 2000. "The Shonubi Case as an Example of the Legal System's Failure to Appreciate Statistical Evidence." In *Statistical Science in the Courtroom,* ed. J. L. Gastwirth, pp. 405–14. New York: Springer-Verlag.

Hájek, A. 1997. "'Mises Redux'—Redux: Fifteen Arguments Against Finite Frequentism." *Erkenntnis* 45: 209–27.

———. Forthcoming. "Conditional Probability is the Guide of Life." In *Probability is the Very Guide of Life,* ed. H. E. Kyburg and M. Thalos. Chicago: Open Court.

Izenman, A. J. 2000. "Introduction to Two Views on the Shonubi Case." In *Statistical Science in the Courtroom,* ed. J. L. Gastwirth, pp. 393–404. New York: Springer-Verlag.

———. 2000a. "Assessing the Statistical Evidence in the Shonubi Case." In *Statistical Science in the Courtroom,* ed. J. L. Gastwirth, pp. 415–43. New York: Springer-Verlag.

Jeffrey, R. C. 1983. *The Logic of Decision.* Chicago: University of Chicago Press.

———. 1992. "Mises Redux." Reprinted in *Probability and the Art of Judgement,* Cambridge: Cambridge University Press, pp. 192–202.

Kyburg, H. E. 1974. *The Logical Foundations of Statistical Inference.* Dordrecht: Reidel.

Lewis, D. 1986. "A Subjectivist's Guide to Objective Chance." Reprinted in *Philosophical Papers,* vol. 2, D. Lewis, pp. 83–113. Oxford: Oxford University Press.

Mayo, D. G. Forthcoming. "Uncertainty and Values in the Responsible Interpretation of Risk Evidence: Beyond Clean Hands vs. Dirty Hands." *Risk Analysis.*

Mellor, D. H. 1971. *The Matter of Chance.* New York: Cambridge University Press.

Papineau, D. 1995. "Probabilities and the Many-Minds Interpretation of Quantum Mechanics." *Analysis* 55: 239–46.

Reichenbach, H. 1949. *The Theory of Probability: An Inquiry into the Logical and Mathematical Foundations of the Calculus of Probability.* Berkeley: University of California Press.

Resnik, M. D. 1987. *Choices: An Introduction to Decision Theory.* Minneapolis: University of Minnesota Press.

Tillers, P. 1997. "Introduction: Three Contributions to Three Important Problems in Evidence Scholarship." *Cardozo Law Review* 18: 1875–89.

———. 1998. "United States v. Shonubi: A Statistical Oddity?" 1 February 2003 <http://www.tillers.net/shonubi.html>.

Tribe, L. H. 1971. "Trial by Mathematics: Precision and Ritual in the Legal Process." *Harvard Law Review* 84: 1329–93.

van Fraassen, B. C. 1980. *The Scientific Image.* Oxford: Clarendon.

von Mises, R. 1957. *Probability Truth and Statistics.* 2nd ed. London: Macmillan.

CASES CITED

United States v. Shonubi: Shonubi V: 962 F.Supp. 370 (E.D.N.Y. 1997); *Shonubi IV:* 103 F.3d 1085 (2d Cir. 1997); *Shonubi III:* 895 F.Supp. 460 (E.D.N.Y. 1995); *Shonubi II:* 998 F.2d 84 (2d Cir. 1993); *Shonubi I*: 802 F.Supp. 859 (E.D.N.Y. 1992).

16

Explaining Things Probabilistically

WESLEY C. SALMON

This contribution was one of the last things Wesley Salmon wrote before his untimely accidental death in April 2001. Salmon was among the first people we asked to contribute to our Monist *issue on Probability as a Guide in Life, since he was among the best known, most respected, and most frequent contributors to issues involving probability, statistics, and explanation. In his contribution, he focused on the question of whether legitimate explanations of particular facts even exist. Salmon concludes that these explanations can be legitimate only if a highly intuitive principle—that if C explains an event of type E it cannot explain an occurrence of type E′ incompatible with E. For example, if treatment with penicillin explains recovery in one instance, it cannot also explain the lack of recovery in another instance. Salmon provides a number of examples that serve to throw doubt on this seemingly intuitive principle, while at the same time allowing that some people might prefer to forgo statistical explanations rather than sacrifice the principle.*

[—The Editors]

* * *

Human beings crave explanations of all sorts of things. If "probability is our very guide of life," then probability must play a crucial role in explanation. There are, of course, many types of explanations, and scientific explanations are no doubt in the minority; nevertheless, they are sometimes enormously important. Carl G. Hempel and Paul Oppenheim's 1948 classic, "Studies in the Logic of Explanation," characterized one form of *deductive* explanation with considerable precision, as well as another, which they dealt with much less formally. They also explicitly acknowledged the need for statistical laws and *statistical* forms of scientific explanation (1965 [1948], pp. 250–51), a topic lying beyond the scope of that essay.

Hempel's magisterial "Aspects of Scientific Explanation" (1965, pp. 331–496), included detailed treatments of two types of statistical explanation, as well as the two types of deductive explanation treated in the 1948 article. In his "covering law" conception of scientific explanation, Hempel distinguished deductive-nomological (D-N) explanations, which involve subsumption under universal laws of nature, from statistical explanations, which involve subsumption under statistical laws. In both of these categories, he distinguished explanations of particular facts (or events)[1] from those of general regularities. Thus, under the heading of statistical explanation, he distinguished between inductive-statistical (I-S) explanations of particulars and deductive-statistical (D-S) explanations of statistical regularities. Although I see no philosophically interesting distinction between D-N and D-S explanations of regularities by deduction from regularities of broader scope, I shall retain Hempel's distinction between the two types for purposes of the present discussion.

Although all four types of covering law explanation have been objects of severe criticism, I shall not dwell on these critiques here. A detailed survey can be found in Salmon 1990. In this essay, I am interested in comparing statistical explanations of statistical generalizations with statistical explanations of particular facts; indeed, I shall examine the question of whether legitimate explanations of this latter sort even exist. Let me make it clear from the outset that I am *not* confining my attention to Hempel's I-S model; the question addresses *any* form of statistical explanation of particular facts.

Hempel's discussion of D-S explanation occupies slightly more than one page (1965, pp. 380–81). In the concluding paragraph, he writes, "Ultimately, however, statistical laws are meant to be applied to particular occurrences and to establish explanatory and predictive connections among them" (p. 381). The following section, dealing with I-S explanation, occupies 32 pages. This discrepancy in size results from two considerations, I think. First, as Hempel makes amply clear, the introduction of inductive arguments in place of deductive arguments brings with it a host of difficulties. About this factor there can be no doubt. It also signifies, I believe, Hempel's conviction that I-S explanations are more important than those of D-S form. The word "ultimately" in the sentence quoted above reinforces this impression.

Hempel's construction of the I-S model is based on a close analogy with D-N explanations of particular facts. A D-N explanation of any fact is a deductive *argument* showing that the fact to be explained—the explanandum—was necessary, given the explanatory facts. An I-S explanation is an inductive *argument* showing that the explanandum is highly probable, given the explanatory facts. Hempel included both forms in the general characterization of an explanation of any particular fact as "an argument to the effect that the event to be explained was to be expected in view of the explanatory facts" (1962a, p. 10).

Hempel clearly recognized that the introduction of inductive arguments entailed serious consequences. He saw, for example, that the requirement of total evidence, which is normally imposed on inductive arguments, would be disastrous for explanation, because we usually know that a particular event has already occurred before we try to explain it. Thus, under the requirement of total evidence, the explanandum is already part of our background knowledge, so it would also appear in the explanans. The argument would therefore be trivially deductive. It would not even qualify as a D-N explanation, because whatever law might have been invoked would not occur *essentially* in the explanans. Total evidence must be cut back in some appropriate fashion. His *requirement of maximal specificity* was designed to do that job.

Hempel also identified a problem that he called *the ambiguity of I-S explanation.* He illustrates the problem by means of a now-famous example, offering two I-S explanations with mutually compatible premises that lead to contradictory conclusions. In one case, the conclusion is that a patient recovers quickly from a streptococcus infection; in the other case, the conclusion is that the same patient does not recover quickly from the infection. This sort of situation can never arise with deductive explanations. If two deductive arguments have mutually contradictory conclusions, they must have mutually inconsistent premises. Hempel asks how we can decide which of the two explanations is the correct one. He did not notice an extraordinarily simple answer, namely, the correct explanatory argument is the one that has a true conclusion. We can simply ascertain whether the recovery was quick or not. The fact that Hempel overlooked this answer suggests, correctly, I think, that he was actually troubled by a different question. Alberto Coffa (1974) pointed this out and suggested that the really troubling difficulty is the choice of a reference class for the statistical law that is invoked.

Another obvious difficulty arises from Hempel's *high probability requirement,* namely, how high is high enough? Any choice among the plausible values seems highly arbitrary. Richard Jeffrey (1969) recognized that the magnitude of the probability has nothing to do with the goodness of an explanation. He pointed to typical cases in which there are two possible outcomes, one having a high probability, the other having a low probability. What is important, he emphasized, is that the two outcomes are produced by the same stochastic mechanism, and when we understand that mechanism we understand outcomes of both types equally well. When we look at the situation in this way, we see, as Jeffrey emphasized, that statistical explanations—in many cases, at least—are not arguments. The view that they are arguments was so deeply ingrained in the received view of explanation that one could designate it as *the third dogma of empiricism.*

My immediate response to Hempel's I-S model was that *statistical relevance*, rather than high probability, is the key to statistical explanation. This recognition led me to advocate the statistical-relevance (S-R) model of explanation (Salmon 1971). The basic idea can be sketched as follows. To explain a particular fact, one begins with an initial reference class to which it belongs. In Hempel's example, the individual in question belongs to the class of people with strep infections. He explains the quick recovery by citing the fact that this person was treated with penicillin. Thus, he partitions the initial class into two subclasses, namely, those treated with penicillin and those not so treated. Those treated with penicillin have a high probability (but not quite certainty) of quick recovery; for those who do not receive penicillin the probability is much lower. However, an additional relevant factor is lurking in the background. Some strep infections are penicillin-resistant, while others are not. Therefore, a further partition should be imposed on the initial reference class. As I read it, Hempel's *requirement of maximal specificity* is intended to demand that an I-S explanation incorporate all relevant information that is in principle available prior to the occurrence of the event to be explained. If the probability is high enough—how high remains a mystery—then the explanation is successful.

The S-R model requires that all *and only* relevant factors be included in the explanans, but it does not require that the probability of the explanandum relative to the explanans be high. The basic difference can be seen in examples similar in principle to Hempel's strep example. Suppose a person who had been troubled by a neurotic symptom undergoes psychotherapy and experiences relief from the symptom during the course of treatment. Suppose further that those who undergo the treatment in question have a high probability of relief. It is tempting to say that the treatment explains the relief; however, if the probability of relief with the treatment is equal to the spontaneous remission rate for that particular problem, it is misleading—to say the least—to claim that the treatment explains the cure. Thus, a high probability is not *sufficient* for a legitimate statistical explanation.

Henry Kyburg (1965) cleverly pointed out that the same problem of explanatory irrelevance applies even to D-N explanations. My own favorite example, which has the same fundamental character as Kyburg's, is the case of the man who explains his failure to become pregnant on the basis of his regular consumption of his wife's birth control pills. Since human males—in contrast to male sea horses—cannot become pregnant, the consumption of oral contraceptives is statistically and explanatorily irrelevant.

Psychotherapy can also be invoked to show that high probability is not *necessary* for statistical explanation. Consider a different person with a different psychological problem. Even though the probability of recovery under treatment may be small (less than one-half), if it is appreciably higher than the spontaneous remission rate for that particular problem, the treatment is at least part of the explanation of recovery. In this case, the treatment is statistically and explanatorily relevant. So, statistical relevance, not high probability, is the key to statistical explanation. I later argued that S-R explanations require causal underpinning as well, but this fact is beside the point for present purposes.

There is a strong temptation to consider the foregoing explanations of recovery from strep infections and neurotic symptoms as incomplete because of our ignorance of additional relevant factors and to suppose that, with more complete knowledge, we could construct D-N explanations of the phenomena in question. Indeed, this reference to our knowledge situation and our possible ignorance of relevant factors led Hempel to enunciate his thesis of *essential epistemic relativity of I-S explanation*. From this principle Coffa and I concluded that ultimately, for Hempel, there is no such thing as a genuine I-S explanation; what is disguised as statistical explanation of particular facts is actually incomplete D-N explanation. An I-S explanation is an enthymeme; when you supply the missing premises you have, not a valid enthymeme, but a valid deductive argument.

To avoid this thicket of problems, let us turn to an example that has a good chance of being irreducibly statistical. Its statistical character results not from our ignorance but from the physical features of the situation. Carbon-14, which is widely used by archaeologists and others to date remains of living materials, has a half-life of 5,730 years. This means that any given C^{14} atom has a probability of one-half of decaying in that period of time and a probability of three-quarters of decaying in 11,460 years. According to our best current theories, there is no further factor that determines which atom will decay and which will not. If a C^{14} atom does decay within 11,460 years, the advocate of I-S explanation might accept 3/4 as a probability large enough for such an explanation; if not, we can obviously extend the time period so as to reach a probability of decay that is acceptably large—as close to unity as anyone might wish. But let's stick with 11,460 years for purposes of illustration. As Jeffrey incisively pointed out, if we claim the ability to explain the decay of one atom of C^{14}, it would be strange to deny that we understand the fact that another such atom remained intact for the same period. In each case, the stochastic mechanism is the same; it generates one kind of result in a majority of cases and another kind of result in a minority of cases. To say that we understand one, but not the other, seems to be a manifestation of a strange sort of prejudice. Though the majority may rule, to use a political metaphor, the rights of minorities must not be infringed.

This consideration brings us face-to-face with a fundamental philosophical principle that has been stated explicitly by many authors, and is, I believe, held implicitly by many others. Let us call it Principle 1:

> If, in one instance, circumstances of type C explain an occurrence of type E, then, in another instance, circumstances of the same type C cannot explain an occurrence of a different type E′, where type E′ is incompatible with type E.

However, if we agree that we have an explanation of the decay of a C^{14} atom in a period of 11,460 years, and then, applying the Jeffrey symmetry principle, conclude that we have an equally good explanation of the fact that another C^{14} atom remained intact during the same period, we have obviously violated Principle 1. This conflict is not to be taken lightly.

A return to Hempel's I-S model and its high-probability requirement is not tempting. There are, it seems to me, two apparently viable alternatives. On the one hand, we can reject Principle 1, counterintuitive as this may appear. This is the approach I have opted for. On the other hand, we can deny that there are any statistical explanations of particular facts. Following this path, we can say that science provides us with statistical laws, some of which can be explained by derivation from more fundamental statistical laws, but it cannot explain particular occurrences. In informal discussion, Ronald Giere elegantly phrased this approach as follows: Science explains how the world works, but it doesn't explain what happens. This is tantamount to admitting Hempel's D-S model, but rejecting the I-S model, the S-R model, or any other pattern of statistical explanation of particular events.

Before embracing this second alternative, we should take into consideration the use of statistics in dealing with large, but finite, collections. For example, Giere (1997, pp. 210–12) offers a clear account of a famous Canadian study of the effects of saccharin on the incidence of bladder cancer in rats. In the first stage of the study, bladder cancer occurred in more members of the experimental group (which ingested saccharin) than in the control group (which received no saccharin), but the difference was too small to be considered statistically significant. The difference could have been due to chance. In the second stage of the experiment, the incidence in the experimental group was sufficiently higher than that in the control group for the experimenters to conclude that the ingestion of saccharin was very probably the cause of bladder cancer in that group. In the opinion of the experimenters, the ingestion of saccharin explained the bladder cancer in the rats that fell victim to that disease. If my interpretation is correct, the ingestion of saccharin explains the occurrence of bladder cancer in individual rats and its incidence in a finite group. A statistical distribution in a finite sample is not a *general regularity* — it is essentially a single case. Of course, an inductive inference was made on the basis of this study, so one could maintain that the result is the statistical regularity that ingestion of saccharin in certain dosages causes bladder cancer in a certain percentage of rats.

I should like to mention a second example drawn from my own experience. Many years ago, I was hired as a consultant on a study of the effects of alcohol on human subjects. Vast quantities of data were gathered, and thousands of coefficients of correlation were calculated. My colleagues (who, along with the institutions that supported this research, will remain unnamed) searched the results for coefficients of correlation that were significant at the 0.05 and 0.01 levels, fixing upon them as indicative of important findings. My analysis of the data showed that about one out of twenty coefficients of correlation was significant at the 0.05 level and about one in a hundred at the 0.01 level. Where they saw scientifically meaningful (possibly causal) relationships, I saw mere statistical fluctuations, attributable to chance. We were offering conflicting statistical explanations of finite collections of outcomes. The issue had considerable practical importance regarding funding for further research and the continuation of the project.

By dogged determination, it may be possible to carry through the argument that, in theoretical science, all statistical explanations are explanations of statistical regularities rather than particular facts. For example, Davisson and Germer were puzzled by the distribution of electrons recoiling from nickel crystals. Their experiment involved a finite number of electrons, but the quantum-mechanical explanation of their observed data applied to the behavior of all electrons diffracted by crystals.

I do not believe that this viewpoint can be upheld in fields of applied science. In Salmon 1978, I discussed "operation Smoky," a case in which military personnel witnessed atomic bomb tests at relatively close range. The test was conducted in 1957; twenty years later the incidence of leukemia among the participants was found to be markedly higher than in the population at large. The statistical explanation of these particular cases of leukemia was that they were the result of radiation to which the participants were exposed during the test. We should note that the probabilities involved are small—among the 2,235 soldiers participating in the test, eight contracted leukemia. More recently, many cases have been tried in the courts in the U.S.A., claiming damages from cigarette manufacturers for lung cancer victims. States, as well as individuals or groups of individuals, are bringing these legal actions. States, for example, are suing to compensate for medical expenses they have incurred as a result of cigarette smoking *in their own finite populations.* The general pattern is clear; decisions must frequently be made on statistical grounds to assign responsibility for given outcomes in particular cases.

My opponent may, however, protest my violation of Principle 1. We will be reminded of Molière's famous example involving the 'dormitive virtue' of opium. However, we do not need Principle 1 to protect us from such pseudo-explanations. To say that opium produces sleep because of its dormitive virtue is a tautology, so it cannot have (scientific) explanatory power. Laws invoked in scientific explanations must have empirical content.

Next, we will be reminded that the will of God is often invoked to 'explain' whatever happens. Again, I would reply that we do not need Principle 1 to protect us; it is sufficient to point out that the 'law' in this case is untestable, so it cannot have scientific status. Indeed, I should say that the principle that *whatever* happens is because of the will of God is also essentially a tautology, so it cannot have (scientific) explanatory import.

Finally, psychoanalytic 'explanations' of filial behavior may be cited. Because of the Oedipus complex, boys are supposed to have great animosity toward their fathers. This 'explains' hostile attitudes and behavior. If, however, a boy behaves affectionately toward his father, this is 'explained' as a reaction formation. The child so fears his hostility that he cannot manifest it; consequently, he behaves in the opposite manner. The law involved in this example is not a tautology; neutral or indifferent behavior is an unexplained possibility. But the much more serious question is whether there is sufficient empirical evidence to accept the law—or theory—involved in this example. Even if we do not confer scientific status on psychoanalytic theory, it still makes sense to ask for evidence that it is true. Again, Principle 1 is not required.

Abandoning Principle 1, I feel no compunction at saying that the theory of radioactive decay explains why one atom of C^{14} decays in a given period of time, while another identical atom in exactly the same relevant circumstances remains intact for the same period of time. After a rather extensive review of the literature on scientific explanation, and after considerable thought about the question, I have not found any convincing reason for retaining Principle 1 if our world is genuinely indeterministic. Twentieth-century science gave us strong—though perhaps not absolutely conclusive—reason to believe that it is. We should, it seems to me, keep open the possibility that modern physics is right regarding this issue. The theme of this volume is *probability as a guide of life.* In this context, it is unthinkable to confine attention entirely to theoretical science. In life, we seek explanations of individual events and of limited collections of events. We do so for many reasons, often to bring about desirable states of affairs and prevent undesirable ones, but sometimes just to satisfy natural human curiosity about particular facts. As Antoine Arnauld (1964, p. 330) said so succinctly, "Our minds are unsatisfied unless they know not only *that* a thing is but *why* it is." We have seen, however, that if we are to fulfill our practical needs and satisfy this intellectual hunger in an age that demands statistical explanations of particular facts, we must relinquish a time-honored philosophical maxim.

WESLEY C. SALMON
University of Pittsburgh
and Kyoto University

NOTES

1. From this point on, I shall construe "fact" as including events within its denotation. No distinction between facts and events will have any real bearing on the following discussion.

REFERENCES

Arnauld, Antoine. 1964. *The Art of Thinking*. Indianapolis: Bobbs-Merrill.

Coffa, J. Alberto. 1974 "Hempel's Ambiguity." *Synthese* 28: 141–63.

Giere, Ronald. 1997. *Understanding Scientific Reasoning*. 4th ed. Fort Worth, Texas: Harcourt Brace.

Hempel, Carl G. 1962. "Explanation in Science and in History."In *Frontiers of Science and Philosophy*, ed. Robert G. Colodny, pp. 7–34. Pittsburgh: University of Pittsburgh Press,

———.1965. *Aspects of Scientific Explanation and Other Essays in the Philosophy of Science*. New York: Free Press.

Hempel, Carl G., and Paul Oppenheim. 1948. "Studies in the Logic of Explanation." *Philosophy of Science* 15: 135–75. Reprinted in Hempel 1965.

Jeffrey, Richard C. 1969. "Statistical Explanation vs. Statistical Inference." In *Essays in Honor of Carl G. Hempel*, ed. Nicholas Rescher, pp. 104–13. Dordrecht: D. Reidel. Reprinted in Salmon 1971.

Kyburg, Henry. 1965. "Comment." *Philosophy of Science* 32: 147–51.

Salmon, Wesley C. 1971. *Statistical Explanation and Statistical Relevance*. Pittsburgh: University of Pittsburgh Press.

———. 1978. "Why Ask, 'Why?'? An Inquiry Concerning Scientific Explanation." *Proceedings and Addresses of the American Philosophical Association* 51: 683–705.

———. 1990. *Four Decades of Scientific Explanation*. Minneapolis: University of Minnesota Press.

Index

ability attributions
  and closest-world semantics, 76
  and kinds of trials, 76
ability predicates, 65–67
AGM revision, 80–81
Alchourrón, C., 72
altruism, 165, 178–80
approximate distribution claims, 249–50, 251
Aristotle, x, xvi, 53
Arnauld, Antoine, 357
Ayer, A. J., 43, 44, 53–54

Batterman, R., 153, 161
Bayes, Thomas, 38, 238
Bayesianism, xv–xvi, 123–24, 135, 136, 145
  and decision theory, 141–42
  and frequentism, 120
  problem of, 132
  as violating probability calculus, 124
Bayes nets, 253–54, 266, 271
  and causation, 254–56, 260
  and caveats on causes, 260
Bayes-nets methods, 254, 266
  and prima-facie causes, 267
Bayes's theorem, 91, 92, 123, 125, 130–31, 133
  problem for, 129
belief
  as decision making, xv
  as wagering, xiii–xiv, xv
Bentham, Jeremy, xv
Berkeley, George, 70
Bernoulli, Daniel, xiv, 244
Bernoulli, James, 38, 70
  Ars Conjectandi, 75
Bernoulli, Nicolas, xiv
Bernoulli's theorem, 38–39, 41–42, 245
Bertrand, Jean Louis François, 187, 189
Blyth, C. R., 165
Boscovitch, Roger, 242, 243–44, 245, 246, 247
Braithewaite, Richard, 235
Broad, C. D., 34, 52, 53
brute-force connections, 255
Buchdahl, Gerd, 254
Butler, Bishop J., 136, 142, 155, 206, 218
Butterfield, J., 153

calculus of probability, 121
carbon-14, 353, 356
Cardano, Giralamo, xi
Carnap, Rudolf, xii, xiii, xvi, 91, 138, 141, 144, 145, 146, 188, 189, 193, 279
Carroll, J., 207, 215–17, 227

Cartwright, Nancy, 165, 166, 212, 301, 309, 315–18, 322–24
Casscells, W., 120
Cassini, Jacques, 242, 247
causal decision theory, 206, 218–19, 221–22, 226
causal generalizations, 205, 212
  and generic sentences, 215–17
  and good advice, 226–27
  as guide to life, 206, 220
  and subjectivity, 227
causal inference, difficulty of, 176–77
causality/causation
  actual, 207–8
    narrow, 208–9
    wide, 208–9
  antireductionist view, 301, 308–15, 318–22
  asymmetry of, 310–11
  and background conditions, 212–13
  bootstrapping method, 312, 315
  and cancellations, 258, 264–65
  caveats to, 266
  and common causes, 321
  and contextual unanimity condition, 212
  deep structure of, 308–9, 313
  deeper structure of, 308–9, 313
  and dependence, 267–72
  and dispositional properties, 65
  and explanation, xvii
  finer grain structure, 309, 314
  general/type-level, 207
  the how of, 318–31
  in macroeconomics, 264
  metaphysics of, 299
  negative, 301, 302
  prima facie, 256, 260, 263
  probabilistic accounts/analyses of, xvi–xvii, 177–78, 205, 209–12, 213, 253, 272, 301, 303–4, 305
  and probabilistic dependence, 255–72
  reductionist views of, xvi, 298–99, 300–301, 305–6, 308–25
  and screening off, 310
  semantic view, 297
  singular/token, 207
  tendencies, 207
    narrow, 208–9
    wide, 208–9
causal Markov condition, 254, 269, 270
causal minimal condition, 254
causal processes, 302–3
causal relevance, as primitive relation, 210
causal tendencies, 207–8
causation. *See* causality/causation
cause and effect, as category, 296–97
causes. *See also* causality/causation
  as chance-raisers, 299
  as objective chances, 302
Caws, Peter, 44
centering condition, 75
chance
  and chaos theory, 160–61
  as conditional, 237
  counterfeit, 157–58
  and determinism, 157–58, 159
  dilemma of, 153–54
  objective, 154–55, 157–62
  relative to perception, 159–60
chaos theory, and chance, 160–61
Church, Alonzo, 186
classical syllogism, 39
Coffa, J. Alberto, 24, 351, 353
Cohen, M. R., 166
common cause, 268
conceivability criterion, of logical possibility, 35
conditional judgments
  and closest-world semantics, 76
  and dispositionability statements, 82
  of modality, 77–78, 79
  and truth-values, 77–78
conditionals
  and closest-world semantics, 72, 74
  consistency-preserving, 79–81
    and truth values, 81
  and dispositions/abilities, 73–78

as modal judgments, 71–72
as nonmonotonic, 73
truth conditions for, 70–71
and truth-values, 72, 73
contextual unanimity requirement, 212, 217
Cosmides, Leda, 120, 121, 123, 125–26, 127–29, 133
problem for, 129–31
Cotes, Roger, 241

data analysis, methods of, 241
Davidson, Donald, 67
Davisson, Clinton Joseph, 355
decision theory, xv
and Bayesianism, 141–42
and chance, 153
and degrees of belief, 153
and utilities, 340–41
decision under risk, theory of, xi
deductive inference
defense of, 36
as monotonic, 36
deductive-nomological (D-N) explanations, 350–51, 352, 353
deductive-statistical (D-S) explanations, 350
de Finetti, Bruno, xii, 84, 138, 191
DeMoivre, 238
density principle, and single-case probability, 24
Descartes, René, x, xvi, 49, 295
determinism, and probability, 75
diminishing marginal utility of money, xiv
direct inference, 39
epistemic symmetry in, 52
and fair sampling, 47–49, 50
and the future, 53–54
and judgments of serious possibility, 84
and the modal barrier, 52–55
objections to, 37–38, 43–44
and randomness, 45–46, 48–49
rationality of, 52
and representative samples, 46
and sample spaces, 64
and thesis of linear attrition, 44, 54–55
disciplinary reasoning, xv–xvi
Disjunctive Normal Form, 144
disposition predicates, 65–67
placeholder view of, 67–68, 73
dispositions
and closest-world semantics, 72–73, 74
as monotonic, 73–74
Dretske, Fred, 43–44
Dudman, V., 71, 76
Dupré, J., 212, 213, 214, 222, 227, 228
dynamic rationality, 155–56
dilemma of, 156

Earman, John, 136, 142, 153–54
A Primer on Determinism, 154
Eells, Ellery, 207, 212, 214, 217, 227, 278, 281
Einstein, Albert, 130, 132, 200, 300, 306, 307
Empiricus, Sextus, 41
error probabilities, 90, 93
errors, and probability density function, 286–87
error statistical account, 90
essential epistemic relativity of I-S explanations, 353
Euler, Leonhard, 241, 246
evidential decision theory, 218
expected utility, xiv
doctrine of, xv
explanation
and causality, xvii
purpose of, 12
types of, 349–50
explanation-seeking why-questions, 13

fair sampling, 46
and chance, problems of, 47
faithfulness, in cause/effect, 256, 260, 261, 263, 264, 265
fallibility, x

Fermat, Pierre de, 137
Fetzer, James, 278, 280, 281
  Scientific Knowledge, 283, 288
Finite-Frequency Theory, 127
Fisher, R. A., 218
Ford, J., 161
Foster, John, 43, 44
freedom, and deliberation, 53
frequentism. *See* probability: frequency interpretation
Frequentist Hypothesis, 121
Friedman, Michael, 47
Frigg, Roman, 258–59

Gambler's Fallacy, 249
games of chance, 137
  and degree of belief, 138
Gärdenfors, P., 72
Gastwirth, J. L., 341
Gauss, Karl Friedrich, 244, 287
Germer, Lester H., 355
Gibbard, A., 76
Giere, Ronald, 190, 278, 354
Gigerenzer, Gerd, 121
Gillies, Donald, 161, 283, 288
  Philosophical Theories of Probability, 277
Gisin, N., 153
Glymour, Clark, 256, 260, 261, 267, 268, 270, 305
Goldstein, Michael, 193, 247
goods, xv
Grable, Betty, 283
Graboys, T. B., 120
Granger, C., 256
Guilford, J., 247–48
  Psychometric Methods, 247

Hacking, Ian, 103, 283
Hao Wang, 50
Harman, Gilbert, 146
Harper, Bill, 183
Hausman, Daniel, 269
Hempel, Carl G., 4, 27, 349–50, 353
  critique of, 22–24
  and determinism, 25
  on D-S explanations, 350–51
  epistemic explanation in, 23–24
  high probability requirement, 351
  on inductive arguments, 351
  on I-S explanations, 350–51
  maximally specific predicate, 20
  revised explication in, 25
  revised requirement of maximal specificity, 20–21
  and single-case problem, 23
  and statistical ambiguity, 21–22
  on statistical explanation, 19
  on statistical relevance, 19, 22
Herodotus, 55
Hesslow, G., 258
heuristics, 120
Hild, Matthias, 191
Hitchcock, C., 207
Holmes, Sherlock, 145
Hoover, Kevin, 264
Horowitz, Vladimir, 284
Howson, Colin, 38, 143
Hume, David, ix–x, xv, xvi, 65, 205, 271, 298, 312
  Abstract, 35
  on causality, xvi, 296
  dilemma in, 50
  Enquiry Concerning Human Understanding, x, xvi, 35
  on inductive inference, 33–35, 37
    response to, 42
  influence of, 34
  on probability, 238
    response to, 52
  on probable arguments, 35
  problem of induction, 295
Humphreys, P. , 212
Hunt, G., 161
Husserl, Edmund, 296
Huygens, Christiaan, xi, xiii, xiv

if-sentences, as disposition statements, 71
indeterminism, 356
induction/inductive inference
  criticisms of, 50

defense of, 42
and guarantee of success, 51–52
justification of, 51
as logic of confirmation, 91
and nonmonotonicity, 36
and probability, 89–92, 93
problems of, 34–35, 36, 38, 47
and rationality, 51
and reference classes, 37–38
as severe testing, 90, 95–97, 102–3, 107
skeptical challenges to, 36–37
inductive arguments, and high probability requirements, 25–26
inductive behavior, statistical tests as guide for, 94–95
inductive inference. *See* induction/inductive inference
inductive learning, error statistics as guide to, 95
inductive-statistical (I-S), explanations, 350–51
inference
Bayesian, 38–39
direct, 37–38, 39, 43, 44, 45–46, 47–49, 50, 52–55, 64, 84
and guarantee of success, 51–52
inductive, 34–38, 42, 50–52, 89
inverse, 38–39
and rationality, 51
inference to the absence of error, 101
insurance, probability in, xi, 284–86, 292
inverse inference, 38–39
critics of, 38
irreducibility, 154
Irzik, Gurol, 311, 315
Izenman, A. J., 341

Jaynes, E. T., 138
Jeffrey, Richard, 218, 220, 351, 353
Jeffreys, Harold, 138
Jones, R., 161
judging possibility/impossibility, and belief transformation, 79
judgments of serious possibility, grounding of, 83–84

Kadane, Jay, 235
Kahneman, D., 120
Kant, Immanuel, xvi, 295–96
Kelly, Kevin, 235
Keynes, John Maynard
Treatise on Probability, 146
Kneale, W. L., 157
Kolmogorov, A. N., 195, 198
Foundations of Probability, 62
on objective probability, 63
Kolmogorov probability theory, 183
Krips, H., 153, 161
Kyburg, Henry, 45–46, 84, 161, 235, 352

Laplace, Pierre Simon, xi, xii, 70, 138, 244, 245
learning from errors, 102–3
least squares method, 241, 244, 245, 247
Legendre, Adrien Marie, 241, 242, 244
Leibniz, Gottfried Wilhelm, x, xvi
Levi, Isaac, 45, 46, 47, 158
Lewis, David, 72, 73, 74, 75, 154, 157, 161, 183, 192–93, 222–23, 297
on chance, 158–59
on counterfeit chance, 158
on objective chance, 158–59
Locke, John, 251
logic of confirmation, 89, 91

Mackie, J. L.
The Cement of the Universe, 297
Maimonides, 136
Makinson, D., 72
Malebranche, Nicolas, xvi
Mayer, Johann, 241, 246
Mayo, Deborah, 141
Mellor, D. H., 153, 154, 156, 157–58, 159, 161, 297
on chance, revised view, 159–60

The Matter of Chance, 157–58, 159–60
Mere, Chevalier de la, 137
Mill, John Stuart, xv, 70
Miller, David W., 283
modal direct inference, problem of, 82
modularity, 269
Molière, Jean Baptiste, 356
Moore's paradox, 193
Morgenstern, Oskar, xv
Theory of Games and Economic Behavior, xi

Nagel, Ernest, 45, 50, 166, 187
Neumann, John von, xv
Theory of Games and Economic Behavior, xi
Newcomb problems, 218, 219
Neyman, Jerzy, 94, 139–40
Neyman-Pearson (NP) tests, 90, 93–94, 95
Norton, John, 235
Nozick, R., 218

objective chance, 154–55, 160
accounts of, 157–62
and determinism, 155, 157, 158
as time-indexical, 161
Oppenheim, Paul, 349

Papineau, David, 302, 304, 305, 310, 311, 315, 317
paradox, 165–66
Pappus, 247
Pareto dominance, 213
Pascal, Blaise, xiii–xiv, xv, 136, 137
Pearl, Judea, 165, 256, 257, 261–62, 263, 264, 267, 269, 30
Peirce, C. S., 68, 70, 72
Popper, Karl, xv, 190, 199, 278, 283
on induction, 100
on severity, 99–100
Popper functions, 183, 199
possibility, and objective modalities, 69–70
practical reasoning, xv–xvi
prediction, purpose of, 12
Prigogine, I., 161
Principal Principle (PP), 158, 159, 192–93, 222–26
and reference-class problem, 223–25
Principle of Direct Probability, 192–93, 194
principle of indifference, xii, 49
principle of precision, 280
principle of richness, 281–82
principle of specificity, 281
Principle 1, 354, 356
probabilistic dependence, and causality, 255–72
probability
and acts and outcomes, 143–45
and approximate distributions, 249–50
a priori interpretation, 50
attributions in, and kinds of trials, 75–76
Bayesian interpretation, xii–xiii, 92, 123, 135, 141–42, 251
calculus of, 121
and causation/causality, xvi–xvii, 177–78, 205, 209–12, 213, 253, 263, 272, 303–4, 305
and chance, 278
and choice behavior, 135
classical, 187–88
and coherence, 143
conditional, 183, 184, 237, 290–91
as primitive, 195–98, 199
and ratio formula, 199
constraints on, 193
and counting possibilities, 138
and decision theory, 240–41
and degrees of belief, 142–43, 238
and determinism, 75
empirical, 279
epistemic interpretation, 50
evidential interpretation, 135, 146–49, 279, 282
expected outcome formula for, xi
and expert functions, 192–93, 194, 195

and explanation, xvii
finite frequency interpretation, 51, 127
fluid dynamic model of, 305–10
formula for reduction, 304–5
and frequency, distinction between, 26
and frequency data, 138–41
frequency interpretation of, xii, 4–6, 10–11, 92–93, 122–23, 125–26, 136, 155, 183, 199, 251
  and Bayesianism, 120
  limiting, 186, 238
  problems for, 10–12, 13–14, 17–18, 132, 139, 141, 155–56
  reference-class problem in, 185–87
  relative, 187
  in testing, 93–95
and games of chance, 137
as guide to life, 90–91, 136, 140, 144, 206, 235–37, 253, 284, 292
history of interpretations of, 137–43
and incoherent beliefs, 145
and inductive inference, 89–92, 93
instrumental, 240
and insurance, xi, 284–86, 292
logical interpretation of, 127, 141, 145–46, 188–90, 279
as logical relation, 147
and mathematical expectation, 136, 137–38
and mathematical statistics, 240–41
mathematics of, xi
and maximizing expected utility, 144
objective, 63, 84, 278
paradoxes of, 187
and percentages, 167–68
and permissible predicates, 280
personal, 155
philosophical study of, x, 248
physical, 155
and propensities, 155–56, 277, 278, 283–84
propensity interpretation, 190–91, 199, 238, 282, 287–88, 291, 292
and quantum mechanics, 278, 291, 293
and random sampling, 49–50, 140
and ratio analysis, 195–98
and reference class, 135, 139, 183–85, 187, 191, 193, 194–95, 197–98, 199, 200, 205, 277, 280, 288, 331–32, 338–39
  conditions for choosing, 280–82
  in frequentism, 184–87
  and objective probability, 222
  principles of, 282
  and sample space, 63–64
  and science, 237–38
  and screening off, 304–5
  in Shonubi case, 335–40
  and single-case chance, 153, 222–23, 277
  and single-case problem, 3, 6–7, 11, 133, 135, 157, 278, 282, 287–88, 292, 338–39
    and density principle, 24
    and epistemic explication, 24–25
  standard views of, xii
    shortcomings, of, xiii
  and statistics, 140
subjective account of, 92, 141–42, 191
and subjective degree of belief, 123–24, 126–27, 141–42
and subjectivity/objectivity, 251
theory of, xi
and truth, 244–45
unconditional, 197–98, 199
unphilosophical account of, 248
probability attributions, and kinds of trials, 75–76
probability calculus, 121
propensities, 155–56, 278
propensity criterion

of causal relevance, 26–27
and determinism, 27
psychometrics, 238–39
Ptolemy, 247

quantitative reductions, 296

Ramsey, Frank, xii, 79, 80, 81, 138, 142, 143, 145, 154, 191
Ramsey Revision, 80–81, 84
randomness
question of, 45
statistical approach to, 45
value of, 236
Rasch, Greg, 239
Rasch model, 239, 250
reasoning, as decision making, xv–xv
reason-seeking why-questions, 12–13
Recovery Condition, 80–81
reducibility, meanings of, 154
reference-class problem. *See* probability: and reference class
Reflection Principle, 193
Reichenbach, Hans, 92, 127, 128–29, 139, 157, 165, 176, 254, 297
on probability, 5–6
frequency interpretation of, 4–6, 27
on single-case prediction, 12
on single-case probability, 3–4, 5, 6, 7–9
representative samples, 46
requirement of maximal specificity, 352
Rule of Acceptance (RA), 111
Rule of Induction by Enumeration, 127, 128
Rule of Rejection (RR), 110
Russell, Bertrand, 51, 70, 122, 127, 128, 195

Salmon, Wesley C., 4, 23, 27, 89, 91, 100, 124, 127, 128, 146, 154, 157, 159, 235, 302, 329
critique of, 16–18
on dynamic rationality, 154–55
as frequentist, 92–93
on Hempel, 19, 24–25
ontic explication in, 24
on probability, 155–56
on propensity, 156
on single-case reference class, 14–16
sample-space predicates, 79
sampling
fair, 46, 47
representative, 46
Savage, L. J., 143, 145
Scheines, Richard, 256, 260, 261, 267, 268, 270, 305
Scotist Realism, 68
Seidenfeld, Teddy, 235
severe tests, 97–99
in induction, 90, 95–97, 102–3, 107
statistical methods as tools for, 103–8
severity principle, 90, 100–101
Shafer, Glenn, 258
Shonubi, Charles, 331–34
and reference-class problem, 335–40
and single-case probability, 337–38
and standard of evidence, 342
and utilities issues, 341
Simpson, E. H., 166
Simpson setups, 181
boundary conditions for, 168–70
Simpson's Paradox, xvii, 165, 176, 194, 256, 257
and altruism, 178
and causation, 178
and classically valid arguments, 170–72
as countermodel, 170–71
in data sets, 174–75
in dynamic settings, 178–81
example of, 166–67
and normalizing data, 169–70
and skewed weights, 169

single-case explanation, problems of, 3–4, 21, 26
single-case problem. *See* probability: single-case problem
Skyrms, Brian, 165, 166, 213, 219
Smith, C. A. B., 146
Sober, Elliot, 165, 178, 207, 212, 213, 217, 301
Spearman, Charles, 247–48
Spirtes, Peter, 256, 260, 261, 264, 267, 268, 270, 305
Spohn, Wolfgang, 253, 254, 257, 265, 266, 271
stability, in cause/effect, 256, 257, 261, 263
Stalnaker, R., 72
state descriptions, xii
statistical evidence, 334–35
statistical explanations, 350, 352, 355
  and probability, 353
statistical inference
  and reference classes, 175–77
  theories of, 175–76
statistical mechanics, 154
statistical methods, as tools for severe testing, 103–8
statistical regularities, 355
statistical relevance, and causal relevance, distinction between, 25
statistical-relevance (S-R) model/explanations, 352, 353
Stigler, Stephen, 241, 244, 246
  History of Statistics, 235
stochastic direct inference, problem of, 83
Stockton, John, 200
Stone, M., 161
St. Petersburg Paradox, xiv
Suppes, Patrick, 161, 256
Sure Thing Principle of Decision Theory, 165, 166, 170, 172–73
syllogisms, 39–41
  classical, 39–41
  premise in, problem of, 40–41
  proportional, 40
  statistical, 40
symmetry thesis, of prediction/explanation, 3
  as unsound, 4

theoretical reasoning, xv–xvi
theory of relativity, 306, 307
thesis of linear attrition, 44
Thurstone, L. L., 247–48
Tillers, P., 335, 341
Tooby, John, 120, 121, 123, 125–26, 127–29, 133
  problem for, 129–31
Trent, Jane, 237
Tversky, A., 120

uncertain but bounded error, 242–43, 245, 247–48, 250
  computational defect in, 247
  in finite frequency, 250
United States v. Shonubi, 331
Urbach, Peter, 38, 143

value, xiv, xv
van Fraassen, Bas, 154, 183, 187, 193
Venn, John, 184, 186, 187
Verma, Thomas, 269
von Mises, Richard, xii, 63, 186–87, 337–38
von Neumann, John, xv
von Plato, J., 161

Weatherson, Brian, 189
Weinstein, Jack B., 332–34, 341
Williams, Donald, 39, 41, 50, 55
Wisdom, J. O., 48, 52, 53, 55
Woodward, James, 269

Yule, G. U., 166